THE SEMANTICS OF DESTRUCTIVE LISP

CSLI
Lecture Notes
Number 5

THE SEMANTICS OF DESTRUCTIVE LISP

Ian A. Mason

CSLI CENTER FOR THE STUDY
OF LANGUAGE
AND INFORMATION

CSLI was founded early in 1983 by researchers from Stanford University, SRI International, and Xerox PARC to further research and development of integrated theories of language, information, and computation. CSLI headquarters and the publication offices are located at the Stanford site.

CSLI/SRI International	**CSLI/Stanford**	**CSLI/Xerox PARC**
333 Ravenswood Avenue	Ventura Hall	3333 Coyote Hill Road
Menlo Park, CA 94025	Stanford, CA 94305	Palo Alto, CA 94304

Printed in the United States

94 93 92 91 90 89 88   5 4 3 2

Library of Congress Catalog Card Number 86–72170
ISBN 0–937073–05–9
ISBN 0–937073–06–7 (pbk.)

I am deeply grateful to:

Solomon Feferman for agreeing to undertake the task of being my teacher, and for his interest, encouragement, and support.

Carolyn Talcott for her insight, enthusiasm, and patience, without which I could not have brought this work to completion.

The Stanford Philosophy Department and John McCarthy for supporting me over the past five years.

Jon Barwise, Alex Bronstein, Ross Casley, Jussi Ketonen, Bill Scherlis, Dave Touretzky, Rodney Topor, Richard Waldinger and Richard Weyhrauch for pointing out mistakes, absurdities and algorithms, as well as showing much appreciated interest.

Palo Verde Gardens and its residents for providing an idyllic place to live and work for the past four years.

My friends Martin, Dave, Katie, Joe, Ludo, Annick, Helen, Peter and Gian, who have all helped me in various ways in the course of this work.

Susan.

My mother and sister.

I dedicate this book to the memory of my father.

Contents

Chapter 1

Introduction

In this work we shall present some aspects of the semantics of destructive Lisp, as a case study in reasoning about programs which destructively manipulate data. By destructive Lisp we do not mean simply pure Lisp but one that fully takes into account the subtleties and advantages of the traditional implementation of the underlying data structure, the so-called S-expression domain (S-expression is an abbreviation of Symbolic expression). Thus we are not interested in nice logical approximations but rather with reconciling both theory and practice. More to the point, we aim to improve practice via theory. Unlike its rivals the theory neatly separates control from data and provides a framework for many areas of research. The following are just a few examples of the areas — which are quite well developed in the pure case — in which we wish to obtain results.

- Program specification.
- Program derivation, from such specifications.
- Program verification, proving programs meet certain specifications.
- Program transformations, both compiling and optimization.
- Analysis of properties of algorithms, both intensional and extensional.

This work constitutes some of our efforts in these areas. In both this work and the theory it describes we have tried to emphasize the interplay between these areas, particularly the first four. Indeed one of the aims of this book is to replace the old paradigm

$$\text{Verification} = \text{Hand Simulation} + \text{Induction},$$

which is implicitly and explicitly dominant in the existing literature, by one which is closer to the aims and spirit of *inferential* programming. Namely

$$\text{Verification} = \text{Transformation} + \text{Induction}.$$

Inferential programming was introduced in (Scherlis and Scott, 1983) and emphasizes the role of derivation in programming practice. To be explicit:

> *Our basic premise is that the ability to construct and modify programs will not improve without a new and comprehensive look at the entire programming process. Past theoretical research, say, in the logics of programs, has*

tended to focus on methods for reasoning about individual programs; little has been done, it seems to us, to develop a sound understanding of the process of programming — the process by which programs evolve in concept and in practice. At present, we lack the means to describe the techniques of program construction and improvement in ways that properly link verification, documentation and adaptability.

The attitude that takes these factors and their dynamics into account we propose to call inferential programming.

Before we proceed further in our discussion of inferential programming and this new paradigm we point out two other connections between these areas. Firstly, on a naive level, verification of programs and derivation of programs can be viewed as *duals* of one another. In verification one proves that a given program meets or satisfies a certain specification. In derivation one does the reverse — from specifications one derives programs which accomplish the task. When such specifications are just simple-minded or well known programs that perform the required calculation or construction the connection between derivation and verification is most apparent. Program transformation is thus seen to be the vehicle of both activities. The process of derivation or verification consists in a sequence of program transformations which, presumably, preserve the appropriate extensional or intensional properties of the programs involved. This analogy, justifiably, places verification in a more favorable light than that which some have cast upon it. Its defect is that it ignores the fact that derivation, on the face of it, is a substantially more difficult task. In verification the programs are predetermined while in derivation not only are they evolving, but also the *direction* in which they are evolving changes. Also in verification one can work with an equivalence relation but in derivation the relation cannot be symmetric, rather one must take some notion of computational progress into account. We regard verification as an integral part of program derivation and feel there is little future in verification, viewed as the *historical* task of formally verifying well known existing programs. Verification is used in this paper as a testing ground for a formal framework of program derivation and transformation.

Secondly, often the verification of one program will increase the programmer's understanding to such an extent that they can write related programs that are more efficient. A good example, when the programmer is a machine, can be seen in (Goad, 1980), where the task of *specializing* an algorithm is accomplished by specializing and pruning the correctness proof of the initial algorithm. The resulting algorithm is often an order of magnitude more efficient than the one obtained by directly specializing and pruning the algorithm itself. Here the transformational approach has obvious advantages over the hand simulation approach. This is because it is at a more abstract level, and hence reveals more structure in both the algorithm and the transformations used. In the hand simulation approach it is often hard to see the forest for the trees.

Program verification, we hope, will eventually disappear as a discipline separate from program derivation. The process of deriving a program from an abstract specification will also serve as a verification of the derived program. It will share all the properties of the specification that the intermediate transformations preserved. Thus verification is incorporated into the study of derivation and transformation, and the study of transformations is central to both activities. This theme is developed further in (Scherlis and Scott, 1983) where the authors say:

> *The traditional correctness proof — that a program is consistent with its specifications — does not constitute a derivation of the program. Conventional proofs, as currently presented in the literature, do little to justify the structure of the program being proved, and they do even less to aid in the development of new programs that may be similar to the program that was proved. That is, they neither explicate existing programs nor aid in their modification and adaptation.*
>
> *We intend that program derivations serve as conceptual or idealized histories of the development of programs. That is, a program derivation can be considered an idealized record of the sequence of design decisions that led to a particular realization of a specification. . . . . .*

And in their conclusions the authors say:

> *Stripped down to essentials, our claim is that the programs of the future will in fact be descriptions of program derivations. Documentation methods based on stepwise-refinement methodologies are already strong evidence that there is movement toward this approach. These documentation methods also provide support for the hypothesis that program derivations offer a more intuitive and revealing way of explaining programs than do conventional proofs of correctness. The proofs may succeed in convincing the reader of the correctness of an algorithm without giving him any hint of why the algorithm works or how it came about. On the other hand, a derivation may be thought of as an especially well-structured constructive proof of correctness of the algorithm, taking the reader step by step from an initial abstract algorithm he accepts as meeting the specifications of the problem to a highly connected and efficient implementation of it.*

One virtue of our new paradigm is that it emphasizes the role of transformation rather than the low-level hand simulation approach. Transformations developed and studied in the process of verification are equally applicable in the more productive process of derivation. The style is also more amenable to automation than the hand simulation variety. The dominance of the hand simulation school is largely a consequence of their preoccupation with extensional relations. To retain a transformational approach in the transition from purely applicative languages to those with side effects one must also make the transition from extensional to intensional equivalence relations. Thus we claim that the limitations of the hand simulation school rests upon their mistaken emphasis on extensionality.

1.1. A Little History

We have chosen to work in a Lisp-like world for many reasons. The most immediate is that it allows us to contrast our destructive version with the purely applicative fragment, pure Lisp, and the issues that arise in an enriched environment. More importantly, however, is that we shall, wherever possible, use pure Lisp as our specification language. Lisp is the second oldest programming language still in active use today, being slightly younger than Fortran. Its father, John McCarthy, began work on the first implementation of Lisp at the newly founded (by McCarthy and Minsky) MIT Artificial Intelligence Project in the fall of 1958. Although work on Lisp, or at least the ideas from which it arose date back as early as 1955. The first implementation was on the IBM 704 computer and accounts for the names of the Lisp primitives. For example we have the **C**ontents of the **A**ddress part of the **R**egister, the **C**ontents of the **D**ecrement part of the **R**egister, **RePL**ace the **C**ontents of the **A**ddress and **RePL**ace the **C**ontents of the **D**ecrement. It has been suggested that the only reason such odd names have survived is the ability to pronounce compositions of them, such as *cdadr*, *cddr* and *cadr*. Interesting discussions of the early history can be found in (McCarthy, 1978) and (Stoyan, 1984). McCarthy, in (McCarthy, 1980), describes the features of Lisp which in his mind characterize it as a programming language:

1. *Computing with symbolic expressions rather than numbers.*
2. *Representation of symbolic expressions and other information by list structure in computer memory.*
3. *Representation of information on paper, from keyboards and in other external media mostly by multi-level lists and sometimes by S-expressions. It has been important that any kind of data can be represented by a single general type.*
4. *A small set of selector and constructor operations expressed as functions, i.e. car, cdr, and cons.*
5. *Composition of functions as a tool for forming more complex functions.*
6. *The use of conditional expressions for getting branching into function definitions.*

7. *The recursive use of conditional expressions as a sufficient tool for building computable functions.*

8. *The use of λ-expressions for naming functions.*

9. *The storage of information on the property lists of atoms.*

10. *The representation of Lisp programs as Lisp data that can be manipulated by object programs. This has prevented the separation between system programmers and application programmers. Everyone can improve his Lisp, and many of these improvements have developed into improvements to the language.*

11. *The conditional expression interpretation of the Boolean connectives.*

12. *The Lisp function eval that serves both as a formal definition of the language and as an interpreter.*

13. *Garbage collection as the means of erasure.*

14. *Minimal requirements for declarations so that Lisp statements can be executed in an on-line environment without preliminaries.*

15. *Lisp statements as a command language in an online environment.*

1.2. The Underlying Data Structure

Let us begin by describing the underlying data structure of pure Lisp and comparing this with that of destructive Lisp. The underlying data structure of pure Lisp, $\mathbb{S}_{wf}$, is easily describable and appears in many guises other than its traditional one, for example in (Moschovakis, 1969) the author developed independently a notion of *prime computability* over an arbitrary algebraic structure. His system is strikingly similar to conventional pure Lisp, both in spirit and style, thus providing evidence for the fundamental nature of Lisp. The underlying data structure in pure Lisp is simply obtained from the set of atoms, $\mathbb{A}$, by closing it under a pairing operation. Thus the celebrated isomorphism:

$$\mathbb{S}_{wf} \cong \mathbb{A} \cup (\mathbb{S}_{wf} \times \mathbb{S}_{wf}).$$

In pure Lisp the functions *car* and *cdr* are simply the first and second projection functions on pairs and are undefined on atoms. *cons* is the pairing function. *equal* determines whether two atoms or pairs are identical, i.e. whether or not their *car*s and *cdr*s are *equal* while *atom* tells us whether the object in question is either an atom or a pair. Thus the underlying data structure of pure Lisp can be thought of as a traditional first order structure:

$$< \mathbb{S}_{wf}, cons, car, cdr, atom, equal, \mathtt{T}, \mathtt{NIL} > .$$

It is thus a *static* object, in the sense that the nature of an object does not change in time. The data structure has other nice properties. For example the theory of this structure has been shown to be decidable (Tenney, 1972), (McKinsey and Tarski, 1946). Also in (Oppen, 1978) it is shown that the quantifier free part of this theory is decidable in linear time. Another important property of the data structure is that it is built up inductively, thus allowing strong principles of induction to be used in verifying programs. One last important principle is that Leibniz's law holds for programs; *equal* expressions can be replaced by *equal* expressions in an expression to obtain an *equal* expression:

Leibniz's Law $e_0(\bar{x}) \equiv e_1(\bar{x}) \rightarrow e(\bar{x}, e_0(\bar{x})) \equiv e(\bar{x}, e_1(\bar{x}))$.

This principle has the consequence that correctness proofs in pure Lisp are very much of the *transformation* plus *induction* variety. The content of Leibniz's principle is that it lays the foundation for a calculus of program transformations. Any program that is obtained from another by replacing a portion by another Lisp equal one is guaranteed to have all the extensional properties the original had. It also allows equational verification and derivation. The underlying semantics can be pushed somewhat into the background, serving merely as a *justification* for the transformations and induction principles involved.

This is not to say that pure Lisp does not have its disadvantages. The most glaring, perhaps, is the fact that it is theoretical rather than practical. It could also be argued that the simplicity of the data structure and the resulting computation theory has, perhaps, helped perpetuate the myth that there is one *single* notion of *equivalence* between programs, which is by and large an extensional notion, and as a consequence one single notion of *equivalence* preserving transformations. It also gives unjustified emphasis to *extensional* properties of programs, since the intensional relations can easily be transformed into extensional properties of related (or *derived*) programs (Talcott, 1985b). This relationship between extensional and intensional properties of programs is certainly not true in the destructive case.

In destructive Lisp we have almost exactly the opposite situation. The language is actual, efficient, but until now did not have an elegant or even nice theory surrounding it. In destructive Lisp the data domain is similar to that of pure Lisp but more complex. It consists of two types of objects, atoms and cons cells. Atoms are either numbers or symbols, with two special symbols `T` and `NIL` playing the role of booleans, `T` for *true* and `NIL` for *false*. In this book we shall usually ignore any structure $\mathbb{A}$ might have, other than containing the integers, and shall concentrate on the other type of object, cons cells. A cons cell is essentially an ordered pair of names or addresses of other S-expressions. These addresses or names are usually called *pointers*, the first one is called the *car pointer* and the second the *cdr pointer*. This indirect reference allows for non well-founded or cyclic S-expressions, an aspect of this data structure that is becoming more and more in

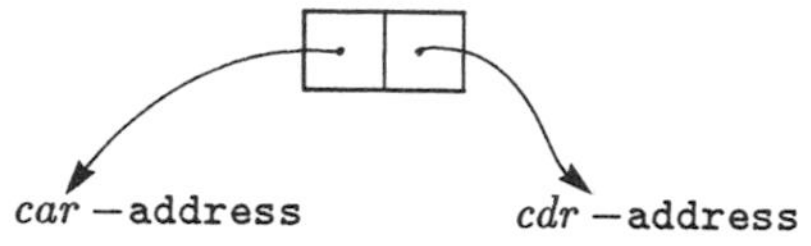

Figure 1. A Cons Cell

vogue. Cons cells are traditionally represented by boxes and pointers diagrams in the manner shown in figure 1.

The basic underlying data operations

$$atom,\ int,\ add1,\ sub1,\ eq,\ cons,\ car,\ cdr,\ rplaca,\ rplacd,$$

are easily describable with this picture in mind. *atom* is the characteristic function, using the booleans T and NIL, of the atoms. *eq* just tests whether two data objects, either cons cells or atoms, are literally identical. *cons* takes two arguments and creates a new cons cell which contains pointers to the arguments, in the order given. *car* and *cdr* just return the object pointed two by the first and second pointers in a cons cell, they are not defined on atoms. The operations *rplaca* and *rplacd* destructively alter an already existing cons cell in the following fashion: given two arguments, the first of which must be a cons cell, *rplaca* will alter the contents of the first argument so that its *car* pointer now points to the second argument. *rplacd* similarly alters the *cdr* pointer. Notice that the use of *rplaca* and *rplacd* allow one to construct cons cells which point back to themselves. They also actually change the nature of existing objects. Thus these operations force us from a static model to a *dynamic* one, the S-expression memory structure. In the next chapter we introduce the general notion of a memory structure, the S-expression memory structure being just a particular example. One of the problems in developing a theory for destructive Lisp is the failure of Leibniz's Law. A simple example of this is

$$cons(cons(\mathtt{T},\mathtt{T}), cons(\mathtt{T},\mathtt{T})) \equiv \mathtt{let}\{x \leftarrow cons(\mathtt{T},\mathtt{T})\}\ cons(x,x).$$

When we apply Leibniz's law with $e(y) = rplaca(car(y), \mathtt{NIL})$ we obtain the obviously false conclusion:

$$cons(cons(\mathtt{NIL},\mathtt{T}), cons(\mathtt{T},\mathtt{T})) \equiv \mathtt{let}\{x \leftarrow cons(\mathtt{NIL},\mathtt{T})\}\ cons(x,x).$$

Thus simple syntactic manipulations, on the face of it, seem prohibited in the destructive case. This does much to explain why the vast majority of verification proofs of destructive programs in the literature are of the hand simulation variety. Thus a first step in justifying our paradigm is to recover Leibniz's Law. This is done by making the transition from extensional relations to intensional ones.

Another problem is that the operations *rplaca* and *rplacd* do not depend solely on the pointwise *isomorphism* type of their arguments. Even though x_0 and x_1 may be isomorphic objects we cannot conclude that $rplaca(x_0, y)$ and $rplaca(x_1, y)$ will return isomorphic objects. These operations not only depend on the isomorphism type of their arguments but also on how they sit together, for example if they share structure or not. Structure sharing between objects, detectable using *eq*, and cyclic or non-well-founded structures make the underlying data structure in this version of Lisp substantially more complex than in the pure case. The nature of the operations prohibit viewing the data structure, in any natural way (an example of an *unnatural* way would be to incorporate an explicit time parameter), as a traditional first order algebraic structure; rather it is a particular example of a Memory Structure, a mathematical object used to model both the *dynamic* state of various types of Random Access Memories and the operations upon them. Another example of the increased complexity is that in opposition to the pure case there seems to be no obvious schema for defining primitive recursive functions, see (Moschovakis, 1969). Since non-well-foundedness substantially complicates the problem of totality, simple recursion must be replaced by recursion with respect to a spanning tree. This is also reflected in the more complex induction principles that are required. Another aspect where pure Lisp and destructive Lisp differ is in the richness of the control primitives. In pure Lisp the only control primitive other than function application is the branching primitive, `if`. In destructive Lisp we also require a lexical variable binding primitive, `let`, and for ease of reading, a sequencing primitive `seq`.

One of the main aims of this work is to overcome the problems just indicated and develop a theory as mathematically elegant as the pure Lisp case.

1.3. An Outline

This work is divided into eleven chapters. The first, this one, serves as an introduction. The second chapter deals with the underlying model, both of the data structure and the computation theory. We introduce a mathematical model called a *memory structure*. It will be the basis for the semantics of the various languages we shall introduce and study. We then define, over an arbitrary memory structure, a language and corresponding computation system. In chapter three we introduce several equivalence relations and give some simple examples of their properties and use. The most important of these equivalence relations is that of *strong isomorphism*, which unlike the others is preserved under many standard syntactic manipulations. In fact implicit in our work is the claim that strong isomorphism is to destructive Lisp what Lisp equality is to pure Lisp. These equivalence relations have the property that it is effectively decidable whether or not two expressions that contain no recursively defined functions are so related. Chapter four then provides a plethora of examples concerning these relations, mostly of the intensional relation, strong isomorphism. These examples range from very simple programs to more complicated programs that have been the subject of many papers in the existing literature. Chapter five deals with certain theoretical results concerning memory structures and destructive Lisp in particular. The effectiveness theorems amongst others are proved in this chapter. In chapter six we use these equivalence relations to compare the strengths and weaknesses of various fragments of Lisp. In chapter seven we examine rules for deriving or transforming programs, in the spirit of (Scherlis, 1980). The next three chapters are devoted to three complicated programming examples. The first is an extended example based on the Robson marking algorithm; we also give an alternative proof of the correctness of the Robson copying algorithm (Robson, 1977) to the one given in (Mason and Talcott, 1985). The second example deals with an important feature of Lisp, namely that Lisp programs are Lisp data and that there is a universal program, *eval*. This allows us to define an *internal* programming language with somewhat richer features, such as self destructing *macros*, than our *external* computation theory. The final example deals with an efficient data editing program. The final chapter then summarizes the main results and draws some conclusions concerning the present and future work. A succinct treatment of many of the highlights of this book can be found in (Mason, 1986). This work grew out of the work described in (Mason and Talcott, 1985) and (Mason, 1985) and is a companion to (Talcott, 1985a).

1.4. Notation

We complete this chapter by describing some of our notation. The usual notation for set membership and function application is used. Let $\mathbb{D}$, $\mathbb{D}_0$, $\mathbb{D}_1$, $\ldots \mathbb{D}_{\mathrm{n}}$ be sets, then $\mathbb{D}_0 \oplus \mathbb{D}_1$ is the (disjoint) union of $\mathbb{D}_0$ and $\mathbb{D}_1$. $\mathbb{D}_0 \otimes \ldots \otimes \mathbb{D}_{\mathrm{n}-1}$ is the set of n-tuples with i^{th} element from $\mathbb{D}_{\mathrm{i}}$ for $i < n$. We write $\mathbb{D}^{(n)}$ for $\mathbb{D}_0 \otimes \ldots \otimes \mathbb{D}_{\mathrm{n}-1}$ when each $\mathbb{D}_{\mathrm{i}}$ is $\mathbb{D}$. $\mathbb{D}^*$ is the set of finite sequences of elements of $\mathbb{D}$,

$$\mathbb{D}^* = \bigcup_{n \in \omega} \mathbb{D}^{(n)}.$$

Some notation for sequences follows. ϵ is the empty sequence, the unique element of $\mathbb{D}^{(0)}$ for any domain $\mathbb{D}$. For $d, d_0, \ldots, d_{n-1}, d'_0, \ldots, d'_{m-1} \in \mathbb{D}$, the sequence of length n with i^{th} element d_i for $i < n$ is written $[d_0, \ldots, d_{n-1}]$. Let $v = [d_0, \ldots, d_{n-1}]$, $u = [d'_0, \ldots, d'_{m-1}]$ and $i < n$ then $|v|$ is the length of v while $v{\downarrow}_i$ is the ith element of v, namely d_i. $v * u \underset{\mathrm{df}}{=} [d_0, \ldots, d_{n-1}, d'_0, \ldots, d'_{m-1}]$ is the concatenation of v and u. We identify d with the singleton sequence $[d]$. Note that $(u * v) * w = u * (v * w)$ and $[\ ] = \epsilon$.

$\mathbf{P}_\omega \mathbb{D}$ is the domain of finite subsets of $\mathbb{D}$. $[\mathbb{D}_0 \rightarrow \mathbb{D}_1]$ is the set of total functions from $\mathbb{D}_0$ to $\mathbb{D}_1$, and $[\mathbb{D}_0 \rightsquigarrow \mathbb{D}_1]$ is the set of partial functions. If $\mu \in [\mathbb{D}_0 \rightsquigarrow \mathbb{D}_1]$, then δ_μ is the domain of μ and ρ_μ is its range. For $d_0 \in \mathbb{D}_0, d_1 \in \mathbb{D}_1$, and $\mu \in [\mathbb{D}_0 \rightsquigarrow \mathbb{D}_1]$ we let

$$\mu\{d_0 \leftarrow d_1\}$$

be the map μ_0 such that $\delta_{\mu_0} = \delta_\mu \cup \{d_0\}$, $\mu_0(d_0) = d_1$ and $\mu_0(d) = \mu(d)$ for $d \neq d_0, d \in \delta_\mu$.

Some particular sets that we shall use frequently are as follows. $\mathbb{Z}$ is the set of integers and $z, z_0, \ldots$ range over $\mathbb{Z}$. $\mathbb{N} = \{0, 1, 2, \ldots\}$ is the set of natural numbers and $n, n_0, \ldots$ range over $\mathbb{N}$. We consider a natural number to be the set of numbers less than it; thus the less-than relation, $<$, is simply the membership relation, $\in$, of set theory. We let $\mathbb{T} = \{0, 1\}^*$ be the complete binary tree, i.e. the set of finite sequences of 0's and 1's. We use 1^n to denote the sequence in $\mathbb{T}$ that consists of exactly n ones. Note that $1^0 = \epsilon$. We shall adopt the convention that trees grow downward and $\sigma, \sigma_0, \ldots$ will range over $\mathbb{T}$. We use two partial orderings on $\mathbb{T}$. The initial segment relation, $<$, and the Brouwer-Kleene linear ordering, $\prec$. $\sigma_0 < \sigma_1$ is taken to mean that σ_1 is *below* σ_0 in $\mathbb{T}$, while $\sigma_0 \prec \sigma_1$ means that σ_0 is *before* σ_1 in $\mathbb{T}$. The *below* relation is defined by

$$\sigma_0 < \sigma_1 \ \leftrightarrow\ \exists \sigma \neq \epsilon\ (\sigma_1 = \sigma_0 * \sigma)$$

and the *before* relation is defined by

$$\sigma_0 \prec \sigma_1 \ \leftrightarrow\ \sigma_0 < \sigma_1 \ \vee\ \exists \sigma, \sigma_2, \sigma_3 (\sigma_0 = \sigma * 0 * \sigma_2 \ \wedge\ \sigma_1 = \sigma * 1 * \sigma_3).$$

The *before* relation is also known as the depth-first ordering.

Chapter 2

The Basic Theory of Memory Structures

In this chapter we shall develop the basis, or model theory, upon which all our work will be built. The models (semantics) of this theory, the so called memory structures, are the subject of the first section. In the second section we define a language and corresponding computation theory.

2.1. Memory Structures

In this section we introduce the notion of a memory structure over a set $\mathbb{A}$ of atoms. The purpose is to model the memory of a Random Access Machine (RAM) and to study the abstract structures typically represented in such machines. The memory of a RAM can be thought of as a collection of locations or cells (at any particular time this collection will of course be finite). The machine uses these cells or locations to store various types and quantities of objects. There are machine instructions for accessing and updating the contents of memory cells. Some objects are intended to represent abstract quantities such as numbers, boolean vectors, characters, etc., and there are machine instructions for computing functions on these abstract entities, such as arithmetic operations and boolean functions. The exact nature and number of the objects storable in each location varies from machine to machine; we shall abstract away from this machine dependent aspect of memory. Consequently we shall assume that our hypothetical machine can store a sequence of objects (the sequence being of arbitrary finite length), each object of which is either an atom from $\mathbb{A}$ or the address of another location in memory. An address in this sense is simply some specification of a location by which the machine can access that location (and its contents). Again the precise nature of these addresses will vary from machine to machine, and so again we shall abstract away from these implementation dependent details.

In this work we shall be mainly concerned with S-expression memories that can only store pairs of objects in each location; however we shall treat the general case first, leaving S-expression memory structures as a particular example. This is because the theory we develop can easily be extended to handle other data structures such as arrays, records, vectors and probably even xectors (Hillis, 1985).

Let $\mathbb{A}$ be some fixed set of atoms and $\mathbb{C}$ some countably infinite set disjoint from $\mathbb{A}$. $\mathbb{C}$ is the set of memory cells of our hypothetical machine. The elements of the sequences that are stored in these cells are the *memory values* and we denote them by $\mathbb{V}$. Thus $\mathbb{V} = \mathbb{A} \oplus \mathbb{C}$. A memory μ is a function from a finite subset of $\mathbb{C}$ to the set of sequences of memory values, $\mathbb{V}^* = (\mathbb{A} \oplus \mathbb{C})^*$. Since we wish $\mu(c)$ to represent the contents of the location c in the memory μ, we also require that those cells which occur amongst the contents of cells are also cells in our memory. Thus we define a *memory* μ to be a finite map such that

$$\mu \in [\delta_\mu \rightarrow (\delta_\mu \oplus \mathbb{A})^*].$$

where δ_μ, the domain of μ, is a finite subset of $\mathbb{C}$. The set of all memories over $\mathbb{A}$ and $\mathbb{C}$ is denoted by $\mathbb{M}_{(\mathbb{A},\mathbb{C})}$.

Now suppose that $\mathbb{M}$ is a set of memories. A *memory object* of $\mathbb{M}$ is a pair

$$[v_0, \ldots, v_{n-1}] \,;\, \mu$$

such that μ is a memory in $\mathbb{M}$ and the sequence $[v_0, \ldots, v_{n-1}]$ satisfies $v_i \in \delta_\mu \oplus \mathbb{A}$ for $i \in n$. Thus a memory object is a memory together with a sequence of memory values which *exist* in that memory. The reason we consider sequences of memory values and not just singletons is twofold. Firstly, we often want to apply a memory operation or defined function to several arguments all of which we assume exist in one and the same memory, and, secondly, the behavior of many of the memory operations is not determined simply by the pointwise nature of its arguments but also by how they *sit* with one another — for example, if they share structure. Hence when defining equivalence relations the pointwise approach is next to useless. A *memory structure* is defined to be a set of memories $\mathbb{M}$ together with a set of operations $\mathbb{O}$, which are allowed to be partial, on those memory objects of $\mathbb{M}$. The operations model the machine instructions for manipulating objects. We usually refer to a memory structure by its collection of memories $\mathbb{M}$, taking the operations to be implicit. We also abuse notation and refer to the set of memory objects of a particular collection of memories $\mathbb{M}$ simply by $\mathbb{M}$; context and notation should always prevent confusion. One last abuse of notation is that by $\mathbb{M}^{(n)}$ we *always* mean the collection of memory objects whose sequence of memory values is of length n. For ease of reading we let $\mu, \mu_0, \ldots$ range over memories, $v, v_0, \ldots$ range over $\mathbb{V}$, $a, a_0, \ldots$ range over $\mathbb{A}$ and $c, c_0, \ldots$ range over $\mathbb{C}$.

2.1.1. Definition of a Memory Structure $\mathbb{M}$

We can summarize the above definitions as follows:

- $\mathbb{A}$ and $\mathbb{C}$ are disjoint sets, $\mathbb{C}$ is countable, and $\mathbb{V} = \mathbb{A} \oplus \mathbb{C}$ is the set of memory values.
- A memory is a finite map μ from $\mathbb{C}$ to $\mathbb{V}^*$ such that $\mu \in [\delta_\mu \rightarrow (\delta_\mu \oplus \mathbb{A})^*]$. The set of all memories over $\mathbb{A}$ and $\mathbb{C}$ is denoted by $\mathbb{M}_{(\mathbb{A},\mathbb{C})}$.

- Let $\mathbb{M}$ be a set of memories. A memory object of $\mathbb{M}$ is a tuple $v_0, \ldots, v_{n-1} ; \mu$ such that μ is a memory in $\mathbb{M}$ and $v_i \in \delta_\mu \oplus \mathbb{A}$ for $i \in n$.
- We write $[v_0, \ldots, v_{n-1}] ; \mu \in \mathbb{M}^{(n)}$ to emphasize the length of the memory value sequence.
- A memory structure is a set of memories $\mathbb{M}$ together with a set of operations $\mathbb{O}$ on memory objects of $\mathbb{M}$.

2.1.2. The S-expression Memory Structure

As a particular example of a memory structure we now present the S-expression memory structure. It should be very familiar to those readers acquainted with any Lisp-like language. We often assume that the integers $\mathbb{Z}$ are contained in $\mathbb{A}$. $\mathbb{A}$ will always be assumed to contain two non-numeric atoms `T` and `NIL`, representing *true* and *false*. `NIL` is also used to represent the empty list. We shall also assume that there are an unlimited collection of non-numeric atoms other than the two just mentioned. We shall usually denote them by strings of upper case letters `IN THIS FONT`. Thus for our purposes the following are also in $\mathbb{A}$:

`INFINITY, M10, THIS:ATOM,...`

The set of S-expression memories, $\mathbb{M}_{sexp}$, is defined by:

$$\mathbb{M}_{sexp} = \{\mu \in \mathbb{M}_{(\mathbb{A},\mathbb{C})} \mid \mu \in [\delta_\mu \nrightarrow \mathbb{V}^{(2)}]\}.$$

Thus, as we mentioned earlier, the S-expression memory can only store pairs of memory values in its memory locations. It is traditional to call these *binary* cells *Cons cells*. To complete our specification of the S-expression memory structure we need only describe the operations $\mathbb{O}_{sexp}$.

$$\mathbb{O}_{sexp} = \{int, atom, add1\,, sub1\,, eq, cons, car, cdr, rplaca, rplacd\},$$

the definitions of which are: *int* and *atom* are characteristic functions (recognizers) of $\mathbb{Z}$ and $\mathbb{A}$, respectively. *eq* is the characteristic function of equality.

$$int(v\,;\mu) = \begin{cases} \mathtt{T}\,;\mu & \text{if } v \in \mathbb{Z} \\ \mathtt{NIL}\,;\mu & \text{if } v \notin \mathbb{Z} \end{cases}$$

$$atom(v\,;\mu) = \begin{cases} \mathtt{T}\,;\mu & \text{if } v \in \mathbb{A} \\ \mathtt{NIL}\,;\mu & \text{if } v \notin \mathbb{A} \end{cases}$$

$$eq(v_0, v_1\,;\mu) = \begin{cases} \mathtt{T}\,;\mu & \text{if } v_0 = v_1 \\ \mathtt{NIL}\,;\mu & \text{if } v_0 \neq v_1 \end{cases}$$

add1 and *sub1* are the successor and predecessor functions on $\mathbb{Z}$.

$$add1(z\,;\mu) = z + 1\,;\mu$$
$$sub1(z\,;\mu) = z - 1\,;\mu$$

The *cons* operation is a pair constructing function and *car* and *cdr* are the corresponding projections. Note that *cons* enlarges the domain of the memory by *selecting* a new location from *free storage* and making the arguments of the function its contents. The method of *selection* is of no concern to us, but can be assumed to be random for the time being. The free storage of a memory μ is just another name for $\mathbb{C} - \delta_\mu$.

$$cons(v_0, v_1\,;\mu) = c\,;\mu_0 \quad \text{where} \quad c \notin \delta_\mu \quad \text{and} \quad \mu_0 = \mu\{c \leftarrow [v_0, v_1]\}$$
$$car(c\,;\mu) = v_0\,;\mu \quad \text{given} \quad \mu(c) = [v_0, v_1]$$
$$cdr(c\,;\mu) = v_1\,;\mu \quad \text{given} \quad \mu(c) = [v_0, v_1]$$

The destructive memory operations *rplaca* and *rplacd* update the contents of a pre-existing location in memory. The domain of the resulting memory object is unchanged. By the use of these functions one can obtain memory objects that store their own locations.

If $\mu(c) = [v_0, v_1]$ then

$$rplaca(c, v\,;\mu) = c\,;\mu_0 \quad \text{where} \quad \mu_0 = \mu\{c \leftarrow [v, v_1]\}$$
$$rplacd(c, v\,;\mu) = c\,;\mu_0 \quad \text{where} \quad \mu_0 = \mu\{c \leftarrow [v_0, v]\}$$

In some cases we shall not be interested in the value of the *rplacx* operations, $x \in \{a, d\}$, so for convenience we define the operations *setcar* and *setcdr*.

$$setcar(c, v\,;\mu) = \mu\{c \leftarrow [v, \mu(c)\!\downarrow_1]\}$$
$$setcdr(c, v\,;\mu) = \mu\{c \leftarrow [\mu(c)\!\downarrow_0, v]\}$$

Note that $rplacx(c, v\,;\mu) = c\,;setcxr(c, v\,;\mu)$ for $x \in \{a, d\}$.

2.1.3. Summary of the Definition of $\mathbb{M}_{sexp}$

- $\mathbb{A}$ and $\mathbb{C}$ are disjoint sets, $\mathbb{C}$ is countable, and $\mathbb{V} = \mathbb{A} \oplus \mathbb{C}$ is the set of memory values.
- A *Lisp memory* is a finite map μ from $\mathbb{C}$ to $\mathbb{V}^{(2)}$ such that $\mu \in [\delta_\mu \to (\delta_\mu \oplus \mathbb{A})^{(2)}]$. The set of all Lisp memories over $\mathbb{A}$ and $\mathbb{C}$ is denoted by $\mathbb{M}_{sexp}$.

- A memory object of $\mathbb{M}_{sexp}$ is a pair

$$[v_0, \ldots, v_{n-1}] ; \mu$$

consisting of a memory μ in $\mathbb{M}_{sexp}$ and a sequence of memory values which exist in that memory, in other words $v_i \in \delta_\mu \oplus \mathbb{A}$ for $i \in n$.

- We write $[v_0, \ldots, v_{n-1}] ; \mu \in \mathbb{M}_{sexp}^{(n)}$ to emphasize the length of the memory value sequence.

- The S-expression memory structure consists of the Lisp memories $\mathbb{M}_{sexp}$ together with the set of Lisp data operations $\mathbb{O}_{sexp}$ on these memory objects,

$$\mathbb{O}_{sexp} = \{int, atom, add1\,, sub1\,, eq, cons, car, cdr, rplaca, rplacd\}.$$

2.1.4. Fragments of $\mathbb{M}_{sexp}$

Two familiar examples of memory structures are obtained by considering the following two sets of memory operations on $\mathbb{M}_{sexp}$:

$$\mathbb{O}_{pure} = \{int, atom, add1\,, sub1\,, atom{:}eq, cons, car, cdr\}$$

$$\mathbb{O}_{pure+} = \{int, atom, add1\,, sub1\,, eq, cons, car, cdr\}$$

All the operations are as defined previously except *atom:eq* which is, the characteristic function of, equality on $\mathbb{A}$:

$$atom{:}eq(v_0, v_1 ; \mu) = \begin{cases} \mathtt{T} ; \mu & \text{if } v_0 = v_1 \text{ and } v_0, v_1 \in \mathbb{A} \\ \mathtt{NIL} ; \mu & \text{otherwise} \end{cases}$$

We call the memory structure with operations $\mathbb{O}_{pure}$ the *pure Lisp* memory structure, denoted by $\mathbb{M}_{pure}$. Finally we denote the memory structure with operations $\mathbb{O}_{pure+}$ by $\mathbb{M}_{pure+}$. Notice that these memory structures all have the same set of memories, consequently a simple comparison of functions definable in each structure is possible.

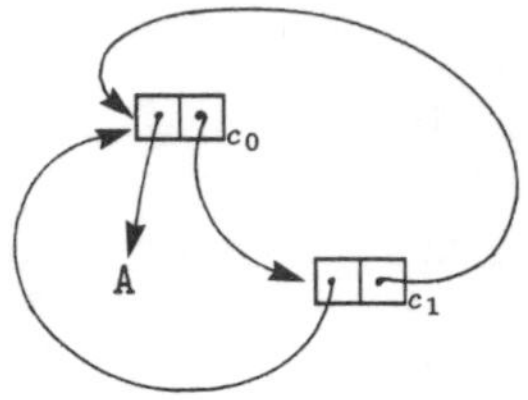

Figure 2. A Simple S-expression

2.1.5. A Low Level Lisp Data Structure

Another example of a memory structure can be obtained by considering a low level implementation of Lisp, one in which cons cells have *mark* and *field bits*. Such a memory structure is required to express and prove properties of such fundamental Lisp programs as the *mark and sweep garbage collection*, and programs it uses such as the Deutsch-Shorr-Waite marking algorithm. The mark and field bits in this version only take on two values, 0 or 1. Thus we have the following set of memories, $\mathbb{M}_{mfsexp}$.

$$\mathbb{M}_{mfsexp} = \{\mu \in \mathbb{M}_{(\mathbb{A},\mathbb{C})} \mid \mu \in [\delta_\mu \rightarrow \{0,1\}^{(2)} \times \mathbb{V}^{(2)}]\}$$

$$\mathbb{O}_{mfsexp} = \mathbb{O}_{sexp} \cup \{m, setm, f, setf\}$$

Over this structure *car* and *cdr* access the third and fourth elements and m returns the value of the mark bit, while f returns the field value. *cons* returns a new cell with the mark and field bits set initially to 0. *setm* and *setf* simply update the mark and field bits, respectively. The rest of the operations are the obvious modifications.

2.1.6. The Derived Tree Function $\lambda x.(v\,;\mu)_x$

There is a very simple way of regarding an S-expression memory object as a labelled, possibly infinite, rational tree. For example consider the S-expression depicted in figure 2.

If we regard elements of the binary tree, $\mathbb{T}$, as describing possible paths through this structure, (0 representing the *car* direction, 1 the *cdr* direction), then we can represent the structure by the subtree of $\mathbb{T}$ consisting of all possible paths through it, labelling these paths by the elements of $\mathbb{V}$ at their ends. Thus paths that are labelled by atoms will be terminal and those labelled by cells will

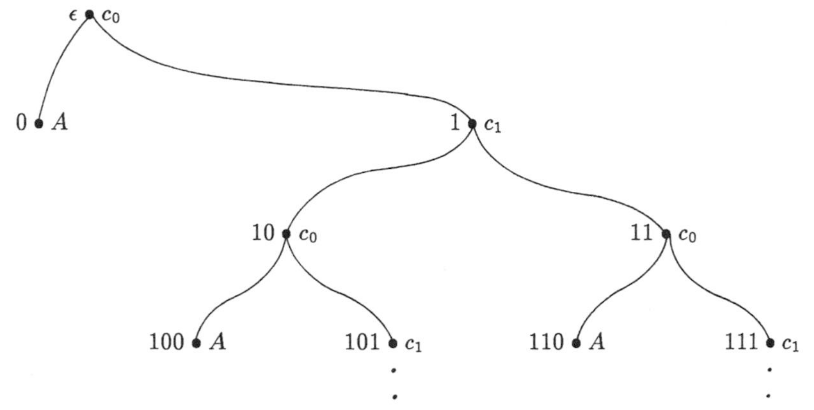

Figure 3. The Rational Tree

have exactly two immediate subtrees. For example the tree associated with the structure in figure 2 is pictured in figure 3.

This way of viewing S-expressions is made explicit by the following. For $v\,;\mu \in \mathbb{M}_{sexp}$ we define a partial function

$$\lambda x.(v\,;\mu)_x$$

from $\mathbb{T}$ to $\mathbb{V}$ and its domain

$$\delta_{\lambda x.(v;\mu)_x}$$

by induction on $\mathbb{T}$:

$$(v\,;\mu)_\sigma = \begin{cases} v & \text{if } \sigma = \epsilon, \text{ the empty word in } \mathbb{T} \\ \mu((v\,;\mu)_{\sigma_0})\downarrow_i & \text{if } \sigma = \sigma_0 * i,\ i \in 2 \text{ and } (v\,;\mu)_{\sigma_0} \in \mathbb{C} \end{cases}$$

When referring to the tree function $\lambda x.(v\,;\mu)_x$ we drop the λ and simply write $(v;\mu)$. Thus, $(v;\mu)$ is the function from $\mathbb{T}$ to $\mathbb{V}$ with the smallest domain satisfying:

- $\epsilon \in \delta_{(v;\mu)}$ and $(v\,;\mu)_\epsilon = v$

and if $\sigma \in \delta_{(v;\mu)}$ and $(v\,;\mu)_\sigma = c \in \mathbb{C}$ then

- $\sigma * j \in \delta_{(v;\mu)}$, and
- $(v\,;\mu)_{\sigma * j} = \mu(c)\downarrow_j$ for $j \in 2$.

Our notation in this regard is derived from that of (Moschovakis, 1969).

We call $(v\,;\mu)$ the *derived tree function*, or the *labelled tree* that is defined by $v\,;\mu$. Note that the following are true for these functions.

Proposition: For any $v\,;\mu \in \mathbb{M}_{sexp}$

0. $\delta_{(v;\mu)}$ is a non-empty subtree of $\mathbb{T}$.
1. If $\sigma * j \in \delta_{(v;\mu)}$ for $j \in 2$ then $(v\,;\mu)_\sigma \in \mathbb{C}$, and conversely if $(v\,;\mu)_\sigma \in \mathbb{C}$ then $\sigma * j \in \delta_{(v;\mu)}$ for $j \in 2$.

Furthermore if $\sigma_0 * \sigma_1 \in \delta_{(v;\mu)}$ then

2. $\sigma_0 \in \delta_{(v;\mu)}$ and $\sigma_1 \in \delta_{((v;\mu)_{\sigma_0};\mu)}$
3. $(v\,;\mu)_{\sigma_0 * \sigma_1} = ((v\,;\mu)_{\sigma_0}\,;\mu)_{\sigma_1}$

We shall sometimes refer to σ (when σ is in the domain of the derived tree function of a memory object $v\,;\mu$) as a *car-cdr* chain in $v\,;\mu$, for the obvious reason that $(v\,;\mu)_\sigma$ is the atom or cell one obtains by a suitable composition of the memory operations *car* and *cdr*. Thus we can define the notion of the cells of a memory object which are accessible by *car-cdr* chains. We define $\mathbf{Cells}_\mu(v)$ to be the set of cells that are reachable from $v\,;\mu$ by travelling along any *car-cdr* chain, and $\mathbf{Cells}_\mu^<(v)$ to be the set of cells reachable from $v\,;\mu$ by travelling along any non-empty *car-cdr* chains. Thus

$$\mathbf{Cells}_\mu(v) \underset{\text{df}}{=} \{c \in \mathbb{C} \mid (\exists\sigma)(v\,;\mu)_\sigma = c\}$$

$$\mathbf{Cells}_\mu^<(v) \underset{\text{df}}{=} \{c \in \mathbb{C} \mid (\exists\sigma \neq \epsilon)(v\,;\mu)_\sigma = c\}$$

We also let $\mathbf{Cells}_\mu(\bar{v}) \underset{\text{df}}{=} \bigcup_{i \in |\bar{v}|} \mathbf{Cells}_\mu(\bar{v}\downarrow_i)$ and $\mathbf{Cells}_\mu^<(\bar{v}) \underset{\text{df}}{=} \bigcup_{i \in |\bar{v}|} \mathbf{Cells}_\mu^<(\bar{v}\downarrow_i)$. We shall often regard $\mathbf{Cells}_\mu(\bar{v})$ as a sequence rather than a set, ordered in some particular fashion. For this and other reasons we define the notion of a spanning tree and fix a particular one for such purposes.

2.1.7. Spanning Trees

For $c\,;\mu \in \mathbb{M}_{sexp}$ we say that X is a *connected* subset of $\mathbf{Cells}_\mu(c)$ if X is the image of a subtree of $\mathbb{T}$ under the map $(c\,;\mu)$. For X, a connected subset of $\mathbf{Cells}_\mu(c)$, we define a *spanning tree* for X at $c\,;\mu$ to be a set $S \subset \mathbb{T}$ having the following properties:

1. $(\forall v \in X)(\exists! \sigma \in S)(c\,;\mu)_\sigma = v$, and
2. S is a subtree of $\mathbb{T}$.

For convenience we say that a cell c_i is left (right) *terminal* with respect to a spanning tree S (at $c\,;\mu$) if $\exists\sigma \in S \quad c_i = (c\,;\mu)_\sigma$ but $\sigma * 0$ ($\sigma * 1$) is not an element of S. For example in the Robson marking algorithm that we examine later on we use *terminal* to mean terminal with respect to the left-first spanning tree. There are various well known spanning trees for graphs (Aho, Hopcroft and Ullman, 1974). We shall be using the left-first spanning tree in this book. The left-first spanning tree of $\mathbf{Cells}_\mu(v)$ can be defined as follows. For $c \in \mathbf{Cells}_\mu(v)$ the function $\mathbf{Left}_{v;\mu}$:$[\mathbf{Cells}_\mu(v) \nrightarrow \mathbb{T}]$ chooses the least path in μ from v to c with respect to the Brouwer-Kleene ordering ($\preceq$).

$$\mathbf{Left}_{v;\mu}(c) = \sigma \;\rightarrow\; (v\,;\mu)_\sigma = c \wedge \forall\sigma_0((v\,;\mu)_{\sigma_0} = c \rightarrow \sigma \preceq \sigma_0).$$

The left first spanning tree of $v\,;\mu$ is then the image of $\mathbf{Left}_{v;\mu}$ and is denoted by $\Lambda_{v;\mu}$.

$$\Lambda_{v;\mu} \underset{\text{df}}{=} \{\mathbf{Left}_{v;\mu}(c) \,|\, c \in \mathbf{Cells}_\mu(v)\}$$

The left-first spanning tree of $\mathbf{Cells}_\mu(\bar{v})$ can be defined similarly as follows, assuming $|\bar{v}| = k$. For $c \in \mathbf{Cells}_\mu(\bar{v})$ the function $\mathbf{Left}_{\bar{v};\mu}$: $\mathbf{Cells}_\mu(\bar{v}) \nrightarrow k \times \mathbb{T}$ chooses the least path in μ from $\bar{v}$ to c with respect to the lexicographic ordering, $\leq$, of $n \times \mathbb{T}$, the ordering on $n = \{0, 1, \ldots, n-1\}$ being the usual one and the ordering on $\mathbb{T}$ being the Brouwer-Kleene ordering ($\preceq$).

$$\mathbf{Left}_{\bar{v};\mu}(c) = [i, \sigma] \rightarrow (\bar{v}{\downarrow_i}\,;\mu)_\sigma = c \wedge (\forall\sigma_0, j)((\bar{v}{\downarrow_j}\,;\mu)_{\sigma_0} = c \rightarrow [i, \sigma] \leq [j, \sigma_0]).$$

The left-first spanning tree of $\bar{v}\,;\mu$ is then the image of $\mathbf{Left}_{\bar{v};\mu}$ and is denoted by $\Lambda_{\bar{v};\mu}$.

$$\Lambda_{\bar{v};\mu} \underset{\text{df}}{=} \{\mathbf{Left}_{\bar{v};\mu}(c) \,|\, c \in \mathbf{Cells}_\mu(\bar{v})\}$$

When we consider $\mathbf{Cells}_\mu(\bar{v})$as a sequence we always assume that it is ordered in this left first fashion.

Now given that S is a spanning tree for X at $c\,;\mu$ and $c_0 \in X$, we say that c_1 *lies below* c_0 in S if $\exists\sigma_0, \sigma_1 \in \mathbb{T}$ such that

1. $\sigma_0, \sigma_1 \in S$
2. $(c\,;\mu)_{\sigma_i} = c_i$, for $i \in 2$, and
3. $\sigma_0 \leq \sigma_1$ in $\mathbb{T}$.

Similarly we can talk about c_0 being above, to the left, or to the right of c_1 in S. We also put

$$S(c_0) = \{c_1 \mid c_1 \text{ lies below } c_0 \text{ in } S\}.$$

Observe that $S(c_0) \subseteq X$ and that if c_1 lies below c_0 in S then $S(c_1) \subseteq S(c_0)$ with equality holding only when $c_0 = c_1$.

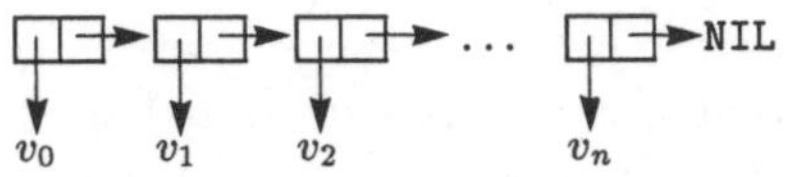

Figure 4. A Typical List

2.1.8. Subdomains of $\mathbb{M}_{sexp}$

We can now define some well known subsets of $\mathbb{M}_{sexp}$. The first, $\mathbb{M}_{wf}$, is the class of well-founded S-expressions and is defined using the tree function:

Definition: We say that $v;\mu$ is a *well-founded* S-expression, written $v;\mu \in \mathbb{M}_{wf}$, if $\delta_{(v;\mu)}$ is a well-founded tree. In other words

$$(\forall c \in \mathbf{Cells}_\mu(v))c \notin \mathbf{Cells}_\mu^<(c).$$

It is important to notice that if $c^* \in \mathbf{Cells}_\mu(c)$ and $c\,;\mu \in \mathbb{M}_{wf}$ then

$$\mathbf{Cells}_\mu(c^*) \subseteq \mathbf{Cells}_\mu(c)$$

with equality holding only when $c^* = c$. This provides a very simple measure upon which to perform induction.

Definition: There are two different notions of *list* depending on whether one allows cyclic lists. We shall refer to the non-cyclic version as $\mathbb{M}_{list}$ and the possibly infinite variety by $\mathbb{M}_{elist}$.

$$v\,;\mu \in \mathbb{M}_{list} \;\leftrightarrow\; (\exists n \in \mathbb{N})(v\,;\mu)_{1^n} = \mathtt{NIL}.$$

Thus $c\,;\mu$ is in $\mathbb{M}_{list}$ iff some *cdr*-chain leads to an atom and this atom is NIL. Thus the typical non-empty list can be represented as in figure 4.

The collection of possibly cyclic lists, $\mathbb{M}_{elist}$, is defined as follows:

$$v\,;\mu \in \mathbb{M}_{elist} \;\leftrightarrow\; (\forall n \in \mathbb{N})(1^n \in \delta_{(v;\mu)} \;\wedge\; (v\,;\mu)_{1^n} \in \mathbb{A} \rightarrow (v\,;\mu)_{1^n} = \mathtt{NIL}).$$

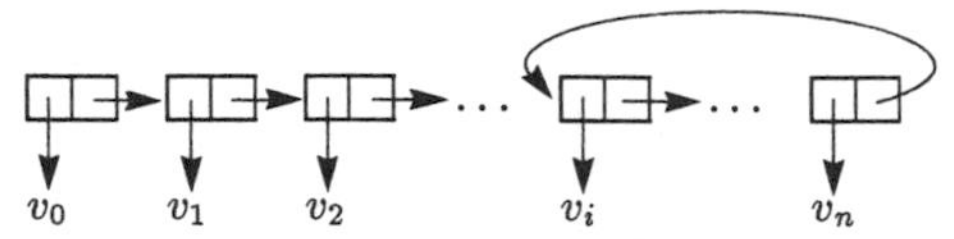

Figure 5. A Typical Cyclic List

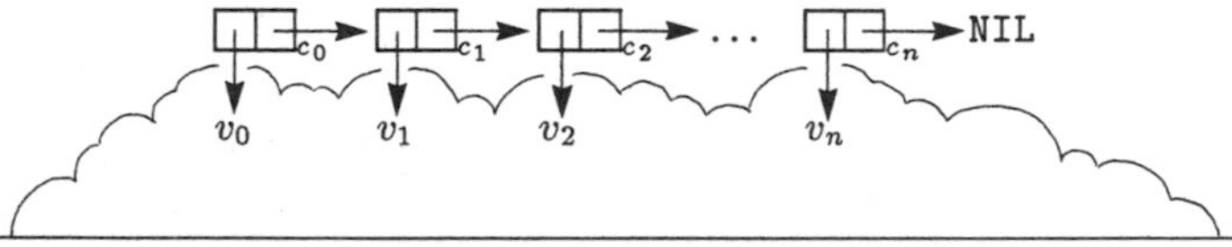

Figure 6. A Typical Pure List, $c_i \notin \mathbf{Cells}_\mu(v_j)$.

Thus a typical element of $\mathbb{M}_{elist} - \mathbb{M}_{list}$ is represented in figure 5.

To make talking about lists somewhat easier we have the following notation. The set of cells that are reachable from a non-NIL elist, $c\,;\mu \in \mathbb{M}_{elist}$, only by using the the function *cdr* is called the *spine* of the list. Namely

$$\mathbf{Spine}_\mu(c) = \{(c\,;\mu)_{1^n} \mid 1^n \in \delta_{(c;\mu)}\} - \{\texttt{NIL}\}.$$

Suppose $c_0\,;\mu_0 \in \mathbb{M}_{list}$ is such that

$$\mathbf{Spine}_{\mu_0}(c_0) = \{c_0 \ldots c_n\}$$

with $\mu_0(c_i) = [v_i\ ,\ c_{i+1}]$ for $i \in n$ and $\mu_0(c_n) = [v_n\ ,\ \texttt{NIL}]$. Then we say $c_0\,;\mu_0$ represents the Lisp list $(v_0\ v_1\ v_2\ \ldots\ v_n)$, represented diagramatically as in figure 6.

We call the v_i the elements of the list $c_0\,;\mu_0$ and put $\mathbf{Elements}_{\mu_0}(c_0) = [v_0, \ldots, v_n]$. We say $c_0\,;\mu_0$ is a *pure* list if $\mathbf{Spine}_{\mu_0}(c_0)$ is disjoint from the set

$$\bigcup_{v_i \in \mathbf{Elements}_{\mu_0}(c_0)} \mathbf{Cells}_{\mu_0}(v_i).$$

A pure list is determined up to *isomorphism* (to be defined later) by the sequence of its elements.

2.2. Computing over Memory Structures

Thus far we have described the underlying data structure. We now turn to the syntax of our language and its subsequent semantics. This we do in three steps. We first define a class of expressions, $\mathbb{E}$, in a lexically scoped Lisp-like language. Secondly using these expressions we specify how functions are to be defined. Finally we define a certain class of objects, called *memory object descriptions,* which are pairs consisting of an expression with no free variables, together with a memory in which every cons cell appearing in the expression exists in that memory, i.e. is in its domain. On these objects we define a *sequential reduction relation* which determines the computation that these memory object descriptions describe. Using this reduction relation on memory object descriptions we can describe the partial functions that are determined by our definitions. The basic rules for computation are given by a *reduction* relation on memory object descriptions, $e_0\,;\mu_0 \gg^D e_1\,;\mu_1$. This relation is generated by two sets of rules, the primitive cases and the congruence cases. That is, $\gg^D$ is the least transitive relation containing the primitive cases and closed under the congruence conditions. The primitive cases correspond to primitive machine instructions for branching, sequencing, variable binding, execution of memory structure operations and function call. The congruence cases are rules for reducing sub-expressions in order to reduce descriptions to primitive cases. They determine which sub-expression may be reduced and the effect of that reduction on the description containing it. The computation theory as defined in this section holds for an arbitrary memory structure; however, the reader may find it helpful to keep the S-expression memory structure in mind since it is the example that we are most interested in.

2.2.1. The Set of Memory Expressions

The set of expressions of our language, $\mathbb{E}$, is defined as follows. Let $\mathbb{X}$ and $\mathbb{F}$ be disjoint countable sets. Elements of $\mathbb{X}$ are memory variable symbols and range over memory values. Elements of $\mathbb{F}$ are function symbols, each with an associated finite arity. Finally there are constant symbols for the atoms and memory operations of $\mathbb{M}$. However, we shall not make any attempt to distinguish between an atom or operation and the constant that denotes it. We use x, x_0, ... for elements of $\mathbb{X}$, f, f_0, ... for elements of $\mathbb{F}$, and e, e_0, ... for memory expressions. The set of *memory expressions* is defined inductively to be the smallest set $\mathbb{E}$ containing

- $\mathbb{V} = \mathbb{A} \oplus \mathbb{C}$,
- $\mathbb{X}$,

and closed under the following formation rules:

- if $e_{test}, e_{then}, e_{else} \in \mathbb{E}$ then $\mathtt{if}(e_{test}, e_{then}, e_{else}) \in \mathbb{E}$;

- if $e_1, \ldots, e_n, e_{body} \in \mathbb{E}$ and $x_1, \ldots, x_n \in \mathbb{X}$ are distinct then
$$\texttt{let}\{x_1 \leftarrow e_1, \ldots, x_m \leftarrow e_m\}e_{body} \in \mathbb{E};$$
- if $e_1, \ldots, e_n \in \mathbb{E}$ then $\texttt{seq}(e_1, \ldots, e_n) \in \mathbb{E}$;
- if ϑ is either an n-ary memory operation or n-ary function symbol from $\mathbb{F}$, and $e_1, \ldots, e_n \in \mathbb{E}$ then $\vartheta(e_1, \ldots, e_n) \in \mathbb{E}$;

Although we have allowed cells, or at least constant symbols denoting them, to appear in expressions, we warn the reader that this will only occur in special contexts. These contexts, which will be defined shortly, are called *memory object descriptions.* The reason for these restrictions is quite simple. If we allowed arbitrary cells to appear in expressions then those expressions could only be evaluated or have meaning in a context, or more appropriately a memory, in which those cells were defined. We shall repeat this warning when we define the appropriate contexts.

The only variable binding operation is `let`. $\texttt{let}\{y_1 \leftarrow e_1, \ldots, y_m \leftarrow e_m\}e_{body}$ binds the free occurrences of y_i to the value returned by e_i in e_{body}. It can thus be thought of as either a *substitution* primitive or else simply a more readable form of λ-*application* since

$$\texttt{let}\{y_1 \leftarrow e_1, \ldots, y_m \leftarrow e_m\}e_{body}$$

is equivalent to

$$(\lambda y_1, y_2, \ldots y_m . e_{body})[e_1, e_2, \ldots e_m].$$

The $\{y_1 \leftarrow e_1, \ldots, y_m \leftarrow e_m\}$ part of a `let` expression is called the *binding expression.* For a memory expression e the set of free variables in e, $FV(e)$, is defined in the usual manner. We say that e is *closed* if $FV(e)$ is empty. $e\{y_1 \leftarrow v_1, \ldots, y_m \leftarrow v_m\}$ is the result of substituting free occurrences of the y_i in e by the values v_i, or to be more precise the constant symbols denoting them.

Definition: We call an expression which contains no $f \in \mathbb{F}$ or $c \in \mathbb{C}$ a *primitive term* or more often simply a *term.*

In addition to the basic constructs of our language, we also use constructs like `and`, `not`, `or` and `ifn`. They are taken to be the usual Lisp abbreviations or *macros*, namely:

$$\texttt{and}(e_1, e_2) \underset{\text{df}}{=} \texttt{if}(e_1, e_2, \texttt{NIL})$$

$$\texttt{or}(e_1, e_2) \underset{\text{df}}{=} \texttt{let}\{t_1 \leftarrow e_1\}\texttt{if}(t_1, t_1, e_2)$$

$$\texttt{not}(e) \underset{\text{df}}{=} \texttt{if}(e, \texttt{NIL}, \texttt{T})$$

$$\texttt{ifn}(e_{test}, e_{then}, e_{else}) \underset{\text{df}}{=} \texttt{if}(e_{test}, e_{else}, e_{then})$$

In addition we have a *cond*-like construct $\mathtt{ifs}$, where

$$\mathtt{ifs}(e_0^0, e_1^0, \ldots, e_0^n, e_1^n) \underset{\mathrm{df}}{=} \mathtt{if}(e_0^0, e_1^0, \mathtt{if}(e_0^1, e_1^1 \ldots \mathtt{if}(e_0^n, e_1^n, \mathtt{NIL}) \ldots))).$$

We also write expressions such as

$$\mathtt{let}_{0 \leq j \leq n}\{x_j \leftarrow e_j\}e_{body} \text{ to denote } \mathtt{let}\{x_0 \leftarrow e_1, \ldots, x_n \leftarrow e_n\}e_{body}$$

and

$$\mathtt{seq}_{0 \leq j \leq n}(e_j) \text{ to denote } \mathtt{seq}(e_0, \ldots, e_n).$$

We shall discuss macros in more detail in chapter 9.

2.2.2. Function Definitions

A system of memory function definitions D is a collection of equations of the form

$$D = \begin{cases} f_0(\bar{x}_0) \leftarrow e_0 \\ \ldots\ldots \\ f_n(\bar{x}_n) \leftarrow e_n \end{cases}$$

that satisfies the following conditions:

- Each $\bar{x}_i = [x_0^i, \ldots x_{m_i-1}^i]$ is a sequence, without repetitions, of variables from $\mathbb{X}$ of length m_i.
- f_i is an m_i-ary function symbol from $\mathbb{F}$.
- e_i must be a memory expression such that the free variables of e_i are a subset of $\bar{x}_i$, the only function symbols that occur in e_i are among $f_0, \ldots, f_n$, and no $c \in \mathbb{C}$ occurs in any of the e_i.

We are somewhat liberal in what we use as variables and function symbols, using words with suggestive names. As an example of typical definitions we give those of *append*, *memq* and *inplace:reverse*:

append(u, v) ← if(u, *cons*(*car*(u), *append*(*cdr*(u)), v)), v)

memq(element, list) ←
    if(list,
        if(*eq*(element, *car*(list)), T, *memq*(element, *cdr*(list))),
        NIL)

$$\mathit{inplace{:}reverse}(\mathtt{u}) \leftarrow \mathit{in{:}rev}(\mathtt{u}, \mathtt{NIL})$$

$$\mathit{in{:}rev}(\mathtt{u}, \mathtt{v}) \leftarrow \mathtt{if}(\mathtt{u}, \mathit{in{:}rev}(\mathit{cdr}(\mathtt{u}), \mathit{rplacd}(\mathtt{u}, \mathtt{v})), \mathtt{v}))$$

The *append* program as written here simply copies the spine of its first argument and attaches it to the second argument. Notice that the definition actually is in the pure fragment $\mathbb{M}_{pure}$. The *memq* program, written in the $\mathbb{M}_{pure^+}$ fragment, simply determines whether or not its first argument is a member of the second argument, which is supposed to be a list. *inplace:reverse* destructively reverses a list; in some Lisp dialects this function is called *nreverse*, see (Pitman, 1983), (Touretzky, 1983) or (Steele, 1984).

If D is the system of definitions

$$D = \begin{cases} f_0(\bar{x}_0) \leftarrow e_0 \\ \ldots\ldots \\ f_n(\bar{x}_n) \leftarrow e_n \end{cases}$$

then we say D is a *tail-recursive* system if and only if no function symbol f_i, which is defined in D, appears in D either in:

1. the test-expression of an `if` expression,
2. a binding expression of a `let` expression,
3. an expression other than the last in a `seq` , or
4. an expression that is an argument to a function or operation symbol in D.

It is well known that functions so defined can be implemented on low-level machines without the use of a stack; for a logical treatment see (Tucker, 1980) or (Friedman, 1971) and for a discussion relating to compiling (Steele and Sussman, 1976). For example, the *memq* and *inplace:reverse* definitions above are both tail recursive whereas the *append* program and the following definition of the list length function

$$\mathit{length}(\mathtt{list}) \leftarrow \mathtt{if}(\mathtt{list}, \mathit{add1}(\mathit{length}(\mathit{cdr}(\mathtt{list}))), \mathtt{0})$$

are not tail-recursive. However the following system, which defines an *extensionally* equivalent *length* function, is tail-recursive.

$$\mathit{length}(\mathtt{list}) \leftarrow \mathit{len}(\mathtt{list}, \mathtt{0})$$

$$\mathit{len}(\mathtt{list}, \mathtt{n}) \leftarrow \mathtt{if}(\mathtt{list}, \mathit{len}(\mathit{cdr}(\mathtt{list}), \mathit{add1}(\mathtt{n})), \mathtt{n})$$

2.2.3. Memory Object Descriptions and $\gg^D$

A closed memory expression together with a *suitable* memory describes the computation of a memory object. Such pairs are called *memory object descriptions.* To make the notion of suitable precise, we fix a system of function definitions

$$D = \begin{cases} f_0(\bar{x}_0) \leftarrow e_0 \\ \ldots\ldots \\ f_n(\bar{x}_n) \leftarrow e_n \end{cases}$$

Definition: A *memory object description* with respect to D is then defined to be a pair $e\ ;\ \mu$ that satisfies the following conditions:

- e is a closed memory expression, i.e. e contains no free variables
- any c which occurs in e is also in δ_μ, and
- every function symbol $f \in \mathbb{F}$ which occurs in e is defined in D.

Remark: As we have already mentioned when we defined the class of expressions, we shall make the following important convention. Only in the context of memory object descriptions shall we allow expressions to contain cells; thus when we say $e(\bar{x})$ is an expression we shall implicitly be saying that no cell $c \in \mathbb{C}$ occurs in $e(\bar{x})$. It is only when we evaluate $e(\bar{x})$ at some memory object $\bar{v}\ ;\ \mu$ that we shall allow cells to appear in e. By evaluating $e(\bar{x})$ at $\bar{v}\ ;\ \mu$ we mean reducing the memory object description $e(\bar{v})\ ;\ \mu$.

The basic rules for computation are given by the reduction relation $\gg^D$ on memory object descriptions. It is the least transitive relation containing the *single step* reduction relation, $\rightarrow\!\!>^D$, which is generated by the rules given below. As we have already mentioned, the primitive cases correspond to primitive machine instructions for branching, sequencing, variable binding, execution of memory structure operations and function call, while the congruence cases are rules for reducing sub-expressions in order to reduce descriptions to primitive cases. They determine which sub-expression may be reduced and the effect of that reduction on the description containing it. We have adhered to the Lisp convention of call-by-value, and that arguments of functions are evaluated in a left to right order. The reader is reminded that $v, v_0, \ldots$ range over $\mathbb{V}$, and that these are entities which cannot be further evaluated.

Definition: The single step reduction relation, $\rightarrow\!\!>^D$, is defined to be the smallest relation on memory object descriptions that satisfies the following two sets of rules.

• **Primitive cases:**

$$\texttt{if}(v_0, e_{then}, e_{else})\,;\mu \twoheadrightarrow^D \begin{cases} e_{then}\,;\mu & \text{if } v_0 \neq \texttt{NIL} \\ e_{else}\,;\mu & \text{if } v_0 = \texttt{NIL} \end{cases}$$

$$\texttt{seq}(e)\,;\mu \twoheadrightarrow^D e\,;\mu$$

$$\texttt{seq}(v_0, e_1, \ldots, e_m)\,;\mu \twoheadrightarrow^D \texttt{seq}(e_1, \ldots, e_m)\,;\mu$$

$$\texttt{let}\{y_1 \leftarrow v_1, \ldots, y_m \leftarrow v_m\}e\,;\mu \twoheadrightarrow^D e\{y_1 \leftarrow v_1, \ldots, y_m \leftarrow v_m\}\,;\mu$$

$$\vartheta(v_1, \ldots, v_n)\,;\mu \twoheadrightarrow^D v_0\,;\mu_0$$

if ϑ is a memory operation and $\vartheta([v_1, \ldots, v_n]\,;\mu) = v_0\,;\mu_0$

$$\vartheta(v_1, \ldots, v_n)\,;\mu \twoheadrightarrow^D e\{y_1 \leftarrow v_1, \ldots, y_n \leftarrow v_n\}\,;\mu \qquad \text{if } \vartheta(y_1, \ldots, y_n) \leftarrow e \text{ is in } D.$$

• **Congruence cases:** If $e_a\,;\mu_a \twoheadrightarrow^D e_b\,;\mu_b$ then

$$\texttt{if}(e_a, e_{then}, e_{else})\,;\mu_a \twoheadrightarrow^D \texttt{if}(e_b, e_{then}, e_{else})\,;\mu_b$$

$$\texttt{seq}(e_a, \ldots)\,;\mu_a \twoheadrightarrow^D \texttt{seq}(e_b, \ldots)\,;\mu_b$$

$$\texttt{let}\{y_1 \leftarrow v_1, \ldots, y_{j-1} \leftarrow v_{j-1}, y_j \leftarrow e_a, \ldots, y_m \leftarrow e_m\}e\,;\mu_a \twoheadrightarrow^D$$
$$\qquad \texttt{let}\{y_1 \leftarrow v_1, \ldots, y_{j-1} \leftarrow v_{j-1}, y_j \leftarrow e_b, \ldots, y_m \leftarrow e_m\}e\,;\mu_b$$

$$\vartheta(v_1, \ldots, v_{j-1}, e_a, \ldots, e_m)\,;\mu_a \twoheadrightarrow^D \vartheta(v_1, \ldots, v_{j-1}, e_b, \ldots, e_m)\,;\mu_b$$

As we have already stated, the *reduction relation* on memory object descriptions, $e_0\,;\mu_0 \gg^D e_1\,;\mu_1$, is the transitive closure of the single step relation. We say $e\,;\mu$ *evaluates* to $v_0\,;\mu_0$ if $e\,;\mu \gg^D v_0\,;\mu_0$ for some $v_0 \in \mathbb{V}$. To emphasize D we sometimes say $e\,;\mu$ *evaluates* to $v_0\,;\mu_0$ with respect to D when $e\,;\mu \gg^D v_0\,;\mu_0$ for some $v_0 \in \mathbb{V}$. More often than not, though, we leave D implicit and simply write $e\,;\mu \gg v_0\,;\mu_0$.

We can now easily describe the functions determined by our definition D. Namely if ϑ is defined in D and $(y_1, \ldots, y_n)$ are its arguments then the corresponding partial function

$$\vartheta^D\colon \mathbb{M}_{sexp}^{(n)} \rightsquigarrow \mathbb{M}_{sexp}$$

is defined by

$$\vartheta^D([v_1, \ldots, v_n]\,;\mu) = v_0\,;\mu_0 \underset{\text{df}}{\equiv} \vartheta(v_1, \ldots, v_n)\,;\mu \gg^D v_0\,;\mu_0.$$

2.2.4. Remarks

• It is easy to see that for any memory object description, at most one of the single step rules applies. Thus the single step relation is functional as is the corresponding evaluation relation $e\,;\mu_0 \gg^D v\,;\mu_1$.

• We use memory operation and function symbols in two contexts: in terms denoting memory objects and in memory object descriptions. In the term context we include the memory as an argument while in the memory object description the memory is not included in the argument. For example, $car(c\,;\mu)$ is a term and $car(c)\,;\mu$ is a memory object description, and we have $car(c)\,;\mu \gg^D car(c\,;\mu)$. The two uses of operation and function symbols should cause no confusion.

• The values of the binding expressions of a `let` construct are evaluated in sequence. Then the free occurences of the variables in the body of the expression are replaced by the corresponding values. The binding expressions are evaluated in their original environment and not the one being created by the `let`. So, for example,

$$\texttt{let}\{x_0 \leftarrow e_0, x_1 \leftarrow e_1\}e_{body}$$

will not always reduce to the same value as

$$\texttt{let}\{x_0 \leftarrow e_0\}\texttt{let}\{x_1 \leftarrow e_1\}e_{body}.$$

The `seq` construct provides for sequencing of computations. It is similar to the `PROGN` construct of Lisp . We should point out that `seq` is definable in terms of `let` since

$$\texttt{seq}(e_0, e_1, \ldots, e_n)$$

is equivalent to

$$\texttt{let}\{x_0 \leftarrow e_0, x_1 \leftarrow e_1, \ldots, x_n \leftarrow e_n\}x_n$$

Definition by cases is handled by the `if` construct. Notice that as usual in Lisp any non-`NIL` value of the test is considered *true*.

• We have not included a means of dynamically assigning values to variables, such as the Lisp `SETQ` mechanism. For present purposes the inclusion of such mechanisms mainly complicates the semantics, while it does not enlarge the class of *definable* functions. They become interesting in a computation theory where functions can be returned as values.

• Our notion of memory structure is essentially that of (Burstall, 1972), although the presentations are somewhat different. Burstall treats computations described by flowchart programs and develops proof rules for proving properties of certain list and tree like memories. We treat computations described by systems of recursive definition and prove properties of the functions described by these computations. In this book we treat a larger variety of programs acting on much less restricted domains. We focus on mathematical properties of the S-expression domain and only develop formal proof-rules as a by-product of such activity. We should also remark that some of our notation and methods are derived in spirit from (Topor, 1979), although in the world he created, cells had mark and field bits.

2.2.5. Example of a Computation

Consider the following pictorial example of the process of evaluating a memory object description. Suppose that

$$cons(\mathtt{A}, cons(\mathtt{B}, \mathtt{NIL}))\ ;\ \emptyset \gg c_0\ ;\ \mu,$$

then we can represent $c_0\ ;\ \mu$ by the boxes and pointers diagram shown in figure 7 (here $\emptyset$ denotes the empty memory). Then the memory object description $inplace{:}reverse(c_0)\ ;\ \mu$ evaluates in the fashion depicted in figure 8.

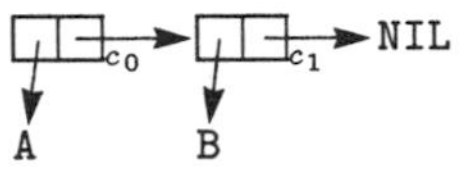

Figure 7. The Boxes and Pointers picture of $c_0\ ;\ \mu$

2.2.6. Functions and Transformations on Expressions

To complete this section we describe some functions and transformations on expressions that will prove useful later. The first is the rank function on expressions. It will often be used when proving facts about primitive terms.

Definition: The *rank* of an expression, $r(e)$, is defined by induction on the complexity of expressions as follows.

$$r(e) = \begin{cases} \infty & \text{if } e = \vartheta(e_1, \ldots, e_{j-1}) \text{ and } \vartheta \in \mathbb{F}, \\ 0 & \text{if } e \in \mathbb{X} \cup \mathbb{A}, \\ 1 + r(e_0) + \mathbf{Max}\{r(e_1), r(e_2)\} & \text{if } e = \mathtt{if}(e_0, e_1, e_2), \\ 1 + r(e_0) + \ldots + r(e_n) & \text{if } e = \mathtt{seq}(e_0, \ldots e_n), \\ 1 + r(e_0) + \ldots + r(e_n) + r(e) & \text{if } e = \mathtt{let}\{y_0 \leftarrow e_0, \ldots, y_n \leftarrow e_n\}e, \\ 1 + r(e_1) + \ldots + r(e_n) & \text{if } e = \vartheta(e_1, \ldots, e_n) \text{ and } \vartheta \in \mathbb{O}. \end{cases}$$

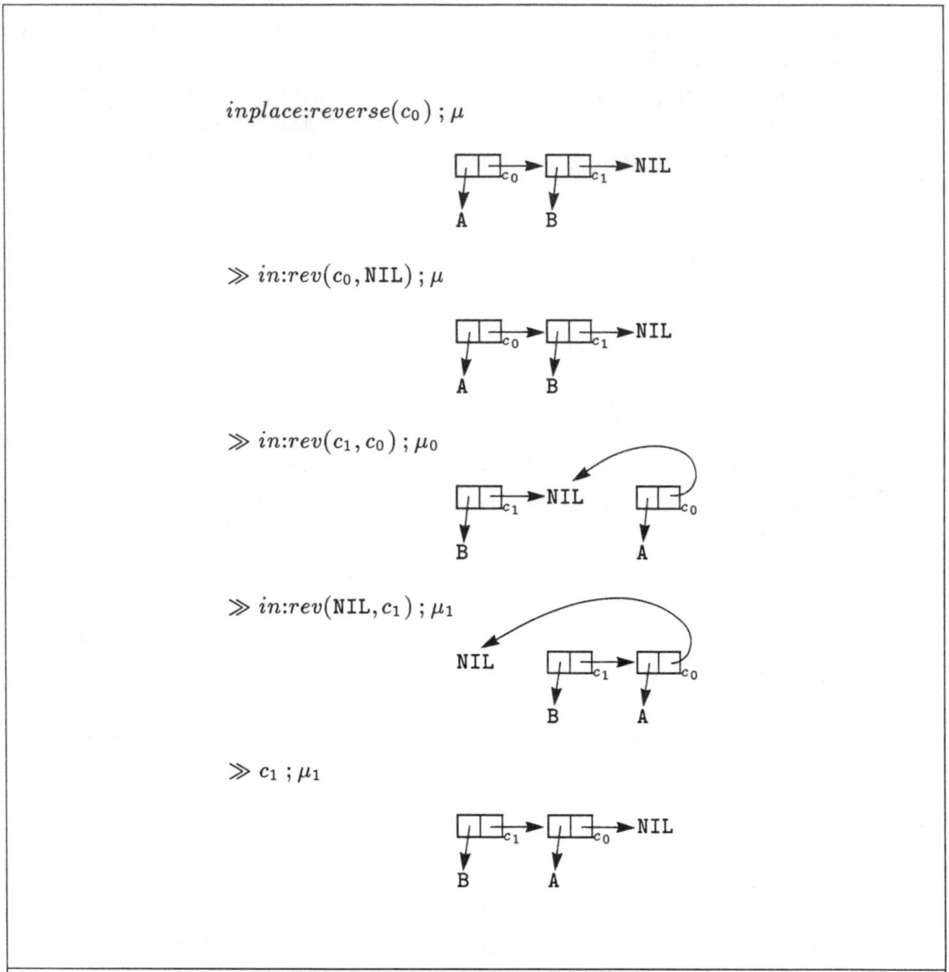

Figure 8. The Evaluation of $inplace{:}reverse(c_0)\ ;\ \mu$

The simplest result concerning this rank function is the following:

Proposition: If $e(\bar{x}) \in \mathbb{E}$ and $\bar{v}\ ;\ \mu \in \mathbb{M}_{sexp}{}^{|\bar{x}|}$ are such that $e(\bar{v})\ ;\ \mu \gg v^*\ ;\ \mu^*$ via a single step reduction sequence of length N, then $N \leq r(e(\bar{x}))$.

The next example is a transformation on expressions named after the *unfold* transformation in (Burstall and Darlington, 1977).

Definition: The *unfolding*, $e^{\bowtie}$, of an expression e with respect to the definition D is defined by:

$$e^{\bowtie} = \begin{cases} e & \text{if } e \in \mathbb{X} \cup \mathbb{V}, \\ \mathtt{if}(e^{\bowtie}_{test}, e^{\bowtie}_{then}, e^{\bowtie}_{else}) & \text{if } e = \mathtt{if}(e_{test}, e_{then}, e_{else}), \\ \mathtt{seq}(e^{\bowtie}_0, \ldots e^{\bowtie}_n) & \text{if } e = \mathtt{seq}(e_0, \ldots e_n), \\ \mathtt{let}\{y_0 \leftarrow e^{\bowtie}_0, \ldots, y_n \leftarrow e^{\bowtie}_n\} e^{\bowtie}_{body} & \text{if } e = \mathtt{let}\{y_0 \leftarrow e_0, \ldots, y_n \leftarrow e_n\} e_{body}, \\ \vartheta(e^{\bowtie}_1, \ldots, e^{\bowtie}_n) & \text{if } e = \vartheta(e_1, \ldots, e_n) \text{ and } \vartheta \in \mathbb{O}_{sexp}, \\ \mathtt{let}\{y_0 \leftarrow e^{\bowtie}_0, \ldots, y_n \leftarrow e^{\bowtie}_n\} e_{\vartheta} & \text{if } e = \vartheta(e_1, \ldots, e_n) \text{ and } \vartheta(\bar{y}) \leftarrow e_{\vartheta} \in D, \\ \vartheta(e^{\bowtie}_1, \ldots, e^{\bowtie}_n) & \text{otherwise .} \end{cases}$$

Iterations of the unfolding operation are defined as follows: $e^{\bowtie^0} = e$ and $e^{\bowtie^n} = (e^{\bowtie^{n-1}})^{\bowtie}$. Another such transformation is the *skeleton*, $e^{\wr}$, of an expression e and is defined, as was the unfolding, by induction on the complexity of terms.

$$e^{\wr} = \begin{cases} e & \text{if } e \in \mathbb{X} \cup \mathbb{V}, \\ \mathtt{if}(e^{\wr}_{test}, e^{\wr}_{then}, e^{\wr}_{else}) & \text{if } e = \mathtt{if}(e_{test}, e_{then}, e_{else}), \\ \mathtt{seq}(e^{\wr}_0, \ldots e^{\wr}_n) & \text{if } e = \mathtt{seq}(e_0, \ldots e_n), \\ \mathtt{let}\{y_0 \leftarrow e^{\wr}_0, \ldots, y_n \leftarrow e^{\wr}_n\} e^{\wr}_{body} & \text{if } e = \mathtt{let}\{y_0 \leftarrow e_0, \ldots, y_n \leftarrow e_n\} e_{body}, \\ \vartheta(e^{\wr}_1, \ldots, e^{\wr}_n) & \text{if } e = \vartheta(e_1, \ldots, e_n) \text{ and } \vartheta \in \mathbb{O}_{sexp}, \\ \mathtt{NIL} & \text{if } e = \vartheta(e_1, \ldots, e_n) \text{ and } \vartheta \in \mathbb{F}. \end{cases}$$

These two transformations will prove useful later. Notice that $e^{\wr}$ is always a primitive term. A simple result concerning these transformations is:

Proposition: If $e(\bar{x}) \in \mathbb{E}$ is such that all $f \in \mathbb{F}$ which occur in it are defined in D and $\bar{v} \,;\, \mu \in \mathbb{M}_{sexp}{}^{|\bar{x}|}$ satisfies $e(\bar{v}) \,;\, \mu \gg v^* \,;\, \mu^*$ via a single step reduction sequence of length N, then $(e^{\bowtie^N})^{\wr}(\bar{v}) \,;\, \mu \gg v^* \,;\, \mu^*$ via a single step sequence of length $\leq N$.

The next example is a transformation on *pure* or *pure*$^+$ definitions that is generated by a transformation on expressions. It has to do with so-called *derived* functions. The idea is this: suppose we have a definition D

$$D = \begin{cases} f_0(\bar{x}_0) \leftarrow e_0 \\ \ldots\ldots \\ f_n(\bar{x}_n) \leftarrow e_n \end{cases}$$

and a memory operation or function symbol $\theta \in \mathbb{O}_{pure^+} \cup \{f_0, \ldots, f_n\}$, Then one wishes to construct a definition $D^{\sharp\theta}$ of the form

$$D^{\sharp\theta} = \begin{cases} f_0^{\sharp\theta}(\bar{x}_0) \leftarrow e_0^{\sharp\theta} \\ \ldots\ldots \\ f_n^{\sharp\theta}(\bar{x}_n) \leftarrow e_n^{\sharp\theta} \end{cases}$$

in such a way that $f_i^{\sharp\theta}$ and f_i have exactly the same arity and domain. Furthermore $f_i^{\sharp\theta}(\bar{v})\ ;\ \mu$ is to compute the number of *calls to* θ that occur in the process of evaluating $f_i(\bar{v})\ ;\ \mu$. For example if $\theta = cons$ and $f_i(\bar{v})\ ;\ \mu \gg^D u\ ;\ \mu^*$ then $f_i^{\sharp\theta}(\bar{v})\ ;\ \mu \gg^{D^{\sharp\theta}} N\ ;\ \mu^{**}$ where

$$N = |\delta_{\mu^*} - \delta_\mu|.$$

Before we give the transformation it should be noticed that we are defining it only for definitions in $\mathbb{M}_{pure+}$. Although it can be done in general, the solution is not as elegant and we leave it as a programming problem for the so-inclined reader. The first step is to define a transformation on expressions. Like those above this is done by induction on the complexity of expressions.

$$e^{\sharp\theta} = \begin{cases} 0 & \text{if } e \in \mathbb{X} \cup \mathbb{V}, \\ e_0^{\sharp\theta} + \ldots + e_n^{\sharp\theta} & \text{if } e = \mathtt{seq}(e_0, \ldots e_n), \\ \mathtt{seq}(\vartheta(e_0, \ldots, e_n), e_0^{\sharp\theta} + \ldots + e_n^{\sharp\theta}) & \text{if } e = \vartheta(\bar{e}), \vartheta \in \mathbb{O}_{sexp} \text{ and } \vartheta \neq \theta, \\ \mathtt{seq}(\vartheta(e_0, \ldots, e_n), 1 + e_0^{\sharp\theta} + \ldots + e_n^{\sharp\theta}) & \text{if } e = \vartheta(e_1, \ldots, e_n) \text{ and } \vartheta = \theta, \\ e_0^{\sharp\theta} + \ldots + e_n^{\sharp\theta} + f^{\sharp\theta}(\bar{e}) & \text{if } e = f(\bar{e}) \text{ and } f \in \mathbb{F}, \\ \mathtt{if}(e_{test}, e_{test}^{\sharp\theta} + e_{then}^{\sharp\theta}, e_{test}^{\sharp\theta} + e_{else}^{\sharp\theta}) & \text{if } e = \mathtt{if}(e_{test}, e_{then}, e_{else}), \\ e_0^{\sharp\theta} + \ldots + e_n^{\sharp\theta} + \mathtt{let}_{0 \le j \le n}\{y_j \leftarrow e_j\}e_{body}^{\sharp\theta} & \text{if } e = \mathtt{let}_{0 \le j \le n}\{y_j \leftarrow e_j\}e_{body}\ . \end{cases}$$

We then define $D^{\sharp\theta}$ to be as above. Rather than spend the time making the notion of *the number of calls to* θ precise, we simply state part of the main result concerning this transformation in the case when $\theta = cons$:

Proposition: If D is a *pure*$^+$-definition, $e(\bar{x}) \in \mathbb{E}$ and $\bar{v}\ ;\ \mu \in \mathbb{M}_{sexp}{}^{|\bar{x}|}$ then $e(\bar{v});\mu$ denotes with respect to D if and only if $e^{\sharp\theta}(\bar{v});\mu$ denotes with respect to $D^{\sharp\theta}$. Furthermore if $\theta = cons$ and $f_i(\bar{v})\ ;\ \mu \gg^D u\ ;\ \mu^*$ then $f_i^{\sharp cons}(\bar{v})\ ;\ \mu \gg^{D^{\sharp cons}} N\ ;\ \mu^{**}$, where $N = |\delta_{\mu^*} - \delta_\mu|$.

We shall use these derived functions in the next chapter to describe a whole family of intensional equivalence relations. We shall also illustrate how they can be used to prove intensional properties of simple programs in Chapter 4.

Chapter 3

Equivalence Relations

Equivalence relations on expressions and terms are central to our approach. *Operations on programs need meanings to transform and meanings to preserve,* (Talcott, 1985b and 1986), and the study of various notions of equivalence is simply a study of the various *meanings*. As we have mentioned before, we regard verification of programs and derivation of programs as duals of one another. In verification one proves that a given program meets or satisfies a certain specification. In derivation one does the reverse — from specifications one derives programs which accomplish the task. Often such specifications are just simple-minded or well known programs that perform the required calculation or construction. When this is the case, satisfying a specification or accomplishing a task can be formulated and proved using these equivalence relations. Without exception these equivalence relations are generated by equivalence relations on memory object descriptions. There are two different types of equivalence relations one can define on memory object descriptions and terms. First are the *extensional* ones, which are generated by equivalence relations on memory objects and are thus really properties of the function or transformation denoted by the expression. Second are the *intensional* ones, which not only depend on value of the memory object description but how the memory has been transformed in the process of evaluating it.

The latter class turns out to have a much more manageable theory than the former. We give two examples of the former, namely isomorphism and Lisp equality, and one of the latter, namely strong isomorphism. It will become apparent to the reader that strong isomorphism stands to destructive Lisp as Lisp equality stands to pure Lisp; in fact we shall prove a theorem to that effect.

The chapter is organized as follows. In the first section we examine the extensional relations and their properties, or lack of them. Then in the second section we describe the basic properties of the intensional approach, concentrating, as we have already mentioned, on strong isomorphism. In the third section we prove the fundamental property of this relation, the Substitution Theorem. In the fourth section we provide a wealth of syntactic manipulations that preserve strong isomorphism. For contrast, we also provide analogous principles for pure Lisp. Finally we give a simple example of the use of the strong isomorphism relation.

3.1. Isomorphism and Lisp Equality

In this section we describe two extensional equivalence relations, Lisp equality and isomorphism. Both of these are equivalence relations on memory objects, memory object descriptions and expressions, and are generated in a uniform fashion from their behavior on memory objects. Thus we describe in general how to extend an equivalence relation on memory objects to one that includes memory object descriptions and expressions, consequently we need only define Lisp equality and isomorphism on memory objects.

Supposing $\sim$ is an equivalence relation on memory objects, we extend $\sim$ to memory object descriptions and expressions in the following fashion.

1. **Memory object descriptions:** Two memory object descriptions $e_0 ; \mu_0$ and $e_1 ; \mu_1$ are said to be $\sim$-related, again written $e_0 ; \mu_0 \sim e_1 ; \mu_1$, iff either they both fail to denote or else they denote $\sim$-related memory objects.
2. **Expressions:** Two expressions $e_0(\bar{x})$ and $e_1(\bar{x})$ are $\sim$-related, $e_0(\bar{x}) \sim e_1(\bar{x})$, iff $\forall\ \bar{v} ; \mu \in \mathbb{M}_{sexp}$ we have that $e_0(\bar{v}) ; \mu \sim e_1(\bar{v}) ; \mu$.
3. **Subdomains:** By 1 and 2, expressions and terms are $\sim$-related iff whenever they denote they denote $\sim$-related objects. We also say that two expressions $e_0(\bar{x})$ and $e_1(\bar{x})$ are $\sim$-related on a subdomain, X, of $\mathbb{M}_{sexp}$, written

$$e_0(\bar{x}) \sim e_1(\bar{x}) \quad \text{on} \quad X,$$

iff $(\forall \bar{v} ; \mu \in X) \ \ (e_0(\bar{v}) ; \mu \sim e_1(\bar{v}) ; \mu)$.

These extensional relations are useful when one is specifying and proving properties of programs viewed as functions; we shall give some examples of such shortly. For the reader whose thirst is not quenched, (Mason and Talcott, 1985) contains many more examples than we shall present here. The actual algebraic definition of these relations on memory objects uses the tree function $(v ; \mu)$ associated with $v ; \mu$. We say memory objects $\bar{v}_0 ; \mu_0$ and $\bar{v}_1 ; \mu_1$ are isomorphic, written

$$\bar{v}_0 ; \mu_0 \cong \bar{v}_1 ; \mu_1,$$

if and only if their respective boxes and pointers diagrams are the same. In other words they are graph theoretically isomorphic via a map which preserves atomic values. This is stated precisely in the following.

Definition: If $[v_0, \ldots, v_n] ; \mu$, $[v_0^*, \ldots, v_n^*] ; \mu^* \in \mathbb{M}_{sexp}^{(n+1)}$ we say $[v_0, \ldots, v_n] ; \mu$ is *isomorphic* to $[v_0^*, \ldots, v_n^*] ; \mu^*$, written

$$[v_0, \ldots, v_n] ; \mu \cong [v_0^*, \ldots, v_n^*] ; \mu^*,$$

if there is a bijection $h : \mathbb{V} \to \mathbb{V}$ which is the identity on $\mathbb{A}$, maps $\mathbb{C} \to \mathbb{C}$ and is such that

$$h \circ (v_i \,;\, \mu) = (v_i^* \,;\, \mu^*)$$

as partial functions, for every $i \in n + 1$. Here $\circ$ denotes function composition.

The fact that isomorphism between terms can be axiomatized is expressed by the following result, which is proved in Chapter 5.

Theorem: (Effectiveness of $\cong$) There is a decision procedure which determines whether or not two primitive terms are isomorphic.

Remark: This theorem does not hold for arbitrary expressions, simply because

$$\mathtt{if}(\vartheta(x), \mathtt{T}, \mathtt{T}) \cong \mathtt{T}$$

holds iff ϑ is total, where ϑ is any defined function.

Two memory objects $\bar{v}_0 \,;\, \mu_0$ and $\bar{v}_1 \,;\, \mu_1$ are said to be *Lisp equal* iff they have exactly the same *car-cdr* chains, and whenever one chain ends in an atom in one it ends in the same atom in the other. This is formulated precisely by:

Definition: We say $v_0 \,;\, \mu_0$ and $v_1 \,;\, \mu_1$ are *Lisp equal*, written

$$v_0 \,;\, \mu_0 \equiv v_1 \,;\, \mu_1,$$

iff

- $(v_0 \,;\, \mu_0)$ and $(v_1 \,;\, \mu_1)$ have the same domains

and

- $(v_0 \,;\, \mu_0)_\sigma = a$ iff $(v_1 \,;\, \mu_1)_\sigma = a$, for $\sigma \in \delta_{(v;\mu_1)}$, $a \in \mathbb{A}$.

Finally we say $[v_0, \ldots, v_n] \,;\, \mu \equiv [v_0^*, \ldots, v_n^*] \,;\, \mu^*$ if for each $0 \leq i \leq n$ we have that $v_i \,;\, \mu \equiv v_i^* \,;\, \mu^*$.

An important point to observe is that S-expression memory operations preserve isomorphism. For example,

$$[c, v] \,;\, \mu \cong [c^*, v^*] \,;\, \mu^* \;\to\; \mathit{rplaca}(c, v \,;\, \mu) \cong \mathit{rplaca}(c^*, v^* \,;\, \mu^*).$$

This is certainly not true for Lisp equality. Note that isomorphism and Lisp equality also differ in that

$$\bigwedge_{0 \leq i \leq n} v_i \,;\, \mu \equiv v_i^* \,;\, \mu^* \;\to\; [v_0, \ldots, v_n] \,;\, \mu \equiv [v_0^*, \ldots, v_n^*] \,;\, \mu^*$$

while

$$\bigwedge_{0 \leq i \leq n} v_i \,;\, \mu \cong v_i^* \,;\, \mu^* \;\not\rightarrow\; [v_0, \ldots, v_n] \,;\, \mu \cong [v_0^*, \ldots, v_n^*] \,;\, \mu^*.$$

The former unlike the latter does not take structure sharing into account.

Two examples: The following are simple examples of these two relations on primitive terms.

1. $cons(cons(\mathtt{T},\mathtt{T}), cons(\mathtt{T},\mathtt{T})) \equiv \mathtt{let}\{x \leftarrow cons(\mathtt{T},\mathtt{T})\}\; cons(x,x)$. The values of these two expressions are represented in figure 9.

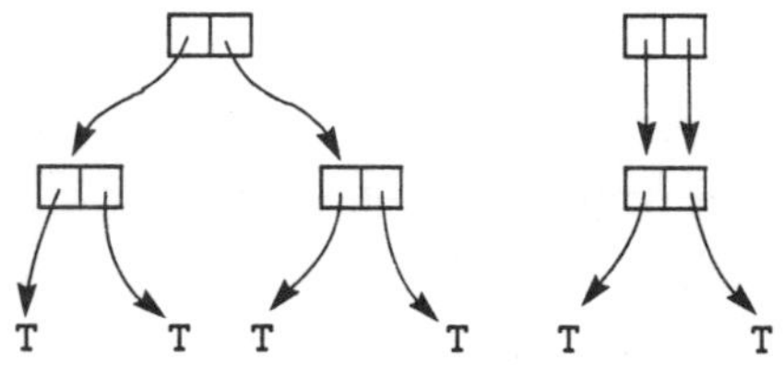

Figure 9. Example 1.

Note that we clearly have

$$cons(cons(\mathtt{T},\mathtt{T}), cons(\mathtt{T},\mathtt{T})) \not\cong \mathtt{let}\{x \leftarrow cons(\mathtt{T},\mathtt{T})\}\; cons(x,x).$$

2. $\mathtt{if}(atom(x), \mathtt{T}, rplacd(rplaca(x,\mathtt{T}),\mathtt{T})) \cong \mathtt{if}(atom(x), \mathtt{T}, cons(\mathtt{T},\mathtt{T}))$.

Note these examples show that $e_0 \sim e_1$ does not imply that $e(\bar{x}, e_0) \sim e(\bar{x}, e_1)$ when $\sim$ is either $\cong$ or $\equiv$. In the case of the first example $e(y) = rplaca(car(y), \mathtt{NIL})$ suffices and in the second case $e(x,y) = rplaca(y,x)$ is sufficient. Thus we do not have Leibniz's Law for these two relations. Consequently to prove properties of expressions using these two relations one must explicitly carry the memory around, dissecting it when necessary (i.e. hand simulation + induction). Perfect examples of this, and the disadvantages thereof, can be found in (Mason and Talcott, 1985). Notice that $v_0 \,;\, \mu_0 \equiv v_1 \,;\, \mu_1$ means that $v_0 \,;\, \mu_0$ and $v_1 \,;\, \mu_1$ *print* the same (for typical Lisp printing algorithms). As we have already mentioned we have the following simple result:

Proposition:

1. $\equiv$ and $\cong$ are both equivalence relations, on memory objects, memory object descriptions and expressions.
2. If $v_0 \,;\, \mu_0 \cong v_1 \,;\, \mu_1$ then $v_0 \,;\, \mu_0 \equiv v_1 \,;\, \mu_1$. The converse is false.
3. If D is a definition in either $\mathbb{M}_{sexp}$, $\mathbb{M}_{pure^+}$ or $\mathbb{M}_{pure}$ and ϑ is a function defined in D then the partial function determined by this definition preserves isomorphism. By this we mean that if $[v_0, \ldots, v_n] \,;\, \mu \cong [v_0^*, \ldots, v_n^*] \,;\, \mu^*$ then $\vartheta(v_0, \ldots, v_n) \,;\, \mu \cong \vartheta(v_0^*, \ldots, v_n^*) \,;\, \mu^*$ whenever either (equivalently both) denote.

The third clause in this proposition would be false if we did not abide by our convention that expressions do not contain cells. These properties in a sense characterize isomorphism. It is the weakest equivalence relation generated from an equivalence relation on memory objects that satisfies this proposition. For consider the following result, the proof of which is left to the reader.

Theorem: Suppose that $\sim$ is an equivalence relation on memory objects, memory object descriptions and expressions such that

0. $e_0(\bar{v}_0) \,;\, \mu_0 \sim e_1(\bar{v}_0) \,;\, \mu_0$ implies that either both sides fail to denote, or else they denote memory objects which are $\sim$-related.
1. $(\forall \bar{v} \,;\, \mu \in \mathbb{M}_{sexp})(e_0(\bar{v}) \,;\, \mu \sim e_1(\bar{v}) \,;\, \mu) \longleftrightarrow e_0(\bar{x}) \sim e_1(\bar{x})$.
2. $(\forall\, a_0, a_1 \in \mathbb{A})\ ((a_0 \,;\, \mu_0 \sim a_1 \,;\, \mu_1) \rightarrow (a_0 = a_1))$.
3. The relation $\sim$ satisfies a very weak Leibniz's Law

$$(\forall e_0(\bar{x}), e_1(\bar{x}) \in \mathbb{M}_{sexp})(\forall \bar{v}_0 \,;\, \mu_0, \bar{v}_1 \,;\, \mu_1 \in \mathbb{M}_{sexp})$$

$$\bar{v}_0 \,;\, \mu_0 \sim \bar{v}_1 \,;\, \mu_1 \,\wedge\, e_0(\bar{x}) \sim e_1(\bar{x}) \,\rightarrow\, e_0(\bar{v}_0) \,;\, \mu_0 \sim e_1(\bar{v}_1) \,;\, \mu_1.$$

Then

$$e_0 \sim e_1 \,\rightarrow\, e_0 \cong e_1.$$

Actually clause 2 in this theorem is not necessary (hint: use the partial nature of *car* to distinguish between atoms and cells, `if` to distinguish `NIL` from all other atoms and, finally, *eq* to distinguish distinct atoms). In (Mason and Talcott, 1985) it is shown that Lisp equality agrees with the usual notion on $\mathbb{M}_{wf}$. Consider the following well known $\mathbb{M}_{pure}$ program

$$\begin{array}{l} equal(\mathtt{u},\mathtt{v}) \leftarrow \\ \quad \mathtt{if}(\mathtt{or}(atom(\mathtt{u}), atom(\mathtt{v})), \\ \qquad atom{:}eq(\mathtt{u},\mathtt{v}), \\ \qquad \mathtt{and}(equal(car(\mathtt{u}), car(\mathtt{v})), \\ \qquad\quad equal(cdr(\mathtt{u}), cdr(\mathtt{v})))). \end{array}$$

Equality Theorem: *equal* is a total function from $\mathbb{M}_{wf}^{(2)}$ to $\mathbb{M}_{wf}$, having values amongst NIL, T. Further, if $v_0 ; \mu,\ v_1 ; \mu \in \mathbb{M}_{wf}$ then the following are equivalent:

1. $equal(v_0, v_1) ; \mu \cong \mathtt{T} ; \mu$
2. $v_0 ; \mu \equiv v_1 ; \mu$
3. $v_0 = v_1$ or else $v_0, v_1 \in \mathbb{C}$ and $car(v_0);\mu \equiv car(v_1);\mu \wedge cdr(v_0);\mu \equiv cdr(v_1);\mu$.

The proof is found below. Note that $\equiv$ cannot agree with *equal* on the whole of $\mathbb{M}_{sexp}$ because the simple recursive program will fail to terminate on many, but not all, cyclic structures. We should also point out that more model theoretic definitions of these two equivalence relations are possible, but we shall not do this just yet. For $v_0, v_1 \in \mathbb{V}$ we say $v_0 \equiv v_1$ iff either v_0 and $v_1 \in \mathbb{C}$ or else $v_0 = v_1$. Using this we have the following simple pointwise characterization of $\equiv$.

Proposition : The following are equivalent

1. $v_0 ; \mu_0 \equiv v_1 ; \mu_1$
2. $\delta_{(v_0;\mu_0)} = \delta_{(v_1;\mu_1)} = \gamma$ and $(\forall \sigma \in \gamma)\ ((v_0 ; \mu_0)_\sigma \equiv (v_1 ; \mu_1)_\sigma)$.

Notice that this together with simple properties of the derived tree function implies

Proposition : If $c_0 ; \mu$ and $c_1 ; \mu \in \mathbb{M}_{sexp}$ then the following are equivalent

1. $c_0 ; \mu \equiv c_1 ; \mu$
2. $(c_0 ; \mu)_i ; \mu \equiv (c_1 ; \mu)_i ; \mu$ for $i \in 2$.

In other words two S-expressions are Lisp equal iff their *car*s and *cdr*s are. The proofs of these two propositions are trivial.

Proof of Equality theorem: We prove that 1 is equivalent to 2, the rest then follows easily from the preceding propositions. This is done by induction on

$$r(v_0, v_1 ; \mu) = |\mathbf{Cells}_\mu(v_0)| \times |\mathbf{Cells}_\mu(v_1)|.$$

Base case: $r(v_0, v_1\,;\mu) = 0$. In this case $v_i \in \mathbb{A}$ for at least one $i \in 2$, and so

$$equal(v_0, v_1)\,;\mu \gg atom{:}eq(v_0, v_1)\,;\mu.$$

Since we have that $atom{:}eq(v_0, v_1)\,;\mu \gg \mathtt{T}\,;\mu$ iff $v_0 = v_1$, since both are in $\mathbb{A}$, and $v_0\,;\mu \equiv v_1\,;\mu$ iff $v_0 = v_1$ the theorem is true in this case.

Induction step: Suppose $r(v_0, v_1\,;\mu) > 0$ and that the theorem is true for any $v_2, v_3\,;\mu_0 \in \mathbb{M}_{wf}$ of less rank. Thus v_0 and $v_1 \in \mathbb{C}$ and

$$equal(v_0, v_1)\,;\mu \gg \mathtt{and}(equal(car(v_0), car(v_1)), equal(cdr(v_0), cdr(v_1)))\,;\mu$$

If we let $v_{ia} = \mu(v_i)\!\downarrow_0$ and $v_{id} = \mu(v_i)\!\downarrow_1$, for $i \in 2$ then we have

$$equal(v_0, v_1)\,;\mu \gg \mathtt{and}(equal(v_{0a}, v_{1a}), equal(cdr(v_0), cdr(v_1)))\,;\mu.$$

Now since $v_i \in \mathbb{M}_{wf}$ we have that $r(v_{0a}, v_{1a}\,;\mu), r(v_{0d}, v_{1d}\,;\mu) < r(v_0, v_1\,;\mu)$. There are two cases to consider.

Case 1: If $v_0\,;\mu \equiv v_1\,;\mu$ then by the previous proposition, $v_{0a}\,;\mu \equiv v_{1a}\,;\mu$ and $v_{0d}\,;\mu \equiv v_{1d}\,;\mu$. So in this case

$$equal(v_0, v_1)\,;\mu \gg \mathtt{and}(\ \mathtt{T}, equal(cdr(v_0), cdr(v_1)))\,;\mu \gg equal(v_{0d}, v_{1d})\,;\mu \gg \mathtt{T}\,;\mu.$$

Case 2: If $v_0;\mu \not\equiv v_1;\mu$ then, again by the previous proposition, either $v_{0a};\mu \not\equiv v_{1a};\mu$ or $v_{0d}\,;\mu \not\equiv v_{1d}\,;\mu$. Suppose $v_{0a}\,;\mu \not\equiv v_{1a}\,;\mu$ then

$$equal(v_0, v_1)\,;\mu \gg \mathtt{and}(\mathtt{NIL}, equal(cdr(v_0), cdr(v_1)))\,;\mu.$$

However, if $v_{0a}\,;\mu \equiv v_{1a}\,;\mu$, then

$$equal(v_0, v_1)\,;\mu \gg equal(cdr(v_0), cdr(v_1))\,;\mu \gg \mathtt{NIL}\,;\mu.$$

□**Theorem**

One other remark is that the above proof can easily be modified to show that the more efficient version of *equal* given below also satisfies this theorem.

```
equal(u,v) ←
     if(eq(u,v),T,if(or(atom(u),atom(v)),
                     NIL,
                     and(equal(car(u),car(v)),
                         equal(cdr(u),cdr(v)))))
```

The following result is slightly stronger than the corresponding result for pure Lisp; this is because in the following we must take structure sharing and cyclicity into account. It will be proved in Chapter 5.

Theorem: (Effectiveness of $\equiv$) There is a decision procedure which determines whether or not two primitive terms are Lisp equal.

As in the case of isomorphism this result does not hold for expressions. The following simple result is used in the proof of the effectiveness theorem. It provides a simple minded way of determining whether or not two objects are Lisp equal.

Proposition: For $v_i \,;\, \mu_i \in \mathbb{M}_{sexp}$, $i \in 2$ the following are equivalent:

1. $v_0 \,;\, \mu_0 \not\equiv v_1 \,;\, \mu_1$.
2. There is a $\sigma \in \mathbb{T}$ with the following two properties. Firstly,

$$|\sigma| \leq |\mathbf{Cells}_{\mu_0}(v_0)| \times |\mathbf{Cells}_{\mu_1}(v_1)|.$$

   Secondly, either exactly one of $(v_0 \,;\, \mu_0)_\sigma$ and $(v_1 \,;\, \mu_1)_\sigma$ is an atom or else they are both atoms and they are distinct.

Proof: Clearly 2 implies 1, hence it suffices to prove the other implication. Suppose that $v_0 \,;\, \mu_0 \not\equiv v_1 \,;\, \mu_1$ and that $\sigma \in \mathbb{T}$ is a *car-cdr* chain of least length such that either exactly one of $(v_0 \,;\, \mu_0)_\sigma$ and $(v_1 \,;\, \mu_1)_\sigma$ is an atom or else they are both distinct atoms. Furthermore suppose that

$$k = |\sigma| > |\mathbf{Cells}_{\mu_0}(v_0)| \times |\mathbf{Cells}_{\mu_1}(v_1)|.$$

Then let $\sigma_0, \sigma_1, \ldots, \sigma_k$ be the list of all the initial segments of σ in such an order that $|\sigma_i| = i$. Now for $j < k$ we have that

$$[(v_0 \,;\, \mu_0)_{\sigma j}, (v_1, \mu_1)_{\sigma j}] = [c^0_j, c^1_j] \in \mathbf{Cells}_{\mu_0}(v_0) \times \mathbf{Cells}_{\mu_1}(v_1).$$

Consequently by a simple counting argument we have that $\exists j_0 < j_1 < k$ such that

$$[c^0_{j_0}, c^1_{j_0}] = [c^0_{j_1}, c^1_{j_1}].$$

As a result we have, by putting $\sigma = \sigma_{j_0} * \sigma^* * \sigma^{**}$ where $|\sigma^*| > 0$ and $\sigma_{j_1} = \sigma_{j_0} * \sigma^*$, that

$$(v_i, \mu_i)_{\sigma_{j_0} * \sigma^{**}} = (v_i \,;\, \mu_i)_\sigma,$$

for $i \in 2$ thus contradicting our choice of σ. $\Box$**Proposition**

3.2. Strong Isomorphism

These extensional relations are not strong enough for many purposes. For example in program transformations and the like one is not just concerned with the value of an expression but also with the effect it has on memory. It is also desirable to have a relation between expressions which satisfies Leibniz's Law, allowing syntactical manipulations in verifications and derivations. For this we define the stronger notion of two terms $e_0(\bar{x})$ and $e_1(\bar{x})$ being strongly isomorphic, written

$$e_0(\bar{x}) \simeq e_1(\bar{x}),$$

which is true if they are not only isomorphic but also they make, up to this isomorphism and the production of garbage, exactly the same modifications to the memory they are evaluated in. By garbage we mean cells constructed in the process of evaluation that are not accessible from either the result or the, possibly modified, arguments. This entails that the isomorphism must map newly created cells to newly created cells and be the identity on old ones. The relation is then extended to expressions in the same way as in the extensional case. For example neither of the two examples of isomorphic and Lisp equal expressions given previously are strongly isomorphic. This relation is used in specifying and constructing program transformations and we shall define it and study its elementary properties in this and subsequent sections.

Definition: Two memory object descriptions $e_0(\bar{v})\,;\mu$ and $e_1(\bar{v})\,;\mu$ are said to be *strongly isomorphic*, written

$$e_0(\bar{v})\,;\mu \simeq e_1(\bar{v})\,;\mu,$$

iff either they both fail to denote or else they both denote, and for $w_i\,;\mu_i$ with

$$e_i(\bar{v})\,;\mu \gg w_i\,;\mu_i$$

for $i \in 2$, there is a bijection

$$h : \mathbb{V} \to \mathbb{V}$$

which is the identity on

$$\mathbb{A} \oplus \mathbf{Cells}_\mu(\bar{v})$$

and maps

$$\mathbb{C} \to \mathbb{C}$$

so that the following two properties hold:

- $w_0\,;\mu_0 \cong w_1\,;\mu_1$ via h.
- $\mathbf{Cells}_\mu(\bar{v})\,;\mu_0 \cong \mathbf{Cells}_\mu(\bar{v})\,;\mu_1$ via h.

Remarks:

1. In the second condition we are regarding $\mathbf{Cells}_\mu(\bar{v})$ as a sequence, ordered in the left first spanning tree.
2. It follows from the second condition, by a simple pasting argument and the fact that μ_0 must agree with μ on $\delta_\mu - \mathbf{Cells}_\mu(\bar{v})$, that we actually have

$$\delta_\mu \,;\, \mu_0 \cong \delta_\mu \,;\, \mu_1 \text{ via such an } h.$$

Definition: Two expressions $e_0(\bar{x})$ and $e_1(\bar{x})$ are said to be *strongly isomorphic*, written

$$e_0(\bar{x}) \simeq e_1(\bar{x}),$$

iff $(\forall \bar{v} \,;\, \mu \in \mathbb{M}_{sexp}) \;\; (e_0(\bar{v}) \,;\, \mu \simeq e_1(\bar{v}) \,;\, \mu)$.

Exercises: The following examples of properties of the memory operations and the basic control primitives are simple instructive exercises. We shall examine more properties of strong isomorphism in the penultimate section of this chapter.

0. $\mathtt{seq}(rplaca(x, y_0), rplaca(x, y_1)) \simeq rplaca(x, y_1)$, and similarly with *rplacd*.
1. $\mathtt{seq}(rplaca(x, y), x) \simeq rplaca(x, y)$, similarly for *rplacd*.
2. $car(cons(x, y)) \simeq x$, similarly for *cdr*.
3. $rplaca(cons(z, y), x) \simeq cons(x, y)$, similarly for *rplacd*.
4. $car(rplaca(x, y)) \simeq \mathtt{seq}(rplaca(x, y), y)$, and similarly for *rplacd*.
5. $rplaca(x, car(x)) \simeq x$ when $x \in \mathbb{C}$, and again we have an analogous version involving *rplacd* and *cdr*.

A simple example of a transformation which preserves strong isomorphism is that of unfolding, defined in 2.2.6:

Unfolding Theorem: For any expression $e(\bar{x})$, $e(\bar{x}) \simeq e^{\bowtie}(\bar{x})$.

Fact: $\simeq$ is an equivalence relation on both memory object descriptions and expressions.

Theorem: (Effectiveness of $\simeq$) There is a decision procedure which determines whether or not two terms are strongly isomorphic.

Remarks: The theorem is proved in Chapter 5. Yet again the theorem does not hold for arbitrary expressions, simply because

$$\mathtt{if}(\vartheta(x), \mathtt{T}, \mathtt{T}) \simeq \mathtt{T}$$

holds iff ϑ is total, where ϑ is any purely defined function.

The main motivation for studying this relation is given by the following theorem. It and its corollaries describe fundamental syntactic manipulations that preserve strong isomorphism. Later we shall show that it is the smallest relation satisfying this theorem.

Substitution Theorem: If $e^0_{body}(\bar{x},\bar{y}) \simeq e^1_{body}(\bar{x},\bar{y})$, $|\bar{x}| = k+1$ and $e^0_i(\bar{y}) \simeq e^1_i(\bar{y})$, for $0 \leq i \leq k$ then

$$\mathtt{let}_{0\leq i\leq k}\{x_i \leftarrow e^0_i(\bar{y})\}e^0_{body}(\bar{x},\bar{y}) \simeq \mathtt{let}_{0\leq i\leq k}\{x_i \leftarrow e^1_i(\bar{y})\}e^1_{body}(\bar{x},\bar{y}).$$

Remarks: Notice that while $eq(x,x) \simeq \mathtt{T}$ we have $eq(cons(y,y), cons(y,y)) \simeq$ `NIL` which is why we have formulated the theorem in the above fashion. The following corollaries follow with a minimum of effort and are left as exercises.

Corollary 1: (Sequencing theorem) If $e^0_i(\bar{x}) \simeq e^1_i(\bar{x})$, for $0 \leq i < k$ then

$$\mathtt{seq}_{0\leq i<k}(e^0_i(\bar{y})) \simeq \mathtt{seq}_{0\leq i<k}(e^1_i(\bar{y})).$$

Proof: Use the fact that

$$\mathtt{seq}(e_0, e_1, \ldots, e_n) \simeq \mathtt{let}\{x_0 \leftarrow e_0, x_1 \leftarrow e_1, \ldots, x_n \leftarrow e_n\}x_n.$$

□Corollary 1

Corollary 2: (Composition theorem) If $e^0_i(\bar{x}) \simeq e^1_i(\bar{x})$, for $0 \leq i < k$ and ϑ is either an n-ary memory operation or an n-ary function symbol then

$$\vartheta(e^0_0(\bar{y}), \ldots, e^0_{k-1}(\bar{y})) \simeq \vartheta(e^1_0(\bar{y}), \ldots, e^1_{k-1}(\bar{y})).$$

Proof: Use the unfolding theorem. □Corollary 2

Corollary 3: (Branching theorem) If $e^0_i(\bar{x}) \simeq e^1_i(\bar{x})$, for $0 \leq i < 3$ then

$$\mathtt{if}(e^0_0(\bar{y}), e^0_1(\bar{y}), e^0_2(\bar{y})) \simeq \mathtt{if}(e^1_0(\bar{y}), e^1_1(\bar{y}), e^1_2(\bar{y})).$$

Proof: Show that $\mathtt{if}(x, e_0, y) \simeq \mathtt{if}(x, e_1, y)$ and $\mathtt{if}(x, y, e_0) \simeq \mathtt{if}(x, y, e_1)$. Then use the following two facts:

$$\mathtt{if}(e_0, e_1, e_2) \simeq \mathtt{let}\{x_0 \leftarrow e_0\}\mathtt{if}(x_0, e_1, e_2),$$

$$\mathtt{if}(x_0, e_1, e_2) \simeq \mathtt{let}\{x_1 \leftarrow \mathtt{if}(x_0, e_1, x_0), x_2 \leftarrow \mathtt{if}(x_0, x_0, e_2)\}\mathtt{if}(x_0, x_1, x_2)$$

□Corollary 3

The most useful consequence of the Substitution Theorem is Leibniz's Law; replacing a subexpression of an expression by a strongly isomorphic one preserves strong isomorphism:

Theorem: (Leibniz's Law) Supposing $e_i(\bar{x}), e(\bar{x}, y)$ are expressions, $i \in 2$, then,

$$e_0(\bar{x}) \simeq e_1(\bar{x}) \rightarrow e(\bar{x}, e_0(\bar{x})) \simeq e(\bar{x}, e_1(\bar{x})).$$

Remark: Clearly the Substitution Theorem is implied by Leibniz's Law. They are actually equivalent as the following proof reveals.

Proof: We begin by proving two special cases as lemmas. The statement of the first lemma requires the following:

Definition: A variable z, that occurs only once in an expression $e(z)$, is said to be an *immediate subexpression* of $e(z)$ iff the only proper subexpression of $e(z)$ in which z occurs is z itself.

Lemma 1: Supposing $e_i(\bar{x}), e(\bar{x}, y)$ are expressions, $i \in 2$, and the only occurrence of y is as an immediate subexpression of $e(\bar{x}, y)$. Then

$$e_0(\bar{x}) \simeq e_1(\bar{x}) \rightarrow e(\bar{x}, e_0(\bar{x})) \simeq e(\bar{x}, e_1(\bar{x})).$$

Proof of Lemma 1: This is an immediate consequence of the Substitution Theorem and its corollaries $\Box_{\textbf{Lemma 1}}$.

Lemma 2: Supposing $e_i(\bar{x}), e(\bar{x}, y)$ are expressions, $i \in 2$, and y occurs exactly once in $e(\bar{x}, y)$. Then

$$e_0(\bar{x}) \simeq e_1(\bar{x}) \rightarrow e(\bar{x}, e_0(\bar{x})) \simeq e(\bar{x}, e_1(\bar{x})).$$

Proof of Lemma 2: Assume the hypothesis of the lemma, then for some $n \in \mathbb{N}$ there is a sequence

$$e^0(\bar{x}, z_0), \quad e^1(\bar{x}, z_1), \quad e^2(\bar{x}, z_2), \quad e^3(\bar{x}, z_3), \quad \ldots, e^n(\bar{x}, z_n)$$

such that

1. z_i occurs only once in $e^i(\bar{x}, z_i)$ and that occurrence is as an immediate subexpression, and
2. $e(\bar{x}, y) = e^0(\bar{x}, e^1(\bar{x}, e^2(\bar{x}, e^3(\bar{x}, e^4(\ldots, e^n(\bar{x}, y)))\ldots)))$.

Now by lemma 1 we have that

$$e^n(\bar{x}, e_0(\bar{x})) \simeq e^n(\bar{x}, e_1(\bar{x})).$$

Using this as well as Lemma 1 again gives

$$e^{n-1}(\bar{x}, e^n(\bar{x}, e_0(\bar{x}))) \simeq e^{n-1}(\bar{x}, e^n(\bar{x}, e_1(\bar{x}))).$$

Thus $n-1$ more applications of Lemma 1 will show that

$$e^0(\bar{x}, e^1(\bar{x}, e^2(\bar{x}, e^3(\bar{x}, e^4(\ldots, e^n(\bar{x}, e_0(\bar{x})))\ldots)))$$

is strongly isomorphic to

$$e^0(\bar{x}, e^1(\bar{x}, e^2(\bar{x}, e^3(\bar{x}, e^4(\ldots, e^n(\bar{x}, e_1(\bar{x})))\ldots))),$$

and, by 2 above, this is just

$$e(\bar{x}, e_0(\bar{x})) \simeq e(\bar{x}, e_1(\bar{x})).$$

□**Lemma 2**

Now to prove the general case assume that y occurs exactly m times in $e(\bar{x}, y)$ and choose

$$z_1, z_2, \ldots, z_m$$

to be distinct variables that do not occur in either $e(\bar{x}, y), e_0(\bar{x})$ or $e_1(\bar{x})$. Let $e^*(\bar{x}, \bar{z})$ be the expression obtained from $e(\bar{x}, y)$ by replacing the ith occurrence of y by z_i for each i, $0 < i \leq m$. Thus one application of Lemma 1 shows that

$$e^*(\bar{x}, e_0(\bar{x}), z_2, \ldots, z_m) \simeq e^*(\bar{x}, e_1(\bar{x}), z_2, \ldots, z_m).$$

A second application shows that

$$e^*(\bar{x}, z_1, e_0(\bar{x}), z_3, \ldots, z_m) \simeq e^*(\bar{x}, z_1, e_1(\bar{x}), z_3, \ldots, z_m).$$

Now applying Lemma 1 to the right hand side of this last equation gives

$$e^*(\bar{x}, e_0(\bar{x}), e_1(\bar{x}), z_3, \ldots, z_m) \simeq e^*(\bar{x}, e_1(\bar{x}), e_1(\bar{x}), z_3, \ldots, z_m).$$

And applying it to the left hand side of the equation before it gives

$$e^*(\bar{x}, e_0(\bar{x}), e_0(\bar{x}), z_3, \ldots, z_m) \simeq e^*(\bar{x}, e_0(\bar{x}), e_1(\bar{x}), z_3, \ldots, z_m).$$

Putting these two together gives

$$e^*(\bar{x}, e_0(\bar{x}), e_0(\bar{x}), z_3, \ldots, z_m) \simeq e^*(x, e_1(x), e_1(x), z_3, \ldots, z_m).$$

Continuing this line of reasoning eventually gives

$$e^*(\bar{x}, e_0(\bar{x}), e_0(\bar{x}), e_0(\bar{x}), \ldots, e_0(\bar{x})) \simeq e^*(\bar{x}, e_1(\bar{x}), e_1(\bar{x}), e_1(\bar{x}), \ldots, e_1(\bar{x})).$$

This is the same as saying

$$e(\bar{x}, e_0(\bar{x})) \simeq e(\bar{x}, e_1(\bar{x})).$$

□**Theorem**

The following surprising connection between isomorphism and strong isomorphism falls out of the proof of the effectiveness theorems. It states that if $e_i(\bar{x}), i \in 2$ are two primitive terms which are isomorphic and also have the property that they can take on arbitrarily large values (by this it is meant that the number of cells accessible from their value can be arbitrarily large) then the expressions are in fact strongly isomorphic on a large definable subset of $\mathbb{M}_{sexp}$; this definable subset also has the property that the values $e_i(\bar{x})$ take on its complement are bounded in size. Thus we can conclude, modulo when the $e_i(\bar{x})$ take on values smaller than a certain size, that

$$e_0(\bar{x}) \simeq e_1(\bar{x}).$$

Although the theorem has very little practical import, it does show how surprisingly close are isomorphism and strong isomorphism. In contrast Lisp equality and isomorphism are miles apart, as the preceding section indicated. To make the statement of the theorem readable we first give a definition.

Definition: If $e(\bar{x})$ is an expression we say it is *bounded* iff $(\exists n \in \mathbb{N})(\forall \bar{v} \,;\, \mu \in \mathbb{M}_{sexp})(\forall v^* \,;\, \mu^* \in \mathbb{M}_{sexp})$ we have

$$(e(\bar{v}) \,;\, \mu \gg v^* \,;\, \mu^*) \;\rightarrow\; |\mathbf{Cells}_{\mu^*}(v^*)| \leq n.$$

$e(\bar{x})$ is said to be *unbounded* iff it is not bounded, or in symbols iff $(\forall n \in \mathbb{N})(\exists \bar{v};\mu \in \mathbb{M}_{sexp})(\exists v^* \,;\, \mu^* \in \mathbb{M}_{sexp})$ such that

$$(e(\bar{v}) \,;\, \mu \gg v^* \,;\, \mu^*) \;\wedge\; (|\mathbf{Cells}_{\mu^*}(v^*)| > n).$$

The theorem indicated above is stated precisely as follows, it is proved in chapter 5.

Theorem: (Unbounded Isomorphism Theorem) If $e_i(\bar{x}), i \in 2$ are primitive terms such that

$$e_0(\bar{x}) \cong e_1(\bar{x})$$

and the $e_i(\bar{x})$ are unbounded, then there is a $\mathbb{M}_{pure^+}$ term $\theta(\bar{x})$ which is total on $\mathbb{M}_{sexp}{}^{|\bar{x}|}$, does not alter or enlarge the memory it is evaluated in, takes only the values T or NIL, and is such that

1. $e_0(\bar{x}) \simeq e_1(\bar{x})$ on $\{\bar{v} \,;\, \mu \mid \theta(\bar{v}) \,;\, \mu \gg \mathtt{T} \,;\, \mu\}$
2. $e_i(\bar{x})$ is bounded on $\{\bar{v} \,;\, \mu \mid \theta(\bar{v}) \,;\, \mu \gg \mathtt{NIL} \,;\, \mu\}$

Remarks:

- Note that the conclusion 1. can be stated simply as

$$\mathtt{if}(\theta(\bar{x}), e_0(\bar{x}), \mathtt{T}) \simeq \mathtt{if}(\theta(\bar{x}), e_1(\bar{x}), \mathtt{T})$$

- Conclusion 2. can also be simply stated as

$$\mathtt{if}(\theta(\bar{x}), \mathtt{T}, e_i(\bar{x})) \text{ is bounded.}$$

- Also note that as a consequence we also have that $\theta(\bar{x})$ evaluates to the value T for arbitrarily large arguments, or in symbols

$$(\forall n \in \mathbb{N})(\exists \bar{v} \,;\, \mu \in \mathbb{M}_{sexp})(\theta(\bar{v}) \,;\, \mu \gg \mathtt{T} \,;\, \mu) \wedge (|\mathbf{Cells}_{\mu}(\bar{v})| > n).$$

- Finally, it also falls out of the proof that on

$$\{\bar{v} \,;\, \mu \mid \theta(\bar{v}) \,;\, \mu \gg \mathtt{NIL} \,;\, \mu\}$$

  the possible values of $e_i(\bar{x})$ are bounded by

$$n = 2^{\mathbf{Max}_{i \in 2}\{r(e_i(\bar{x}))\}} + \mathbf{Max}_{i \in 2}\{r(e_i(\bar{x}))\}.$$

Another corollary of the proof of the effectiveness theorems is the following criterion for a term to be unbounded

Corollary: If $e(\bar{x})$ is a term and for some $\bar{v} \,;\, \mu$ we have that $e(\bar{v}) \,;\, \mu \gg v^* \,;\, \mu^*$ with

$$|\mathbf{Cells}_{\mu^*}(v^*)| > 2^{r(e(\bar{x}))} + r(e(\bar{x})).$$

then $e(\bar{x})$ is unbounded.

It is probably an appropriate time to prove the following property of strong isomorphism: it is the weakest relation extending Lisp equality that has a Substitution Theorem. And as we have already pointed out, the Substitution Theorem is an equivalent form of Leibniz's Law:

Theorem: Suppose that $\sim$ is an equivalence relation on memory object descriptions and expressions such that:

0. $(\forall \bar{v} ; \mu \in \mathbb{M}_{sexp})(e_0(\bar{v}) ; \mu \sim e_1(\bar{v}) ; \mu) \Longleftrightarrow e_0(\bar{x}) \sim e_1(\bar{x})$.
1. $e_0(\bar{v}) ; \mu \sim e_1(\bar{v}) ; \mu$ implies that $e_0(\bar{v}) ; \mu \equiv e_1(\bar{v}) ; \mu$.
2. If $e_0(\bar{x}), e_1(\bar{x}), e(\bar{x}, y)$ are expressions then

$$e_0(\bar{x}) \simeq e_1(\bar{x}) \ \rightarrow \ e(\bar{x}, e_0(\bar{x})) \simeq e(\bar{x}, e_1(\bar{x})).$$

Then $e_0 \sim e_1 \ \rightarrow \ e_0 \simeq e_1$.

Remarks:

1. Just as in the case for $\cong$ and $\equiv$ 1 can be replaced by the assertion that $e_0 ; \mu \sim e_1 ; \mu$ implies that either they both denote or else they both fail to denote.
2. Since the Substitution Theorem is equivalent to Leibniz's Law, we can replace 2 by the assertion that $\sim$ satisfies the Substitution Theorem. It is this modified version that we prove.

Before we prove this theorem we shall give *one thousand and twenty three* distinct examples of decidable equivalence relations, other than $\simeq$, that satisfy its hypothesis.

Definition: Let $\Theta \subseteq \mathbb{O}_{sexp}$ and define the equivalence relation $\simeq_\Theta$ as follows:

$$e_0(\bar{v}) ; \mu \simeq_\Theta e_1(\bar{v}) ; \mu$$

if and only if the following two conditions hold:

1. $e_0(\bar{v}) ; \mu \simeq e_1(\bar{v}) ; \mu$
2. For each $\theta \in \Theta$ we have that $e_0^{\sharp\theta}(\bar{v}) ; \mu \simeq e_1^{\sharp\theta}(\bar{v}) ; \mu$ where $e^{\sharp\theta}$ is the derived expression defined, or at least described, in Chapter 2.

We then define $e_0(\bar{x}) \simeq_\Theta e_1(\bar{x})$ in the usual way. Note that since we can effectively go from e to $e^{\sharp\theta}$ the decidability of $\simeq_\Theta$ follows from that of $\simeq$. The following is a simple exercise.

Proposition: $\simeq_\Theta$ satisfies the hypothesis of the preceding theorem.

Proof of Theorem: Suppose that $e_0(\bar{x}) \sim e_1(\bar{x})$ and that $\sim$ satisfies the hypothesis of the theorem. Given any $\bar{v} ; \mu \in \mathbb{M}_{sexp}$, we shall show two things.

A. 1. and 2. actually imply $e_0(\bar{v}) ; \mu \cong e_1(\bar{v}) ; \mu$,

and

B. A. together with 2. implies $e_0(\bar{v})\,;\mu \simeq e_1(\bar{v})\,;\mu$,

The theorem then follows from B. together with 0, since the choice of $\bar{v}\,;\mu$ was arbitrary.

Proof of A: Without loss of generality we may assume that

$$e_i(\bar{v})\,;\mu \gg w_i\,;\mu_i, \quad i \in 2.$$

By 1 we have that

$$w_0\,;\mu_0 \equiv w_1\,;\mu_1.$$

Now suppose that

$$w_0\,;\mu_0 \not\cong w_1\,;\mu_1.$$

This implies, again without loss of generality, that there are $\sigma_1, \sigma_2 \in \delta_{(w_0;\mu_0)}$ such that

3. $(w_0\,;\mu_0)_{\sigma_0} = (w_0\,;\mu_0)_{\sigma_1} \in \mathbb{C}$,

and

4. $(w_1\,;\mu_1)_{\sigma_0} \neq (w_1\,;\mu_1)_{\sigma_1}$, both are cells of course.

Now let θ_0 and θ_1 be the compositions of *car*s and *cdr*s that corresponds to the paths σ_0 and σ_1, respectively. Explicitly $\theta_i(w_j);\mu \gg (w_j;\mu_j)_{\sigma_i};\mu$. Put $e_{body}(y)$ to be the expression

$$\texttt{let}\{x_0 \leftarrow \theta_0(y), x_1 \leftarrow \theta_1(y)\}\texttt{seq}(rplaca(x_0, a_0), rplaca(x_1, a_1), cons(x_0, x_1)).$$

Here a_0 and a_1 are any distinct atoms not in $\mathbf{Atoms}_{\mu_0}(w_0) = \mathbf{Atoms}_{\mu_1}(w_1)$. Thus by the substitution theorem we have that

$$\texttt{let}\{y \leftarrow e_0\}e_{body} \sim \texttt{let}\{y \leftarrow e_1\}e_{body}.$$

In particular

$$e_{body}(w_0)\,;\mu_0 \sim e_{body}(w_1)\,;\mu_1,$$

and consequently

$$e_{body}(w_0)\,;\mu_0 \equiv e_{body}(w_1)\,;\mu_1.$$

Letting $e_{body}(w_i)\,;\mu_i \gg c_i\,;\mu_i^*$ it is easily seen that

5. $(c_0\,;\mu_0^*)_{00} = a_1 = (c_0\,;\mu_0^*)_{01}$,

but

6. $(c_1\,;\mu_1)_{00} = a_0$ and $(c_1\,;\mu_1)_{01} = a_1$. This contradicts the fact that $c_0\,,\mu_0^* \equiv c_1\,;\mu_1^*$. Thus $w_0\,;\mu_0 \cong w_1\,;\mu_1$. $\Box_{\mathbf{A}}$.

Proof of B: Now for each v_i in $\bar{v}$ let $\{\theta_i^j\}_{j\in I_i}$ be a finite collection of compositions of *car* and *cdr* with the following properties:

7. For any $c \in \mathbf{Cells}_\mu(v_i)$ there is a $j \in I_i$ such that $\theta_i^j(v_i)\,;\mu \gg c\,;\mu$.

and

8. $\theta_i^j(v_i)\,;\mu$ denotes for every $j \in I_i$.

Now put

$$e_i^*(\bar{x}) = cons(\theta_i^0(x_i), cons(\theta_i^1(x_i), \ldots cons(\theta_i^{I_i-1}(x_i), \mathtt{NIL}))) \ldots))$$

and

$$e_{body}(\bar{y}, z) = cons(y_0, cons(y_1, \ldots cons(y_{|\bar{x}|-1}, cons(z, \mathtt{NIL}))) \ldots))$$

The Substitution Theorem and part **A** then allows us to conclude that

$$\mathtt{let}\{y_0 \leftarrow e_0^*, \ldots y_{|\bar{x}|-1} \leftarrow e_{|\bar{x}|-1}^*, z \leftarrow e_0\} e_{body}(\bar{y}, z)$$

is isomorphic to

$$\mathtt{let}\{y_0 \leftarrow e_0^*, \ldots y_{|\bar{x}|-1} \leftarrow e_{|\bar{x}|-1}^*, z \leftarrow e_1\} e_{body}(\bar{y}, z).$$

Evaluating these two expressions at $\bar{v}\,;\mu$ and interpreting this last condition forces $e_0(\bar{v})\,;\mu \simeq e_1(\bar{v})\,;\mu$. $\Box_{\mathbf{B}}$. $\Box_{\mathbf{Theorem}}$

3.3. The Substitution Theorem

In this section we prove the Substitution Theorem, the statement of which we repeat here for the convenience of the reader.

Substitution Theorem: If $e_{body}^0(\bar{x}, \bar{y}) \simeq e_{body}^1(\bar{x}, \bar{y})$, $|\bar{x}| = k+1$ and $e_i^0(\bar{y}) \simeq e_i^1(\bar{y})$, for $0 \le i \le k$ then

$$\mathtt{let}_{0\le i\le k}\{x_i \leftarrow e_i^0(\bar{y})\} e_{body}^0(\bar{x}, \bar{y}) \simeq \mathtt{let}_{0\le i\le k}\{x_i \leftarrow e_i^1(\bar{y})\} e_{body}^1(\bar{x}, \bar{y}).$$

We begin with a simple lemma, the proof of which we leave as an exercise.

Lemma: If $e_0(\bar{x}) \simeq e_1(\bar{x})$, $\bar{v}_0\,;\mu_0 \cong \bar{v}_1\,;\mu_1$ via h and $e_i(\bar{v}_i)\,;\mu_i \gg w_i\,;\mu_i^*$ for $i \in 2$, then there is a bijection h^*, which is the identity on $\mathbb{A}$ and maps $\mathbb{C} \to \mathbb{C}$, such that

- $h^* = h$ on $\mathbf{Cells}_{\mu_0}(\bar{v}_0)$
- $w_0\,;\mu_0^* \cong w_1\,;\mu_1^*$ via h^*

- $\mathbf{Cells}_{\mu_0}(\bar{v}_0)\,;\mu_0^* \cong \mathbf{Cells}_{\mu_1}(\bar{v}_1)\,;\mu_1^*$ via h^*

Furthermore if $\bar{u}_i \in \delta_{\mu_i}$ for $i \in 2$ with the property that

$$\bar{u}_0\,;\mu_0 \cong \bar{u}_1\,;\mu_1 \quad \text{via } h$$

then we can add the following two requirements.

- $h^* = h$ on $\mathbf{Cells}_{\mu_0}(\bar{u}_0)$
- $\bar{u}_0\,;\mu_0^* \cong \bar{u}_1\,;\mu_1^*$ via h^*

Remark: Notice that the second part follows from the first and the simple observation that if $e_0(\bar{x}) \simeq e_1(\bar{x})$ then these two expressions are also strongly isomorphic:

$$cons(y_0, cons(y_1, \ldots cons(y_m, e_0(\bar{x}))) \ldots))$$
$$cons(y_0, cons(y_1, \ldots cons(y_m, e_1(\bar{x}))) \ldots)).$$

Proof of the Substitution Theorem: Assume the hypothesis of the theorem and pick $\bar{v}\,;\mu \in \mathbb{M}_{sexp}$. Without loss of generality we may assume that there are memory objects

$$\{w_i^j\,;\mu_i^j\}_{j\in 2,\ 0\leq i\leq k}$$

such that

- $e_0^j(\bar{v})\,;\mu \gg w_0^j\,;\mu_0^j$ for $j \in 2$
- $e_i^j(\bar{v})\,;\mu_{i-1}^j \gg w_i^j\,;\mu_i^j$ for $j \in 2$ and $0 < i < k$
- $e_{body}^j(w_0^j, \ldots w_{k-1}^j, \bar{v})\,;\mu_{k-1}^j \gg w_k^j\,;\mu_k^j$,

since the case when the memory object descriptions fail to denote is a simple variation on the following argument. We now construct a sequence of functions

$$\{h_i\}_{i\in k+1}$$

with the following properties, putting

$$\mathbf{D}_i^j = \begin{cases} \mathbf{Cells}_{\mu}(\bar{v}) & \text{for } i = 0 \text{ and } j \in 2 \\ \mathbf{D}_{i-1}^j \cup \mathbf{Cells}_{\mu_{i-1}^j}(\bar{v} * [w_{i-1}^j]) & \text{for } 1 \leq i \leq k,\ j \in 2. \end{cases}$$

0. h_0 is the identity on $\mathbf{D}_0^0$
1. $h_i = h_{i-1}$ on $\mathbf{D}_{i-1}^0$, $0 < i \leq k$.
2. $w_i^0\,;\mu_i^0 \cong w_i^1\,;\mu_i^1$ via h_i, for $0 \leq i \leq k$.

3. $\mathbf{D}_i^0 \,;\, \mu_i^0 \cong \mathbf{D}_i^1 \,;\, \mu_i^1$ via h_i for $0 \leq i \leq k$.

We construct these functions by induction on i. In the case $i = 0$ the function h_0 is given to us by our assumption that $e_0^0(\bar{x}) \simeq e_0^1(\bar{x})$. So supposing we have constructed h_{i-1} we consider two cases, the first is when $i < k$ and the second is when $i = k$. In both cases we show how to construct h_i.

Case 1: By the induction hypothesis we have that

$$\bar{v} \,;\, \mu_{i-1}^0 \cong \bar{v} \,;\, \mu_{i-1}^1 \quad \text{via } h_{i-1}.$$

So by the first part of the lemma we have that there is a function h_i such that

4. $h_i = h_{i-1}$ on $\mathbf{Cells}_{\mu_{i-1}^0}(\bar{v})$
5. $w_i^0 \,;\, \mu_i^0 \cong w_i^1 \,;\, \mu_i^1$ via h_i
6. $\mathbf{Cells}_{\mu_{i-1}^0}(\bar{v}) \,;\, \mu_i^0 \cong \mathbf{Cells}_{\mu_{i-1}^1}(\bar{v}) \,;\, \mu_i^1$ via h_i.

But furthermore we have that $\mathbf{D}_{i-1}^j \subset \delta_{\mu_{i-1}^j}$ and by the induction hypothesis,

$$[w_{i-1}^0] * \mathbf{D}_{i-1}^0 \,;\, \mu_{i-1}^0 \cong [w_{i-1}^1] * \mathbf{D}_{i-1}^1 \,;\, \mu_{i-1}^1 \quad \text{via } h_{i-1}.$$

Thus by the second part of the lemma we can also require that

7. $h_i = h_{i-1}$ on $\mathbf{D}_{i-1}^0 \cup \mathbf{Cells}_{\mu_{i-1}^0}(w_{i-1}^0)$
8. $w_{i-1}^0 \,;\, \mu_i^0 \cong w_{i-1}^1 \,;\, \mu_i^1$ via h_i
9. $\mathbf{D}_{i-1}^0 \,;\, \mu_i^0 \cong \mathbf{D}_{i-1}^1 \,;\, \mu_i^1$ via h_i for $0 \leq i \leq k$.

Now putting 6, 8 and 9 together yields 3. Also 4 and 7 have 1 as a consequence. Thus we are done in this case $\Box_{\textbf{Case 1}}$.

Case 2: This case is almost identical. By the induction hypothesis we have that

$$\bar{v} * \bar{w}^0 \,;\, \mu_{k-1}^0 \cong \bar{v} * \bar{w}^1 \,;\, \mu_{k-1}^1 \quad \text{via } h_{k-1}$$

where $\bar{w}^j = [w_0^j, \ldots, w_{k-1}^j]$, and so by the first part of the lemma we have that there is a function h_k such that

10. $h_k = h_{k-1}$ on $\mathbf{Cells}_{\mu_{k-1}^0}(\bar{v} * \bar{w}^0)$
11. $w_k^0 \,;\, \mu_k^0 \cong w_k^1 \,;\, \mu_k^1$ via h_k
12. $\mathbf{Cells}_{\mu_{k-1}^0}(\bar{v} * \bar{w}^0) \,;\, \mu_k^0 \cong \mathbf{Cells}_{\mu_{k-1}^1}(\bar{v} * \bar{w}^1) \,;\, \mu_k^1$ via h_k.

But furthermore we have that $\mathbf{D}^j_{k-1} \subset \delta_{\mu^j_{k-1}}$, and by the induction hypothesis

$$\mathbf{D}^0_{k-1} \,;\, \mu^0_{k-1} \cong \mathbf{D}^1_{k-1} \,;\, \mu^1_{k-1} \text{ via } h_{k-1}.$$

Thus by the second part of the lemma we can also require that

13. $h_k = h_{k-1}$ on $\mathbf{D}^0_{k-1}$
14. $\mathbf{D}^0_{k-1} \,;\, \mu^0_k \cong \mathbf{D}^1_{k-1} \,;\, \mu^1_k$ via h_k.

These again give the result. □**Case 2.** □**Substitution Theorem**

3.4. Axioms for $\simeq$

In this section we shall present a large collection of principles, which for want of a better word, we shall call *axioms*. We make no claim as to their *independence*. Nor, unfortunately, shall we claim *completeness*. The former because they are not independent, the latter because they are not complete. In fact the difficulty of this and related tasks is the reason for our model theoretic proofs of the effectiveness theorems.

Although it is an implicit aim of this work to show that destructive Lisp is no more complex or mathematically inelegant than pure Lisp, we shall begin by producing the salt with which one must take this aim. We shall provide a simple axiomatization of pure Lisp which the reader may compare to that in the destructive case.

Firstly however we provide the reader with a perspective. We have divided the axioms relating $\simeq$ into groups, depending upon the *principal* entity that the property depends upon. This is a *value* judgment because, for example, the properties of the underlying data operations cannot be formulated without the help of `seq` and sometimes even `let`. It should also be pointed out that even though `seq` can be defined in terms of `let` and even in terms of the underlying data operations, such an economical approach is somewhat harder to comprehend.

3.4.1. Axiomatizing Pure Lisp

Prior to our never-ending list of facts concerning destructive Lisp, we present an axiomatization of pure Lisp. This *equational* theory consists of expressions from

$$\mathbb{O}_{pure} = \{atom, atom{:}eq, cons, car, cdr\},$$

being related by Lisp equality, $\equiv$. The variables are restricted to $\mathbb{M}_{wf}$. Thus when we say that $e_0(\bar{x}) \equiv e_1(\bar{x})$ is true, we actually mean

$$e_0(\bar{x}) \equiv e_1(\bar{x}) \quad \text{on } \mathbb{M}_{wf}.$$

The reason we only include *atom:eq* rather than *eq* in pure Lisp is to retain Leibniz's Law; equals can be replaced by equals to obtain equals.

Leibniz's Law $(\forall e_0(\bar{x}), e_1(\bar{x}), e(\bar{x}, y) \in \mathbb{M}_{pure})(\forall \bar{x} \in \mathbb{M}_{sexp})$

$$e_0(\bar{x}) \equiv e_1(\bar{x}) \rightarrow e(\bar{x}, e_0(\bar{x})) \equiv e(\bar{x}, e_1(\bar{x})).$$

We begin by eliminating the need to consider the control primitives `seq`, `let` and `if`. It is here the difference between pure and destructive Lisp manifests itself. While the principles for pure Lisp are essentially trivial (almost to the point of demonstrating the redundancy of these primitives), those for destructive Lisp are by no means so. Firstly we define

$$e{\downarrow} \iff \exists x(e \equiv x).$$

1. $\mathtt{let}_{0 \le i \le n}\{y_i \leftarrow e_i\}e \equiv e\{y_i \leftarrow e_i\}_{0 \le i \le n}$, where the R.H.S. denotes the expression obtained by simultaneously replacing free occurences of y_i by e_i in e, provided that $e_i{\downarrow}$ for $0 \le i \le n$.
2. $\neg(\mathtt{let}_{0 \le i \le n}\{y_i \leftarrow e_i\}e){\downarrow}$ whenever there is an $0 \le i \le n$ such that $\neg(e_i{\downarrow})$.
3. $\mathtt{seq}(e_0, \ldots, e_n) \equiv e_n$, as long as $e_0{\downarrow}, \ldots e_{n-1}{\downarrow}$
4. $\neg(\mathtt{seq}(e_0, \ldots, e_n){\downarrow})$, whenever there is an $0 \le i \le n$ such that $\neg(e_i{\downarrow})$.
5. $\neg(\mathtt{if}(e_0, e_1, e_2){\downarrow})$, whenever $\neg(e_0{\downarrow})$.
6. $\mathtt{if}(e_0, e_1, e_2) \equiv e_1$ whenever $e_0{\downarrow}$ and $e_0 \not\equiv \mathtt{NIL}$.
7. $\mathtt{if}(e_0, e_1, e_2) \equiv e_2$ whenever $e_0 \equiv \mathtt{NIL}$.

The axioms for the underlying data operations are then easily enumerated. They are almost complete; the incompleteness results simply from our silence on the number of atoms.

0. $atom{:}eq(\mathtt{T}, \mathtt{NIL}) \equiv \mathtt{NIL}$.
1. $atom{:}eq(e_0, e_1) \equiv atom{:}eq(e_1, e_0)$.
2. $atom{:}eq(x, y) \equiv \mathtt{T}$ if and only if $atom(x) \equiv \mathtt{T} \equiv atom(y)$ and $x = y$.
3. $atom{:}eq(x, y) \equiv \mathtt{T}$ or $atom{:}eq(x, y) \equiv \mathtt{NIL}$.

4. $atom(\mathtt{T}) \equiv \mathtt{T}$ and $atom(\mathtt{NIL}) \equiv \mathtt{T}$.
5. $atom(x) \equiv \mathtt{T}$ iff $x \in \mathbb{A}$ and $atom(x) \equiv \mathtt{NIL}$ iff $x \in \mathbb{C}$.
6. $atom(cons(x, y)) \equiv \mathtt{NIL}$.
7. $car(cons(x, y)) \equiv x$.
8. $cdr(cons(x, y)) \equiv y$.
9. If $atom(x) \equiv \mathtt{NIL}$ then $cons(car(x), cdr(x)) \equiv x$.
10. $cons(x, y) \not\equiv \sigma(cons(x, y))$ for any non-trivial composition σ of *car*s and *cdr*s.
11. $atom(x) \equiv \mathtt{T}$ iff $car(x) \equiv x$.
12. $atom(x) \equiv \mathtt{T}$ iff $cdr(x) \equiv x$.

3.4.2. The Principal Subexpression Theorem

We begin our study of destructive Lisp with some definitions that will be used in expressing certain properties. The two main notions to be defined are that of a *gentle* expression, being one that does not alter any memory it is evaluated in, and that of a expression being a *principal* subexpression of a given expression. By the latter is meant a subexpression which must be evaluated first, prior to evaluating the whole. Both these notions will be used heavily in our formulation of the axioms.

Definition: We will call a term or expression $e(\bar{x})$, in $\mathbb{E}$, *gentle* iff for every $i \in |\bar{x}|$, $\mathsf{seq}(e(\bar{x}), \bar{x}{\downarrow_i}) \simeq \bar{x}{\downarrow_i}$. The reason we call them *gentle* is because of their failure to alter memory.

The first and somewhat obvious result is the following, the proof of which we leave as an exercise.

Proposition: The following are equivalent.

1. $e(\bar{x})$ is gentle.
2. $\mathsf{seq}(e(\bar{x}), \mathtt{T}) \simeq \mathtt{T}$.

Before we begin our endurance test of truth we make one more definition.

Definition: We say that the variable z is *principal* in the expression e if and only if one of the following holds:

0. $e = z$,
1. $e = \vartheta(e_0^*, \ldots, e_n^*, e_0, \ldots, e_m)$ and firstly z is principal in e_0, secondly z does not occur in e_i for any $0 < i \leq m$, and finally $e_i^* \in \mathbb{V} \cup (\mathbb{X} - \{z\})$.

2. $e = \mathtt{if}(e_0, e_1, e_2)$ and either z occurs principally in e_0 and does not occur in either e_1 or e_2, or else $e_0 \in \mathbb{V} \cup (\mathbb{X} - \{z\})$ and z is principal in both e_1 and e_2,

3. $e = \mathtt{seq}(e_0^*, \ldots e_n^*, e_0, \ldots e_m)$ and firstly z is principal in e_0, secondly z does not occur in e_i for any $0 < i \leq m$, and finally $e_i^* \in \mathbb{V} \cup (\mathbb{X} - \{z\})$, for $0 \leq i \leq n$.

4. $\mathtt{let}\{x_0 \leftarrow e_0^*, \ldots x_n \leftarrow e_n^*, x_{n+1} \leftarrow e_1, \ldots, x_{n+m} \leftarrow e_m\}e$ and firstly z is principal in e_1, secondly z does not occur in e or e_i for any $0 < i \leq m$, thirdly for $0 \leq i \leq n$ $e_i^* \in \mathbb{V} \cup (\mathbb{X} - \{z\})$, and finally z is distinct from the $\bar{x}$.

5. $\mathtt{let}\{x_0 \leftarrow e_0, \ldots x_n \leftarrow e_n\}e$, $e_i \in \mathbb{V} \cup (\mathbb{X} - \{z\})$ and z is principal in e.

The idea behind this definition is the following: If z is principal in $e(z)$ then the first expression to be evaluated in $e(e_0)$ is e_0. We call e_0 in such a situation a *principal subexpression* of e. As a result we have the following theorem, the proof of which is a simple induction on the rank of e.

Principal Subexpression Theorem: If z is principal in $e(z)$ then

1. $\mathtt{seq}(e_0, \ldots, e_{n-1}, e(e_n)) \simeq e(\mathtt{seq}(e_0, \ldots, e_{n-1}, e_n))$,
2. $\mathtt{let}\{z \leftarrow e_0\}e(z) \simeq e(e_0)$.
3. $\mathtt{let}\{x_1 \leftarrow e_1, \ldots, x_n \leftarrow e_n, z \leftarrow e_0\}e(z) \simeq \mathtt{let}\{x_1 \leftarrow e_1, \ldots x_n \leftarrow e_n\}e(e_0)$, provided that e_0 contains no free variables from $\bar{x}$.
4. $e(\mathtt{if}(e_0, e_1, e_2)) \simeq \mathtt{if}(e_0, e(e_1), e(e_2))$.
5. If $\mathtt{let}\{z \leftarrow e_0\}e(z) \simeq \mathtt{let}\{z \leftarrow e_0\}\mathtt{seq}(e(z), z)$ then

$$\mathtt{let}\{z \leftarrow e_0\}\mathtt{seq}(e(z), e_1, \ldots) \simeq \mathtt{let}\{z \leftarrow e(e_0)\}\mathtt{seq}(e_1, \ldots).$$

3.4.3. The Basics

As we have already said, the main motivation for studying $\simeq$ is given by the Substitution Theorem. It and its corollaries describe fundamental syntactic manipulations that preserve strong isomorphism. It is these properties that suggest that the program we are about to undertake will not be ridiculously complicated. In contrast, even though $\cong$ is a decidable relation, the non-existence of *nice* principles regarding it is almost certain, simply because of the non-existence of such syntactic manipulations. Returning to basic manipulations, which we repeat here for the convenience of the reader, if $e^0_{body}(\bar{x}, \bar{y}) \simeq e^1_{body}(\bar{x}, \bar{y})$, $|\bar{x}| = k + 1$, $e^0_i(\bar{y}) \simeq e^1_i(\bar{y})$, for $0 \leq i \leq k$ and ϑ is either an k-ary memory operation or an k-ary function symbol then:

Substitution :

$$\mathtt{let}_{0 \leq i \leq k}\{x_i \leftarrow e^0_i(\bar{y})\}e^0_{body}(\bar{x}, \bar{y}) \simeq \mathtt{let}_{0 \leq i \leq k}\{x_i \leftarrow e^1_i(\bar{y})\}e^1_{body}(\bar{x}, \bar{y}).$$

Sequencing : $\mathtt{seq}_{0\leq i<k}(e_i^0(\bar{y})) \simeq \mathtt{seq}_{0\leq i<k}(e_i^1(\bar{y}))$.

Composition : $\vartheta(e_0^0(\bar{y}),\ldots,e_{k-1}^0(\bar{y})) \simeq \vartheta(e_0^1(\bar{y}),\ldots,e_{k-1}^1(\bar{y}))$.

Branching : $\mathtt{if}(e_0^0(\bar{y}),e_1^0(\bar{y}),e_2^0(\bar{y})) \simeq \mathtt{if}(e_0^1(\bar{y}),e_1^1(\bar{y}),e_2^1(\bar{y}))$.

Unfolding : $e(\bar{x}) \simeq e^{\bowtie}(\bar{x})$.

Leibniz's Law: $e_0(\bar{x}) \simeq e_1(\bar{x}) \rightarrow e(\bar{x},e_0(\bar{x})) \simeq e(\bar{x},e_1(\bar{x}))$.

3.4.4. The Data Operations

The properties of the data operations are quite simple to express and we expect the following list to be fairly close to being complete (we will point out places where there is room for improvement). We begin by enumerating the properties of *rplaca* and *rplacd*, necessitating heavy use of seq. The first two axioms simply state that *rplaca*(x,y) and *rplacd*(x,y) both return the modified x.

0. $\mathtt{seq}(rplaca(x,y),x) \simeq rplaca(x,y)$.
1. $\mathtt{seq}(rplacd(x,y),x) \simeq rplacd(x,y)$.

The next two axioms describe the modifications made to x, and the two after describe what isn't altered.

2. $car(rplaca(x,y)) \simeq \mathtt{seq}(rplaca(x,y),y)$.
3. $cdr(rplacd(x,y)) \simeq \mathtt{seq}(rplacd(x,y),y)$.
4. $car(rplacd(x,y)) \simeq \mathtt{let}\{z \leftarrow car(x)\}\mathtt{seq}(rplacd(x,y),z)$.
5. $cdr(rplaca(x,y)) \simeq \mathtt{let}\{z \leftarrow cdr(x)\}\mathtt{seq}(rplaca(x,y),z)$.

Notice that in these last two the let is important since simply saying

$$car(rplacd(x,y)) \simeq \mathtt{seq}(rplacd(x,y),car(x)),$$

for example, would not be enough. In fact this last equation follows from 0. using the principal subexpression theorem. These last two can also be generalized so that they imply that every other pointer in existing cells, other than the one modified, remains the same. We shall not do this.

The next six axioms are *cancellation* axioms. The first two simply state that modifying the same pointer in x successively is identical to carrying out the single second modification. These properties are used very heavily when proving properties of pointer reversing programs, as will be seen in Chapters 4 and 8. The second two state simple relations between *cons*-ing a new cell and modifying a newly constructed one. The final two just express the fact that altering a pointer so that it now points to what it did previously is no alteration.

6. $\mathsf{seq}(rplaca(x, y_0), rplaca(x, y_1)) \simeq rplaca(x, y_1)$.
7. $\mathsf{seq}(rplacd(x, y_0), rplacd(x, y_1)) \simeq rplacd(x, y_1)$.
8. $rplaca(cons(z, y), x) \simeq cons(x, y)$.
9. $rplacd(cons(x, z), y) \simeq cons(x, y)$.
10. $rplaca(x, car(x)) \simeq x$ when $x \in \mathbb{C}$.
11. $rplacd(x, cdr(x)) \simeq x$ when $x \in \mathbb{C}$.

The next three properties of *rplaca* and *rplacd* are simple *commutativity* properties, stating when the order of these destructive modifications can be changed without any harm.

12. $\mathsf{seq}(rplacd(x_0, x_1), rplaca(x_2, x_3), x_4) \simeq \mathsf{seq}(rplaca(x_2, x_3), rplacd(x_0, x_1), x_4)$.
13. $\mathsf{seq}(rplaca(x_0, x_1), rplaca(x_2, x_3), x_4) \simeq \mathsf{seq}(rplaca(x_2, x_3), rplaca(x_0, x_1), x_4)$, if $x_0 \neq x_2$.
14. $\mathsf{seq}(rplacd(x_0, x_1), rplacd(x_2, x_3), x_4) \simeq \mathsf{seq}(rplacd(x_2, x_3), rplacd(x_0, x_1), x_4)$, if $x_0 \neq x_2$.

The next two assert, in a rather subtle manner, that one cannot modify an atom.

15. $atom(rplaca(e_0, e_1)) \simeq \mathsf{seq}(rplaca(e_0, e_1), \mathtt{NIL})$.
16. $atom(rplacd(e_0, e_1)) \simeq \mathsf{seq}(rplacd(e_0, e_1), \mathtt{NIL})$.

What remains now are simple properties of the remaining operations. The first simply states that *cons* creates a cell, never an atom. The next two are simple facts about the characteristic function of $\mathbb{A}$, *atom*.

17. $atom(cons(x, y)) \simeq \mathtt{NIL}$.
18. $atom(x) \simeq \mathtt{T}$ if $x \in \mathbb{A}$ and $atom(x) \simeq \mathtt{NIL}$ if $x \in \mathbb{C}$.
19. $atom(\mathtt{T}) \simeq \mathtt{T}$ and $atom(\mathtt{NIL}) \simeq \mathtt{T}$.

The following two properties relate the cell constructing operation, *cons*, with the access operations, *car* and *cdr*. Note that $cons(car(x), cdr(x)) \simeq x$ is always *false*, regardless of the nature of x.

20. $car(cons(x, y)) \simeq x$.
21. $cdr(cons(x, y)) \simeq y$.

The next axiom states, again in a necessarily subtle way, that *cons* always creates a new cell. The remaining axioms state simple properties of the identity, *eq*. There are obvious modifications of these axioms for the case of *atom*:*eq*. We leave their statement to the reader's imagination.

22. $eq(cons(e_0, e_1), e_2) \simeq \mathsf{seq}(e_0, e_1, e_2, \mathtt{NIL})$.
23. $eq(e_0, e_1) \simeq eq(e_1, e_0)$ if the e_i are gentle.
24. $eq(x, y) \simeq \mathtt{NIL}$ if $x \neq y$.
25. $eq(x, y) \simeq \mathtt{T}$ if $x = y$.
26. $eq(\mathtt{T}, \mathtt{NIL}) \simeq \mathtt{NIL}$.
27. $atom(eq(e_0, e_1)) \simeq \mathsf{seq}(e_0, e_1, \mathtt{T})$.

3.4.5. Properties of seq

We now commence with the control structure, beginning with seq. The first three properties are the simplest one can think of concerning the *sequencing* primitive: a sequence of one expression is the same as the expression; a sequence within a sequence can be flattened, i.e. nested seq removal; and thirdly, seq can be defined in terms of let.

1. $\mathsf{seq}(e) \simeq e$
2. $\mathsf{seq}(e_0, \ldots, \mathsf{seq}(e_n \ldots e_m), e_k, \ldots) \simeq \mathsf{seq}(e_0, \ldots, e, e_n, \ldots e_m, e_k, \ldots)$
3. $\mathsf{seq}(e_0, e_1, \ldots, e_n) \simeq \mathtt{let}\{x_0 \leftarrow e_0, x_1 \leftarrow e_1, \ldots, x_n \leftarrow e_n\}x_n$

The next six properties all stem from the fact that the value returned by the sequence is the value of the last expression in the sequence. Consequently gentle expressions, when they are defined, can be added and removed from anywhere within the sequence other than the last. The five axioms subsequent to the first allow one to replace an expression in a value-ignoring position by one or more that have the same effect on memory. Note that in the last two of the six, the hypothesis cannot be weakened to $atom(e_n) \simeq \mathsf{seq}(e_n, \mathtt{NIL})$ for reasons of validity.

4. $\mathsf{seq}(e_0(\bar{y}) \ldots, e_n(\bar{y}), e(\bar{y})) \simeq e(\bar{y})$ if $e_i(\bar{y})$ are total gentle terms, $0 \leq i \leq n$.
5. $\mathsf{seq}(e_0, \ldots, cons(e_n, e_{n+1}), \ldots, e_m) \simeq \mathsf{seq}(e_0, \ldots, e_n, e_{n+1}, \ldots, e_m)$.
6. $\mathsf{seq}(e_0, \ldots, eq(e_n, e_{n+1}), \ldots, e_m) \simeq \mathsf{seq}(e_0, \ldots, e_n, e_{n+1}, \ldots, e_m)$.
7. $\mathsf{seq}(e_0, \ldots, atom(e_n), \ldots, e_m) \simeq \mathsf{seq}(e_0, \ldots, e_n, \ldots, e_m)$.
8. If $atom(\mathsf{seq}(e_0, \ldots, e_n)) \simeq \mathsf{seq}(e_0, \ldots, e_n, \mathtt{NIL})$, then

$$\mathsf{seq}(e_0, \ldots, car(e_n), \ldots, e_m) \simeq \mathsf{seq}(e_0, \ldots, e_n, \ldots, e_m).$$

9. If $atom(\mathtt{seq}(e_0, \ldots, e_n)) \simeq \mathtt{seq}(e_0, \ldots, e_n, \mathtt{NIL})$, then

$$\mathtt{seq}(e_0, \ldots, cdr(e_n), \ldots, e_m) \simeq \mathtt{seq}(e_0, \ldots, e_n, \ldots, e_m).$$

The final two properties concern somewhat different manipulations of seq. The first describes when one can *push a* seq *inside an expression.* And the last allows one to commute gentle expressions with one another, regardless of whether they are defined.

10. If z is principal in $e(z)$ then $\mathtt{seq}(e_0, \ldots, e_{n-1}, e(e_n)) \simeq e(\mathtt{seq}(e_0, \ldots, e_{n-1}, e_n))$.

11. If e_{n-1} and e_n are gentle then

$$\mathtt{seq}(e_0, \ldots, e_{n-1}, e_n, \ldots, e_m) \simeq \mathtt{seq}(e_0, \ldots, e_n, e_{n-1}, \ldots, e_m).$$

A shortcoming in our axioms regarding seq is in their dealing with the problem of commuting expressions. Our only relevant axiom was this last one. It is clear that this is not exhaustive, but an elegant description of when such a principle is valid has eluded us. One final axiom, which we include for interest rather than anything else, demonstrates that seq is in fact definable without recourse to let.

12 $\mathtt{seq}(e_0, \ldots, e_n)$ is strongly isomorphic to

$$\underbrace{cdr(cdr(\ldots cdr}_{n\ \ cdr\ s}(car(cons(e_0, cons(e_1, \ldots, cons(e_n, \mathtt{NIL})))\ldots)))$$

3.4.6. Properties of if

The branching construct, if, and its properties are well understood, see for example (Bloom and Tindell, 1983),(Guessarian and Meseguer, 1985) or Chapter 5, and so we shall not dwell upon them here.

1. $\mathtt{if}(\mathtt{NIL}, e_0, e_1) \simeq e_1$.
2. $\mathtt{if}(\mathtt{T}, e_0, e_1) \simeq e_0$.
3. $\mathtt{if}(e_0, e_1, e_1) \simeq \mathtt{seq}(e_0, e_1)$
4. Suppose that $e_0 \simeq \mathtt{seq}(e_0, \mathtt{NIL})$ implies that $e_2 \simeq e_2^*$ then $\mathtt{if}(e_0, e_1, e_2) \simeq \mathtt{if}(e_0, e_1, e_2^*)$.
5. Suppose that $e_0 \not\simeq \mathtt{seq}(e_0, \mathtt{NIL})$ implies that $e_1 \simeq e_1^*$ then $\mathtt{if}(e_0, e_1, e_2) \simeq \mathtt{if}(e_0, e_1^*, e_2)$.
6. Suppose that $e_0 \simeq \mathtt{seq}(e_0, \mathtt{NIL})$ then $\mathtt{if}(e_0, e_1, e_2) \simeq \mathtt{seq}(e_0, e_2)$.
7. Suppose that $e_0 \not\simeq \mathtt{seq}(e_0, \mathtt{NIL})$ then $\mathtt{if}(e_0, e_1, e_2) \simeq \mathtt{seq}(e_0, e_1)$.
8. $\vartheta(\bar{x}_0, \mathtt{if}(e_0, e_1, e_2), \bar{x}_1) \simeq \mathtt{if}(e_0, \vartheta(\bar{x}_0, e_1, \bar{x}_1), \vartheta(\bar{x}_0, e_2, \bar{x}_1))$.

3.4.7. Properties of let

The lexically scoped variable binding operation, `let`, is by far the most difficult of the control primitives to describe axiomatically. Even though we shall show it is possible in Chapter 5, we have but scratched the surface here. The first property is a simple consequence of the *lexical* nature of `let`.

1. $\mathtt{let}\{x_0 \leftarrow e_0\}\mathtt{let}\{x_1 \leftarrow e_1\}e \simeq \mathtt{let}\{x_0 \leftarrow e_0, x_1 \leftarrow e_1\}e$, as long as x_0 does not occur free in e_1.

The next three properties are the simplest forms of `let` elimination we have found. They are by no means the end of the story. There are many other cases when one can eliminate or introduce a `let` but we have not found any elegant way of describing them. Basically there are only two reasons why a `let` cannot be eliminated. The first is when it is used to obtain a pointer to an object about to become inaccessible. For example

$$\mathtt{let}\{y \leftarrow \mathit{car}(x)\}\mathtt{seq}(\mathit{rplaca}(x, z), \ldots).$$

The second is when it is used to obtain a pointer to the value of an expression e that when evaluated twice produces distinct answers. For example

$$\mathtt{let}\{y \leftarrow \mathit{cons}(\mathtt{T}, \mathtt{T})\}\ \mathit{cons}(y, y).$$

Another example of when a `let` cannot be eliminated is illustrated by the following fact. It states that, in a sense, all primitive terms have inverses. The obvious version without the `let` is of course false.

Proposition: For any term $e(\bar{x})$ there are terms $e_i(\bar{x})$ in $\mathbb{M}_{pure^+}$ for $0 \leq i \leq n$ and a term $e^{-1}(\bar{x}, \bar{y})$ such that

$$\mathtt{let}_{0 \leq i \leq n}\{y_i \leftarrow e_i(\bar{x})\}\mathtt{seq}(e(\bar{x}), e^{-1}(\bar{x}, \bar{y})) \simeq \mathtt{T}.$$

We would be delighted if someone produced an elegant characterization of when a `let` can be eliminated. At the end of this section we give some other examples of when a `let` can be eliminated. The list of properties of `let` continues as follows.

2. If the x_i do not occur in e, then the following two expressions are strongly isomorphic

$$\mathtt{let}\{x_0 \leftarrow e_0, \ldots x_n \leftarrow e_n, y_0 \leftarrow e_0^*, \ldots, y_m \leftarrow e_m^*\}e$$

$$\mathtt{seq}(e_0, \ldots e_n, \mathtt{let}\{y_0 \leftarrow e_0^*, \ldots, y_m \leftarrow e_m^*\}e).$$

3a. If z is principal in $e(z)$ then

$$\texttt{let}\{z \leftarrow e_0\}e(z) \simeq e(e_0).$$

3b. If z is principal in $e(z)$ and e_0 contains no free variables from $\bar{x}$ then

$$\texttt{let}\{x_1 \leftarrow e_1, \ldots, x_n \leftarrow e_n, z \leftarrow e_0\}e(z) \simeq \texttt{let}\{x_1 \leftarrow e_1, \ldots x_n \leftarrow e_n\}e(e_0).$$

4. $\texttt{let}\{y_0 \leftarrow e_0, \ldots, x \leftarrow v, \ldots y_n \leftarrow e_n\}e(x, \bar{y}) \simeq \texttt{let}_{0 \leq i \leq n}\{y_i \leftarrow e_i\}e(v, \bar{y})$.

The next axiom is more a property of function application than that of `let`, but we include it here because of its importance and because it follows from the axioms above.

5. $\vartheta(e_0, e_1, \ldots, e_n) \simeq \texttt{let}\ \{x_0 \leftarrow e_0, x_1 \leftarrow e_1, \ldots, x_n \leftarrow e_n\}\vartheta(\bar{x})$.

The next two axioms pretty much speak for themselves; they turn out to be very useful when proving properties of programs. They can, of course, be generalized and the axiom following them is one such generalization.

6. $\texttt{let}\{x \leftarrow e\}\texttt{seq}(\mathit{rplaca}(x, y), e_0, \ldots) \simeq \texttt{let}\{x \leftarrow \mathit{rplaca}(e, y)\}\texttt{seq}(e_0, \ldots)$.
7. $\texttt{let}\{x \leftarrow e\}\texttt{seq}(\mathit{rplaca}(x, y), e_0, \ldots) \simeq \texttt{let}\{x \leftarrow \mathit{rplaca}(e, y)\}\texttt{seq}(e_0, \ldots)$.
8. If $\texttt{let}\{x \leftarrow e\}e_0(x) \simeq \texttt{let}\{x \leftarrow e\}\texttt{seq}(e_0(x), x)$ and x is principal in $e_0(x)$ then

$$\texttt{let}\{x \leftarrow e\}\texttt{seq}(e_0(x), e_1, \ldots) \simeq \texttt{let}\{x \leftarrow e_0(e)\}\texttt{seq}(e_1, \ldots).$$

The last axiom gives a sufficient condition for commuting binding expressions. It is clear that this condition is not necessary, but again an elegant description of when such principles are valid has escaped us.

9. If e_{n-1} and e_n are gentle then

$$\texttt{let}\{\ldots, x_{n-1} \leftarrow e_{n-1}, x_n \leftarrow e_n, \ldots\}e \simeq \texttt{let}\{\ldots, x_n \leftarrow e_n, x_{n-1} \leftarrow e_{n-1}, \ldots\}e.$$

We finish off this section with some more complex cases of valid `let`-elimination and introduction, which require some definitions. The first is that of an expression being a predicate; not only must it be gentle but it must also not enlarge the domain of the memory which it is evaluated in.

Definition: An expression $e(\bar{x})$ is said to be a *predicate* if for every memory object $\bar{v}\,;\mu$ if

$$e(\bar{v})\,;\mu \gg v^*\,;\mu^*$$

then

$$\mu = \mu^*.$$

It is often said that a good programmer will only use *predicates* as test clauses in `if` expressions,see for example page 29 of (Pitman, 1983). We sympathize with this standpoint, and indeed that is why we have called them predicates. The following proposition gives a simple necessary and sufficient for a primitive term to be strongly isomorphic to a predicate, its proof requires the techniques developed in Chapter 5.

Proposition: If $e(\bar{x})$ is a gentle term and for every memory object description $\bar{v}\,;\mu$ we have that either $e(\bar{v})\,;\mu$ does not denote or else it either denotes an atom or else a cell in μ, then there is a predicate $e^*(\bar{x})$ such that

$$e(\bar{x}) \simeq e^*(\bar{x}).$$

The next definition is that of a variable, x, occurring in a stable position in an expression, $e(\bar{x})$. The definition is designed to make sure that the nature of x will not be changed in the evaluation of e up to the point it appears in the expression.

Definition: An occurrence of a variable in an expression e is said to be stable if no *rplaca* or *rplacd* is evaluated before that occurrence of x is evaluated. This is defined formally as follows. Suppose $e(z)$ is an expression in which the variable z occurs freely exactly once and does not occur bound. Then we say *z is stable in* $e(z)$ if one of the following conditions holds.

0. $e = z$,
1. $e = \vartheta(e_0^*, \ldots, e_n^*, e_0, \ldots, e_m)$, z is stable in e_0 and $\mathtt{seq}(e_0^*, \ldots, e_n^*)$ is gentle.
2. $e = \mathtt{if}(e_0, e_1, e_2)$ and either z is stable in e_0 or else e_0 is gentle and z is stable in either e_1 or e_2,
3. $e = \mathtt{seq}(e_0^*, \ldots e_n^*, e_0, \ldots e_m)$, z is stable in e_0, and $\mathtt{seq}(e_0^*, \ldots, e_n^*)$ is gentle,
4. $\mathtt{let}\{x_0 \leftarrow e_0^*, \ldots x_n \leftarrow e_n^*, x_{n+1} \leftarrow e_1, \ldots, x_{n+m} \leftarrow e_m\}e$, z is stable in e_1, and $\mathtt{seq}(e_0^*, \ldots, e_n^*)$ is gentle,
5. $\mathtt{let}\{x_0 \leftarrow e_0, \ldots x_n \leftarrow e_n\}e$, z is stable in e, and $\mathtt{seq}(e_0, \ldots, e_n)$ is gentle.

An occurrence of a variable, x, that occurs more than once in e is said to be stable at that occurrence if when we replace it by a new variable, z, in that occurrence, then z occurs in a stable position in the so obtained expression. Note for example that x is stable in the expression $rplaca(x, x)$ because in our version of Lisp we evaluate the arguments of a function call before carrying out the function call. The final definition is that of a strict subexpression of an expression. The idea is simple, a strict subexpression of an expression is one which must be evaluated in order to evaluate the whole expression.

Definition: The strict subexpressions of an expression e consist of the collection $\varrho(e)$ defined inductively as follows:

$$\varrho(e) = \begin{cases} \{e\} & \text{if } e \in \mathbb{X} \cup \mathbb{V}; \\ \{e\} \cup \varrho(e_0) & \text{if } e = \mathtt{if}(e_0, e_1, e_2) \\ \{e\} \cup \bigcup_i \varrho(e_i) & \text{if } e = \begin{cases} \vartheta(e_0, \ldots e_m) & \text{with } \vartheta \in \mathbb{O} \cup \mathbb{F} \text{ or} \\ \mathtt{seq}(e_0, \ldots e_m) \end{cases} \\ \{e\} \cup \bigcup_i \varrho(e_i) \cup \varrho(e_{body}) & \text{if } e = \mathtt{let}_{0 \le i \le m}\{y_i \leftarrow e_i\} e_{body} \end{cases}$$

Using these three definitions we can state the following valid form of `let`-elimination.

Proposition: Suppose that every occurrence of x is stable in $e(x)$, x occurs at least once in a strict position, and that e_0 is a predicate. Then

$$\mathtt{let}\{x \leftarrow e_0\} e(x) \simeq e(e_0).$$

Furthermore we can alter the assumptions slightly to cover the case when e_0 is not a predicate but is gentle.

Proposition: Suppose that x occurs only once in $e(x)$ and that occurrence is both stable and strict; also suppose that e_0 is a gentle expression. Then

$$\mathtt{let}\{x \leftarrow e_0\} e(x) \simeq e(e_0).$$

In both of these simple cases we can drop the assumption concerning strictness provided that the expression e_0 is total. Also the assumption that x can only occur once in the second proposition can be weakened. This is because if, for example,

$$e(x) = \mathtt{if}(e_{test}, e_{then}, e_{else})$$

and x did not occur in e_{test} then we would only need to require that it occurs at most once in *both* e_{then} and e_{else}. To make this explicit we make the following definition of a variable occurring *uniquely* in an expression.

Definition: We say that the variable z is *unique* in the expression e if and only if one of the following holds:

0. $e = z$,
1. $e = \vartheta(e_0^*, \ldots, e_n^*, e_0, \ldots, e_m)$ and firstly z is unique in e_0, secondly z does not occur in e_i for any $0 < i \le m$ nor in e_i^* for $0 \le i \le n$

2. $e = \texttt{if}(e_0, e_1, e_2)$ and either z occurs uniquely in e_0 and does not occur in either e_1 or e_2, or else it does not occur in e_0 and if it occurs in either e_1 or e_2, then it occurs uniquely.

3. $e = \texttt{seq}(e_0^*, \ldots e_n^*, e_0, \ldots e_m)$ and firstly z is unique in e_0, secondly z does not occur in e_i for any $0 < i \leq m$ nor in e_i^* for $0 \leq i \leq n$.

4. $\texttt{let}\{x_0 \leftarrow e_0^*, \ldots x_n \leftarrow e_n^*, x_{n+1} \leftarrow e_1, \ldots, x_{n+m} \leftarrow e_m\}e$ and firstly z is unique in e_1, secondly z does not occur in e, e_i for any $0 < i \leq m$ or in e_i^* for $0 \leq i \leq n$, and z is distinct from the $\bar{x}$.

5. $\texttt{let}\{x_0 \leftarrow e_0, \ldots x_n \leftarrow e_n\}e$, z does not occur in e_i for $0 \leq i \leq n$, z is distinct from the $\bar{x}$ and z is unique in e.

With this definition we can generalize the previous proposition to

Proposition: Suppose that x occurs uniquely in $e(x)$ and every occurrence is stable. Furthermore suppose that either there is a strict occurrence of x or else e_0 is total. Also suppose that e_0 is a gentle expression. Then

$$\texttt{let}\{x \leftarrow e_0\}e(x) \simeq e(e_0).$$

There are other issues concerning `let` elimination that we have not touched upon here. The most important is when, from a point of view of efficiency, is it better to introduce or eliminate a `let`. A discussion of some of the issues can be found in (Steele, 1976) and (Steele, 1977a).

3.4.8. Call by Value and Domain axioms

These axioms again are somewhat self-evident and, yet again, probably not exhaustive especially, once again, in the case of `let`. Note that because evaluating expressions can alter the course of nature, these axioms are more complex than their pure counterparts. We define $e\downarrow$ to mean

$$e \not\simeq car(\mathtt{T}).$$

1. Whenever there is an $0 \leq i \leq n$ such that $\neg(\texttt{seq}(e_0, \ldots, e_i)\downarrow)$ we have

$$\neg(\texttt{let}_{0 \leq i \leq n}\{y_i \leftarrow e_i\}e)\downarrow.$$

2. Whenever there is an $0 \leq i \leq n$ such that $\neg(\texttt{seq}(e_0, \ldots, e_i)\downarrow)$ we have

$$\neg(\texttt{seq}(e_0, \ldots, e_n)\downarrow).$$

3. $\neg(\mathtt{if}(e_0, e_1, e_2)\downarrow)$, whenever $\neg(e_0\downarrow)$.
4. $\neg(\vartheta(e_0, \ldots, e_n)\downarrow)$, whenever there is an $0 \leq i \leq n$ such that $\neg(\mathtt{seq}(e_0, \ldots, e_i)\downarrow)$.
5. $cons(x, y)\downarrow$.
6. $atom(x) \simeq \mathrm{T}$ implies that $\neg(car(x)\downarrow)$ and $\neg(cdr(x)\downarrow)$.
7. $atom(x) \simeq \mathrm{T}$ implies that $\neg(rplaca(x, y)\downarrow)$ and $\neg(rplacd(x, y)\downarrow)$.

3.5. An Example of a Proof

We chose the *defined:eq* program as our first real example of the use of strong isomorphism for four reasons. Firstly it is a very simple program, involving no recursion, that accomplishes an easily specified task. The second reason is that the correctness proof is quite subtle, and involves several delicate manipulations. Thirdly, each step in the proof is a simple combination of the axioms in the preceding section. Finally it demonstrates that the only natural fragments of destructive Lisp are $\mathbb{M}_{pure}$, $\mathbb{M}_{pure^+}$ and $\mathbb{M}_{sexp}$. We shall refer to the axioms in a systematic and self-explanatory fashion. For example do4. refers to the fourth axiom concerning the data operations, namely

4. $car(rplacd(x, y)) \simeq \mathtt{let}\{z \leftarrow car(x)\}\mathtt{seq}(rplacd(x, y), z)$.

While seq1. refers to the first property of seq, namely

1. $\mathtt{seq}(e) \simeq e$

We begin, by force, with the definition of the program *defined:eq*.

$$
\begin{array}{l}
defined{:}eq(\mathtt{x}, \mathtt{y}) \leftarrow \\
\quad \mathtt{if}(\mathtt{or}(atom(\mathtt{x}), atom(\mathtt{y})), \\
\quad\quad atom{:}eq(\mathtt{x}, \mathtt{y}), \\
\quad\quad \mathtt{let}\{\mathtt{oldx} \leftarrow car(\mathtt{x}), \mathtt{oldy} \leftarrow car(\mathtt{y})\} \\
\quad\quad\quad \mathtt{seq}(rplaca(\mathtt{x}, \mathrm{T}), \\
\quad\quad\quad\quad rplaca(\mathtt{y}, \mathtt{NIL}), \\
\quad\quad\quad\quad \mathtt{let}\{\mathtt{answer} \leftarrow atom{:}eq(car(\mathtt{x}), car(\mathtt{y}))\} \\
\quad\quad\quad\quad\quad \mathtt{seq}(rplaca(\mathtt{x}, \mathtt{oldx}), rplaca(\mathtt{y}, \mathtt{oldy}), \mathtt{answer}))).
\end{array}
$$

The theorem that we prove is, predictably, the following:

Theorem: $defined{:}eq(x, y) \simeq eq(x, y)$.

Proof of Theorem: Clearly the result will be true when either x or y are atoms. Consequently we need only consider the case when they are both cells. We can simplify the problem even further by observing that by eq23 and eq24 the theorem is equivalent to the following two statements:

1. $defined\text{:}eq(x, y) \simeq \texttt{NIL}$ whenever $x \neq y$.
2. $defined\text{:}eq(x, y) \simeq \texttt{T}$ whenever $x = y$.

We prove these in the order stated.

Proof of 1: Suppose that both x and y are distinct cells with $\texttt{x}_\texttt{a}$ and $\texttt{y}_\texttt{a}$ their respective cars. Evaluating the body of *defined:eq*, simplifying the `if` and eliminating the `let` in this context results in:

$$\begin{array}{l} \texttt{seq}(rplaca(x, \texttt{T}), \\ \quad rplaca(y, \texttt{NIL}), \\ \quad \texttt{let}\{answer \leftarrow atom\text{:}eq(car(x), car(y))\} \\ \qquad \texttt{seq}(rplaca(x, \texttt{x}_\texttt{a}), rplaca(y, \texttt{y}_\texttt{a}), answer))) \end{array}$$

It is this expression that, we shall demonstrate, is strongly isomorphic to `NIL`.

$$\begin{array}{l} \texttt{seq}(rplaca(x, \texttt{T}), \\ \quad rplaca(y, \texttt{NIL}), \\ \quad \texttt{let}\{answer \leftarrow atom\text{:}eq(car(x), car(y))\} \\ \qquad \texttt{seq}(rplaca(x, \texttt{x}_\texttt{a}), rplaca(y, \texttt{y}_\texttt{a}), answer))). \end{array}$$

Pushing the `seq` inside the `let` produces (seq10)

$$\begin{array}{l} \simeq \texttt{let}\{answer \leftarrow \texttt{seq}(rplaca(x, \texttt{T}), rplaca(y, \texttt{NIL}), atom\text{:}eq(car(x), car(y))\} \\ \qquad \texttt{seq}(rplaca(x, \texttt{x}_\texttt{a}), rplaca(y, \texttt{y}_\texttt{a}), answer))). \end{array}$$

And now pushing the `seq` inside the *atom:eq* yields (seq10)

$$\begin{array}{l} \simeq \texttt{let}\{answer \leftarrow atom\text{:}eq(\texttt{seq}(rplaca(x, \texttt{T}), rplaca(y, \texttt{NIL}), car(x)), car(y))\} \\ \qquad \texttt{seq}(rplaca(x, \texttt{x}_\texttt{a}), rplaca(y, \texttt{y}_\texttt{a}), answer))). \end{array}$$

Commuting the two calls to *rplaca* gives (do13, seq2)

$$\begin{array}{l} \simeq \texttt{let}\{answer \leftarrow atom\text{:}eq(\texttt{seq}(rplaca(y, \texttt{NIL}), rplaca(x, \texttt{T}), car(x)), car(y))\} \\ \qquad \texttt{seq}(rplaca(x, \texttt{x}_\texttt{a}), rplaca(y, \texttt{y}_\texttt{a}), answer))). \end{array}$$

Now eliminating the call to *car*, (seq10, do2, do0, seq2)

$$\begin{array}{l} \simeq \texttt{let}\{answer \leftarrow atom\text{:}eq(\texttt{seq}(rplaca(y, \texttt{NIL}), rplaca(x, \texttt{T}), \texttt{T}), car(y))\} \\ \qquad \texttt{seq}(rplaca(x, \texttt{x}_\texttt{a}), rplaca(y, \texttt{y}_\texttt{a}), answer))). \end{array}$$

Popping the seq out of the *atom:eq* results in (seq10)

$$\simeq \texttt{let}\{answer \leftarrow \texttt{seq}(rplaca(y,\texttt{NIL}), rplaca(x,\texttt{T}), atom{:}eq(\texttt{T}, car(y)))\}$$
$$\texttt{seq}(rplaca(x,\texttt{x}_\texttt{a}), rplaca(y,\texttt{y}_\texttt{a}), answer))).$$

Commuting the calls to *rplaca* has the consequence that (do13, seq2)

$$\simeq \texttt{let}\{answer \leftarrow \texttt{seq}(rplaca(x,\texttt{T}), rplaca(y,\texttt{NIL}), atom{:}eq(\texttt{T}, car(y)))\}$$
$$\texttt{seq}(rplaca(x,\texttt{x}_\texttt{a}), rplaca(y,\texttt{y}_\texttt{a}), answer))).$$

Now commuting the, *gentle*, arguments to the *atom:eq* call gives (do23)

$$\simeq \texttt{let}\{answer \leftarrow \texttt{seq}(rplaca(x,\texttt{T}), rplaca(y,\texttt{NIL}), atom{:}eq(car(y), \texttt{T}))\}$$
$$\texttt{seq}(rplaca(x,\texttt{x}_\texttt{a}), rplaca(y,\texttt{y}_\texttt{a}), answer))).$$

Pushing the seq back inside the *atom:eq* call gives (seq10)

$$\simeq \texttt{let}\{answer \leftarrow atom{:}eq(\texttt{seq}(rplaca(x,\texttt{T}), rplaca(y,\texttt{NIL}), car(y)), \texttt{T})\}$$
$$\texttt{seq}(rplaca(x,\texttt{x}_\texttt{a}), rplaca(y,\texttt{y}_\texttt{a}), answer))).$$

Again eliminating the call to *car* produces (seq10, seq2, do2, do0)

$$\simeq \texttt{let}\{answer \leftarrow atom{:}eq(\texttt{seq}(rplaca(x,\texttt{T}), rplaca(y,\texttt{NIL}), \texttt{NIL}), \texttt{T})\}$$
$$\texttt{seq}(rplaca(x,\texttt{x}_\texttt{a}), rplaca(y,\texttt{y}_\texttt{a}), answer))).$$

Pulling the seq out of the *atom:eq* for the last time leaves (seq10)

$$\simeq \texttt{let}\{answer \leftarrow \texttt{seq}(rplaca(x,\texttt{T}), rplaca(y,\texttt{NIL}), atom{:}eq(\texttt{NIL}, \texttt{T})\}$$
$$\texttt{seq}(rplaca(x,\texttt{x}_\texttt{a}), rplaca(y,\texttt{y}_\texttt{a}), answer))).$$

Simplifying the *atom:eq* call, (do27)

$$\simeq \texttt{let}\{answer \leftarrow \texttt{seq}(rplaca(x,\texttt{T}), rplaca(y,\texttt{NIL}), \texttt{NIL})\}$$
$$\texttt{seq}(rplaca(x,\texttt{x}_\texttt{a}), rplaca(y,\texttt{y}_\texttt{a}), answer))).$$

Now pulling the seq out of the let, again for the last time, (seq10)

$$\begin{aligned}\simeq \texttt{seq}(&rplaca(x,\texttt{T}),\\ &rplaca(y,\texttt{NIL}),\\ &\texttt{let}\{answer \leftarrow \texttt{NIL}\}\\ &\quad \texttt{seq}(rplaca(x,\texttt{x}_\texttt{a}), rplaca(y,\texttt{y}_\texttt{a}), answer))).\end{aligned}$$

We can now eliminate the let in favor of the following (let4, seq2)

$$\simeq \mathtt{seq}(rplaca(x, \mathtt{T}),\ rplaca(y, \mathtt{NIL}),\ rplaca(x, \mathbf{x_a}),\ rplaca(y, \mathbf{y_a}),\ \mathtt{NIL}))).$$

Commuting the calls to *rplaca* results in (do13, seq2)

$$\simeq \mathtt{seq}(rplaca(x, \mathtt{T}),\ rplaca(x, \mathbf{x_a}),\ rplaca(y, \mathtt{NIL}),\ rplaca(y, \mathbf{y_a}),\ \mathtt{NIL}))).$$

Cancelling the redundant modification of y yields (do6, do10, seq2)

$$\simeq \mathtt{seq}(rplaca(x, \mathtt{T}), rplaca(x, \mathbf{x_a}), \mathtt{NIL}))).$$

Similarly cancelling the modification of x provides (do6, do10, seq2)

$$\simeq \mathtt{seq}(\mathtt{NIL}).$$

The simplest property of **seq** gives the desired result, (seq1)

$$\simeq \mathtt{NIL}.$$

$\square_1$.

Proof of 2.: Suppose that x and y, both cells, are in fact identical, and for simplicity the *car* of x is $\mathbf{x_a}$. In this case we can immediately simplify the body of *defined:eq* to:

$$\mathtt{seq}(rplaca(x, \mathtt{T}),\ rplaca(x, \mathtt{NIL}),\ \mathtt{let}\{answer \leftarrow atom{:}eq(car(x), car(x))\}\ \mathtt{seq}(rplaca(x, \mathbf{x_a}), rplaca(x, \mathbf{x_a}), answer))).$$

Eliminating the redundant calls to *rplaca* gives (do6, seq2)

$$\simeq \mathtt{seq}(rplaca(x, \mathtt{NIL}),\ \mathtt{let}\{answer \leftarrow atom{:}eq(car(x), car(x))\}\ \mathtt{seq}(rplaca(x, \mathbf{x_a}), answer))).$$

Pushing the **seq** inside the **let** produces (seq10)

$\simeq$ let$\{answer \leftarrow$ seq$(rplaca(x,$ NIL$),\ atom{:}eq(car(x), car(x))\}$
seq$(rplaca(x, \mathtt{x_a}), answer)))$.

Pushing the seq inside the *atom:eq* call produces, (seq10)

$\simeq$ let$\{answer \leftarrow atom{:}eq(seq(rplaca(x,$ NIL$), car(x)), car(x))\}$
seq$(rplaca(x, \mathtt{x_a}), answer)))$.

Eliminating the *car* call gives (seq10, seq2, do2, do0)

$\simeq$ let$\{answer \leftarrow atom{:}eq(seq(rplaca(x,$ NIL$),$ NIL$), car(x))\}$
seq$(rplaca(x, \mathtt{x_a}), answer)))$.

Popping the seq out once again, (seq10)

$\simeq$ let$\{answer \leftarrow$ seq$(rplaca(x,$ NIL$), atom{:}eq($NIL$, car(x))\}$
seq$(rplaca(x, \mathtt{x_a}), answer)))$.

Commuting the gentle arguments to *atom:eq*, (do23)

$\simeq$ let$\{answer \leftarrow$ seq$(rplaca(x,$ NIL$), atom{:}eq(car(x),$ NIL$)\}$
seq$(rplaca(x, \mathtt{x_a}), answer)))$.

Pushing the seq inside yet again (seq10)

$\simeq$ let$\{answer \leftarrow atom{:}eq(seq(rplaca(x,$ NIL$), car(x)),$ NIL$)\}$
seq$(rplaca(x, \mathtt{x_a}), answer)))$.

Eliminating the call to *car*, (seq10, seq2, do2, do0)

$\simeq$ let$\{answer \leftarrow atom{:}eq(seq(rplaca(x,$ NIL$),$ NIL$),$ NIL$)\}$
seq$(rplaca(x, \mathtt{x_a}), answer)))$.

Popping the seq, (seq10)

$\simeq$ let$\{answer \leftarrow$ seq$(rplaca(x,$ NIL$), atom{:}eq($NIL, NIL$)\}$
seq$(rplaca(x, \mathtt{x_a}), answer)))$.

Simplifying the call to *atom:eq*, (do25)

$\simeq$ let$\{answer \leftarrow$ seq$(rplaca(x,$ NIL$),$ T$)$
seq$(rplaca(x, \mathtt{x_a}), answer)))$.

Pulling the seq out for the very last time leaves (seq10)

$\simeq$ seq$(rplaca(x,$ NIL$),$ let$\{answer \leftarrow$ T$\}$seq$(rplaca(x, \mathtt{x_a}), answer)))$.

Forsaking the let for something simpler, (let4, seq2)

$\simeq$ seq$(rplaca(x,$ NIL$), rplaca(x, \mathtt{x_a}),$ T$)$.

Ending with a whimper rather than a bang, (do6, do10, seq2)

$\simeq$ `seq(T).`

$\simeq$ `T.`

$\square_2$. $\square$**Theorem**

Chapter 4

A Plethora of Simple Examples

In this chapter we use the equivalence relations that we have introduced to prove properties of and verify some well known programs. We begin with those programs which can be verified, without causing too much pain, using the extensional relations. We then go on to treat an wider class of programs that can be verified using strong isomorphism. This is used as an excuse to show that proving properties in this case is very similar to the trivial pure Lisp case. In other words the proofs are of the transformation plus induction variety. We also make an effort to show how such increased understanding can be utilized to write new programs, as well as suggest the *duality* between program verification and program derivation or transformation. Since we have not given a complete axiomatization of strong isomorphism our approach in proofs will be somewhat model theoretic.

4.1. Example 0: The *inplace:reverse* Program

Consider the simple minded pure definition of *reverse*.

$$slow{:}reverse(\mathtt{u}) \leftarrow$$
$$\mathtt{ifn}(\mathtt{u}, \mathtt{NIL}, append(slow{:}reverse(cdr(\mathtt{u})), cons(car(\mathtt{u}), \mathtt{NIL})))$$

In (Scherlis, 1980) and in Chapter 7 the following well known tail recursive version is derived from the simple minded and slow one.

$$reverse(\mathtt{u}) \leftarrow rev(\mathtt{u}, \mathtt{NIL})$$
$$rev(\mathtt{u}, \mathtt{v}) \leftarrow \mathtt{ifn}(\mathtt{u}, \mathtt{v}, rev(cdr(\mathtt{u}), cons(car(\mathtt{u}), \mathtt{v})))$$

It is easy to see that these two versions are equivalent in a very strong sense, in fact it easily shown that

Theorem: $reverse(x) \simeq slow{:}reverse(x)$.

In this example, though, we are more interested in the following refinement of *reverse* . Let us restrict our attention to pure lists. If u is indeed a pure list, then the cell u belongs to neither $\mathbf{Cells}(cdr(u))$ nor $\mathbf{Cells}(cons(car(u), v))$, provided that it is not in $\mathbf{Cells}(v)$. Thus the cell u under these circumstances is disjoint from the value of $rev(cdr(u), cons(car(u), v))$. Consequently rather than create a new cell via the *cons* we could, while preserving isomorphism in the value, recycle the cell u. This leads to the definition:

$$inplace{:}reverse(\mathtt{u}) \leftarrow in{:}rev(\mathtt{u}, \mathtt{NIL})$$

$$in{:}rev(\mathtt{u}, \mathtt{v}) \leftarrow \mathtt{if}(\mathtt{u}, in{:}rev(cdr(\mathtt{u}), rplacd(\mathtt{u}, \mathtt{v})), \mathtt{v}))$$

The following theorem is a simple result that we shall prove in this section.

Theorem: $reverse(x) \cong slow{:}reverse(x) \cong inplace{:}reverse(x)$ on pure lists.

We begin with the following result, adapted from (Mason and Talcott, 1985).

Theorem: If $c_0 ; \mu_0 \in \mathbb{M}_{list}$ represents the Lisp list

$$(v_0 \; v_1 \; v_2 \; \ldots \; v_n)$$

with

$$\mathbf{Spine}_{\mu_0}(c_0) = \{c_0 \ldots c_n\}$$

then

$$inplace{:}reverse(c_0) ; \mu_0 \gg c_n ; \mu_{n+1}$$

where

1. $c_n ; \mu_{n+1}$ represents the Lisp list $(v_n \; v_{n-1} \; \ldots \; v_2 \; v_1 \; v_0)$.
2. $\mathbf{Spine}_{\mu_{n+1}}(c_n) = \{c_n \ldots c_0\}$,
3. $\mu_1 = setcdr(c_0, \; \mathtt{NIL} ; \; \mu_0)$, and
4. $\mu_{i+1} = setcdr(c_i, \; c_{i-1} ; \; \mu_i)$, for $i \in n+1$. In addition as a consequence of 3 and 4 we have
5. $\delta_{\mu_0} = \delta_{\mu_{n+1}}$ with μ_{n+1} differing from μ_0 only on $\{c_i\}_{i \in n+1}$.

Corollary 1: $inplace{:}reverse(inplace{:}reverse(c_0 ; \mu_0)) = c_0 ; \mu_0$

Corollary 2: $reverse(x) \cong slow{:}reverse(x) \cong inplace{:}reverse(x)$ on pure lists.

Notice that unless $c_0 ; \mu_0$ is a pure list we will not have that $v_i ; \mu_{n+1} \equiv v_i ; \mu_0$, in other words *inplace:reverse* may alter the elements of the original list. However a little careful thought on the matter reveals that there is no particularly obvious candidate for the epitaph *reverse* of a list in such structure sharing situations.

Proof of Theorem: We shall show by induction on i that

P1. $in{:}rev(c_0, \mathtt{NIL}) ; \mu_0 \gg in{:}rev(c_{i+1}, c_i) ; \mu_{i+1} \gg in{:}rev(\mathtt{NIL}, c_n) ; \mu_{n+1}$

P2. $i < j \leq n \rightarrow \mu_0(c_j) = \mu_{i+1}(c_j)$

P3. $0 \leq j < i \rightarrow \mu_{i+1}(c_j) = \mu_{j+1}(c_j)$

Note that

- for $0 < j \leq n$ $\mu_0(c_j) = [v_j, c_{j+1}]$ and $\mu_{j+1}(c_j) = [v_j, c_{j-1}]$
- for any $c\,;\mu \in \mathsf{M}_{list}$ with $u\,;\mu = cdr(c)\,;\mu$ we have by computation

$$
\begin{aligned}
&in{:}rev(c,v)\,;\mu \gg \\
&\quad \gg \mathtt{if}(c, in{:}rev(cdr(c), rplacd(c,v)), v)\,;\mu \\
&\quad \gg in{:}rev(u, rplacd(c,v))\,;\mu \\
&\quad \gg in{:}rev(u,c)\,; setcdr(c, v\,;\mu)
\end{aligned}
$$

- since $c_0\,;\mu_0 \in \mathsf{M}_{list}$ we have $c_i \neq c_j$, whenever $i \neq j$, and $i, j \in n+1$.

Case $i = 0$: By computation, since $c_1\,;\mu_0 = cdr(c_0);\mu_0$ and $\mu_1 = setcdr(c_0, \mathtt{NIL}; \mu_0)$ we have

$$in{:}rev(c_0, \mathtt{NIL})\,;\mu_0 \gg in{:}rev(c_1, c_0)\,;\mu_1.$$

Thus P1 holds for $i = 0$. Since μ_1 differs from μ_0 only on c_0 we have that

$$\mu_0(c_s) = \mu_1(c_s) \text{ for } 0 < s \leq n$$

so P2 holds. P3 is vacuous.

Induction step: Suppose $0 < i < n$ and

$$in{:}rev(c_0, \mathtt{NIL})\,;\mu_0 \gg in{:}rev(c_i, c_{i-1})\,;\mu_i$$

with μ_j satisfying P2 for $i-1 \leq j \leq n$ and P3 for $0 \leq j < i-1$. Thus $c_{i+1}\,;\mu_i = cdr(c_i)\,;\mu_0 = cdr(c_i)\,;\mu_i$. By computation again we have

$$in{:}rev(c_i, c_{i-1})\,;\mu_i \gg in{:}rev(c_{i+1}, c_i)\,;\mu_{i+1}$$

where $\mu_{i+1} = setcdr(c_i, c_{i-1}\,;\mu_i)$. P2 and P3 hold for μ_{i+1} because it only differs from μ_i on c_i.

Termination case: So far we have shown that for $0 \leq i \leq n$

$$in{:}rev(c_0, \mathtt{NIL})\,;\mu_0 \gg in{:}rev(c_i, c_{i-1})\,;\mu_i$$

with μ_j satisfying P2 for $i \leq j \leq n$ and P3 for $0 \leq j < i$. Thus P2 and P3 are proved and $cdr(c_n)\,;\mu_n = \mathtt{NIL}\,;\mu_n$. By computation we have

$$in{:}rev(c_n, c_{n-1})\,;\mu_n \gg in{:}rev(\mathtt{NIL}, c_n)\,;\mu_{n+1}$$

where $\mu_{n+1} = setcdr(c_n, c_{n-1} ; \mu_n)$.

$\Box$**P1,P2,P3**

The theorem now follows from the above and the simple observation that

$$inplace{:}reverse(c_0) ; \mu_0 \gg in{:}rev(c_0, \mathtt{NIL}) ; \mu_0 \gg c_n ; \mu_{n+1}.$$

$\Box$**Theorem**

We will treat these versions of reversing lists in more detail later, using strong isomorphism. Notice that we can use the derived functions to express simple intensional properties of these programs. The following are simple examples of this phenomenon which we leave as exercises for the reader.

Exercises:

1. $append^{\sharp cons}(x, y) \cong length(x)$
2. $slow{:}reverse^{\sharp cons}(x) \cong \mathtt{let}\{y \leftarrow length(x)\} \frac{(y+1) \cdot y}{2}$
3. $reverse^{\sharp cons}(x) \cong length(x)$
4. $inplace{:}reverse^{\sharp cons}(x) \cong 0$ on $\mathbb{M}_{list}$, note that doing this exercise also requires defining the $\sharp$ transformation on $\mathbb{M}_{sexp}$ rather than just $\mathbb{M}_{pure^+}$.

4.2. Example 1: The Recursive *copy* Program

In this example we deal with the traditional recursive copying program that one learns about in introductory Lisp courses.

```
recursive:copy(u) ←
      if(atom(u),
         u,
         cons(recursive:copy(car(u)), recursive:copy(cdr(u))))
```

The following is a simple induction on $|\mathbf{Cells}^{<}_{\mu}(c)|$.

Theorem: $recursive{:}copy(x) \equiv x$ on $\mathbb{M}_{wf}$, Furthermore if $recursive{:}copy(c) ; \mu \gg c^* ; \mu^*$ then

1. $\mathbf{Cells}_{\mu}(c) \cap \mathbf{Cells}_{\mu^*}(c^*) = \emptyset$
2. $|\mathbf{Cells}_{\mu}(c)| \leq |\mathbf{Cells}_{\mu^*}(c^*)|$

In general this is not the most useful copying algorithm. It has three obvious defects:

• Firstly *recursive:copy* only constructs a copy which is Lisp equal ($\equiv$) but not necessarily isomorphic ($\cong$) to the original. In fact the copy obtained by using this recursive program is the *least compact* S-expression (up to isomorphism) which is Lisp equal to the original. By least compact we mean that the copy will possess no cellular structure sharing. So, for some suitable $c\,;\mu$ we actually have that

$$|\mathbf{Cells}_{\mu^*}(c^*)| = 2^{|\mathbf{Cells}_\mu(c)|} - 1.$$

• Secondly, and perhaps most importantly, *recursive:copy* will not terminate on, let alone copy, cyclic S-expressions.

• Finally, its recursive nature means that it will use up stack proportional to the maximum depth of its argument, and so on large structures it may run out of free storage. Also since it does not recognize shared structure it will often duplicate calls to itself.

4.3. Example 2: Substitution Programs

This example was suggested to me by Dave Touretzky, who is thanked for his interest. We consider two versions of the substitution function, beginning with the standard one; see for example (McCarthy, 1962a). The approach taken in this program is that to make substitutions in a cons tree one copies the entire tree, except of course for the substructures one is replacing. The actual program is:

```
subst(x, y, z) ←
    ifs(eq(z, y),    x,
        atom(z),     z,
        T,           cons(subst(x, y, car(z)), subst(x, y, cdr(z))))
```

The fact that *subst* completely copies the tree is sometimes used by Lisp hackers when substitution is not the goal, e.g. consider the following equivalent but slower definition of *recursive:copy*

```
recursive:copy(x) ← subst(NIL, NIL, x).
```

Also notice that *eq* is used rather than *equal* in the base case; there is no real agreement amongst (and even within) the various Lisp dialects as to this point, see for example (Pitman, 1983) or (Brooks and Gabriel, 1984). The following are simple properties of *subst*; we leave the proofs as exercises.

Theorem: Suppose $[v_x, v_y, v_z]\,;\mu_0 \in \mathbf{M}_{wf}$ then

1. If $subst(v_x, v_y, v_z)\,;\mu_0 \gg v_1\,;\mu_1$ and $\sigma \in \mathbb{T}$ is such that $(v_z\,;\mu_0)_\sigma = v_y$ then $(v_1\,;\mu_1)_\sigma = v_x$.
2. If $occur(v_y, v_z)\,;\mu_0 \gg \texttt{NIL}\,;\mu_0$ then $v_z\,;\mu_0 \equiv v_1\,;\mu_1$.
3. $subst(x, y, subst(x, y, z)) \equiv subst(subst(x, y, x), y, z)$

Here the program *occur* does the obvious thing, namely it checks whether or not the first argument can be reached by a *car*-*cdr* chain, including the trivial one, through the second argument.

```
occur(x, y) ←
      if(eq(x, y), T, if(atom(y),
                         NIL,
                         or(occur(x, car(y)),
                            occur(x, cdr(y)))))
```

Formally *occur* satisfies the following:

Proposition: If $[v_x, v_y]\,;\mu \in \mathbb{M}_{wf}$ then $occur(v_x, v_y)\,;\mu$ denotes either $\texttt{NIL}\,;\mu$ or $\texttt{T}\,;\mu$ and the following are equivalent:

1. $occur(v_x, v_y)\,;\mu \gg \texttt{T}\,;\mu$
2. $\exists\sigma \in \delta_{(v_y;\mu)}$ such that $v_x = (v_y\,;\mu)_\sigma$.

The next version we call *lazy:subst*, although a better but more cumbersome name would be *no:change:no:work:subst*. This version only creates new cons cells when it is necessary, consequently the resulting S-expression shares as much structure with the original S-expression in which the substitutions are taking place. A reference to it may be found in (Brooks and Gabriel, 1984).

```
lazy:subst(x, y, z) ←
    ifs(eq(z, y),    x,
        atom(z),     z,
        T,           let{  a ← lazy:subst(x, y, car(z)),
                           d ← lazy:subst(x, y, cdr(z))}
                       if(and(eq(a, car(z)),
                              eq(d, cdr(z))),
                          z,
                          cons(a, d)))
```

The crucial facts about *lazy:subst* are summarized in the following theorem. Note that part two expresses that the result of carrying out $lazy{:}subst(x, y, z)$ shares as much structure with z as possible. These results will be proved as corollaries of slightly stronger results concerning applications of the notion of *strong isomorphism.*

Theorem: Suppose $[v_x, v_y, v_z] ; \mu_0 \in \mathbb{M}_{wf}$ and

$$lazy{:}subst(v_x, v_y, v_z) ; \mu_0 \gg v_1 ; \mu_1$$

then

1. $subst(x, y, z) \equiv lazy{:}subst(x, y, z)$.
2. If $\sigma \in \delta_{v_z;\mu_0}$ is such that

$$occur(v_y, (v_z ; \mu_0)_\sigma) ; \mu_0 \gg \mathtt{NIL} ; \mu_0$$

then

$$(v_z ; \mu_0)_\sigma = (v_1 ; \mu_1)_\sigma.$$

Furthermore if $v_y \in \mathbb{A}$ then we can relax the assumption to simply that $(v_z ; \mu_0)_\sigma ; \mu_0 \equiv (v_1 ; \mu_1)_\sigma ; \mu_1$.

Note that since both programs are defined in the $\mathbb{M}_{pure^+}$ fragment they will leave their arguments unchanged. A treatment of destructive substitution programs, which are somewhat more complicated, can be found in (de Champeaux, 1978) and (de Champeaux and de Bruin, 1981).

4.4. Example 3: A Sophisticated Length Program

In this example we deal with a length function which not only calculates the length of a list, but also detects whether the list is *cyclic* or, less appropriately but more commonly, *infinite*. A reference to it may be found in (Steele, 1984).

```
elength(list) ← elen(list, list, 0)
elen(slow, fast, n) ←
    ifs(null(fast),                              n,
        null(cdr(fast)),                         n + 1,
        and(eq(fast, slow), not(eq(n, 0))),      INFINITY,
        T,                                       elen(cdr(slow),
                                                      cdr(cdr(fast)),
                                                      n + 2))
```

The key fact about *elength* is given in the next statement.

Theorem: The following holds:

$$elength(x) \simeq \begin{cases} length(x) & \text{on } \mathbb{M}_{list} \\ \texttt{INFINITY} & \text{on } \mathbb{M}_{elist} - \mathbb{M}_{list} \end{cases}$$

and $elength(x)$ recurs at most $|\mathbf{Spine}(x)|$ times.

Proof of theorem: We leave the proof that $elength(x) \simeq length(x)$ on $\mathbb{M}_{list}$ as an exercise, and only outline the more difficult case. Suppose that

$$c_0 \; ; \mu \in \mathbb{M}_{elist} - \mathbb{M}_{list}.$$

This assumption implies that for $n \in \mathbb{N}$, $1^n \in \delta_{(c_0;\mu)}$ and $(c_0 \; ; \mu)_{1^n} \in \mathbb{C}$. Consequently, letting $c_i = (c_0 \; ; \mu)_{1^i}$ we have by the finiteness of $\delta_{(c_0;\mu)}$ that

$$\{[m_0, m_1] \in \mathbb{N}^{(2)} \mid m_1 > 0 \text{ and } c_{m_0} = c_{m_0+m_1}\}$$

is non-empty. Now choose $[m_0, m_1]$ to be the lexicographically least element of this set, and put x to be the smallest solution to the integer equation

$$0 = m_0 + x \qquad [\text{mod } m_1].$$

The list $c_0 \; ; \mu$ can then be represented by figure 10.

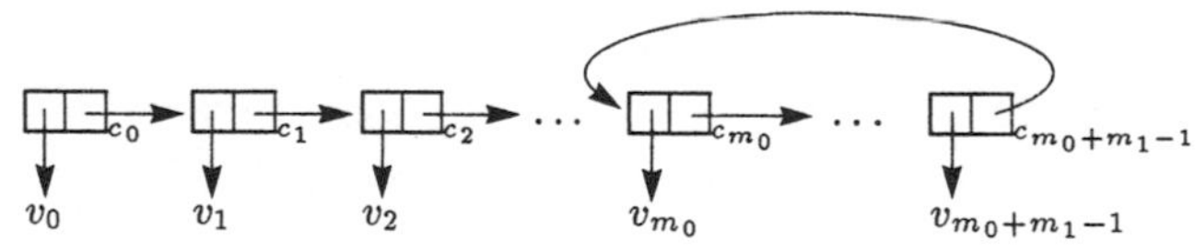

Figure 10. $c_0 \; ; \mu$

Now observe that while $c_j \neq c_{2j}$ for $0 < j < i$ we have that

$$elen(c_0, c_0, 0) ; \mu \gg elen(c_i, c_{2i}, 2i) ; \mu.$$

Letting $k = m_0 + x$ we claim

1. $c_k = c_{2k}$, and
2. $c_j \neq c_{2j}$ for $0 < j < k$.

It is easy to verify that, by our choice of notation, 1. is equivalent to

$$k = 2k \qquad [\text{mod } m_1]$$

which is true by virtue of our choice of x. Now suppose there is a j with $0 < j < k$ and $c_j = c_{2j}$; then by our choice of notation we would have

$$0 = j \qquad [\text{mod } m_1].$$

Now if $j < m_0$ then we would contradict our choice of $[m_0, m_1]$. On the other hand if $m_0 \leq j < m_0 + x$ then we would contradict our choice of x. Consequently no such j exists and we are done.

□**Theorem**

4.5. Example 4: The *iterative:append* Program

Consider the following two versions of the list append *function*, the first being the traditional pure version.

$$append(\mathtt{u}, \mathtt{v}) \leftarrow \mathtt{if}(\mathtt{u}, cons(car(\mathtt{u}), append(cdr(\mathtt{u})), \mathtt{v})), \mathtt{v})$$

The problem with this definition is that to perform the *cons* in the non-trivial case we must first compute the result of *append*-ing the *cdr* of the first argument onto the second. This is easily seen to entail that *append* will use up stack proportional to the length of its first argument. The second is an iterative version written using *rplacd*. It utilizes the destructive operations in the following way. Instead of waiting around for the result of doing the *append* of the *cdr* of the first argument before it can do the *cons*, it performs the *cons* with a, possibly, dummy *cdr* value and later on in the computation rectifies this haste. The result is a program that need not use any stack.

$$iterative{:}append(\mathtt{u},\mathtt{v}) \leftarrow$$
$$\mathtt{ifn}(\mathtt{u},\mathtt{v},\mathtt{let}\{\mathtt{w} \leftarrow cons(car(\mathtt{u}),\mathtt{v})\}\mathtt{seq}(it{:}app(cdr(\mathtt{u}),\mathtt{w},\mathtt{v}),\mathtt{w})))$$
$$it{:}app(\mathtt{u},\mathtt{w},\mathtt{v}) \leftarrow$$
$$\mathtt{ifn}(\mathtt{u},\mathtt{u},\mathtt{let}\{\mathtt{z} \leftarrow cons(car(\mathtt{u}),\mathtt{v})\}$$
$$\mathtt{seq}(rplacd(\mathtt{w},\mathtt{z}), it{:}app(cdr(\mathtt{u}),\mathtt{z},\mathtt{v})))$$

Notice that while this system of definitions is not tail recursive, it can easily be made so by adding an extra parameter `val` to *it:app*, modifying the definitions appropriately. The following result could and should be taken as verification of the correctness of the *iterative:append* program, since we are reducing its behavior to that of a very simple program.

Theorem: $iterative{:}append(\mathtt{u},\mathtt{v}) \simeq append(\mathtt{u},\mathtt{v})$

Proof: Clearly if $\mathtt{u} = \mathtt{NIL}$ then the theorem is true, so suppose that $\mathtt{u} \in \mathbb{M}_{list} - \{\mathtt{NIL}\}$. We prove the following lemma by induction on the length of u.

Lemma: $append(\mathtt{u},\mathtt{v}) \simeq \mathtt{let}\{\mathtt{w} \leftarrow cons(car(\mathtt{u}),\mathtt{v})\}\mathtt{seq}(it{:}app(cdr(\mathtt{u}),\mathtt{w},\mathtt{v}),\mathtt{w})$

Proof of Lemma:

Base Case: $car(\mathtt{u}) = x$ and $cdr(\mathtt{u}) = \mathtt{NIL}$ here we have

$$\mathtt{let}\{\mathtt{w} \leftarrow cons(car(\mathtt{u}),\mathtt{v})\}\mathtt{seq}(it{:}app(cdr(\mathtt{u}),\mathtt{w},\mathtt{v}),\mathtt{w}) \simeq$$

$$\simeq \mathtt{let}\{\mathtt{w} \leftarrow cons(x,\mathtt{v})\}\mathtt{seq}(it{:}app(\mathtt{NIL},\mathtt{w},\mathtt{v}),\mathtt{w}),$$

since $car(\mathtt{u}) \simeq x$ and $cdr(\mathtt{u}) \simeq \mathtt{NIL}$.

$$\simeq \mathtt{let}\{\mathtt{w} \leftarrow cons(x,\mathtt{v})\}\mathtt{seq}(\mathtt{NIL},\mathtt{w}),$$

by unfolding and simplifying the $it{:}app(\mathtt{NIL},\mathtt{w},\mathtt{v})$ *call.*

$$\simeq \mathtt{let}\{\mathtt{w} \leftarrow cons(x,\mathtt{v})\}\mathtt{w},$$

since $\mathtt{seq}(\mathtt{NIL},\mathtt{w}) \simeq \mathtt{w}$.

$$\simeq cons(x,\mathtt{v})$$

$$\simeq append(\mathtt{u},\mathtt{v})$$

□**Base Case**

Induction Step: Suppose $car(\mathtt{u}) = x$ and $cdr(\mathtt{u}) = \mathtt{u}_0$ with $\mathtt{u}_0 \in \mathbb{M}_{list} - \{\mathtt{NIL}\}$, then

$$\mathtt{let}\{\mathtt{w} \leftarrow cons(car(\mathtt{u}), \mathtt{v})\}\mathtt{seq}(it{:}app(cdr(\mathtt{u}), \mathtt{w}, \mathtt{v}), \mathtt{w}) \simeq$$

$$\simeq \mathtt{let}\{\mathtt{w} \leftarrow cons(x, \mathtt{v})\}\mathtt{seq}(it{:}app(\mathtt{u}_0, \mathtt{w}, \mathtt{v}), \mathtt{w}),$$

since $car(u) \simeq x$ and $cdr(u) \simeq u_0$.

Now

$$\mathtt{seq}(it{:}app(\mathtt{u}_0, \mathtt{w}, \mathtt{v}), \mathtt{w}) \simeq$$

$$\simeq \mathtt{seq}(\mathtt{let}\{\mathtt{z} \leftarrow cons(car(\mathtt{u}_0), \mathtt{v})\}\mathtt{seq}(rplacd(\mathtt{w}, \mathtt{z}), it{:}app(cdr(\mathtt{u}_0), \mathtt{z}, \mathtt{v})), \mathtt{w}),$$

by unfolding the *it:app* call.

$$\simeq \mathtt{seq}(\mathtt{let}\{\mathtt{z} \leftarrow cons(car(\mathtt{u}_0), \mathtt{v})\}\mathtt{seq}(it{:}app(cdr(\mathtt{u}_0), \mathtt{z}, \mathtt{v}), rplacd(\mathtt{w}, \mathtt{z})), \mathtt{w}),$$

since w is not visible in $it{:}app(cdr(\mathtt{u}_0), \mathtt{z}, \mathtt{v})$.

Also note that

$$\mathtt{let}\{\mathtt{z} \leftarrow cons(car(\mathtt{u}_0), \mathtt{v})\}\mathtt{seq}(it{:}app(cdr(\mathtt{u}_0), \mathtt{z}, \mathtt{v})\ rplacd(\mathtt{w}, \mathtt{z})) \simeq$$

$$\simeq \mathtt{let}\{\mathtt{z} \leftarrow \mathtt{let}\{\mathtt{w}_0 \leftarrow cons(car(\mathtt{u}_0), \mathtt{v})\}\mathtt{seq}(it{:}app(cdr(\mathtt{u}_0), \mathtt{w}_0, \mathtt{v}), \mathtt{w}_0)\}\ rplacd(\mathtt{w}, \mathtt{z}),$$

by using some simple properties of the `let` construct.

$$\simeq \mathtt{let}\{\mathtt{z} \leftarrow append(\mathtt{u}_0, \mathtt{v})\}\ rplacd(\mathtt{w}, \mathtt{z}),$$

by the induction hypothesis.

Thus we have

$$\mathtt{let}\{\mathtt{w} \leftarrow cons(car(\mathtt{u}), \mathtt{v})\}\mathtt{seq}(it{:}app(cdr(\mathtt{u}), \mathtt{w}, \mathtt{v}), \mathtt{w}) \simeq$$

$$\simeq \mathtt{let}\{\mathtt{w} \leftarrow cons(car(\mathtt{u}), \mathtt{v})\}\mathtt{seq}(\mathtt{let}\{\mathtt{z} \leftarrow append(\mathtt{u}_0, \mathtt{v})\}\ rplacd(\mathtt{w}, \mathtt{z}), \mathtt{w})$$

$$\simeq \mathtt{let}\{\mathtt{w} \leftarrow cons(car(\mathtt{u}), \mathtt{v})\}\mathtt{seq}(rplacd(\mathtt{w}, append(\mathtt{u}_0, \mathtt{v})), \mathtt{w}),$$

eliminating the inner `let` for something simpler.

$$\simeq \mathtt{let}\{\mathtt{w} \leftarrow cons(car(\mathtt{u}), \mathtt{v})\}\ rplacd(\mathtt{w}, append(\mathtt{u}_0, \mathtt{v})),$$

since $rplacd(\mathtt{w}, \ldots)$ returns w.

$$\simeq rplacd(cons(car(\mathtt{u}), \mathtt{v}), append(\mathtt{u}_0, \mathtt{v})),$$

again eliminating the `let` for something simpler.

$$\simeq cons(car(\mathtt{u}), append(\mathtt{u}_0, \mathtt{v})),$$

using simple properties of *cons* and *rplacd*.

$$\simeq append(\mathtt{u}, \mathtt{v})$$

□Lemma

The theorem now follows by observing that if $u, v; \mu \in \mathbb{M}_{sexp}$ with $u; \mu \notin \mathbb{M}_{list}$ then neither

$$append(u, v)\ ;\ \mu$$

nor

$$iterative{:}append(u, v)\ ;\ \mu$$

will denote. □Theorem

An immediate consequence of this theorem is that any equation proved to be true of *append* carries over to the *iterative:append* program. For example the following express fundamental properties of *append* and by the above are also true of *iterative:append*.

Theorem:

- $append(\mathtt{NIL}, v) \simeq append(v, \mathtt{NIL}) \simeq v$ on $\mathbb{M}_{list}$
- $append(cons(x, \mathtt{NIL}), v) \simeq cons(x, v)$
- $append(u_0, append(u_1, u_2)) \simeq append(append(u_0, u_1), u_2)$

These properties are fundamental in the sense that in pure Lisp they characterize the extensional behavior of *append*. The following is proved by a simple induction on the length of the list x.

Proposition: Suppose f satisfies the above theorem, (with $\simeq$ replaced by $\equiv$). Then

$$f(x, y) \equiv append(x, y) \text{ on } \mathbb{M}_{list}.$$

However these properties do not characterize *append* in the stronger sense that such an f must be strongly isomorphic to *append*, as the next example indicates. In fact there are an infinite number of, albeit artificial, examples of non-strongly isomorphic functions which satisfy the above theorem.

4.6. Example 5: The *nconc* Program

This example deals with the *nconc* program. We are only concerned with its behavior on $\mathbb{M}_{list}$ which is reflected in our definition.

$nconc(\mathtt{u}, \mathtt{v}) \leftarrow \mathtt{ifn}(\mathtt{u}, \mathtt{v}, \mathtt{seq}(nconc1(\mathtt{u}, \mathtt{v}), \mathtt{u}))$

$nconc1(\mathtt{u}, \mathtt{v}) \leftarrow \mathtt{if}(cdr(\mathtt{u}), nconc1(cdr(\mathtt{u}), \mathtt{v}), rplacd(\mathtt{u}, \mathtt{v})))$

This program is similar to the *append* program except that rather than copy the top level or spine of the list u it simply modifies the original u so that the last cell in its spine now points to v rather than `NIL`. Thus we cannot show that $nconc(u, v)$ and $append(u, v)$ are strongly isomorphic. What we can do is to verify that it has similar algebraic properties to those of the normal *append* program. In a later example we will give another type of verification proof whereby we show

$$nconc(copy{:}list(x), y) \simeq append(x, y)$$

for a list copying program *copy:list*. Notice that, like our iterative version of the *append* program, *nconc* as written above is not tail recursive. The addition of one extra argument, the value parameter, to the *nconc1* program is all that is needed to transform the definition into a tail recursive one.

Theorem:

- $nconc(\mathtt{NIL}, v) \simeq nconc(v, \mathtt{NIL}) \simeq v$ on $\mathbb{M}_{list}$
- $nconc(cons(x, \mathtt{NIL}), v) \simeq cons(x, v)$
- $nconc(u_0, nconc(u_1, u_2)) \simeq nconc(nconc(u_0, u_1), u_2)$ as long as the $u_i \in \mathbb{M}_{list}$ have disjoint spines.

Remarks:

- Note that if $u_0 \in \mathbb{M}_{list} - \{\mathtt{NIL}\}$ then $nconc(u_0, u_0)$ will be cyclic.
- The condition in the associativity result is thus necessary since

  $$nconc(u_0, nconc(u_0, cons(\mathtt{NIL}, \mathtt{NIL}))) \not\simeq nconc(nconc(u_0, u_0), cons(\mathtt{NIL}, \mathtt{NIL}))$$

  because the right hand side, unlike the left hand side, fails to denote.
- Actually a seemingly weaker condition is sufficient to obtain associativity of *nconc*. We only need that the last cell in the spine of u_i is distinct from the last one in the spine of $u_j, 0 \leq i < j \leq 2$, since this easily seen to imply that the spines must be disjoint. This condition can then be stated in terms of the behavior of the program *last* which is the defined as follows:

  $$last(\mathtt{list}) \leftarrow \mathtt{if}(\mathtt{list}, \mathtt{if}(cdr(\mathtt{list}), last(cdr(\mathtt{list})), \mathtt{list}), \mathtt{list}).$$

  We need only require that

  $$eq(last(u_i), last(u_j)) \simeq \mathtt{NIL} \text{ for } 0 \leq i < j \leq 2.$$

Proof of Theorem: The first two properties are simple exercises. We prove the third by induction on the length of u_0.

Base Case: $u_0 = \mathtt{NIL}$, so

$$nconc(u_0, nconc(u_1, u_2)) \simeq$$

$$\simeq nconc(\mathtt{NIL}, nconc(u_1, u_2))$$

$$\simeq nconc(u_1, u_2),$$

by the first property.

$$\simeq nconc(nconc(\mathtt{NIL}, u_1), u_2)),$$

again by the first property.

$$\simeq nconc(nconc(u_0, u_1), u_2))$$

□**Base Case**

Induction Step: Suppose that the theorem holds for all lists of length less than $u_0 \in \mathbb{M}_{list} - \{\mathtt{NIL}\}$. We consider two possibilities: 1. $cdr(u_0) \neq \mathtt{NIL}$ and 2. $cdr(u_0) = \mathtt{NIL}$. In the first case we have

$$nconc(u_0, nconc(u_1, u_2)) \simeq$$

$$\simeq \mathsf{seq}(nconc1(u_0, nconc(u_1, u_2)), u_0),$$

by unfolding and simplifying the outer *nconc* call.

$$\simeq \mathsf{seq}(nconc1(cdr(u_0), nconc(u_1, u_2)), u_0),$$

by unfolding and simplifying the *nconc1* call.

$$\simeq \mathsf{seq}(\mathsf{seq}(nconc1(cdr(u_0), nconc(u_1, u_2)), cdr(u_0)), u_0),$$

inserting a superfluous **seq** and a defined pure term.

$$\simeq \mathsf{seq}(nconc(cdr(u_0), nconc(u_1, u_2)), u_0),$$

by folding the inner **seq**.

$$\simeq \mathsf{seq}(nconc(nconc(cdr(u_0), u_1), u_2)), u_0),$$

using the induction hypothesis.

$$\simeq \mathsf{seq}(nconc(cdr(nconc(u_0, u_1)), u_2)), u_0),$$

by pulling the *cdr* outside.

$$\simeq \mathsf{seq}(cdr(nconc(nconc(u_0, u_1), u_2)), u_0),$$

again by pulling the *cdr* outside.

$$\simeq \texttt{seq}(nconc(nconc(u_0, u_1), u_2), u_0),$$

removing the useless *cdr* call.

$$\simeq nconc(nconc(u_0, u_1), u_2).$$

$\Box_1$.

While in the second case we have that

$$nconc(u_0, nconc(u_1, u_2)) \simeq rplacd(u_0, nconc(u_1, u_2)).$$

Thus this case follows from

Claim: If $u_0, u_1, u_2 \in \mathsf{M}_{list}$ have disjoint spines and $cdr(u_0) = \texttt{NIL}$ then

$$rplacd(u_0, nconc(u_1, u_2)) \simeq nconc(nconc(u_0, u_1), u_2)$$

Proof of Claim: This is a direct derivation, we consider three cases: 1. $u_1 = \texttt{NIL}$, 2. $cdr(u_1) = \texttt{NIL}$ and 3. $cdr(u_1) \neq \texttt{NIL}$ In the first situation we have

$$rplacd(u_0, nconc(u_1, u_2)) \simeq$$

$$\simeq rplacd(u_0, u_2)$$

$$\simeq nconc(u_0, u_2)$$

$$\simeq nconc(nconc(u_0, \texttt{NIL}), u_2)$$

$$\simeq nconc(nconc(u_0, u_1), u_2).$$

In the second case we have

$$rplacd(u_0, nconc(u_1, u_2)) \simeq$$

$$\simeq rplacd(u_0, rplacd(u_1, u_2))$$

$$\simeq \texttt{seq}(rplacd(u_1, u_2), rplacd(u_0, u_1))$$

$$\simeq \texttt{seq}(rplacd(u_0, u_1), rplacd(u_1, u_2), u_0),$$

since by assumption $eq(u_0, u_1) \simeq \texttt{NIL}$.

$$\simeq \texttt{let}\{w \leftarrow rplacd(u_0, u_1)\}\texttt{seq}(rplacd(u_1, u_2), w)$$

$$\simeq \texttt{let}\{w \leftarrow rplacd(u_0, u_1)\}\texttt{seq}(rplacd(cdr(w), u_2), w)$$

$$\simeq \texttt{let}\{w \leftarrow nconc(u_0, u_1)\}\texttt{seq}(rplacd(cdr(w), u_2), w)$$

$$\simeq \texttt{let}\{w \leftarrow nconc(u_0, u_1)\}\texttt{seq}(nconc1(w, u_2), w)$$

$$\simeq nconc(nconc(u_0, u_1), u_2).$$

Finally in the last case we have

$$
\begin{aligned}
&\mathit{rplacd}(u_0, \mathit{nconc}(u_1, u_2)) \simeq \\
&\quad \simeq \mathit{rplacd}(u_0, \mathsf{seq}(\mathit{nconc1}(u_1, u_2), u_1)) \\
&\quad \simeq \mathsf{seq}(\mathsf{seq}(\mathit{nconc1}(u_1, u_2), u_1), \mathit{rplacd}(u_0, u_1)), \\
&\qquad \text{since the spines of } u_0, u_1 \text{ and } u_2 \text{ are all disjoint.} \\
&\quad \simeq \mathsf{seq}(\mathit{nconc}(u_1, u_2), \mathit{rplacd}(u_0, u_1)) \\
&\quad \simeq \mathsf{seq}(\mathit{nconc}(u_1, u_2), \mathit{nconc}(u_0, u_1)) \\
&\quad \simeq \mathit{nconc}(\mathit{nconc}(u_0, u_1), u_2).
\end{aligned}
$$

$\square_{\text{Claim}}$ $\square_2$ $\square_{\text{Theorem}}$

4.7. Example 6: The List Reversing Programs Revisited

This example deals in more depth with the various reverse programs that have already been introduced. The main one we shall be concerned with is the *inplace:reverse* program that reverses a list by cdr-ing down it reversing the pointers as it goes. Firstly recall the two other examples, *reverse* and *slow:reverse*. The following result we leave as an exercise.

Lemma: $\mathit{rev}(u, v) \simeq \mathit{append}(\mathit{rev}(u, \mathtt{NIL}), v)$.

Corollary: $\mathit{slow{:}reverse}(x) \simeq \mathit{reverse}(x)$.

In this example we show that *inplace:reverse* has properties similar to those possessed by the *reverse* program. Because *inplace:reverse* modifies the nature of its arguments we cannot prove a relation like $\mathit{reverse}(x) \simeq \mathit{inplace{:}reverse}(x)$. However the fact that it satisfies analogous properties can in a sense be taken as *verification*. In particular we prove the following two theorems. The first property is self explanatory. The second is related to the well know relationship between *append* and *reverse*, namely

$$\mathit{reverse}(\mathit{append}(u, v)) \simeq \mathit{append}(\mathit{reverse}(v), \mathit{reverse}(u)).$$

Another method of verification that we shall mention later is to show

$$\mathit{inplace{:}reverse}(\mathit{copy{:}list}(x)) \simeq \mathit{reverse}(x).$$

Theorem A: $\mathit{inplace{:}reverse}(\mathit{inplace{:}reverse}(u)) \simeq u$ on $\mathbb{M}_{list}$.

Theorem B: If $u, v \in \mathbb{M}_{list}$ have disjoint spines then

$$inplace{:}reverse(nconc(u,v)) \simeq nconc(inplace{:}reverse(v), inplace{:}reverse(u)).$$

We prove these results using the following lemma, the *nconc*-ified version of the *rev* lemma above.

Main Lemma: If $u, v \in \mathbb{M}_{list}$ have disjoint spines then

$$in{:}rev(u,v) \simeq nconc(in{:}rev(u, \mathtt{NIL}), v).$$

Note that this lemma allows us to write a faster program for the specialized task of *nconc*-ing the destructive reversal of a list onto another list. Namely computing

$$nconc(inplace{:}reverse(x), y),$$

in Maclisp, (Pitman, 1983), (Touretzky, 1983), produces a function called *nreconc*. The faster version is given by

$$nreconc(\mathbf{x}, \mathbf{y}) \leftarrow in{:}rev(\mathbf{x}, \mathbf{y}),$$

and is a simple example of how verification of one program can lead to the writing of more efficient related programs.

Proof of Main Lemma: This is by induction on the length of $u \in \mathbb{M}_{list}$. As usual we leave the trivial base case to the reader. So, suppose that the lemma is true for u_d, the *cdr* of u.

$$in{:}rev(u,v) \simeq$$

$$\simeq in{:}rev(u_d, rplacd(u,v))$$

$$\simeq nconc(in{:}rev(u_d, \mathtt{NIL}), rplacd(u,v)),$$

by the induction hypothesis.

$$\simeq nconc(in{:}rev(u_d, \mathtt{NIL}), nconc(rplacd(u, \mathtt{NIL}), v))$$

$$\simeq nconc(nconc(in{:}rev(u_d, \mathtt{NIL}), rplacd(u, \mathtt{NIL})), v),$$

since *nconc* is associative under the conditions of the lemma.

$$\simeq nconc(in{:}rev(u_d, rplacd(u, \mathtt{NIL})), v),$$

again by the induction hypothesis.

$$\simeq nconc(in{:}rev(u, \mathtt{NIL}), v)$$

□**Main Lemma**

We shall prove Theorem B, which is then shown to imply Theorem A, by using the main lemma and the following consequence of it.

Corollary: If $u, v \in \mathbb{M}_{list}$ have disjoint spines then

$$in{:}rev(v, in{:}rev(u, \mathtt{NIL})) \simeq in{:}rev(nconc(u, v), \mathtt{NIL}).$$

Proof of Corollary: This is by induction on the length of v, Rather than do the base case we shall assume that the reader can verify the result for themselves in the cases when v is either NIL or a list of length one. We do the induction step: Assume that v is a list of length > 1, $cdr(v) = v_d$, $v_d \neq \mathtt{NIL}$ and that u and v satisfy the hypothesis.

$$in{:}rev(v, in{:}rev(u, \mathtt{NIL})) \simeq$$

$$\simeq in{:}rev(v_d, rplacd(v, in{:}rev(u, \mathtt{NIL})))$$

$$\simeq in{:}rev(v_d, nconc(rplacd(v, \mathtt{NIL}), in{:}rev(u, \mathtt{NIL}))),$$

by a simple property of *nconc* and *rplacd*.

$$\simeq in{:}rev(v_d, nconc(in{:}rev(rplacd(v, \mathtt{NIL}), \mathtt{NIL}), in{:}rev(u, \mathtt{NIL}))),$$

since it is easily seen that $rplacd(v, \mathtt{NIL}) \simeq in{:}rev(rplacd(v, \mathtt{NIL}), \mathtt{NIL})$.

$$\simeq in{:}rev(v_d, in{:}rev(rplacd(v, \mathtt{NIL}), in{:}rev(u, \mathtt{NIL}))),$$

by the main lemma.

$$\simeq in{:}rev(v_d, in{:}rev(nconc(u, rplacd(v, \mathtt{NIL})))),$$

by the induction hypothesis.

$$\simeq in{:}rev(nconc(nconc(u, rplacd(v, \mathtt{NIL})), v_d)),$$

again by the induction hypothesis.

$$\simeq in{:}rev(nconc(u, nconc(rplacd(v, \mathtt{NIL}), v_d), \mathtt{NIL}),$$

since the associativity of *nconc* is applicable in this case.

$$\simeq in{:}rev(nconc(u, v), \mathtt{NIL}),$$

by a simple cancellation property.

□**Corollary**

Proof of Theorem B: This is a direct derivation.

$$nconc(inplace{:}reverse(v), inplace{:}reverse(u)) \simeq$$

$$\simeq nconc(in{:}rev(v, \mathtt{NIL}), in{:}rev(u, \mathtt{NIL}))$$

$$\simeq in{:}rev(v, in{:}rev(u, \mathtt{NIL})),$$

by the main lemma.

$$\simeq in{:}rev(nconc(u, v), \mathtt{NIL}),$$

by the corollary.

$$\simeq inplace{:}reverse(nconc(u, v))$$

$\square_{\textbf{Theorem B}}$

Proof of Theorem A: We prove this by induction on the length of u. The base case is trivial so suppose that it holds for lists of less length than u. Clearly we may assume that

$$u = nconc(u_0, u_1)$$

for two lists u_0, u_1 of less length than u. We prove

$$inplace{:}reverse(inplace{:}reverse(nconc(u_0, u_1))) \simeq nconc(u_0, u_1)$$

$$inplace{:}reverse(inplace{:}reverse(nconc(u_0, u_1))) \simeq$$

$$\simeq inplace{:}reverse(nconc(inplace{:}reverse(u_1), inplace{:}reverse(u_0))),$$

by theorem B.

$$\simeq nconc(inplace{:}reverse(inplace{:}reverse(u_0)),$$
$$inplace{:}reverse(inplace{:}reverse(u_1))),$$

again by theorem B.

$$\simeq nconc(u_0, u_1),$$

by the induction hypothesis.

$\square_{\textbf{Theorem A}}$.

4.8. Example 7: List Copying Programs

Often copying all of an object is not required; for example when the object is a pure list it is sufficient for many purposes to merely copy the spine of the list. In Common Lisp this function is called *Copy-List*, see (Steele, 1984) for example; its task is to copy only in the *cdr* direction. A simple version of this function is given as follows:

$$rec{:}copy{:}list(\mathtt{x}) \leftarrow \mathtt{if}(atom(\mathtt{x}), \mathtt{x}, cons(car(\mathtt{x}), rec{:}copy{:}list(cdr(\mathtt{x})))).$$

However a more efficient version can be written in a style similar to the *iterative:append* program. This version is tail recursive and is given by the following definition.

$$\begin{array}{l} copy{:}list(\mathtt{x}) \leftarrow \\ \quad \mathtt{if}(atom(\mathtt{x}), \mathtt{x}, \mathtt{let}\{\mathtt{w} \leftarrow cons(car(\mathtt{x}), cdr(\mathtt{x}))\} \\ \qquad\qquad it{:}copy{:}list(cdr(\mathtt{x}), \mathtt{w}, \mathtt{w})) \\ it{:}copy{:}list(\mathtt{x}, \mathtt{y}, \mathtt{val}) \leftarrow \\ \quad \mathtt{if}(atom(\mathtt{x}), \mathtt{val}, \mathtt{let}\{\mathtt{w} \leftarrow cons(car(\mathtt{x}), cdr(\mathtt{x}))\} \\ \qquad\qquad \mathtt{seq}(rplacd(\mathtt{y}, \mathtt{w}) \\ \qquad\qquad\quad it{:}copy{:}list(cdr(\mathtt{x}), \mathtt{w}, \mathtt{val}))) \end{array}$$

Notice that regardless of whether or not x is a pure list, both

$$copy{:}list(x) \text{ and } rec{:}copy{:}list(x)$$

will be pure lists. Duplicating the methods of the *iterative:append* example allow us to prove the following theorem. Again, as in the *iterative:append* example, it should be taken as verifying the more complex *copy:list* program.

Theorem: $rec{:}copy{:}list(x) \simeq copy{:}list(x)$.

A simple induction on the length of the pure list demonstrates the first part of the following proposition, the second part is then an immediate consequence of it and the above theorem.

Proposition:

1. $rec{:}copy{:}list(x) \cong x$ via a map f which is the identity on **Elements**(x), for any pure list x.
2. $copy{:}list(x) \cong x$ via a map f which is the identity on **Elements**(x), for any pure list x.

Proof of 1: As we have already mentioned the proof is by induction on the length of the list $v\ ;\mu$. The base case, when $v = \texttt{NIL}$, is trivial so we do the induction step. Suppose $v\ ;\mu \in \mathbb{M}_{list}$ is a pure list of length $n+1$ and that $rec{:}copy{:}list(u)\ ;\mu_0 \cong u\ ;\mu_0$ via a map f which is the identity on $\mathbf{Elements}_{\mu_0}(u)$ for pure lists, $u\ ;\mu_0$, of shorter length. Then letting $v_a\ ;\mu = car(v)\ ;\mu$ and $v_d\ ;\mu = cdr(v)\ ;\mu$ we have that

$$rec{:}copy{:}list(v)\ ;\mu \gg cons(v_a, rec{:}copy{:}list(v_d))\ ;\mu.$$

Now by induction we have that $rec{:}copy{:}list(v_d)\ ;\mu \cong v_d\ ;\mu$ via a map f which is the identity on $\mathbf{Elements}_\mu(v_d)$. Assume that $rec{:}copy{:}list(v_d)\ ;\mu \gg v_d^*\ ;\mu^*$ then

$$rec{:}copy{:}list(v)\ ;\mu \gg cons(v_a, v_d^*)\ ;\mu^* \gg v^*\ ;\mu^{**}.$$

Defining f^* as follows gives the result

$$f^*(x) = \begin{cases} x & \text{if } x \in \mathbb{A} \cup \mathbf{Elements}_\mu(v), \\ v^* & \text{if } x = v, \\ f(x) & \text{if } x \in \mathbf{Spine}_\mu(v_d), \\ g(x) & \text{otherwise.} \end{cases}$$

Here g is any bijection from $\mathbb{C} - \mathbf{Cells}_\mu(v) \to \mathbb{C} - \mathbf{Cells}_{\mu^{**}}(v^*)\ \Box_1$.

The following example and exercises use *copy:list* to exhibit obvious relationships between programs we have already studied. In the next section we shall discuss queues and use similar methods to prove properties of *efficient queue operations.*

Theorem: $inplace{:}reverse(copy{:}list(x)) \simeq reverse(x)$

Proof of Theorem: The theorem follows directly from the following lemma, which we prove by induction on the length of the list x.

Lemma: $in{:}rev(rec{:}copy{:}list(x), y) \simeq rev(x, y)$

Proof of Lemma: We leave the base case, when $x = \texttt{NIL}$, to the reader. The induction step proceeds thus. Suppose that x is a non-empty list and that the lemma is true for all lists of shorter length. Then

$in{:}rev(rec{:}copy{:}list(x), y) \simeq$

pulling the *rec:copy:list* call out gives

$\simeq \texttt{let}\{u \leftarrow rec{:}copy{:}list(x)\} in{:}rev(u, y).$

Unfolding and simplifying the *rec:copy:list* call leaves

$$\simeq \texttt{let}\{u \leftarrow cons(car(x), rec{:}copy{:}list(cdr(x)))\} in{:}rev(u, y).$$

Unfolding and simplifying the *in:rev* call leaves

$$\simeq \texttt{let}\{u \leftarrow cons(car(x), rec{:}copy{:}list(cdr(x)))\}$$
$$in{:}rev(cdr(u), rplacd(u, y)).$$

Pulling the call to *rec:copy:list* out leaves

$$\simeq \texttt{let}\{w \leftarrow rec{:}copy{:}list(cdr(x))\}$$
$$\texttt{let}\{u \leftarrow cons(car(x), w)\} in{:}rev(cdr(u), rplacd(u, y)).$$

And since $cdr(u) = w$,

$$\simeq \texttt{let}\{w \leftarrow rec{:}copy{:}list(cdr(x))\}$$
$$\texttt{let}\{u \leftarrow cons(car(x), w)\} in{:}rev(w, rplacd(u, y)).$$

Using a simple property of *rplacd*,

$$\simeq \texttt{let}\{w \leftarrow rec{:}copy{:}list(cdr(x))\}$$
$$\texttt{let}\{u \leftarrow cons(car(x), w)\} in{:}rev(w, \texttt{seq}(rplacd(u, y), u)).$$

Pulling the `seq` out from the *in:rev* call,

$$\simeq \texttt{let}\{w \leftarrow rec{:}copy{:}list(cdr(x))\}$$
$$\texttt{let}\{u \leftarrow cons(car(x), w)\} \texttt{seq}(rplacd(u, y), in{:}rev(w, u)).$$

By another simple fact we have

$$\simeq \texttt{let}\{w \leftarrow rec{:}copy{:}list(cdr(x))\}$$
$$\texttt{let}\{u \leftarrow rplacd(cons(car(x), w), y)\} in{:}rev(w, u).$$

Cancelling the *rplacd* call,

$$\simeq \texttt{let}\{w \leftarrow rec{:}copy{:}list(cdr(x))\} \texttt{let}\{u \leftarrow cons(car(x), y)\} in{:}rev(w, u).$$

Commuting the `let` s produces

$$\simeq \texttt{let}\{u \leftarrow cons(car(x), y)\} \texttt{let}\{w \leftarrow rec{:}copy{:}list(cdr(x))\} in{:}rev(w, u).$$

`let` elimination gives

$$\simeq \texttt{let}\{u \leftarrow cons(car(x), y)\} in{:}rev(rec{:}copy{:}list(cdr(x)), u).$$

A single use of our induction hypothesis yields

$$\simeq \texttt{let}\{u \leftarrow cons(car(x), y)\} rev(cdr(x), u).$$

`let` elimination once more,

$$\simeq rev(cdr(x), cons(car(x), y)).$$

Folding finalizes things,

$\simeq rev(x, y)$.$\Box_{\mathbf{Lemma}}\Box_{\mathbf{Theorem}}$

Exercises:

0. Using the previous result deduce that $inplace{:}reverse(x) \cong reverse(x)$ when x is a pure list.
1. $copy{:}list(x) \simeq append(x, \mathtt{NIL})$ on $\mathbb{M}_{list}$
2. Show that $nconc(copy{:}list(x), y) \simeq append(x, y)$ and then deduce that when x and y are pure lists with disjoint spines $nconc(x, y) \cong append(x, y)$.
3. $\mathsf{seq}(rplacd(last(x), y), x) \simeq nconc(x, y)$ for $x \in \mathbb{M}_{list}, x \neq \mathtt{NIL}$.
4. $last(nconc(x, y)) \simeq \mathsf{seq}(nconc(x, y), last(y))$ for $x \neq \mathtt{NIL} \neq y$.
5. $last(append(x, y)) \simeq last(y)$ for $x \neq \mathtt{NIL} \neq y$.
6. $nreconc(copy{:}list(x), y) \simeq append(reverse(x), y)$

4.9. Example 8: Queue Representation and Manipulation

In this example we describe and prove properties of queues and queue operations in $\mathbb{M}_{sexp}$. This example was motivated by the following passage in (Cartwright, Hood and Matthews, 1981).

> *It is noteworthy that all practical dialects of LISP (such as LISP 1.6 and MACLISP) include a multitude of impure operations (e.g rplaca, rplacd) which directly modify the pointer and record structures representing S-expressions. The semantics of these operations cannot be described at the abstract level of S-expressions; they have meaning only at the level of the underlying implementation.*
>
> *Despite the logical complexity of impure operations, they are indispensable in many practical applications because they enable the programmer to write much more efficient programs. As an illustration, consider the problem of maintaining a queue in Pure LISP. The standard solution is to store the queue as a linear list, inserting new elements at the end and removing elements from the front. The operations of inspecting and removing the first element require only constant time. Inserting an element at the end of the list, however, requires time proportional to the length of the list. By using sophisticated data structures and algorithms, it is*

possible to reduce the asymptotic time bound, but the resulting programs are much more complicated. [1]

On the other hand, if we allow impure (destructive) operations, we can improve the efficiency of the simple linear list solution so that all operations take only constant time. The modification is obvious: maintain a pointer to the last record of the list representation and use the pointer to destructively update the list (using rplacd) when inserting a new element. It is not only more efficient than the Pure LISP solutions, but it seems logically simpler as well. Nevertheless, it is difficult to prove that the impure solution actually implements a queue. The Pure Lisp solutions have simpler proofs because they are expressed at a much higher level of abstraction.

The idea in this example will be to represent a queue as a cons cell, the *car* of which is a pure list that stores the contents of the queue. The *cdr* will then point to the last cell in the spine of this pure list. Thus our representation is only a minor modification of the one suggested above, in that we store the head and tail pointers together in a single cell. Diagramatically a queue, in our scheme of things, is pictured in figure 11.

The cell c_{queue} will be called the *queue cell*, the cells $c_0, c_1, \ldots, c_n$ are called the *spine* of the queue and the objects $v_0, v_1, \ldots, v_n$ are the *elements* of the queue and are assumed to be disjoint from the spine and the queue cell. An empty queue is anything isomorphic to the value of *cons*(NIL, NIL). We shall denote the collection of all queues by $\mathbb{M}_{queue}$, and we shall define six different operations on queues. They are *front*, *pop*, *push:front*, *push:rear*, *copy:queue* and *rotate*. Explicitly:

1. **Front** returns the first element of the pure list stored in the *car* of a *non-empty* queue. In other words it returns the *first element* of a non-empty queue. It is not defined for empty queues and so the user should always test to see whether or not a queue is empty. The actual definition is

   $$front(\mathsf{queue}) \leftarrow car(car(\mathsf{queue}))$$

[1] If we split the queue into two separates lists so that both the head and tail are accessible in constant time, we can reduce the cost of n queue operations from $O(n^2)$ to $O(n)$. A single operation, however, can still require $O(n)$ steps. In particular, removing an element from the queue when the head list is empty involves replacing the head list by the reverse of the tail list- a linear time operation. At the cost of adding more lists to the representation and further complicating the definition of the queue operations, we can reduce the cost of every operation to constant time, producing a real time implementation (Hood and Matthews, 1980). The trick is to distribute the work done in reversing the tail list over a number of operations.

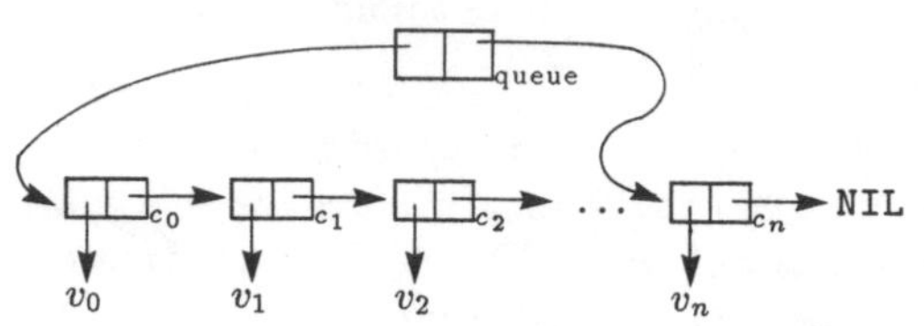

Figure 11. A Typical Queue

2. **Pop** removes the front element from an non-empty queue and returns the modified queue, it is does nothing if the queue is already empty. We give two different versions of this operation. The first is *pure:pop* which is a $\mathbb{M}_{pure+}$ function while the second *pop* is a destructive version. We have made no attempt to make the pure versions as efficient as possible. Their purpose is merely instructive and as the reader may have guessed are used to prove properties of their destructive counterparts. The actual definitions are:

   pure:pop(queue) ←

   if(*eq*(*car*(queue), *cdr*(queue)),

   cons(NIL, NIL),

   cons(*cdr*(*car*(queue)), *cdr*(queue))))

   pop(queue) ←

   if(*eq*(*car*(queue), *cdr*(queue)),

   rplaca(*rplacd*(queue, NIL), NIL),

   rplaca(queue, *cdr*(*car*(queue))))

3. **Push:Front** expects two arguments; the first is supposed to be a new element for the second argument which is a queue. Push:Front then returns a new queue obtained from the second argument by adding the first argument to the front of the list. Notice that for the value of this operation to be a queue as we have defined them we must place certain constraints on the first argument. Namely it must be disjoint from the queue cell as well as the spine of the list. Again we shall give two versions of this operation, a simple minded pure

version *pure:push:front* and a destructive version *push:front*, the definitions being:

```
pure:push:front(v, queue) ←
    let{new:list ← cons(v, car(queue))}
        cons(new:list, last(new:list))
push:front(v, queue) ←
    if(cdr(queue),
       rplaca(queue, cons(v car(queue))),
       seq(rplaca(queue, cons(v, car(queue))),
           rplacd(queue, car(queue))))
```

4. **Push:Rear** expects the same type of arguments as Push:Front. It however returns the queue obtained by placing the first argument at the rear of the second argument's list.

```
pure:push:rear(v, queue) ←
    let{new:list ← append(car(queue), cons(v, NIL))}
        cons(new:list, last(new:list))))
push:rear(v, queue) ←
    if(cdr(queue),
       seq(rplacd(cdr(queue), cons(v, NIL)),
           rplacd(queue, cdr(cdr(queue)))),
       seq(rplaca(queue, cons(v, NIL)),
           rplacd(queue, car(queue))))
```

5. **Queue:Copy** copies the queue cell as well as the spine of the list. The result is a queue that is isomorphic to the original. Note that the elements of the queue are exactly the same (i.e. *eq*) to the original elements. We give two versions; the first is a straightforward recursive version while the second is an iterative version much in the spirit of *iterative:append* and *copy:list*.

```
pure:copy:queue(queue) ←
    let{new:list ← list:copy(car(queue))}
        cons(new:list, last(new:list))
```

```
copy:queue(queue) ←
    if(car(queue),
      let{w ← cons(car(car(queue)), NIL)}
          it:copy:queue(cdr(car(queue)), w, w)),
      cons(NIL, NIL))
it:copy:queue(rest, current, new:queue) ←
    if(rest,
      it:copy:queue(cdr(rest),
                    cdr(rplacd(current, cons(car(rest), NIL))),
                    new:queue),
      cons(new:queue, current)))
```

6. **Rotate** expects a queue and returns a new queue obtained by placing the first element of the queue at the rear. It does nothing if the queue is either empty or contains only one element. Unlike the similar operation described by

   `if(eq(car(queue), cdr(queue)), queue, push:rear(front(queue), pop(queue))),`

   the impure version of Rotate does not create any new cells. Thus a sequence of n rotations on a queue of length n returns exactly the same queue in exactly the same memory. The actual definitions are:

```
pure:rotate(queue) ←
    if(eq(car(queue), cdr(queue)),
      queue,
      let{new:list ← append(cdr(car(queue)),
                            cons(car(car(queue)), NIL))}
         cons(new:list, last(new:list)))
rotate(queue) ←
    if(eq(car(queue), cdr(queue)),
      queue,
      seq(rplacd(cdr(queue), car(queue)),
          rplacd(queue, car(queue)),
          rplaca(queue, cdr(car(queue))),
          rplacd(cdr(queue), NIL),
          queue))
```

The first thing to notice is that all the destructive queue operations take constant time, except of course *copy:queue*. Since we shall demonstrate the correctness of these destructive operations in terms of the program *copy:queue* our first result concerns this cornerstone.

Theorem A: $copy{:}queue(x) \simeq pure{:}copy{:}queue(x)$ on $\mathbb{M}_{queue}$

Just as in the case of *copy:list* this theorem is proven by almost exactly the same methods that were used to to prove that *append* and *iterative:append* are strongly isomorphic. As a consequence we leave the proof as an exercise. The next result demonstrates the connection between the pure and the impure versions of the remaining queue operations.

Theorem B: If $x \in \mathbb{M}_{queue}$ and $y \in \mathbb{M}_{sexp}$ then

1. $pure{:}pop(x) \simeq pop(copy{:}queue(x))$
2. $pure{:}push{:}front(y, x) \simeq push{:}front(y, copy{:}queue(x))$
3. $pure{:}push{:}rear(y, x) \simeq push{:}rear(y, copy{:}queue(x))$
4. $pure{:}rotate(x) \simeq rotate(copy{:}queue(x))$

Proof of Theorem B: We shall only prove 1. and 3. leaving the other two simple variations as exercises. Furthermore, in the light of the previous result, it suffices to prove the results for *pure:queue:copy* rather than the more complex iterative version.

Proof of 1. This is a direct derivation:

$pop(copy{:}queue(x)), \simeq$

which by Theorem A is

$\simeq pop(pure{:}copy{:}queue(x))$

$\simeq pop(\texttt{let}\{\texttt{new:list} \leftarrow list{:}copy(car(x))\}$
$\quad cons(\texttt{new:list}, last(\texttt{new:list}))),$

by unfolding the *pure:copy:queue* call.

$\simeq \texttt{let}\{\texttt{new:list} \leftarrow list{:}copy(car(x))\}$
$\quad \texttt{let}\{\texttt{z} \leftarrow cons(\texttt{new:list}, last(\texttt{new:list}))\}$
$\quad\quad pop(\texttt{z}),$

by pushing the *pop* call in.

$$
\begin{aligned}
\simeq\ & \texttt{let}\{\texttt{new:list} \leftarrow \mathit{list{:}copy}(\mathit{car}(x))\}\\
&\quad \texttt{let}\{\texttt{z} \leftarrow \mathit{cons}(\texttt{new:list}, \mathit{last}(\texttt{new:list}))\}\\
&\qquad \texttt{if}(\mathit{eq}(\mathit{car}(\texttt{z}), \mathit{cdr}(\texttt{z})),\\
&\qquad\quad \mathit{rplaca}(\mathit{rplacd}(\texttt{z}, \texttt{NIL}), \texttt{NIL}),\\
&\qquad\quad \mathit{rplaca}(\texttt{z}, \mathit{cdr}(\mathit{car}(\texttt{z})))),
\end{aligned}
$$

by unfolding the *pop* call.

$$
\begin{aligned}
\simeq\ & \texttt{let}\{\texttt{new:list} \leftarrow \mathit{list{:}copy}(\mathit{car}(x))\}\\
&\quad \texttt{if}(\mathit{eq}(\texttt{new:list}, \mathit{last}(\texttt{new:list})),\\
&\qquad \texttt{let}\{\texttt{z} \leftarrow \mathit{cons}(\texttt{new:list}, \mathit{last}(\texttt{new:list}))\}\\
&\qquad\quad \mathit{rplaca}(\mathit{rplacd}(\texttt{z}, \texttt{NIL}), \texttt{NIL}),\\
&\qquad \texttt{let}\{\texttt{z} \leftarrow \mathit{cons}(\texttt{new:list}, \mathit{last}(\texttt{new:list}))\}\\
&\qquad\quad \mathit{rplaca}(\texttt{z}, \mathit{cdr}(\mathit{car}(\texttt{z})))),
\end{aligned}
$$

by pushing the `let` in and simplifying.

$$
\begin{aligned}
\simeq\ & \texttt{let}\{\texttt{new:list} \leftarrow \mathit{list{:}copy}(\mathit{car}(x))\}\\
&\quad \texttt{if}(\mathit{eq}(\texttt{new:list}, \mathit{last}(\texttt{new:list})),\\
&\qquad \mathit{cons}(\texttt{NIL}, \texttt{NIL}),\\
&\qquad \mathit{cons}(\mathit{cdr}(\mathit{car}(\texttt{new:list})), \mathit{last}(\texttt{new:list}))),
\end{aligned}
$$

again by pushing the `let` in and simplifying.

$$\simeq \mathit{pure{:}pop}(x),$$

by folding.

$\ulcorner_1$.

Proof of 3: The easiest way to prove this is by considering two cases depending on whether or not x is an empty queue ($\mathit{car}(x) = \mathit{cdr}(x) = \texttt{NIL}$). We shall only do the non-empty case, leaving the empty case as an exercise. So assume that $\mathit{car}(x) \neq \texttt{NIL} \neq \mathit{cdr}(x)$ then:

$$\mathit{push{:}rear}(y, \mathit{copy{:}queue}(x)) \simeq$$

which is again by theorem A.

$$\simeq \mathit{push{:}rear}(y, \mathit{pure{:}copy{:}queue}(x))$$

$$
\begin{aligned}
\simeq\ & \mathit{push{:}rear}(y, \texttt{let}\{\texttt{new:list} \leftarrow \mathit{list{:}copy}(\mathit{car}(x))\}\\
&\qquad\qquad \mathit{cons}(\texttt{new:list}, \mathit{last}(\texttt{new:list}))),
\end{aligned}
$$

by unfolding the *pure:copy:queue* call.

```
≃ let{new:list ← list:copy(car(x))}
      let{z ← cons(new:list, last(new:list))}
          push:rear(y, z),
```

by pushing the *push:rear* call in.

```
≃ let{new:list ← list:copy(car(x))}
      let{z ← cons(new:list, last(new:list))}
          if(cdr(z),
             seq(rplacd(cdr(z), cons(y, NIL)),
                 rplacd(z, cdr(cdr(z)))),
             seq(rplaca(z, cons(y, NIL)),
                 rplacd(z, car(z)))),
```

by unfolding the *push:rear* call.

```
≃ let{new:list ← list:copy(car(x))}
      let{z ← cons(new:list, last(new:list))}
          seq(rplacd(last(new:list), cons(y, NIL)),
              new:list
              rplacd(z, cdr(cdr(z)))),
```

by our assumptions on *x* as well as

adding a redundant term to the seq.

```
≃ let{new:list ← list:copy(car(x))}
      let{z ← cons(new:list, last(new:list))}
          seq(nconc(new:list, cons(y, NIL)),
              rplacd(z, cdr(cdr(z)))),
```

by utilizing a previous exercise.

```
≃ let{new:list ← list:copy(car(x))}
      let{z ← cons(new:list, last(new:list))}
          seq(nconc(new:list, cons(y, NIL)),
              rplacd(z, last(new:list))),
```

since *last*(new:list)) = *cdr*(*cdr*(z)).

```
≃ let{new:list ← list:copy(car(x))}
      seq(nconc(new:list, cons(y, NIL)),
          cons(new:list, last(new:list))),
```

by eliminating the `let` and simplifying.

$\simeq$ `let{new:list` $\leftarrow$ *nconc*(*list:copy*(*car*(x)), *cons*(y, `NIL`))}
cons(`new:list`, *last*(`new:list`))),

pushing the *nconc* into the `let`.

$\simeq$ `let{new:list` $\leftarrow$ *append*(*car*(x), *cons*(y, `NIL`))}
cons(`new:list`, *last*(`new:list`))),

again by a previous exercise.

$\simeq$ *pure:push*(y, x),

by folding.

$\square_3$. $\square_{\textbf{Theorem B}}$.

4.10. Example 9: The Substitution Programs Revisited

In this section we shall, using the notion of strongly isomorphic expressions, prove certain facts left unproven previously. In particular we want to prove that *subst* and *lazy:subst* produce answers that are related in the following fashion:

Theorem: For $[v_x, v_y, v_z] ; \mu \in \mathbb{M}_{sexp}$ we have that

$$subst(v_x, v_y, v_z) ; \mu \equiv lazy{:}subst(v_x, v_y, v_z) ; \mu.$$

We do this by showing

Theorem A: $equal(subst(x, y, z), lazy{:}subst(x, y, z)) \simeq \mathtt{T}$ on ${\mathbb{M}_{wf}}^{(3)}$.

The result then follows from the previously mentioned fact that $equal(x, y) \simeq \mathtt{T}$ implies $x \equiv y$. The following are left to the reader as they are simple exercises. The last three allow a short proof of the following, previously left unproven.

Theorem: Suppose $[v_x, v_y, v_z] ; \mu_0 \in \mathbb{M}_{wf}$ and

$$lazy{:}subst(v_x, v_y, v_z) ; \mu_0 \gg v_1 ; \mu_1.$$

Then if $\sigma \in \delta_{v_z;\mu_0}$ is such that

$$occur(v_y, (v_z ; \mu_0)_\sigma) ; \mu_0 \gg \mathtt{NIL} ; \mu_0$$

then

$$(v_z ; \mu_0)_\sigma = (v_1 ; \mu_1)_\sigma.$$

Furthermore if $v_y \in \mathbb{A}$ then we can relax the assumption to

$$(v_z \,;\, \mu_0)_\sigma \,;\, \mu_0 \equiv (v_1 \,;\, \mu_1)_\sigma \,;\, \mu_1.$$

Exercises:

0. $subst(\texttt{NIL}, \texttt{NIL}, x) \simeq recursive{:}copy(x)$.
1. $lazy{:}subst(y, y, x) \simeq x$.
2. $\texttt{if}(occur(y, z), z, lazy{:}subst(x, y, z)) \simeq z$.
3. $car(lazy{:}subst(x, y, z)) \simeq \texttt{if}(eq(y, z), car(x), lazy{:}subst(x, y, car(z)))$
4. $cdr(lazy{:}subst(x, y, z)) \simeq \texttt{if}(eq(y, z), cdr(x), lazy{:}subst(x, y, cdr(z)))$

Proof of Theorem A: This is by induction on the size of z. The base case we leave to the reader as usual. We outline the induction step.

$$equal(subst(x, y, z), lazy{:}subst(x, y, z)) \simeq$$

$$\simeq \texttt{let}\{x_1 \leftarrow subst(\ldots), x_2 \leftarrow lazy{:}subst(\ldots)\}equal(x_1, x_2)$$

$$\simeq \texttt{let}\{x_1 \leftarrow \texttt{ifs}(\ldots), x_2 \leftarrow \texttt{ifs}(\ldots)\}equal(x_1, x_2)$$

by unfolding both the *subst* and the *lazy:subst* calls

$$\begin{aligned}\simeq \texttt{ifs}(&eq(z, y),\ equal(x, x),\\ &atom(z), equal(z, z),\\ &\texttt{T},\quad equal(cons(subst(x, y, car(z)), subst(x, y, cdr(z)),\\ &\qquad\qquad \texttt{let}\{a \leftarrow lazy{:}subst(x, y, car(z)),\\ &\qquad\qquad\quad d \leftarrow lazy{:}subst(x, y, cdr(z))\}\\ &\qquad\qquad \texttt{if}(\ldots))),\end{aligned}$$

By a sequence of simple transformations.

This in turn by elementary properties reduces to showing that when $atom(z) \simeq \texttt{NIL}$ we have

$$\begin{aligned}\texttt{T} \simeq equal(&cons(subst(x, y, car(z)), subst(x, y, cdr(z)),\\ &\texttt{let}\{\ a \leftarrow lazy{:}subst(x, y, car(z)),\\ &\qquad d \leftarrow lazy{:}subst(x, y, cdr(z))\}\\ &\quad \texttt{if}(\texttt{and}(eq(a, car(z)),\\ &\qquad\qquad eq(d, cdr(z))),\\ &\qquad z,\\ &\qquad cons(a, d))))))\end{aligned}$$

This is what we now show.

```
equal(cons(subst(x, y, car(z)), subst(x, y, cdr(z)),
      let{  a ← lazy:subst(x, y, car(z)),
            d ← lazy:subst(x, y, cdr(z))}
         if(and(eq(a, car(z)),
                eq(d, cdr(z))),
            z,
            cons(a, d))))))
```

which by pulling the let out becomes

```
≃ let{a ← lazy:subst(x, y, car(z)), d ← lazy:subst(x, y, cdr(z))}
     equal(cons(subst(x, y, car(z)), subst(x, y, cdr(z)),
           if(and(eq(a, car(z)),
                  eq(d, cdr(z))),
              z,
              cons(a, d))))))
```

now by unfolding and simplifying the *equal* call we obtain

```
≃ let{a ← lazy:subst(x, y, car(z)), d ← lazy:subst(x, y, cdr(z))}
     and(equal(car(cons(subst(x, y, car(z)), subst(x, y, cdr(z))),
               car(if(and(eq(a, car(z)),
                          eq(d, cdr(z))),
                      z,
                      cons(a, d))))),
         equal(cdr(cons(subst(x, y, car(z)), subst(x, y, cdr(z))),
               cdr(if(and(eq(a, car(z)),
                          eq(d, cdr(z))),
                      z,
                      cons(a, d))))))
```

we can now push the *car* and *cdr* calls inside to obtain

$$
\begin{aligned}
\simeq \mathtt{let}\{a \leftarrow lazy{:}subst(x,y,car(z)), d \leftarrow lazy{:}subst(x,y,cdr(z))\}\\
\mathtt{and}(&equal(subst(x,y,car(z)),\\
&\quad \mathtt{if}(\mathtt{and}(eq(a,car(z)),\\
&\qquad eq(d,cdr(z))),\\
&\quad car(z),\\
&\quad car(cons(a,d))))),\\
&equal(subst(x,y,cdr(z)),\\
&\quad \mathtt{if}(\mathtt{and}(eq(a,car(z)),\\
&\qquad eq(d,cdr(z))),\\
&\quad cdr(z),\\
&\quad cdr(cons(a,d))))),
\end{aligned}
$$

simplifying the **if** gives

$$
\begin{aligned}
\simeq \mathtt{let}\{a \leftarrow lazy{:}subst(x,y,car(z)), d \leftarrow lazy{:}subst(x,y,cdr(z))\}\\
\mathtt{and}(&equal(subst(x,y,car(z)),\\
&\quad a),\\
&equal(subst(x,y,cdr(z)),\\
&\quad d))
\end{aligned}
$$

finally we use the induction hypothesis to obtain the result

$$\simeq \mathtt{T}$$

□Theorem A

4.11. Example 10: The Deutsch-Schorr-Waite Marking Algorithm

We chose this example for historical reasons, since there have been many different verification proofs in the literature. It is a version of the famous Deutsch-Schorr-Waite marking algorithm, (Schorr and Waite, 1967) and (Deutsch, 1968), that is used in implementing mark and sweep garbage collection, the usual method for reclaiming useless and unusable *cons* cells in the usual dynamic storage allocation environment. See (Knuth, 1968) or (Schorr and Waite, 1967) for an extensive discussion of garbage collection and marking algorithms. In this example we describe what we believe to be the most convincing, useful and least technical proof. We shall also discuss the other proofs since they all differ from this one. In this example we work within the low level Lisp data structure $\mathbb{M}_{mfsexp}$ introduced earlier. The Deutsch-Shore-Waite marking algorithm uses pointer reversal to avoid using an explicit stack. Pointer reversal is a very powerful technique that is used in destructive memory programming. The idea is quite simple: the program destructively alters the structure it is operating on to store the information that a stack would normally be used for. In this case the algorithm scans the graph in a left-first fashion, marking cells as it proceeds. Since the cells are marked when they are first visited, looping or repeatedly scanning the same subgraph is avoided. A succinct treatment of pointer reversal, or pointer rotation as it is sometimes called, may be found in (Suzuki, 1982). However the notation in that paper follows the unfortunate trend, as exemplified by the Lisp SETF mechanism, see for example (Steele, 1984), (Brooks and Gabriel, 1984) or (Pitman, 1980), of confusing control and data. In this structure our version of the algorithm is given by the following definition.

```
dsw:mark(cell) ← mark(cell, NIL))
mark(cell, stack) ←
    if(terminal(cell),
       pop(cell, stack),
       let{a ↞ car(cell)}
          seq(setm(cell, 1),
              rplaca(cell, stack),
              mark(a, cell)))
pop(cell, stack) ←
    ifn(stack,
        cell,
        if(eq(f(stack), 0),
           let{d ↞ cdr(stack), os ↞ car(stack)}
              seq(setf(stack, 1),
                  rplaca(stack, cell),
                  rplacd(stack, os),
                  mark(d, stack))
           let{os ↞ cdr(stack)}
              seq(setf(stack, 0),
                  rplacd(stack, cell),
                  pop(stack, os))))
terminal(cell) ← or(atom(cell), eq(m(cell), 1))
```

Our verification proof consists in showing that *dsw:mark* is strongly isomorphic to a very simple recursive program. This has several advantages over most proofs.

Firstly, rather than proving that the algorithm meets an equally complicated theoretical specification, our specification, being the simple recursive version below, is by its very nature simpler and does not force the idle reader to grapple with the sometimes overbearing details of the underlying semantics and proof rules. Another reason is that our proof emphasizes the relationship between program verification, program transformation and program derivation, in that because the proof is of a syntactical nature it can be thought of in two ways. The first is the way we are presenting it, a verification of a complex algorithm via a reduction to a very simple algorithm. The second is the reverse or dual, obtaining or deriving a complex more efficient algorithm from a simpleminded or *specifying* algorithm. This very simple algorithm is defined as follows:

```
r1:dsw:mark(cell) ←
    if(terminal(cell),
       cell,
       seq(setm(cell, 1),
           r1:dsw:mark(car(cell)),
           r1:dsw:mark(cdr(cell)),
           cell))
```

As we have already stated, our verification proof simply involves showing that the following holds under certain simple conditions:

Theorem: $dsw{:}mark(x) \simeq r1{:}dsw{:}mark(x)$.

Of the existing proofs in the literature the closest to ours in spirit, but not in style, is that found in (Topor, 1979). Topor's approach is to separate the proof into two essentially distinct parts. The first part involves properties of the underlying data structure, while the second relies on properties of the algorithm itself. The proof itself is of the *intermittent assertions* variety that was first introduced by (Knuth, 1968) and later developed by (Burstall, 1974) and (Manna and Waldinger, 1977). Topor's paper is also interesting in that there he, to some extent, suggests the possibility of our proof, or at least one like it. In (Topor, 1979) he gives three marking algorithms, Algorithm 1, which is a slight variation on our *r1:dsw:mark*, Algorithm 3, being his version of the Deutsch-Schorr-Waite marking algorithm, and in between, Algorithm 2, which we describe by the following definition:

```
r2:dsw:mark(cell) ← seq(r2:mark(cell, NIL), cell)
```

$r2{:}mark$(cell, stack) ←
    if($terminal$(cell),
        if(stack, $r2{:}mark$($cdar$(stack), cdr(stack)), cell),
        seq($setm$(cell, 1),
            $r2{:}mark$(car(cell), $cons$(cell, stack))))

This version is simply a(n almost) tail recursive program obtained from the trivial one by the incorporation of an explicit stack. *dsw:mark* eliminates this storage extravagant feature by storing the stack on the structure being marked. In his conclusions Topor says:

> *An alternative method of proof which has apparently not been used is to first verify Algorithm 2, a purely constructive program, using the present (or any other) method, and then use the techniques of (Milner, 1971) or (Hoare, 1972) to show that the Shorr-Waite algorithm simulates Algorithm 2. In such a proof the representation function describing how the stack of Algorithm 2 is represented in the Schorr-Waite algorithm is defined by*
>
> Rep(X) ←
>   **if** X = NIL **then** empty
>   **else if** f(X) = 0 **then** Rep(car(X))
>   **else** Push(X, Rep(car(X))).
>
> *However the structure of this definition means that the proof of simulation is not completely straightforward but requires yet another inductive argument. Since the proof of Algorithm 2 is almost as long as that of the Schorr-Waite algorithm, the resulting proof is no shorter than the one we have given. This fact suggests that further research into proofs of simulation and the use of data structure is desirable.*

This suggestion is very much in the spirit of our proof. The main differences are that we do not choose Algorithm 2 as our *go-between* but rather the trivial Algorithm 1. Thus our proof is not one of *simulation* but of *actual equivalence*, and does not suffer from the deficiencies that Topor raises. We also do not use the methods of (Milner, 1971) or (Hoare, 1972) but our own.

Most of the other proofs of correctness are of the *inductive assertions* variety as described by (Floyd, 1967). Gries, in a companion paper to Topor's (Gries, 1979), proves the correctness and termination of a version of the algorithm in a rather elegant fashion, although he simplifies the world so as to combine the *mark* and *field* bits as well as exclude the existence of atoms. Other proofs have been given. We mention them briefly: Kowaltowski (Kowaltoski, 1973) extended the techniques of

(Burstall, 1972) to encompass a proof of the marking algorithm; Suzuki (Suzuki, 1976) in his dissertation, describes a machine checked proof that uses recursively defined predicates in his assertions; Morris (Morris, J. H, 1972) gives a more direct analysis similar to that of Topor's; finally a proof using denotational semantics has been given in (Poupon and Wegbreit, 1972). Let **Unmarked**(`cell`) be the set of unmarked cells reachable from `cell` via paths through unmarked cells. We finish this example by proving

Theorem: $dsw{:}mark(x) \simeq \mathrm{r1}{:}dsw{:}mark(x)$, assuming

$$(\forall c \in \mathbf{Unmarked}(x))f(c) = 0.$$

Proof of Theorem:

Lemma: The following are strongly isomorphic under the hypothesis of the theorem:

$$mark(\texttt{cell}, \texttt{stack})$$

$$\texttt{seq}(r1{:}dsw{:}mark(\texttt{cell}), pop(\texttt{cell}, \texttt{stack}))$$

To see that the result follows it suffices to observe that

$$mark(\texttt{cell}, \texttt{NIL}) \simeq r1{:}dsw{:}mark(\texttt{cell})$$

and

$$r1{:}dsw{:}mark(\texttt{cell}) \simeq \texttt{seq}(r1{:}dsw{:}mark(\texttt{cell}), pop(\texttt{cell}, \texttt{NIL}))$$

The proof of the lemma is straightforward, using the following simple commutativity property of *r1:dsw:mark*. This is left to the reader to verify. It expresses the fact that *r1:dsw:mark* does not depend on the contents of a marked cell.

Commutativity Property: If $\vartheta \in \{rplaca, rplacd, setf\}$ and e is any expression then the following expressions are strongly isomorphic.

$$\texttt{if}(eq(m(x), 1), \texttt{seq}(\mathrm{r1}{:}dsw{:}mark(z), \vartheta(x, y), e), \texttt{T})$$

$$\texttt{if}(eq(m(x), 1), \texttt{seq}(\vartheta(x, y), \mathrm{r1}{:}dsw{:}mark(z), e), \texttt{T})$$

Proof of lemma: We prove this lemma by induction on the size of

$$\mathbf{Unmarked}(\texttt{cell}).$$

For convenience we suppose that $m(\texttt{cell}) = 0$, $car(\texttt{cell}) = \texttt{v}_a$ and $cdr(\texttt{cell}) = \texttt{v}_d$. Since the identity clearly holds when `cell` is terminal, we also assume that $f(c) = 0$ whenever $c \in \textbf{Unmarked}(\texttt{cell})$.

$$
\begin{aligned}
&mark(\texttt{cell},\texttt{stack}) \simeq\\
&\quad\simeq \texttt{if}(terminal(\texttt{cell}),\\
&\qquad\quad pop(\texttt{cell},\texttt{stack}),\\
&\qquad\quad \texttt{let}\{\texttt{a} \leftarrow car(\texttt{cell})\}\\
&\qquad\qquad \texttt{seq}(setm(\texttt{cell},1),\\
&\qquad\qquad\quad rplaca(\texttt{cell},\texttt{stack}),\\
&\qquad\qquad\quad mark(\texttt{a},\texttt{cell}))).
\end{aligned}
$$

Evaluating the `let` gives

$$
\begin{aligned}
&\simeq \texttt{if}(terminal(\texttt{cell}),\\
&\qquad pop(\texttt{cell},\texttt{stack}),\\
&\qquad \texttt{seq}(setm(\texttt{cell},1),\\
&\qquad\quad rplaca(\texttt{cell},\texttt{stack}),\\
&\qquad\quad mark(\texttt{v}_a,\texttt{cell}))).
\end{aligned}
$$

Since `cell` has been marked we must have

$$\textbf{Unmarked}(\texttt{v}_a) < \textbf{Unmarked}(\texttt{cell})$$

thus we can use the induction hypothesis to obtain

$$
\begin{aligned}
&\simeq \texttt{if}(terminal(\texttt{cell}),\\
&\qquad pop(\texttt{cell},\texttt{stack}),\\
&\qquad \texttt{seq}(setm(\texttt{cell},1),\\
&\qquad\quad rplaca(\texttt{cell},\texttt{stack}),\\
&\qquad\quad r1{:}dsw{:}mark(\texttt{v}_a)\\
&\qquad\quad pop(\texttt{v}_a,\texttt{cell}))).
\end{aligned}
$$

Unfolding the $pop(\texttt{v}_a,\texttt{cell})$ call

and eliminating the vacuous `ifn` yields

$$
\begin{aligned}
\simeq \texttt{if}(&\mathit{terminal}(\texttt{cell}),\\
&\mathit{pop}(\texttt{cell},\texttt{stack}),\\
&\texttt{seq}(\mathit{setm}(\texttt{cell},1),\\
&\quad\mathit{rplaca}(\texttt{cell},\texttt{stack}),\\
&\quad\mathit{r1{:}dsw{:}mark}(\texttt{v}_a)\\
&\quad\texttt{if}(\mathit{eq}(f(\texttt{cell}),0),\\
&\qquad\texttt{let}\{\texttt{d} \leftarrow \mathit{cdr}(\texttt{cell}), \texttt{os} \leftarrow \mathit{car}(\texttt{cell})\}\\
&\qquad\quad\texttt{seq}(\mathit{setf}(\texttt{cell},1),\\
&\qquad\qquad\mathit{rplaca}(\texttt{cell},\texttt{v}_a),\\
&\qquad\qquad\mathit{rplacd}(\texttt{cell},\texttt{os}),\\
&\qquad\qquad\mathit{mark}(\texttt{d},\texttt{cell}))\\
&\qquad\texttt{let}\{\texttt{os} \leftarrow \mathit{cdr}(\texttt{cell})\}\\
&\qquad\quad\texttt{seq}(\mathit{setf}(\texttt{cell},0),\\
&\qquad\qquad\mathit{rplacd}(\texttt{cell},\texttt{v}_a),\\
&\qquad\qquad\mathit{pop}(\texttt{cell},\texttt{os})))).
\end{aligned}
$$

This simplifies to the following since the field bit is 0

$$
\begin{aligned}
\simeq \texttt{if}(&\mathit{terminal}(\texttt{cell}),\\
&\mathit{pop}(\texttt{cell},\texttt{stack}),\\
&\texttt{seq}(\mathit{setm}(\texttt{cell},1),\\
&\quad\mathit{rplaca}(\texttt{cell},\texttt{stack}),\\
&\quad\mathit{r1{:}dsw{:}mark}(\texttt{v}_a),\\
&\quad\mathit{setf}(\texttt{cell},1),\\
&\quad\mathit{rplaca}(\texttt{cell},\texttt{v}_a),\\
&\quad\mathit{rplacd}(\texttt{cell},\texttt{stack}),\\
&\quad\mathit{mark}(\texttt{v}_d,\texttt{cell}))).
\end{aligned}
$$

Again we can use the induction hypothesis to obtain

$$\simeq \texttt{if}(\mathit{terminal}(\texttt{cell}),\\
\quad \mathit{pop}(\texttt{cell}, \texttt{stack}),\\
\quad \texttt{seq}(\mathit{setm}(\texttt{cell}, 1),\\
\qquad \mathit{rplaca}(\texttt{cell}, \texttt{stack}),\\
\qquad \mathit{r1{:}dsw{:}mark}(\texttt{v}_a),\\
\qquad \mathit{setf}(\texttt{cell}, 1),\\
\qquad \mathit{rplaca}(\texttt{cell}, \texttt{v}_a),\\
\qquad \mathit{rplacd}(\texttt{cell}, \texttt{stack}),\\
\qquad \mathit{r1{:}dsw{:}mark}(\texttt{v}_d),\\
\qquad \mathit{pop}(\texttt{v}_d, \texttt{cell}))).$$

Unfolding and simplifying the $\mathit{pop}(\texttt{v}_d, \texttt{cell})$ call results in

$$\simeq \texttt{if}(\mathit{terminal}(\texttt{cell}),\\
\quad \mathit{pop}(\texttt{cell}, \texttt{stack}),\\
\quad \texttt{seq}(\mathit{setm}(\texttt{cell}, 1),\\
\qquad \mathit{rplaca}(\texttt{cell}, \texttt{stack}),\\
\qquad \mathit{r1{:}dsw{:}mark}(\texttt{v}_a),\\
\qquad \mathit{setf}(\texttt{cell}, 1),\\
\qquad \mathit{rplaca}(\texttt{cell}, \texttt{v}_a),\\
\qquad \mathit{rplacd}(\texttt{cell}, \texttt{stack}),\\
\qquad \mathit{r1{:}dsw{:}mark}(\texttt{v}_d),\\
\qquad \mathit{setf}(\texttt{cell}, 0),\\
\qquad \mathit{rplacd}(\texttt{cell}, \texttt{v}_d),\\
\qquad \mathit{pop}(\texttt{cell}, \texttt{stack}))).$$

Using the commutativity property gives

$\simeq$ `if`(*terminal*(`cell`),
    pop(`cell`, `stack`),
    `seq`(*setm*(`cell`, 1),
        rplaca(`cell`, `stack`),
        rplaca(`cell`, $\mathtt{v}_a$),
        setf(`cell`, 1),
        setf(`cell`, 0),
        rplacd(`cell`, `stack`),
        rplacd(`cell`, $\mathtt{v}_d$),
        r1:dsw:mark($\mathtt{v}_a$),
        r1:dsw:mark($\mathtt{v}_d$),
        pop(`cell`, `stack`))).

Finally cancelling redundant operations gives

$\simeq$ `if`(*terminal*(`cell`),
    pop(`cell`, `stack`),
    `seq`(*setm*(`cell`, 1),
        r1:dsw:mark($\mathtt{v}_a$),
        r1:dsw:mark($\mathtt{v}_d$),
        pop(`cell`, `stack`))).

We obtain the result by folding and a minimum of effort

$\simeq$ `seq`(*r1:dsw:mark*(`cell`), *pop*(`cell`, `stack`)).□**Lemma**□**Theorem**

4.12. Example 11: The Morris Traversal Algorithm

Consider the following simple program that applies the gentle operation *process*, pre-order style, to each cell in **Cells**(`tree`).

rec:traverse(`tree`) ←
    `if`(*atom*(`tree`),
        `tree`,
        `seq`(*process*(`tree`),
            rec:traverse(*car*(`tree`)),
            rec:traverse(*cdr*(`tree`)))).

The Deutsch-Schorr-Waite marking algorithm demonstrates one way to eliminate stack from such a program, assuming the structure being operated on has a mark and field bit. In this section we will look at another way, one that does not need a mark or field bit, but only requires that its input is somewhat *nicer* than the ordinary run of the mill S-expression. The input will be assumed to belong to $\mathbb{M}_{hered}$, which is roughly speaking the collection of all hereditary lists that contain no cellular structure sharing. Explicitly:

Definition: $c\,;\mu \in \mathbb{M}_{sexp}$ is in $\mathbb{M}_{hered}$ if the following two conditions hold

1. $(\forall c_0 \in \mathbf{Cells}_\mu(c))(c_0\,;\mu \in \mathbb{M}_{list})$.
2. $(\forall \sigma_0, \sigma_1)(((c\,;\mu)_{\sigma_0} = (c\,;\mu)_{\sigma_1} \;\wedge\; \sigma_0 \neq \sigma_1) \rightarrow (c\,;\mu)_{\sigma_0} \in \mathbb{A})$.

We also need to assume that the operation *process* does not depend on the contents of its cellular arguments. Actually we need only assume that

$$\mathtt{seq}(rplacd(x, \mathtt{NIL}), process(y), e) \simeq \mathtt{seq}(process(y), rplacd(x, \mathtt{NIL}), e).$$

The no stack version of the above algorithm, restricted to $\mathbb{M}_{hered}$, consists of the following two programs. It is a slightly modified version of (Morris, J. M, 1979). The idea behind the program is quite simple. If we are to traverse `tree` we must traverse the *car* and then the *cdr*. If the car is an atom this reduces to traversing the *cdr*. So assuming that the *car* is not an atom we must traverse it and somehow store the fact that when done with the *car* we have still the *cdr* ahead of us. This is done in the following way. Before we traverse the *car*, which is a list, we alter the *cdr* pointer of the last cell in its spine so that it points back to `tree`. This backward pointer is detected when we finally arrive at this altered cell. Which of course corresponds to the completion of traversing the *car*. The pointer is then restored to `NIL` and we then proceed with marking the *cdr*. The detection of the backward pointers is the job of the auxiliary program *ult*. (I wish to thank Rodney Topor for bringing this algorithm to my attention.)

```
ult(tree, parent) ←
    let{cell ← cdr(tree)}
        if(or(not(cell), eq(cell, parent)),
           tree,
           ult(cell, parent))
```

```
traverse(tree) ←
    if(atom(tree),
       tree,
       if(atom(car(tree)),
          seq(process(tree), traverse(cdr(tree))),
          let{ter ← ult(car(tree), tree)}
             ifn(cdr(ter),
                 seq(process(tree),
                     rplacd(ter, tree),
                     traverse(car(tree))),
                 seq(rplacd(ter, NIL),
                     traverse(cdr(tree))))))
```

The theorem that we shall prove is, predictably:

Theorem: $rec{:}traverse(x) \simeq traverse(x)$ on $\mathbb{M}_{hered}$.

We begin by defining a class of objects, that are relevant to the proof of the theorem. This is necessary since although we wish only to consider hereditary lists, the program forces us to consider a wider class of objects.

Definition of Marked: A cell $c_0 \in \mathbf{Cells}_\mu(c)$ is said to be *marked* in $c\,;\mu$ if it is such that

$$(car(c_0\,;\mu))_{1^n} = c_0$$

for some $n \in \mathbb{N}$.

Definition of Half-marked: An S-expression $c\,;\mu$ is said to be half-marked if the following conditions hold:

1. Either c is marked or else all marked nodes in $c\,;\mu$ are in $\mathbf{Cells}_\mu(cdr(c))$, and each marked node c_i is pointed to by the cdr pointer of exactly one cell, c_i^*, in the spine of $car(c_i)$; also each marked cell is pointed to by at most two other cells.

2. Letting $c_0, \ldots, c_m$ be all the marked nodes in $c\,;\mu$ and μ^* be the memory obtained by evaluating

$$\mathtt{seq}(rplacd(c_0^*, \mathtt{NIL}), \ldots, rplacd(c_m^*, \mathtt{NIL}))$$

in μ, then for any $c^* \in \mathbf{Cells}_\mu(c)$ we have that $c^*\,;\mu^* \in \mathbb{M}_{hered}$.

The point of the auxiliary program *ult* should be clear. Firstly if $c\,;\mu$ is not marked and its car is not an atom, then

$$ult(car(c), c)\,;\mu \simeq last(car(c))\,;\mu.$$

On the other hand if $c\,;\mu$ is marked then using the notation from the definition above we have:

$$ult(car(c), c)\,;\mu \simeq c^*\,;\mu.$$

Lemma: Assuming that

$$\mathsf{seq}(rplacd(x, \mathtt{NIL}), process(y), e) \simeq \mathsf{seq}(process(y), rplacd(x, \mathtt{NIL}), e)$$

then the following hold for any half-marked S-expression.

1. If $c\,;\mu \in \mathsf{M}_{list}$ and is not marked then $traverse(c)\,;\mu \simeq rec{:}traverse(c)\,;\mu$
2. If $c\,;\mu \notin \mathsf{M}_{list}$ is not marked and c_1 is the marked cell in the spine of c, with c_0 the cell prior to c_1 then

$$\begin{aligned} &traverse(c)\,;\mu \\ &\quad\simeq \mathsf{seq}(rplacd(c_0, \mathtt{NIL}), \\ &\qquad\qquad rec{:}traverse(c), \\ &\qquad\qquad traverse(cdr(c_1)))\,;\mu \end{aligned}$$

Proof of Lemma: The proof is by induction on the rank of $c\,;\mu$, the rank in this case is the number of unmarked cells reachable via paths through unmarked cells. The base case is left to the reader as usual, so suppose that 1. and 2. hold for all half-marked objects of less rank than $c\,;\mu$.

Proof of 1. We divide this into two separate cases depending on whether or not $car(c\,;\mu)$ is an atom. The case when it is an atom is straightforward:

$$\begin{aligned} &traverse(c)\,;\mu \\ &\quad\simeq \mathsf{seq}(process(c), \\ &\qquad\qquad traverse(cdr(c)))\,;\mu \end{aligned}$$

by unfolding and simplifying.

$$\begin{aligned} &\simeq \mathsf{seq}(process(c), \\ &\qquad\qquad rec{:}traverse(cdr(c)))\,;\mu \end{aligned}$$

using the induction hypothesis.

$\simeq \mathsf{seq}(\mathit{process}(c),$
$\quad \mathit{car}(c),$
$\quad \mathit{rec}{:}\mathit{traverse}(\mathit{cdr}(c))\ ;\ \mu$

by inserting a defined gentle term.

$\simeq \mathsf{seq}(\mathit{process}(c),$
$\quad \mathit{rec}{:}\mathit{traverse}(\mathit{car}(c)),$
$\quad \mathit{rec}{:}\mathit{traverse}(\mathit{cdr}(c))\ ;\ \mu$

since $\mathit{rec}{:}\mathit{traverse}(x) \simeq x$ on $\mathbb{A}$.

$\simeq \mathit{rec}{:}\mathit{traverse}(c)\ ;\ \mu$

by folding.

So let us suppose that the car of $c\ ;\ \mu$ is not an atom. Consequently it is a list; taking c_0 to be the last cell in its spine, we have:

$\mathit{traverse}(c)\ ;\ \mu$

$\simeq \mathsf{seq}(\mathit{process}(c),$
$\quad \mathit{rplacd}(c_0, c),$
$\quad \mathit{traverse}(\mathit{car}(c))\ ;\ \mu$

by unfolding and simplifying.

$\simeq \mathsf{seq}(\mathit{process}(c),$
$\quad \mathit{rplacd}(c_0, c),$
$\quad \mathit{rplacd}(c_0), \mathtt{NIL}),$
$\quad \mathit{rec}{:}\mathit{traverse}(\mathit{car}(c)),$
$\quad \mathit{traverse}(\mathit{cdr}(c))\ ;\ \mu$

using the induction hypothesis.

$\simeq \mathsf{seq}(\mathit{process}(c),$
$\quad \mathit{rec}{:}\mathit{traverse}(\mathit{car}(c)),$
$\quad \mathit{traverse}(\mathit{cdr}(c))\ ;\ \mu$

cancelling the redundant operations.

$\simeq \mathsf{seq}(\mathit{process}(c),$
$\quad \mathit{rec}{:}\mathit{traverse}(\mathit{car}(c)),$
$\quad \mathit{rec}{:}\mathit{traverse}(\mathit{cdr}(c))\ ;\ \mu$

using the induction hypothesis.

$\simeq rec{:}traverse(c)$

by folding neatly.

$\Box_1$.

Proof of 2. Again we must consider two cases, depending on whether or not the $cdr(c\,;\mu)$ is marked. Beginning with the unmarked case, we leave the case when the car of $c\,;\mu$ is an atom to the reader. Thus let c_a be the last cell in the spine of $car(c\,;\mu)$.

$$
\begin{aligned}
& traverse(c)\,;\mu \\
& \quad \simeq \mathtt{seq}(process(c), \\
& \qquad\qquad rplacd(c_a, c), \\
& \qquad\qquad traverse(car(c))\,;\mu
\end{aligned}
$$

by unfolding and simplifying.

$$
\begin{aligned}
& \simeq \mathtt{seq}(process(c), \\
& \qquad\qquad rplacd(c_a, c), \\
& \qquad\qquad rplacd(c_a), \mathtt{NIL}), \\
& \qquad\qquad rec{:}traverse(car(c)), \\
& \qquad\qquad traverse(cdr(c))\,;\mu
\end{aligned}
$$

using the induction hypothesis.

$$
\begin{aligned}
& \simeq \mathtt{seq}(process(c), \\
& \qquad\qquad rec{:}traverse(car(c)), \\
& \qquad\qquad traverse(cdr(c))\,;\mu
\end{aligned}
$$

cancelling the redundant operations.

$$
\begin{aligned}
& \simeq \mathtt{seq}(process(c), \\
& \qquad\qquad rec{:}traverse(car(c)), \\
& \qquad\qquad rplacd(c_0, \mathtt{NIL}), \\
& \qquad\qquad rec{:}traverse(cdr(c)), \\
& \qquad\qquad traverse(cdr(c_1))\,;\mu
\end{aligned}
$$

using the induction hypothesis.

$$
\begin{aligned}
& \simeq \mathtt{seq}(rplacd(c_0, \mathtt{NIL}), \\
& \qquad\qquad process(c), \\
& \qquad\qquad rec{:}traverse(car(c)), \\
& \qquad\qquad rec{:}traverse(cdr(c)), \\
& \qquad\qquad traverse(cdr(c_1))\,;\mu
\end{aligned}
$$

commuting operations.

$\simeq$ seq($rplacd(c_0, \texttt{NIL})$,
$rec{:}traverse(c)$,
$traverse(cdr(c_1))$; μ

by folding.

Now in the situation where $cdr(c\,;\mu)$ is marked we proceed as follows, noting that $c_0 = c$ and $c_1 = cdr(c)$

$traverse(c)$; μ

$\simeq$ seq($process(c)$,
$rplacd(c_a, c)$,
$traverse(car(c))$; μ

again by unfolding and simplifying.

$\simeq$ seq($process(c)$,
$rplacd(c_a, c)$,
$rplacd(c_a), \texttt{NIL})$,
$rec{:}traverse(car(c))$,
$traverse(cdr(c))$; μ

by utilizing the induction hypothesis.

$\simeq$ seq($process(c)$,
$rec{:}traverse(car(c))$,
$traverse(cdr(c))$; μ

cancelling redundant operations.

$\simeq$ seq($process(c)$,
$rec{:}traverse(car(c))$,
$rplacd(c, \texttt{NIL})$,
$traverse(cdr(c_1))$; μ

unfolding and simplifying.

$\simeq$ seq($rplacd(c, \texttt{NIL})$,
$process(c)$,
$rec{:}traverse(car(c))$,
$traverse(cdr(c_1))$; μ

commuting operations.

$$\simeq \texttt{seq}(rplacd(c, \texttt{NIL}),\; process(c),\; rec{:}traverse(car(c)),\; \texttt{NIL},\; traverse(cdr(c_1))\;;\; \mu$$

inserting a defined term.

$$\simeq \texttt{seq}(rplacd(c, \texttt{NIL}),\; process(c),\; rec{:}traverse(car(c)),\; rec{:}traverse(cdr(c)),\; traverse(cdr(c_1))\;;\; \mu$$

by definition of *rec:traverse*.

$$\simeq \texttt{seq}(rplacd(c, \texttt{NIL}),\; rec{:}traverse(c),\; traverse(cdr(c_1))\;;\; \mu$$

finally folding.

□2. □**Lemma** □**Theorem**

Chapter 5

The Effectiveness Theorems

In this chapter we prove, among other things, the effectiveness theorems. We shall actually prove them in a somewhat more general context than the one in which we stated them in Chapter 3. Take $\mathfrak{A}^*$ to be an arbitrary countable τ-structure, τ a finite similarity type (that being the isomorphism type of a first order language).

$$\mathfrak{A}^* =< A, \phi_0^*, \ldots, \phi_n^*, R_0^*, \ldots, R_m^*, a >_{a \in A}$$

The ϕ_i^* are m_i-ary, possibly partial, operations on A and the R_i^* are n_i-ary relations, we also for convenience assume that $\mathtt{T}, \mathtt{NIL} \notin A$. Since we are going to be dealing with the first order theory of $\mathfrak{A}^*$ the possibly partial nature of the ϕ_i^* is somewhat bothersome. Also because of the emphasis of our approach, regarding them as $m_i + 1$-placed relations in the usual way is also awkward. For these and other reasons we introduce the following modification $\mathfrak{A}$ of $\mathfrak{A}^*$. Let $\mathbb{A} = A \oplus \{\mathtt{T}, \mathtt{NIL}\}$ and put

$$\mathfrak{A} =< \mathbb{A}, \phi_0, \ldots, \phi_n, R_0^?, \ldots R_m^?, \mathtt{T}, \mathtt{NIL}, a >_{a \in A}$$

Here the ϕ_i are total m_i-ary operations obtained by extending ϕ_i^* so that anything in $\mathbb{A}^{m_i} - \delta_{\phi_i^*}$ is mapped to $\mathtt{NIL}$, and $R_i^?$ is the characteristic function, using $\mathtt{T}$ and $\mathtt{NIL}$, of the relation R_i^* as viewed as a relation on $\mathbb{A}$. If we regarded $\mathfrak{A}^*$ as a relational structure then the following would be a simple exercise.

Proposition: $\mathbf{Th}(\mathfrak{A})$ and $\mathbf{Th}(\mathfrak{A}^*)$, the respective first order theories of these structures, are recursive in one another.

As usual we do not spend any time trying to distinguish the element a and the constant symbol that denotes it. The memory structure that we work with in this section, $\mathbb{M}_{\mathfrak{A}}$, is defined as follows. Its memory objects are just those of $\mathbb{M}_{sexp}$ with atoms $\mathbb{A}$. The memory operations are

$$\mathbb{O}_{\mathfrak{A}} = \{\phi_0, \ldots \phi_n, R_0^?, \ldots R_m^?, atom, eq, cons, car, cdr, rplaca, rplacd\}$$

where $\phi_i(\bar{v}\,;\mu) = w\,;\mu$ iff $\bar{v} \in \mathbb{A}^{m_i}$ with $\phi_i(\bar{v}) = w$ and $R_i^?(\bar{v}\,;\mu) = w\,;\mu$ iff $\bar{v} \in \mathbb{A}^{m_i}$ with $R_i^?(\bar{v}) = w$. The effectiveness theorem can be stated as follows. Let $\sim$ be any one of $\equiv, \cong$ or $\simeq$. and $\Delta^{+}_{\sim}(\mathsf{M}_{\mathfrak{A}})$ be the collection of all equations $e_0 \sim e_1$ where the e_i are terms in $\mathsf{M}_{\mathfrak{A}}$ and $e_0 \sim e_1$ is indeed true.

Theorem A: $\Delta^{+}_{\sim}(\mathsf{M}_{\mathfrak{A}})$ is recursive in $\mathbf{Th}^0(\mathfrak{A})$, the quantifier free part of $\mathbf{Th}(\mathfrak{A})$.

As an application of the methods developed to prove this theorem we shall also prove the unbounded isomorphism theorem:

Theorem B: If $e_i(\bar{x}), i \in 2$ are primitive terms such that $e_0(\bar{x}) \cong e_1(\bar{x})$ and the $e_i(\bar{x})$ are unbounded, then there is a term $\theta(\bar{x})$ which is total on $\mathsf{M}_{\mathfrak{A}}^{|\bar{x}|}$, does not alter or enlarge the memory it is evaluated in, takes only the values T or NIL, and which satisfies

1. $e_0(\bar{x}) \simeq e_1(\bar{x})$ on $\{\bar{v}\,;\mu \mid \theta(\bar{v})\,;\mu \gg \mathtt{T}\,;\mu\}$
2. $e_i(\bar{x})$ is bounded on $\{\bar{v}\,;\mu \mid \theta(\bar{v})\,;\mu \gg \mathtt{NIL}\,;\mu\}$

Using the three equivalence relations we can define three logics over $\mathsf{M}_{\mathfrak{A}}$: $\mathcal{L}^{\mathfrak{A}}_{\simeq}$, $\mathcal{L}^{\mathfrak{A}}_{\cong}$ and $\mathcal{L}^{\mathfrak{A}}_{\equiv}$ respectively. If $\mathbf{Th}_{\sim}(\mathsf{M}_{\mathfrak{A}})$ is the collection of $\mathcal{L}^{\mathfrak{A}}_{\sim}$-sentences valid in $\mathsf{M}_{\mathfrak{A}}$ and $\mathbf{Th}^n_{\sim}(\mathsf{M}_{\mathfrak{A}})$ is the subset consisting of sentences of alternation rank less than or equal to n (i.e the quantifier rank when one considers $\forall\bar{x}$ and $\exists\bar{x}$ to be single quantifiers), then we also prove the following two theorems which in opposition to the effectiveness theorems demonstrate the differing complexities of the three equivalence relations. It is not only the failure of a substitution theorem which separates the extensional relations from strong isomorphism but also their logical complexity.

Theorem C: For every $n \in \mathbb{N}$ we have that $\mathbf{Th}^n_{\simeq}(\mathsf{M}_{\mathfrak{A}})$ is recursive in $\mathbf{Th}^n(\mathfrak{A})$.

Theorem D: Regardless of the complexity of $\mathbf{Th}(\mathfrak{A})$, when $\sim$ is either $\cong$ or $\equiv$ we can interpret true arithmetic in $\mathbf{Th}_{\sim}(\mathsf{M}_{\mathfrak{A}})$. Consequently $\mathbf{Th}_{\sim}(\mathsf{M}_{\mathfrak{A}})$ is exactly Δ^1_1 in $\mathbf{Th}(\mathfrak{A})$, when $\mathfrak{A}$ is recursively presented.

5.1. The Underlying Logic

In this section we define the three logics as well as settle some notation. We let $\mathbf{Term}(\mathfrak{A})$ be the set of terms of the τ-structure $\mathfrak{A}$ in the variables

$$\Lambda = \{\alpha, \alpha_0, \ldots, \alpha_i, \ldots\},$$

and if $X \subset \Lambda$ we let $\mathbf{Term}_X(\mathfrak{A})$ be the set of terms which only contain variables from X. The first order language with equality, which we denote by $\mathcal{L}^{\mathfrak{A}}$, is built up from these terms in the usual way. In contrast the language, $\mathcal{L}^{\mathfrak{A}}_{\sim}$, denotes the first order language without equality built up from the atomic formulas from $\mathbb{E}_{\mathfrak{A}}$, and $x \in \mathbb{X}$, using the relation $\sim$ and the operations

$$\neg, \ \wedge, \ \exists x.$$

Explicitly $\mathbb{E}_{\mathfrak{A}}$ is defined inductively to be the smallest set containing both $\mathbb{V} = \mathbb{A} \oplus \mathbb{C}$ and $\mathbb{X} \oplus \Lambda$, closed under the following formation rules:

- If $e_{test}, e_{then}, e_{else} \in \mathbb{E}_{\mathfrak{A}}$ then $\mathtt{if}(e_{test}, e_{then}, e_{else}) \in \mathbb{E}_{\mathfrak{A}}$.
- If $e_1, \ldots, e_n, e_{body} \in \mathbb{E}_{\mathfrak{A}}$ and $x_1, \ldots, x_n \in \mathbb{X}$ are distinct then

$$\mathtt{let}\{x_1 \leftarrow e_1, \ldots, x_m \leftarrow e_m\} e_{body} \in \mathbb{E}_{\mathfrak{A}}.$$

- If $e_1, \ldots, e_n \in \mathbb{E}_{\mathfrak{A}}$ then $\mathtt{seq}(e_1, \ldots, e_n) \in \mathbb{E}_{\mathfrak{A}}$.
- If ϑ is either an n-ary memory operation or n-ary function symbol from $\mathcal{L}^{\mathfrak{A}}$, and $e_1, \ldots, e_n \in \mathbb{E}_{\mathfrak{A}}$ then $\vartheta(e_1, \ldots, e_n) \in \mathbb{E}_{\mathfrak{A}}$.

  The atomic formulas of $\mathcal{L}^{\mathfrak{A}}_{\sim}$ are of the form

$$e_0 \sim e_1$$

where e_0, e_1 are in $\mathbb{E}_{\mathfrak{A}}$. The formulas are then built up from these in the usual manner.

5.1.1. The Quest for a Quantifier

The syntax must now give way to the semantics. The satisfaction relation in this dynamic setting is somewhat subtler than in the usual first order case. Suppose that $\bar{v} \in \mathbb{M}_{\mathfrak{A}}^{|\bar{x}|}$, $e_i(\bar{x}), i \in 2$ are terms in $\mathcal{L}^{\mathfrak{A}}_{\sim}$ and $\theta, \theta_0, \theta_1$ are formulas of $\mathcal{L}^{\mathfrak{A}}_{\sim}$ then the boolean and atomic cases are defined as usual:

- $\mu \models e_0(\bar{x}) \sim e_1(\bar{x}) \ [\bar{v}] \iff e_0(\bar{v}) \,;\mu \sim e_1(\bar{v}) \,; \mu.$
- $\mu \models \neg\theta \ [\bar{v}] \iff \mu \not\models \theta \ [\bar{v}]$
- $\mu \models (\theta_0 \ \wedge \ \theta_1) \ [\bar{v}] \iff \mu \models \theta_0 \ [\bar{v}]$ and $\mu \models \theta_1 \ [\bar{v}]$

  However in the case of the existential quantifier we cannot simply say

- $\mu \models \exists x \ \theta(x, \bar{y}) \ [\bar{v}] \iff \exists v^* \in \mathbb{V}$ such that $\mu \models \theta(x, \bar{y}) \ [v^*, \bar{v}]$

since, firstly for this definition to make sense we must also require that $v^* \in \mathbb{A} \cup \delta_{\mu}$. Secondly, restricting ourselves only to those objects already created seems narrow minded and not in the spirit of the quantifier. The following definition seems natural in the case of the extensional equivalence relations.

Definition: Suppose that $\bar{v} \in \mathbb{M}_{\mathfrak{A}}^{|\bar{x}|}$, $e_i(\bar{x}), i \in 2$ are terms in $\mathcal{L}_{\sim}^{\mathfrak{A}}$ and $\theta, \theta_0, \theta_1$ are formulas of $\mathcal{L}_{\sim}^{\mathfrak{A}}$ then we define $\mu \models \theta[\bar{v}]$ by induction on the complexity of θ as follows:

- $\mu \models e_0(\bar{x}) \sim e_1(\bar{x})\ [\bar{v}] \iff e_0(\bar{v})\,;\mu \sim e_1(\bar{v})\,;\mu.$
- $\mu \models \neg\theta\ [\bar{v}] \iff \mu \not\models \theta\ [\bar{v}]$
- $\mu \models (\theta_0 \wedge \theta_1)\ [\bar{v}] \iff \mu \models \theta_0\ [\bar{v}] \quad \text{and} \quad \mu \models \theta_1\ [\bar{v}]$
- $\mu \models \exists x\ \theta(x, \bar{y})\ [\bar{v}] \iff \exists \mu^* \sqsupseteq \mu,\ \mu^* \in \mathbb{M}_{\mathfrak{A}}$ and a $w \in \delta_{\mu^*} \cup \mathbb{A}$ such that

$$\mu^* \models \theta(x, \bar{y})\ [w, \bar{v}]$$

Remarks:

- Thus in the *dynamic* case the existential quantifier should be read as saying *there is an object, constructible prior to evaluation, such that,* rather than the usual *static* interpretation of *there is an (already existing) object such that.* There is a difference because in any particular memory there is only a finite number of *existing* objects.
- Note that the inclusion of *eq* eliminates the need to treat the logic *with equality* in the case of the extensional relations, since $eq(e_0, e_1) \sim \mathtt{T}$ is equivalent to $e_0 = e_1$ when $\sim$ is either $\equiv$ or $\cong$. We do not include it in the strong isomorphism case since it is not in the spirit of the relation. This is because we must either treat it as an intensional relation which is stronger than $\simeq$ or else an extensional relation which is weaker than $\simeq$. In the latter situation the laws of equality will unfortunately fail.
- As usual we let $\forall x\phi$ abbreviate $\neg\exists x\neg\phi$, but we should warn the reader that not all the usual first order axioms are valid in these dynamic logics. For example the second quantifier axiom in (Chang and Keisler, 1973) which is stated thus:

  2. *If ϕ, ψ are $\mathcal{L}_{\sim}^{\mathfrak{A}}$ formulas and ψ is obtained by freely substituting each free occurrence of x in ϕ by the term t (i.e., no variable free in t shall occur bound in ψ at a place where it is introduced), then*

$$\vdash (\forall x)\phi \rightarrow \psi.$$

is no longer valid in this dynamic situation. A simple example of this is when ϕ is

$$(\forall x)(eq(x, x) \sim \mathtt{T})$$

and t is

$$cons(x, x).$$

The first axiom of (Chang and Keisler, 1973)

1. *If ϕ, ψ are $\mathcal{L}^{\mathfrak{A}}_{\sim}$ formulas and x is a variable not free in ϕ then*

$$\vdash (\forall x)(\phi \to \psi) \to (\phi \to (\forall x)\psi).$$

does, however, remain valid. In the case of $\simeq$ the usual laws of equality, as in (Chang and Keisler, 1973), remain valid.

In the case of the extensional relations, however, there is a simple extension of the first axiom which holds. It makes use of the `let` construct and the following definition of *pushing a* `let` *inside a formula.*

Definition: Suppose that ϕ is a formula in $\mathcal{L}^{\mathfrak{A}}_{\sim}$, e is an expression in $\mathbb{E}_{\mathfrak{A}}$ and x does not occur bound by a quantifier in ϕ. Then we define

$$\texttt{let}\{x \leftarrow e\}\phi$$

by induction on the complexity of ϕ as follows.

$$\texttt{let}\{x \leftarrow e\}\phi = \begin{cases} \texttt{let}\{x \leftarrow e\}e_0 \sim \texttt{let}\{x \leftarrow e\}e_1 & \text{if } \phi = (e_1 \sim e_1), \\ \neg(\texttt{let}\{x \leftarrow e\}\phi_0) & \text{if } \phi = \neg\phi_0, \\ \texttt{let}\{x \leftarrow e\}\theta_0 \wedge \texttt{let}\{x \leftarrow e\}\theta_1 & \text{if } \phi = (\theta_1 \wedge \theta_1), \\ (\exists y)(\texttt{let}\{x \leftarrow e\}\phi_0) & \text{if } \phi = (\exists y)\phi_0. \end{cases}$$

When $\sim$ is either $\cong$ or $\equiv$ then the following modification of the defective rule is valid.

- If ϕ, ψ are $\mathcal{L}^{\mathfrak{A}}_{\sim}$ formulas, ψ is $\texttt{let}\{x \leftarrow e\}\phi$ where $e \in \mathbb{E}_{\mathfrak{A}}$ is gentle, no occurrence of x in ϕ is bound by a quantifier and finally no variable free in e becomes bound in ψ, then $\vdash (\forall x)\phi \to \psi$.

Note that this rule is not valid for the intensional relation, for in the case of strong isomorphism the following sentence is, in a sense unfortunately, valid (because in strong isomorphism new cells must be identified with new cells and old cells with old cells)

$$(\forall x)\neg(x \simeq cons(\mathrm{T}, \mathrm{T})).$$

But

$$\texttt{let}\{x \leftarrow cons(\mathrm{T}, \mathrm{T})\}\neg(x \simeq cons(\mathrm{T}, \mathrm{T}))$$

is clearly false.

It is for this reason we will discuss other interpretations of the existential quantifier in the intensional case. In the case of the extensional equivalence relations we can define the existential quantifier in terms of an infinite disjunction. Let $\mathbb{G}_{\bar{y}}$ be the collection of all gentle terms with free variables amongst the $\bar{y}$, then we have the following proposition.

Proposition: Suppose that $\phi(x, \bar{y})$ is a formula of $\mathcal{L}^{\mathfrak{A}}_{\sim}$ where $\sim$ is either $\equiv$ or $\cong$ then

$$(\exists x)\phi(x, \bar{y}) \Longleftrightarrow \bigvee_{e \in \mathbf{G}_{\bar{y}}} \mathtt{let}\{x \leftarrow e(\bar{y})\}\phi(x, \bar{y}).$$

Again this proposition fails for strong isomorphism, as illustrated by the same example given above. In fact the meaning of the existential quantifier in the intensional case is quite different from the extensional case. Suppose that $e(\bar{y})$ is a term in $\mathbb{E}_{\mathfrak{A}}$ and

$$(\exists x)(x \simeq e(\bar{y}))$$

is valid in $\mathcal{L}^{\mathfrak{A}}_{\simeq}$. Then $e(\bar{y})$ is a *predicate.* Conversely if $e(\bar{y})$ is a predicate then we can conclude that

$$(\exists x)(x \simeq e(\bar{y}))$$

is valid in $\mathcal{L}^{\mathfrak{A}}_{\simeq}$. We could easily strengthen the meaning of the existential quantifier in the case of strong isomorphism by defining it as follows.

First Alternate Definition: Suppose that $\phi(x, \bar{y})$ is a formula of $\mathcal{L}^{\mathfrak{A}}_{\simeq}$ then

$$(\exists x)\phi(x, \bar{y}) \Longleftrightarrow \bigvee_{e \in \mathbf{G}_{\bar{y}}} \mathtt{let}\{x \leftarrow e(\bar{y})\}\phi(x, \bar{y}).$$

In this situation we would have the following consequence; suppose that $e(\bar{y})$ is a term in $\mathbb{E}_{\mathfrak{A}}$ and

$$(\exists x)(x \simeq e(\bar{y}))$$

is valid in $\mathcal{L}^{\mathfrak{A}}_{\simeq}$. Then $e(\bar{y})$ is *gentle.* Conversely if $e(\bar{y})$ is gentle then we can conclude that

$$(\exists x)(x \simeq e(\bar{y}))$$

is valid in $\mathcal{L}^{\mathfrak{A}}_{\simeq}$. We could go even further and define the existential quantifier as a disjunction over all expressions, not just gentle ones.

Second Alternate Definition: Suppose that $\phi(x, \bar{y})$ is a formula of $\mathcal{L}^{\mathfrak{A}}_{\simeq}$ then

$$(\exists x)\phi(x, \bar{y}) \Longleftrightarrow \bigvee_{e \in \mathbb{E}_{\mathfrak{A}}} \mathtt{let}\{x \leftarrow e(\bar{y})\}\phi(x, \bar{y}).$$

In this case we would have that for any expression $e(\bar{x})$ the formula

$$(\exists y)(y \simeq e(\bar{x}))$$

is valid. However we would also have some very weird consequences; an amusing one is the following.

Exercise: Suppose that $\phi(x)$ is a formula in $\mathcal{L}^{\mathfrak{A}}_{\simeq}$ with exactly one free variable, also assume that the variable y does not occur in ϕ, Finally assume that

$$(\exists x)(atom(x) \simeq \texttt{NIL} \wedge \phi(x))$$

is valid. Then show that

$$(\forall x)(\exists y)(atom(x) \simeq \texttt{NIL} \rightarrow \phi(x))$$

is also valid (the variables *are* as they should be).

For no other reason other than uniformity we shall take the definition of the existential quantifier to be the same as in the extensional case. We have not investigated the properties of $\mathcal{L}^{\mathfrak{A}}_{\simeq}$ in the two alternate cases but suspect the results will carry over in some form. In all practical uses of strong isomorphism we have never needed to resort to using the quantifier, consequently we do not feel this is a pressing issue.

5.1.2. An Outline of the Proof of the Effectiveness Theorem

The proof of the effectiveness theorems consists in giving an algorithm which decides whether or not $e_0 \sim e_1 \in \Delta^{\pm}_{\sim}(\mathsf{M}_{\mathfrak{A}})$ given an oracle for $\mathbf{Th}^0(\mathfrak{A})$, and of course verifying the correctness of this algorithm. The algorithm is naturally divided into two parts, the first part is independent of $\sim$, while the second is $\sim$-specific. Before we begin with the first step we give a brief outline of these two steps.

1. This stage is best described as a symbolic evaluation. We reduce a term $e(\bar{x})$ to a finite set describing all its possible answers, in a suitably abstract fashion. We call these answers *symbolic answers*; the fact that there are only a finite number of them allows us to effectively proceed to the second stage. The symbolic reduction relation, $\gg^{\mathsf{S}}$, is defined on triples, $e\,;g\,;\Pi$, called *symbolic descriptions,* these being the symbolic counterpart of a memory object description. e is as usual simply an expression, g is a *partial memory schema* and Π is a set of quantifier free formula from $\mathcal{L}^{\mathfrak{A}}$. The symbolic answers are then just *irreducible* symbolic descriptions. They are of the form $v;g;\Pi$ where v is either a cell or else a term in $\mathfrak{A}$.

2. The second stage is a type of pattern matching process. Given two of these abstract answers we give an algorithm that decides whether or not these abstract answers describe values that are always $\sim$-related. As one would expect the algorithm is simplest when $\sim$ is $\simeq$ and most complex when $\sim$ is $\equiv$. This is done by proving an algebraic relation on these partial answers and showing that it corresponds in a natural sense (Lemma A4) to the equivalence relation under consideration. The decidability of the algebraic relation together with the fact there are only a finite number of these symbolic answers implies the result.

5.2. Partial Memories and Memory Schemata

Before we can define symbolic descriptions and the symbolic reduction relation we need to develop some notation. The principal concepts are those of a partial memory and a partial memory schema. In a nutshell, a partial memory is simply a memory that need not assign contents to every cell.

Definition: A *partial memory* is a finite function, f, with $\delta_f \subset \mathbb{C}$ and

$$\rho_f \subset (\mathbb{A} \oplus \mathbb{C})^{(2)}.$$

The elements of $\mathbf{Cells}_f - \delta_f$ are called *vague cells.* $\mathbf{Cells}_f$ is the set

$$\{c \in \mathbb{C} \mid (\exists \sigma), (\exists v \in \delta_f)(v\,;g)_\sigma = c\}.$$

A typical example of a partial memory is a function obtained from a memory object by forgetting the contents of cells that occur at a certain depth. Most of what we have done carries over immediately to partial memories; however they are not the objects of primary interest. That title belongs to *partial memory schemata*; these are simply partial memories in which one is allowed not only to store cells and atoms but also elements of $\mathbf{Term}(\mathfrak{A})$.

Definition: A *partial memory schema* is a finite function, g, such that $\delta_g \subset \mathbb{C}$ and for some $\bar{\alpha} \in \Lambda$

$$\rho_g \subset (\mathbf{Term}_{\bar{\alpha}}(\mathfrak{A}) \oplus \mathbb{C})^{(2)}.$$

If we let $V_g = \bar{\alpha}$ be all those variables that appear in locations in g, then we regard g as a function from $\mathbb{A}^{|\bar{\alpha}|}$ to the collection of all partial memories. To emphasize this we will often write $g(\bar{\alpha})$. A memory μ is said to be a *completion* of a partial memory f iff $f \sqsubseteq \mu$. It is said to be a completion of a partial memory schema, $g(\bar{\alpha})$, iff $\exists \bar{a} \in \mathbb{A}^{|\bar{\alpha}|}$ such that μ is a completion of $g(\bar{a})$.

In the following we let $v, v_0, \ldots, v_n, \ldots$ range over $\mathbb{C} \oplus \mathbf{Term}(\mathfrak{A})$ (rather than just $\mathbb{V}$), $f, f_0, f_1, \ldots$ range over partial memories and $g, g_0, g_1, \ldots$ range over partial memory schemata. Notice that a partial memory is just a special partial memory schema.

Definition: Supposing g is a partial memory schema, we define the sets

$$\mathbf{Cells}_g(\bar{v}),\ \mathbf{Atoms}_g(\bar{v}),\ \mathbf{Vars}_g(\bar{v}) \text{ and } \mathbf{Values}_g(\bar{v})$$

in the following way:

1. $\mathbf{Cells}_g(v)$ is the set $\{c \in \mathbb{C} \mid (\exists\sigma)(v\,;g)_\sigma = c\}$.
2. $\mathbf{Atoms}_g(v)$ is the set $\{u \in \mathbf{Term}(\mathfrak{A}) \mid (\exists\sigma)(v\,;g)_\sigma = u\}$.
3. $\mathbf{Vars}_g(v)$ is the set $\{\alpha \in \Lambda \mid \alpha$ occurs in $\mathbf{Atoms}_g(v)\}$.
4. $\mathbf{Values}_g(v) = \mathbf{Cells}_g(v) \oplus \mathbf{Atoms}_g(v)$.

And assuming Φ is one of **Cells**, **Atoms**, **Values** or **Vars** then we let

$$\Phi_\mu(\bar{v}) \underset{\text{df}}{=} \bigcup_{i \in |\bar{v}|} \Phi_\mu(\bar{v}{\downarrow}_i).$$

and by Φ_g we mean $\Phi_g(\delta_g)$. Using this notation we can now define:

Definition: A *partial memory object* is a pair $[v_0, \ldots, v_{n-1}]\,; f$ such that f is a partial memory and $v_i \in \mathbb{A} \oplus \mathbf{Cells}_f$ for $i \in n$. A *partial memory object schema* is a pair $[v_0, \ldots, v_{n-1}]\,; g(\bar{\alpha})$ such that $g(\bar{\alpha})$ is a partial memory schema and $v_i \in \mathbf{Cells}_g \oplus \mathbf{Term}_{\bar{\alpha}}(\mathfrak{A})$ for $i \in n$. To emphasize that the sequence $\bar{v}$ may also contain variables (from $\mathbf{Vars}_g$) we usually write $\bar{v}(\bar{\alpha})\,; g(\bar{\alpha})$ to denote such entities.

If $\bar{v}\,; g$ is a partial memory object schema and $n \in \mathbb{N}$ then we say that $\bar{v}\,; g$ is *complete to a depth* n iff for every $\sigma \in \delta_{(\bar{v}{\downarrow}_j;g)}$ with $|\sigma| \leq n$ we have that $(\bar{v}{\downarrow}_j\,; g)_\sigma$ is not a vague cell. If $\bar{v}\,; g$ is complete to a depth n for every $n \in \mathbb{N}$ then we simply say that $\bar{v}\,; g$ is complete. Thus if $\bar{v}\,; g(\bar{\alpha})$ is complete and $\mathbf{Cells}_g = \mathbf{Cells}_g(\bar{v})$ then for any $\bar{a} \in \mathbb{A}^{|\bar{\alpha}|}$ we have that $g(\bar{a})$ is a memory. In preparation to defining symbolic descriptions and the symbolic reduction relation on them we extend the operations in $\mathbb{O}_{\mathfrak{A}}$ to operations on partial memory objects schemata. Up until now we have shown no interest in how the operation *cons* selects a new cell from free storage. For purely technical reasons we no longer continue this practice. To simplify matters we make the following innocuous assumption concerning the behavior of *cons*.

Definition: Suppose that g_0, g_1 are two partial memory schemata and that $\mathbf{Cells}_{g_0} = \mathbf{Cells}_{g_1}$; then we will assume that $cons(v_0, v_1)\,; g_0$ and $cons(v_0, v_1)\,; g_1$ select the same cell from free storage. We also extend this assumption as follows: suppose that $cons(v_0, v_1)\,; f$ returns the new cell c and that μ is a completion of f

with the added property that $c \notin \delta_\mu$. Then we shall also assume that $cons(v_0, v_1); \mu$ returns the same cell c. We call this assumption the *uniform cons property* and henceforth *cons* will be assumed to satisfy it.

Definition: The memory operations in $\mathbb{O}_{\mathfrak{A}}$, other than *eq*, are extended to partial memory object schemata in the following fashion.

$$\phi_i(\bar{v}\,;g) = \phi_i(\bar{v})\,;g \text{ if } \bar{v} \in \mathbf{Term}(\mathfrak{A}).$$

$$R_i^?(\bar{v}\,;g) = R_i^?(\bar{v})\,;g \text{ if } \bar{v} \in \mathbf{Term}(\mathfrak{A}).$$

$\phi_i(\bar{v})$ and $R_i^?(\bar{v})$ are complex terms unless $\bar{v} \in \mathbb{A}$

$$atom(v\,;g) = \begin{cases} \mathtt{T}\,;g & \text{if } v \in \mathbf{Term}(\mathfrak{A}), \\ \mathtt{NIL}\,;g & \text{if } v \in \mathbb{C}. \end{cases}$$

$$cons(v_0, v_1\,;g) = c\,;g_0 \quad \text{where} \quad c \notin \mathbf{Cells}_g \quad \text{and} \quad g_0 = g\{c \leftarrow [v_0, v_1]\}$$

$$car(c\,;g) = v_0\,;g \quad \text{given} \quad g(c) = [v_0, v_1]$$

$$cdr(c\,;g) = v_1\,;g \quad \text{given} \quad g(c) = [v_0, v_1]$$

If $g(c) = [v_0, v_1]$ then

$$rplaca(c, v\,;g) = c\,;g_0 \quad \text{where} \quad g_0 = g\{c \leftarrow [v, v_1]\}$$

$$rplacd(c, v\,;g) = c\,;g_0 \quad \text{where} \quad g_0 = g\{c \leftarrow [v_0, v]\}$$

5.3. The Symbolic Evaluation Relation $\gg^{\mathbb{S}}$

The time is ripe for us to launch into the details of the first step.

Definition: A *partial memory object description schema*, or *symbolic description* for short, is a triple

$$e(\bar{\alpha})\,;g(\bar{\alpha})\,;\Pi(\bar{\alpha})$$

such that

- $e(\bar{\alpha})$ is an expression with no free variables from $\mathbb{X}$ and $\bar{c}$ is the set of cells that occur in $e(\bar{\alpha})$.
- $g(\bar{\alpha})$ is a partial memory schema such that $\bar{c}\,;g$ is complete to a depth $r(e)$.
- $\Pi(\bar{\alpha})$ is a finite set of atomic and negated atomic $\mathcal{L}^{\mathfrak{A}}$ formula, in the variables $\bar{\alpha}$, consistent with $\mathbf{Th}(\mathfrak{A})$.

Note that since a partial memory object is a special partial memory object schema (with $\Pi = \emptyset$), the above definition remains valid in this special case. But, because of our conventions concerning meta-variables, when we say that

$$e\,;f$$

is a symbolic description we mean not only that the above conditions hold, but also that f is a partial memory object. The symbolic reduction relation is then defined in an analogous fashion to the $\gg$ relation. Even though most of the results in this chapter will pertain only to terms, we give the definition in the general case supposing that D is some fixed definition. Relative to this fixed definition we define $\gg^{\mathbb{S}}$ to be the smallest transitive relation containing $\rightarrow\!>^{\mathbb{S}}$. This in turn is defined to be the the smallest relation closed under the following rules. In what follows we use the word consistent to mean consistent with $\mathbf{Th}(\mathfrak{A})$. Recall that we let $v, v_0, \ldots, v_n, \ldots$ range over $\mathbb{C} \oplus \mathbf{Term}(\mathfrak{A})$.

Definition: The single step symbolic reduction relation is defined to be the smallest relation on symbolic descriptions satisfying the following conditions.

- **Primitive cases:**

$$eq(v_0, v_1)\,;g\,;\Pi \rightarrow\!>^{\mathbb{S}} \begin{cases} \texttt{NIL}\,;g\,;\Pi & \text{if } v_0 \neq v_1 \text{ and } v_0 \in \mathbb{V}, \\ \texttt{T}\,;g\,;\Pi & \text{if } v_0 = v_1 \text{ and } v_0 \in \mathbb{V}, \\ \texttt{T}\,;g\,;\Pi^+ & \text{if } v_i \in \mathbf{Term}(\mathfrak{A}) \text{ and } \Pi^+ \text{ is consistent}, \\ \texttt{NIL}\,;g\,;\Pi^- & \text{if } v_i \in \mathbf{Term}(\mathfrak{A}) \text{ and } \Pi^- \text{ is consistent}, \end{cases}$$

where $\Pi^+ = \Pi \cup \{v_0 = v_1\}$ and $\Pi^- = \Pi \cup \{v_0 \neq v_1\}$.

In the last two clauses we assume that one of v_0, v_1 is not in $\mathbb{V}$.

$$\texttt{if}(v_0, e_0, e_1);g;\Pi \rightarrow\!>^{\mathbb{S}} \begin{cases} e_0\,;g\,;\Pi & \text{if } v_0 \neq \texttt{NIL} \text{ and } v_0 \in \mathbb{V}, \\ e_1\,;g\,;\Pi & \text{if } v_0 = \texttt{NIL} \text{ and } v_0 \in \mathbb{V}, \\ e_0\,;g\,;\Pi^+ & \text{if } v_0 \in \mathbf{Term}(\mathfrak{A}) \text{ and } \Pi^+ \text{ is consistent}, \\ e_1\,;g\,;\Pi^- & \text{if } v_0 \in \mathbf{Term}(\mathfrak{A}) \text{ and } \Pi^- \text{ is consistent}, \end{cases}$$

where $\Pi^+ = \Pi \cup \{v_0 \neq \texttt{NIL}\}$ and $\Pi^- = \Pi \cup \{v_0 = \texttt{NIL}\}$.

In the last two clauses we assume that one of v_0, v_1 is not in $\mathbb{V}$.

$\texttt{seq}(e)\,;g\,;\Pi \rightarrow\!>^{\mathbb{S}} e\,;g\,;\Pi$

$\texttt{seq}(v_0, e_1, \ldots, e_m)\,;g\,;\Pi \rightarrow\!>^{\mathbb{S}} \texttt{seq}(e_1, \ldots, e_m)\,;g\,;\Pi$

$\texttt{let}\{y_1 \leftarrow v_1, \ldots, y_m \leftarrow v_m\}e\,;g\,;\Pi \rightarrow\!>^{\mathbb{S}} e\{y_1 \leftarrow v_1, \ldots, y_m \leftarrow v_m\}\,;g\,;\Pi$

$\vartheta(v_1, \ldots, v_n)\,;g\,;\Pi \rightarrow\!>^{\mathbb{S}} v_0\,;g_0\,;\Pi$

if ϑ is a memory operation and $\vartheta([v_1, \ldots, v_n]\,;g) = v_0\,;g_0$

$\vartheta(v_1, \ldots, v_n);g;\Pi \rightarrow\!>^{\mathbb{S}} e\{y_1 \leftarrow v_1, \ldots, y_n \leftarrow v_n\};g;\Pi$ if $\vartheta(y_1, \ldots, y_n) \leftarrow e$ is in D.

- **Congruence cases:** If $e_a\,;g_a\,;\Pi_a \rightarrow\!>^{\mathbb{S}} e_b\,;g\,;\Pi_b$ then

$\texttt{if}(e_a, e_{then}, e_{else})\,;g_a\,;\Pi_a \rightarrow\!>^{\mathbb{S}} \texttt{if}(e_b, e_{then}, e_{else})\,;g_b\,;\Pi_b$

$\texttt{seq}(e_a, \ldots)\,;g_a\,;\Pi_a \rightarrow\!>^{\mathbb{S}} \texttt{seq}(e_b, \ldots)\,;g_b\,;\Pi_b$

$$\texttt{let}\{y_1 \leftarrow v_1, \ldots, y_{j-1} \leftarrow v_{j-1}, y_j \leftarrow e_a, \ldots, y_m \leftarrow e_m\}e \,;\, g_{\mathrm{a}} \,;\, \Pi_{\mathrm{a}} \twoheadrightarrow^{\mathbb{S}}$$
$$\texttt{let}\{y_1 \leftarrow v_1, \ldots, y_{j-1} \leftarrow v_{j-1}, y_j \leftarrow e_b, \ldots, y_m \leftarrow e_m\}e \,;\, g_{\mathrm{b}} \,;\, \Pi_{\mathrm{b}}$$
$$\vartheta(v_1, \ldots, v_{j-1}, e_a, \ldots, e_m) \,;\, g_{\mathrm{a}} \,;\, \Pi_{\mathrm{a}} \twoheadrightarrow^{\mathbb{S}} \vartheta(v_1, \ldots, v_{j-1}, e_b, \ldots, e_m) \,;\, g_{\mathrm{b}} \,;\, \Pi_{\mathrm{b}}$$

We call $v_i \,;\, g_i \,;\, \Pi_i$ when $v_i \in \mathbb{C} \oplus \mathbf{Term}(\mathfrak{A})$ a *symbolic answer,* and say $e \,;\, g \,;\, \Pi$ *evaluates* to $v_i \,;\, g_i \,;\, \Pi_i$ when $e \,;\, g \,;\, \Pi \gg^{\mathbb{S}} v_i \,;\, g_i \,;\, \Pi_i$. It is important to note that if ϑ is a function from $\mathfrak{A}$ and $\bar{v} \notin \mathbf{Term}(\mathfrak{A})^{|\bar{v}|}$ then $\vartheta(\bar{v}) \notin \mathbf{Term}(\mathfrak{A})$ and $\vartheta(\bar{v}) \,;\, \mu$ will not denote. This explains the definition of a symbolic answer. Evaluation is no longer functional since the primitive *eq* and `if` rules can allow two distinct reductions. So suppose that $v_i \,;\, g_i \,;\, \Pi_i, i \in I$ are the set of symbolic answers of $e \,;\, g \,;\, \Pi$ (enumerated without repetition); then we can state several simple facts that we leave for the reader to verify.

Exercises:

0. If $e_0 \,;\, g_0 \,;\, \Pi_0 \twoheadrightarrow^{\mathbb{S}} e_1 \,;\, g_1 \,;\, \Pi_1$, then $e_1 \,;\, g_1 \,;\, \Pi_1$ is a partial memory object description scheme with the same vague cells.
1. If $i, j \in I$ are distinct then Π_i and Π_j are tautologically inconsistent.
2. If e is a total term, or even simply total on completions of g, then
$$\mathbf{Th}(\mathfrak{A}) \models (\bigwedge \Pi) \iff \bigvee_{i \in I} (\bigwedge \Pi_i).$$
3. $e \,;\, g \,;\, \Pi_i \gg^{\mathbb{S}} v_i \,;\, g_i \,;\, \Pi_i$ and this is the only evaluation possible in this case. This *monotonicity* property can be generalized as follows; suppose that
$$e_0 \,;\, g_0 \,;\, \Pi_0 \gg^{\mathbb{S}} e_1 \,;\, g_1 \,;\, \Pi_1$$
and that $\Pi_0 \subset \Pi_2 \subset \Pi_1 \subset \Pi_3$ are all consistent with $\mathbf{Th}(\mathfrak{A})$, then
$$e_0 \,;\, g_0 \,;\, \Pi_2 \gg^{\mathbb{S}} e_1 \,;\, g_1 \,;\, \Pi_1$$
and
$$e_0 \,;\, g_0 \,;\, \Pi_3 \gg^{\mathbb{S}} e_1 \,;\, g_1 \,;\, \Pi_3.$$
As we have already hinted, we will call these relations the monotonicity properties. They shall come in handy later.

We abbreviate $e(\bar{\alpha}) \,;\, g(\bar{\alpha}) \,;\, \emptyset$ to $e(\bar{\alpha}) \,;\, g(\bar{\alpha})$ so that a memory object description is just a special type of symbolic description, as is a partial memory object description. Furthermore $\gg^{\mathbb{S}}$ takes (partial) memory object descriptions to (partial) memory object descriptions, and so, on these objects we write $\gg$ rather than

$\gg^{\mathbb{S}}$. The following is a simple consequence of the above definition and thus this convention should cause no confusion.

Lemma A1: The following are equivalent:

1. $e\,;\mu\,;\emptyset \gg^{\mathbb{S}} v\,;\mu^*\,;\emptyset$.
2. $e\,;\mu \gg v\,;\mu^*$.

One consequence of the uniform *cons* property is that it makes the statement of the connection between symbolic evaluation on symbolic descriptions and partial memory objects particularly simple, as the following lemma demonstrates.

Lemma A2: Suppose that $e(\bar{\alpha})\,;g(\bar{\alpha})\,;\Pi(\bar{\alpha}) \gg^{\mathbb{S}} v(\bar{\alpha})\,;g_0(\bar{\alpha})\,;\Pi_0(\bar{\alpha})$. Then for any $\bar{a} \in \mathbb{A}$ we have that:

$$\mathfrak{A} \models \Pi_0[\bar{a}] \;\rightarrow\; e(\bar{a})\,;g(\bar{a}) \gg^{\mathbb{S}} v(\bar{a})\,;g_0(\bar{a}).$$

The situation is not quite as simple in the case of partial memory object descriptions and memory object descriptions, but here again the uniform *cons* property comes to the rescue.

Lemma A3:

1. Suppose that $e\,;f \gg v\,;f^*$ and μ is a completion of f with the property that δ_μ is disjoint from $\delta_{f^*} - \delta_f$. Then there is a completion μ^* of f^* such that $e\,;\mu \gg v\,;\mu^*$ with the added properties that $\mu^* = \mu$ on $\delta_\mu - \delta_f$ and $\delta_{\mu^*} = \delta_\mu \oplus (\delta_{f^*} - \delta_f)$.
2. Suppose that $e\,;\mu \gg v\,;\mu^*$, μ is a completion of f, $e\,;f$ is a partial memory object description and letting $m = |\delta_{\mu^*} - \delta_\mu|$ we have that

$$\mathtt{seq}(\underbrace{cons(\mathtt{T},\mathtt{T}),\ldots,cons(\mathtt{T},\mathtt{T})}_{m\ times})\,;f \gg c\,;f_m$$

where the $\mathtt{seq}$ consists of m *cons*es and δ_μ is disjoint from $\delta_{f_m} - \delta_f$. Then there exists an f^* such that $e\,;f \gg v\,;f^*$ and μ^* is a completion of f^*.

5.4. The Proofs of Theorems A and B

Theorem A: $\Delta^{+}_{\sim}(\mathbb{M}_{\mathfrak{A}})$ is recursive in $\mathbf{Th}^0(\mathfrak{A})$, the quantifier free part of $\mathbf{Th}(\mathfrak{A})$.

We begin by defining the algebraic counterparts of the equivalence relations on symbolic answers. In the following three definitions and, unless otherwise stated, assume that

1. $e_i(\bar{\alpha})\,;g(\bar{\alpha}) \gg^{\mathbb{S}} v_i(\bar{\alpha})\,;g_i(\bar{\alpha})\,;\Pi_i(\bar{\alpha})$ for $i \in 2$.

2. $\Pi_0(\bar{\alpha}) \cup \Pi_1(\bar{\alpha}) \cup \mathbf{Th}(\mathfrak{A})$ is consistent.
3. $V_i = \mathbf{Cells}_{g_i}(\delta_g * v_i) - \delta_g$ for $i \in 2$.

The first relation we define is $\simeq$ since it is substantially simpler than the remaining two.

Definition A1:($\simeq$) We define $v_0 \,;\, g_0 \,;\, \Pi_0 \simeq v_1 \,;\, g_1 \,;\, \Pi_1$ via h to mean that, putting $Y_i = v_i * \mathbf{Cells}_g$,

$$h : \mathbf{Values}_{g_0}(Y_0) \rightarrow \mathbf{Values}_{g_1}(Y_1)$$

is such that it maps

$$\mathbf{Atoms}_{g_0}(Y_0) \rightarrow \mathbf{Atoms}_{g_1}(Y_1).$$

It is a bijection from

$$V_0 \rightarrow V_1,$$

is the identity on $\mathbf{Cells}_g$, and $\forall c \in \mathbf{Cells}_g$ we also have $h \circ (v_0 \,;\, g_0) = (v_1 \,;\, g_1)$ and $h \circ (c \,;\, g_0) = (c \,;\, g_1)$ as partial functions.

The next two are somewhat more complicated and we first define them when neither $\mathbf{Cells}_{g_0}(v_0)$ nor $\mathbf{Cells}_{g_1}(v_1)$ contain any vague cells, and then extend the definition to the general case.

Definition A2: ($\cong$)

1. Suppose that neither $\mathbf{Cells}_{g_0}(v_0)$ nor $\mathbf{Cells}_{g_1}(v_1)$ contain any vague cells, then we define $v_0 \,;\, g_0 \,;\, \Pi_0 \cong v_1 \,;\, g_1 \,;\, \Pi_1$ via h to mean

$$h : \mathbf{Values}_{g_0}(v_0) \rightarrow \mathbf{Values}_{g_1}(v_1)$$

maps

$$\mathbf{Atoms}_{g_0}(v_0) \rightarrow \mathbf{Atoms}_{g_1}(v_1).$$

It is a bijection from

$$\mathbf{Cells}_{g_0}(v_0) \rightarrow \mathbf{Cells}_{g_1}(v_1),$$

and $h \circ (v_0 \,;\, g_0) = (v_1 \,;\, g_1)$ as partial functions.

2. In the case when there are vague cells we define $v_0 \,;\, g_0 \,;\, \Pi_0 \cong v_1 \,;\, g_1 \,;\, \Pi_1$ via h to mean that $v_0 \,;\, g_0 \,;\, \Pi_0 \simeq v_1 \,;\, g_1 \,;\, \Pi_1$ via h.

Definition A3: ($\equiv$)

1. Suppose that neither $\mathbf{Cells}_{g_0}(v_0)$ nor $\mathbf{Cells}_{g_1}(v_1)$ contain any vague cells, then we define $v_0 \,;\, g_0 \,;\, \Pi_0 \equiv v_1 \,;\, g_1 \,;\, \Pi_1$ via h to mean

$$h : \mathbf{Atoms}_{g_0}(v_0) \rightarrow \mathbf{Atoms}_{g_1}(v_1)$$

is such that $(v_0 ; g_0)$ and $(v_1 ; g_1)$ have the same domain, call it Z. $\forall \sigma \in Z$ if either $(v_0 ; g_0)_\sigma$ or $(v_1 ; g_1)_\sigma$ is in $\mathbf{Term}(\mathfrak{A})$ then $h((v_0 ; g_0)_\sigma) = (v_1 ; g_1)_\sigma \in \mathbf{Th}(\mathfrak{A})$.

2. In the case where there are vague cells we define $v_0 ; g_0 ; \Pi_0 \equiv v_1 ; g_1 ; \Pi_1$ via h to mean, putting $Y_i = v_i * \mathbf{Cells}_g$,

$$h : \mathbf{Atoms}_{g_0}(Y_0) \to \mathbf{Atoms}_{g_1}(Y_1)$$

is such that not only $v_0 ; g_0 ; \Pi_0 \equiv v_1 ; g_1 ; \Pi_1$ via h in the sense of 1. above but also $c ; g_0 ; \Pi_0 \equiv c ; g_1 ; \Pi_1$ via h for every $c \in \mathbf{Cells}_g$, again in the sense of 1. above. Furthermore we require that if $(v_0 ; g_0)_\sigma$ (respectively $(c ; g_0)_\sigma$) is a vague cell then $(v_1 ; g_1)_\sigma$ (respectively $(c ; g_1)_\sigma$) is exactly the same cell, and vice versa.

Remarks:

- Note that in each case h is unique and consequently we often simply write $v_0;g_0;\Pi_0 \sim v_1;g_1;\Pi_1$ and leave h implicit. We also write $v_0;g_0;\Pi_0 \not\sim v_1;g_1;\Pi_1$ when no such h exists.
- In each case it should be clear that the existence or non-existence of such an h is recursive in $\mathbf{Th}^\circ(\mathfrak{A})$. In the case of $\equiv$ the result at the end of 3.1 is useful since it extends easily to partial memory objects.

Definition A4: Suppose that $v_0 ; g_0 ; \Pi_0 \sim v_1 ; g_1 ; \Pi_1$ via h then we define

$$\Gamma(h)$$

to be the set

$$\{t_0 = t_1 \mid t_i \in \mathbf{Term}(\mathfrak{A}) \wedge h(t_0) = t_1\}.$$

Lemma A4: Suppose that

- $e_i(\bar{a}) ; g(\bar{a}) \gg^{\mathbb{S}} v_i(\bar{a}) ; g_i(\bar{a}) ; \Pi_i(\bar{a})$ for $i \in 2$.
- $\bar{a} \in \mathbb{A}^{|\bar{a}|}$ is such that $\mathfrak{A} \models (\Pi_0 \cup \Pi_1)[\bar{a}]$,

then the following are equivalent

1. $v_0 ; g_0 ; \Pi_0 \sim v_1 ; g_1 ; \Pi_1$ via h and $\mathfrak{A} \models \Gamma(h)[\bar{a}]$
2. For any completion, μ, of $g(\bar{a})$ we have $e_0(\bar{a}) ; \mu \sim e_1(\bar{a}) ; \mu$.

Proof of Lemma A4: The lemma is naturally divided into three cases depending on which equivalence relation it is stated for. The first two cases, being $\simeq$ and $\cong$ in that order, we do in detail and leave the third as an exercise for the reader.

Case 1. Strong Isomorphism: Assume the hypotheses of the lemma for $\bar{a} \in \mathbb{A}^{|\bar{a}|}$; we must prove two things and begin by proving that 1. implies 2.

1. $\rightarrow$ 2.: By lemma A2 we have that $e_i(\bar{a})\,;g(\bar{a}) \gg v_i(\bar{a})\,;g_i(\bar{a}),\quad i \in 2$. It now clearly suffices to prove that 2. holds for any μ such that δ_μ is disjoint from $\delta_{g_i} - \delta_g$. Thus choose such a μ. Consequently by lemma A3 there exists completions μ_i of $g_i(\bar{a})$ such that

1. $e_i(\bar{a})\,;\mu \gg v_i(\bar{a})\,;\mu_i$
2. $\mu_i = \mu$ on $\delta_\mu - \delta_g$
3. $\delta_{\mu_i} = \delta_\mu \oplus (\delta_{g_i} - \delta_g)$.

Now the assumption that $v_0(\bar{\alpha})\,;g_0(\bar{\alpha})\,;\Pi_0 \sim v_1(\bar{\alpha})\,;g_1(\bar{\alpha})\,;\Pi_1$ via h induces a map

$$h^*\colon \mathbf{Values}_{g_0(\bar{a})}(v_0(\bar{a}) * \delta_g) \rightarrow \mathbf{Values}_{g_1(\bar{a})}(v_1(\bar{a}) * \delta_g)$$

such that h^* maps V_0 to V_1 and is the identity on $\mathbf{Cells}_g$. Furthermore the assumption that

$$\mathfrak{A} \models \Gamma(h)[\bar{a}]$$

implies that h^* is the identity on $\mathbf{Atoms}_{g_0(\bar{a})}(v_0(\bar{a}) * \delta_g)$ which is thus the same as $\mathbf{Atoms}_{g_1(\bar{a})}(v_1(\bar{a}) * \delta_g)$. Now extend h^* so that it is not only the identity on $\mathbb{A}$ but also on $\delta_\mu - \delta_g$. The resulting map, which we will continue to call h^*, is a bijection by the assumption that δ_μ is disjoint from $\delta_{g_i} - \delta_g$. It is now routine to show that $v_0(\bar{a}) * \delta_\mu\,;\mu_0 \cong v_1(\bar{a}) * \delta_\mu\,;\mu_1$ via h^* is a consequence of 2. and 3. above. $\Box_{1.\rightarrow 2.}$

2. $\rightarrow$ 1.: This direction is almost immediate. Choose μ to be the completion of $g(\bar{a})$ that assigns to any vague cell in g the value [NIL, NIL]. The fact that $e_0(\bar{a});\mu \simeq e_1(\bar{a});\mu$ via h^*, say, and the uniqueness of any h satisfying the first part of 1. is easily seen to imply two things. Firstly, there is such an h. Secondly, $\mathfrak{A} \models \Gamma(h)[\bar{a}]$, sincee h must induce h^*, which is the identity on $\mathbf{Atoms}_{g_0(\bar{a})}(v_0(\bar{a}) * \delta_g)$. $\Box_{2.\rightarrow 1.}$ $\Box_{\textbf{Case 1}}$

Case 2. Lisp Isomorphism: The case where there are no vague cells presents no challenge. For assume the hypotheses of the lemma. Then by lemma A2 we have that $e_i(\bar{a})\,;g(\bar{a}) \gg v_i(\bar{a})\,;g_i(\bar{a}),\quad i \in 2$; furthermore choosing μ such that δ_μ is disjoint from $\delta_{g_i} - \delta_g$, we have by lemma A3 that there exists completions μ_i of $g_i(\bar{a})$ such that

1. $e_i(\bar{a})\,;\mu \gg v_i(\bar{a})\,;\mu_i$
2. $\mu_i = \mu$ on $\delta_\mu - \delta_g$
3. $\delta_{\mu_i} = \delta_\mu \oplus (\delta_{g_i} - \delta_g)$.

Furthermore, since there are no vague cells,

4. $(v_i(\bar{a}) \,;\, g_i(\bar{a})) = (v_i(\bar{a}) \,;\, \mu_i)$ as partial functions.

These, particularly the latter, force the desired equivalence, as the reader can easily verify for themselves. Consequently we only concentrate on the cases when there are vague cells. In this case we have already proved that 1. implies 2. when $\sim$ is $\simeq$, and thus we need only prove that 2. implies 1. when there are vague cells. So suppose that $\mathbf{Cells}_{g_0(\bar{a})}(v_0(\bar{a}))$ contains vague cells and that 2. is true. Let

$$c_0, \ldots, c_m$$

be all the vague cells in g and assume without loss of generality that

$$c_0 \in \mathbf{Cells}_{g_0(\bar{a})}(v_0(\bar{a})).$$

Now choose distinct atoms

$$b_0, \ldots, b_m$$

such that $(\forall i \leq m)\ b_i \notin \mathbf{Atoms}_{g_0(\bar{a})}$, and supposing that $\mathbf{Cells}_g = [c_1^*, \ldots, c_k^*]$, where $k = |\mathbf{Cells}_g|$, choose distinct cells

$$c_{m+1}, \ldots, c_{m+k}$$

disjoint from $\mathbf{Cells}_{g_0} \cup \mathbf{Cells}_{g_1}$. Now consider the completion, μ, of $g(\bar{a})$ which satisfies the following:

- $\mu(c_0) = [c_{m+1}, b_0]$
- $\mu(c_i) = [b_i, b_i]$ for $1 \leq i \leq m$
- $\mu(c_{m+i}) = [c_i^*, c_{m+i+1}]$ for $1 \leq i < k$
- $\mu(c_{m+k}) = [c_k^*, \mathtt{NIL}]$

The structure of μ on $\delta_\mu - \delta_g$ is illustrated in figure 12. Now by lemma A3 there exists completions μ_i of $g_i(\bar{a})$ such that

1. $e_i(\bar{a}) \,;\, \mu \gg v_i(\bar{a}) \,;\, \mu_i$
2. $\mu_i = \mu$ on $\delta_\mu - \delta_g$
3. $\delta_{\mu_i} = \delta_\mu \oplus (\delta_{g_i} - \delta_g)$.

Furthermore since $e_0(\bar{a}) \,;\, \mu \cong e_1(\bar{a}) \,;\, \mu$ we have that there exists an h such that $h : v_0(\bar{a}) \,;\, \mu_0 \cong v_1(\bar{a}) \,;\, \mu_1$, and because $c_0 \in \mathbf{Cells}_{g_0}(v_0)$ we know that $c_0 \in \mathbf{Cells}_{g_1}(v_1)$. Also by the choice of b_0, $h(c_0) = c_0$. Further by the second consequence of lemma A3 above and by the choice of the b_i we must have that $h(c_i) = c_i$ for $0 \leq i \leq m + k$. This in turn implies that $h(c_i^*) = c_i^*$ and thus the desired conclusion follows routinely. $\Box_{2,\rightarrow 1}$. $\Box_{\text{Case 2}}$.

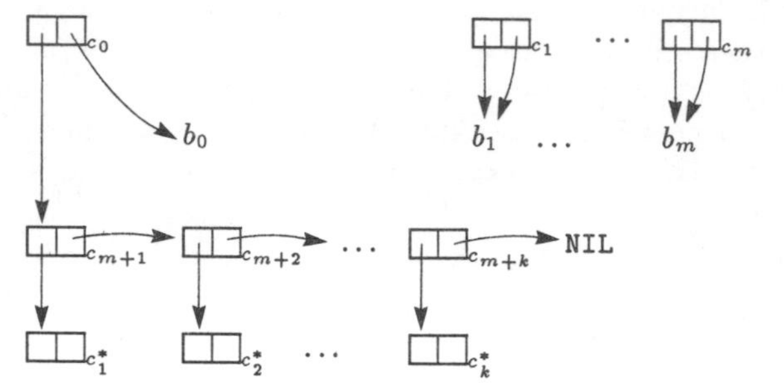

Figure 12. The Structure of μ on $\delta_\mu - \delta_g$

As already mentioned we leave the proof of the third case, i.e. when $\sim$ is $\equiv$, to the reader. Thus we have proved what we have claimed. $\square_{\textbf{Lemma A4}}$

Definition A5: Call a collection

$$\{\bar{v}_i(\bar{\alpha})\,;\,g_i(\bar{\alpha})\}_{i\in I}$$

exhaustive if for each $i, j \in I$ we have that $\bar{v}_i(\bar{\alpha})\,;g_i(\bar{\alpha})$ is a partial memory object schema, $|\bar{v}_i| = |\bar{v}_j|$, and for every $\bar{v};\mu \in \mathbb{M}_{\mathfrak{A}}$ such that $|\bar{v}| = |\bar{v}_i|$ we have that $\exists \bar{a} \in \mathbb{A}$ and $\exists i \in I$ and a completion, μ_i, of $g_i(\bar{a})$ with the property that $\bar{v}\,;\mu \cong \bar{v}_i(\bar{a})\,;\mu_i$.

Proof of Theorem A: Now given $e_j(\bar{x}) \in \mathbb{E}_{\mathfrak{A}}, j \in 2$, choose a finite exhaustive set of partial memory object schemata

$$\{\bar{v}_i(\bar{\alpha})\,;\,g_i(\bar{\alpha})\}_{i\in I}$$

such that for each $i \in I$ we have that $\bar{v}_i(\bar{\alpha})\,;\,g_i(\bar{\alpha})$ is complete to a depth $\mathbf{Max}\{r(e_0), r(e_1)\}$, and $|\bar{x}| = |\bar{v}_i|$. Let

$$\{v_{ij}^k(\bar{\alpha})\,;\,g_{ij}^k(\bar{\alpha})\,;\,\Pi_{ij}^k(\bar{\alpha})\}_{j\in 2, i\in I, k\in K_{ij}}$$

be the set of all symbolic answers of $e_j(\bar{v}_i(\bar{\alpha}));g_i(\bar{\alpha})$ Clearly the sets K_{ij} are finite. The first thing to observe is that

$$(\forall i \in I)(\mathfrak{A} \models (\forall \bar{\alpha})(\bigvee_{k_0\in K_{i0}}(\bigwedge \Pi_{i0}^{k_0})) \Longleftrightarrow (\bigvee_{k_1\in K_{i1}}(\bigwedge \Pi_{i1}^{k_1}))$$

is equivalent to the fact that for any $\bar{v}\,;\mu \in \mathbb{M}_{\mathfrak{A}}^{|\bar{x}|}$ $e_0(\bar{v})\,;\mu$ will denote iff $e_1(\bar{v})\,;\mu$ denotes. Consequently we can assume that for each $k_0 \in K_{i0}$ there is a $k_1 \in K_{i1}$

such that $\Pi_{i0}^{k_0} \cup \Pi_{i1}^{k_1}$ is consistent with $\mathbf{Th}^{\circ}(\mathfrak{A})$ and visa versa, for otherwise $e_0 \sim e_1$ would have no hope of being true. Thus to check whether

$$e_0(\bar{x}) \sim e_1(\bar{x}) \in \Delta_{\sim}^{+}(\mathbb{M}_{\mathfrak{A}})$$

we need only check for each $i \in I$, $k_0 \in K_{i0}$ and $k_1 \in K_{i1}$ such that $\Pi_{i0}^{k_0} \cup \Pi_{i1}^{k_1}$ is consistent with $\mathbf{Th}^{\circ}(\mathfrak{A})$ whether or not

$$v_{i0}^{k_0}(\bar{\alpha})\,;\, g_{i0}^{k_0}(\bar{\alpha})\,;\, \Pi_{i0}^{k_0}(\bar{\alpha}) \sim v_{i1}^{k_1}(\bar{\alpha})\,;\, g_{i1}^{k_1}(\bar{\alpha})\,;\, \Pi_{i1}^{k_1}(\bar{\alpha}).$$

□**Theorem A**

As a corollary to the proof of Theorem A we now prove the unbounded isomorphism theorem.

Theorem B: If $e_i(\bar{x}), i \in 2$ are primitive terms such that

$$e_0(\bar{x}) \cong e_1(\bar{x})$$

and the $e_i(\bar{x})$ are unbounded, then there is a term $\theta(\bar{x})$ which is total on $\mathbb{M}_{\mathfrak{A}}^{|\bar{x}|}$ and takes only the values T or NIL such that

1. $e_0(\bar{x}) \simeq e_1(\bar{x})$ on $\{\bar{v}\,;\,\mu \mid \theta(\bar{v})\,;\,\mu \gg \mathtt{T}\,;\,\mu\}$
2. $e_i(\bar{x})$ is bounded on $\{\bar{v}\,;\,\mu \mid \theta(\bar{v})\,;\,\mu \gg \mathtt{NIL}\,;\,\mu\}$

Remarks:

- Actually the term $\theta(\bar{x})$ does not contain the operations *cons*, *rplacd* or *rplaca* and so we have for any $\bar{v};\mu \in \mathbb{M}_{sexp}{}^{|\bar{x}|}$ that $\theta(\bar{v});\mu \gg \mathtt{T};\mu$ or $\theta(\bar{v});\mu \gg \mathtt{NIL};\mu$.
- 1. can be stated equivalently as $\mathtt{if}(\theta(\bar{x}), e_0(\bar{x}), \mathtt{T}) \simeq \mathtt{if}(\theta(\bar{x}), e_1(\bar{x}), \mathtt{T})$
- 2. can also be stated as $\mathtt{if}(\theta(\bar{x}), \mathtt{T}, e_i(\bar{x}))$ is bounded.
- Also note that as a consequence we also have that $\theta(\bar{x})$ evaluates to the value T for arbitrarily large arguments, or in symbols

$$(\forall n \in \mathbb{N})(\exists \bar{v}\,;\,\mu \in \mathbb{M}_{sexp})(\theta(\bar{v})\,;\,\mu \gg \mathtt{T}\,;\,\mu) \wedge (|\mathbf{Cells}_{\mu}(\bar{v})| > n).$$

- Finally, it also falls out of the proof that on $\{\bar{v};\mu \mid \theta(\bar{v});\mu \gg \mathtt{NIL};\mu\}$ the possible values of $e_i(\bar{x})$ are bounded by $n = 2^m + m$, where $m = \mathbf{Max}_{i\in 2}\{r(e_i(\bar{x}))\}$.

Another corollary of the proof is the following criteria for a term to be unbounded.

Corollary: If $e(\bar{x})$ is a term and for some $\bar{v}\,;\mu$ we have that $e(\bar{v})\,;\mu \gg v^*\,;\mu^*$ with

$$|\mathbf{Cells}_{\mu^*}(v^*)| > 2^{r(e(\bar{x}))} + r(e(\bar{x}))$$

then $e(\bar{x})$ is unbounded.

Proof of Theorem B: Suppose that $e_0(\bar{x}) \cong e_1(\bar{x})$ and choose a finite exhaustive set of partial memory object schemata $\{\bar{v}_i(\bar{\alpha})\,;g_i(\bar{\alpha})\}_{i\in I}$ that are complete to a depth $\mathbf{Max}\{r(e_0), r(e_1)\}$ and assume that $e_j(\bar{v}_i)\,;g_i \gg^{\mathbb{S}} \{v_k\,;g_k\,;\Pi_k\}_{k\in K_{ij}}$. The first thing to observe is that

$$(\forall i\in I)(\mathfrak{A} \models (\forall\bar{\alpha})((\bigvee_{k_0\in K_{i0}}(\bigwedge\Pi_{k_0})) \Longleftrightarrow (\bigvee_{k_1\in K_{i1}}(\bigwedge\Pi_{k_1})))$$

since e_0 is defined exactly when e_1 is. Refine these answers, using the monotonicity properties of $\gg^{\mathbb{S}}$, to sets $\{v_k^j\,;g_k^j\,;\Pi_k\}_{k\in K_i}$, for $j,i\in 2$. So that $e_j(\bar{v}_i)\,;g_i\,;\Pi_k \gg^{\mathbb{S}} v_k^j\,;g_k^j\,;\Pi_k$ for any $k\in K_i$. Now let $\theta(\bar{x})$ be any total $\mathbb{M}_{\mathfrak{A}}$ term such that the following are equivalent:

1. $\theta(\bar{v})\,;\mu \gg \mathtt{T}\,;\mu$.
2. $\exists i\in I, \exists\bar{a}\in\mathbb{A}^{|\bar{\alpha}|}, \exists k\in K_i$ such that
   - $\mathfrak{A} \models \Pi_k[\bar{a}]$.
   - $\bar{v}\,;\mu$ is a completion of $\bar{v}_i(\bar{a})\,;g_i(\bar{a})$.
   - $\mathbf{Cells}_{g_k^j}(v_k^j)$ contains vague cells.

Such a term, indeed actually a predicate in the sense of chapter 3, is easily constructed by examining the symbolic answers

$$\{v_k^j\,;g_k^j\,;\Pi_k\}_{k\in K_i, i\in I, j\in 2}.$$

It is then a simple application of lemma A4 to show that, for such θ:

Lemma B1: $\mathtt{if}(\theta(\bar{x}), e_0(\bar{x}), \mathtt{T}) \simeq \mathtt{if}(\theta(\bar{x}), e_1(\bar{x}), \mathtt{T})$.

□**Theorem B**

5.5. The Proof of Theorem C

Theorem C: For every $n \in \mathbb{N}$ we have that $\mathbf{Th}^n_{\simeq}(\mathbb{M}_{\mathfrak{A}})$ is recursive in $\mathbf{Th}^n(\mathfrak{A})$.

The first result needed in the proof is the following converse to lemma A4. It is important to note that this result does not hold for either of the extensional equivalence relations.

Lemma C1: Suppose that

- $e_i(\bar{\alpha})\,;g(\bar{\alpha}) \gg^{\mathbb{S}} v_i(\bar{\alpha})\,;g_i(\bar{\alpha})\,;\Pi_i(\bar{\alpha})$ for $i \in 2$.
- $v_0\,;g_0\,;\Pi_0 \not\simeq v_1\,;g_1\,;\Pi_1$
- $\bar{a} \in \mathbb{A}^{|\bar{\alpha}|}$ is such that $\mathfrak{A} \models (\Pi_0 \cup \Pi_1)[\bar{a}]$

then for any completion, μ, of $g(\bar{a})$ we have $e_0(\bar{a})\,;\mu \not\simeq e_1(\bar{a})\,;\mu$.

Proof of Lemma C1: It is easy to show that $e_0(\bar{a})\,;\mu \simeq e_1(\bar{a})\,;\mu$ implies that $v_0\,;g_0\,;\Pi_0 \simeq v_1\,;g_1\,;\Pi_1$ when $\bar{a} \in \mathbb{A}^{|\bar{\alpha}|}$ is such that $\mathfrak{A} \models (\Pi_0 \cup \Pi_1)[\bar{a}]$. We leave it to the reader to work out the details. $\square_{\mathbf{Lemma\ C1}}$

Lemma C2: Let t be the term rank of $\phi[\bar{x}] \in \mathcal{L}^{\mathfrak{A}}_{\simeq}$, $\bar{v}\,;\mu \in \mathbb{M}_{\mathfrak{A}}^{|\bar{x}|}$ and take f to be a partial memory such that $(\bar{v}{\downarrow_i}\,;\mu)_\sigma = (\bar{v}{\downarrow_i}\,;f)_\sigma$, for any $|\sigma| \le t$; also for simplicity assume that μ is a completion of f, then the following are equivalent

1. $\mu \models \phi[\bar{v}]$
2. $f \models \phi[\bar{v}]$,

here we define $f \models \phi[\bar{v}]$ to mean that every completion, μ_0, of f satisfies $\mu_0 \models \phi[\bar{v}]$.

Proof of Lemma C2: Clearly 2. implies 1. consequently we need only prove that 1. implies 2. This is done by induction on the complexity of ϕ.

Base Case: Suppose that ϕ is $e_0 \simeq e_1$ and that $\mu \models \phi[\bar{v}]$. We shall leave the case when neither $e_0(\bar{v})\,;\mu$ nor $e_1(\bar{v})\,;\mu$ denote as an exercise. It is a simpler application of lemma A3 than the one we consider. Consequently we shall assume that

$$e_i(\bar{v})\,;\mu \gg w_i\,;\mu_i, i \in 2.$$

Let $M = \mathbf{Max}_{i\in 2}|\delta_{\mu_i} - \delta_\mu|$ and without loss of generality assume that

$$\mathtt{seq}(\underbrace{cons(\mathtt{T},\mathtt{T}),\ldots,cons(\mathtt{T},\mathtt{T})}_{M\ conses})\,;f \gg c\,;f_M$$

and that δ_μ is disjoint from $\delta_{f_M} - \delta_f$. Consequently by lemma A3 there are $f_i, i \in 2$ such that

$$e_i(\bar{v})\,,f \gg w_i\,,f_i, i \in 2,$$

and μ_i is a completion of f_i. This step required the initial assumption on $\bar{v}\,;f$ to ensure that $e_i(\bar{v});f$ was a partial memory object description. Now since $e_0(\bar{v});\mu \simeq e_1(\bar{v})\,;\mu$ there exists an $h{:}\mathbb{V} \to \mathbb{V}$ a bijection which is the identity on $\mathbb{A} \cup \delta_\mu$ such that

1. $h : w_0\,;\mu_0 \cong w_1\,;\mu_1$,
2. $h : \delta_\mu\,;\mu_0 \cong \delta_\mu\,;\mu_1$.

Let h^* be the restriction of h to $\mathbb{A} \cup \delta_f$ and choose μ^* to be any completion of f with δ_{μ^*} disjoint from δ_{f_M}. Again by lemma A3 we have that there exists μ_i^*, completions of f_i^*, such that

$$e_i(\bar{v})\,;\mu^* \gg w_i^*\,;\mu_i^*, i \in 2.$$

Put

$$h^{**} = \begin{cases} h^* & \text{on } \delta_{h^*} \\ id & \text{on } \delta_{\mu_0^*} - \delta_{f_0} \\ g & \text{elsewhere.} \end{cases}$$

where g is any bijection from the free storage of μ_0^* to the free storage μ_1^* and id is the identity. It is then routine to show that

1. $h^{**} : w_0\,;\mu_0^* \cong w_1\,;\mu_1^*$,
2. $h^{**} : \delta_{\mu^*}\,;\mu_0^* \cong \delta_{\mu^*}\,;\mu_1^*$.

□**Base Case.**

Induction Case: The boolean cases are, as usual, immediate. Thus we are left with the case when

$$\phi = \exists x \psi.$$

Suppose that $\mu \models \exists x\psi[\bar{v}]$. Then there is a $\mu^* \sqsupseteq \mu$ and a $w \in \mathbb{A} \cup \delta_{\mu^*}$ such that $\mu^* \models \psi[w^* * \bar{v}]$. Let f^* be the following extension of f:

$$\delta_{f^*} = \delta_f \cup \{c \mid \exists\sigma |\sigma| \leq t \ \wedge \ (w\,;\mu^*)_\sigma = c\}$$

and $f^* = \mu^*$ on δ_{f^*}. By the induction hypothesis we have that $f^* \models \psi[w^* * \bar{v}]$. It is then routine to show that $f \models \exists x\psi[\bar{v}]$. □**Lemma C2**

Lemma C3: Suppose that $\phi[\bar{x}] \in \mathcal{L}^{\mathfrak{A}}_{\simeq}$ is a formula of term rank t and quantifier rank n, $\bar{v}(\bar{a})\,;g(\bar{a})$ is complete to a depth t. Then we can effectively find a finite set, $\Pi(\bar{a})$, of formulas from $\mathcal{L}^{\mathfrak{A}}$ of alternation rank n such that the following are equivalent for any $\bar{a} \in \mathbb{A}^{|\bar{a}|}$:

1. $\mathfrak{A} \models \Pi[\bar{a}]$,
2. $g(\bar{a}) \models \phi[\bar{v}(\bar{a})]$.

Proof of Lemma C3: The proof is by induction on the complexity of ϕ, beginning with the case when ϕ is $e_0 \simeq e_1$. Assume that $e_j(\bar{v})\,;\, g \gg^{\mathbb{S}} \{v_k\,;\, g_k\,;\, \Pi_k\}_{k \in K_j}$, for $j \in 2$. For each j_0, j_1 with $j_i \in K_i$ let $\Gamma_{j_0 j_1}$ be $\bigwedge \Gamma(h)$ if

$$v_{j_0}\,;\, g_{j_0}\,;\, \Pi_{j_0} \simeq v_{j_1}\,;\, g_{j_1}\,;\, \Pi_{j_1} \text{ via } h$$

and $\alpha_0 \neq \alpha_0$ otherwise. Finally putting

$$\Pi = \bigvee_{k_0 \in K_0, k_1 \in K_1} ((\bigwedge \Pi_{k_0}) \wedge (\bigwedge \Pi_{k_1}) \wedge \Gamma_{k_0 k_1})) \vee \neg(\bigvee_{k_j \in K_j, j \in 2} (\bigwedge \Pi_{k_j}))$$

we have the desired result. The boolean cases are again omitted because of their triviality. We finish off by doing the case when ϕ is $\exists y \psi$, and ψ is of less alternation rank. The general case when ϕ is $\exists \bar{y} \psi$ is just as simple, modulo a mess of notation. Let

$$w_0\,;\, g_0(\bar{\alpha} * \bar{\alpha}^*), \ldots, w_d\,;\, g_d(\bar{\alpha} * \bar{\alpha}^*)$$

be such that

1. $g_i(\bar{\alpha} * \bar{\alpha}^*) \sqsupseteq g(\bar{\alpha})$,
2. $w_i\,;\, g_i$ is complete to a depth t,
3. For any $\bar{\alpha}, \mu$ and $w \in \mathbb{A} \cup \delta_\mu$ with $\mu \sqsupseteq g(\bar{\alpha})$ there is a g_s and a $\bar{\alpha}^*$ such that μ is (isomorphic to) a completion of $g_s(\bar{\alpha} * \bar{\alpha}^*)$.

Now by induction let Π_d be the set of formulas obtained for $\psi(y, \bar{x})$ and $w_s * \bar{v}\,;\, g_s(\bar{\alpha} * \bar{\alpha}^*)$. The desired formula is then just:

$$\exists \bar{\alpha}^* (\Pi_0 \vee \Pi_1 \vee \ldots \vee \Pi_d)$$

$\Box$**Lemma C3** $\Box$**Theorem C**

5.6. The Proof of Theorem D

Theorem D: Regardless of the complexity of $\mathbf{Th}(\mathfrak{A})$, when $\sim$ is either $\cong$ or $\equiv$ we can interpret true arithmetic in $\mathbf{Th}_\sim(\mathbb{M}_\mathfrak{A})$. Consequently $\mathbf{Th}_\sim(\mathbb{M}_\mathfrak{A})$ is exactly Δ^1_1 in $\mathbf{Th}(\mathfrak{A})$.

We prove the theorem for $\mathcal{L}^\mathfrak{A}_\cong$; exactly the same proof works for $\mathcal{L}^\mathfrak{A}_\equiv$. To prove that we can interpret true arithmetic in $\mathbf{Th}_\cong(\mathbb{M}_\mathfrak{A})$ we define the relation xEy as follows. It is always false when y is an atom. Supposing that y is a cell, then xEy abbreviates the conjunction of the following two sentences:

1. $atom(x) \simeq \texttt{NIL}$ implies

$$(\exists x_1)\neg(y \cong \texttt{seq}(rplaca(x, x_1), y).$$

2. $atom(x) \simeq \texttt{T}$ implies

$$(\exists w)(atom(w) \cong \texttt{NIL} \wedge wEy \wedge (eq(car(w), x) \cong \texttt{T} \vee eq(cdr(w), x) \cong \texttt{T})).$$

Lemma D1: The following are equivalent

1. $\mu \models (x_0 E x_1)[v_0, c_1]$
2. v_0 is an element of $\mathbf{Values}_\mu(c_1)$.

Thus xEy expresses the fact x is a *substructure* of y. The idea is now quite simple. We shall identify the integer n with anything isomorphic to the value of

$$\begin{array}{l} \texttt{let}\{x_0 \leftarrow cons(\texttt{NIL}, \texttt{NIL})\} \\ \quad \texttt{let}\{x_1 \leftarrow cons(x_0, x_0)\} \\ \qquad \ldots \\ \qquad\quad \texttt{let}\{x_{n-1} \leftarrow cons(x_{n-2}, x_{n-2})\}x_{n-1}, \end{array}$$

making the convention that the number 0 is identified with NIL. The first thing to observe is that if x represents the integer n then $cons(x, x)$ represents the integer $n+1$. Also notice that *equality*, between representations of numbers, is simply $\cong$. Expressing that z represents the sum of x and y is achieved by saying $\exists w$ such that $w \cong z$, yEw, and either $x \cong \texttt{NIL}$ and $z \cong y$ or else ($x \ncong \texttt{NIL}$) and

$$(\exists uEw)(car(u) \cong y \wedge x \cong \texttt{seq}(rplaca((rplacd(u, \texttt{NIL}), \texttt{NIL}), w).$$

What remains is for us to show that we can recognize those objects representing numbers and that we can express that the representation of one number is the product of the representation of two others. The first is trivial since x represents a number iff either

$$x \cong \texttt{NIL}$$

or else

$$\texttt{NIL}\ E\ x \wedge \forall y(yEx \rightarrow (y \cong \texttt{NIL} \vee eq(car(y), cdr(y)) \cong \texttt{T})).$$

We abbreviate this formula by $int(x)$. To express multiplication we need to develop a little notation. We write $x = y$ to mean that $eq(x, y) \cong \texttt{T}$, and $x \cap y = \emptyset$ to mean

$$\neg\exists z(atom(z) \cong \texttt{NIL} \wedge zEx \wedge zEy).$$

Now supposing that x and y represent numbers, we write

$$z : x \to y$$

to mean that z codes up a function from $x+1$ to $y+1$. We express it by saying that $\forall x_0$ such that $atom(x_0) \simeq$ NIL and $x_0 E x$, there exists a unique $z_0 E z$ such that $car(z_0) = x_0$ and $cdr(z_0) E y$. It is an easy exercise to show that we can also express that such a z in fact codes up an injection from x to y. Given that $z : x \to y$ is true we write $z(x_0)$ to denote the cdr of the unique $z_0 E z$ that satisfies $car(z_0) = x_0$ for any $x_0 E x$. The predicate $\otimes(x_m, x_n, x_{m\times n})$ is defined to express:

0. x_m, x_n and $x_{m\times n}$ all represent numbers.
1. x_m, x_n and $x_{m\times n}$ share no cells with one another. This is done by using the predicate $x \cap y = \emptyset$.
2. $\exists z : x_m \to x_{m\times n}$ such that the following hold

$$z(x_m) = x_{m\times n},$$

$$z \text{ is an injection},$$

$$x_n \cong \mathtt{seq}(rplaca(rplacd(z(cdr(x_m)), \mathtt{NIL}), \mathtt{NIL}), z(x_m)),$$

$$(\exists y E x_m)(y = 1 \wedge cdr(z(y)) = x_n),$$

And finally $(\forall y_0, y_1 E x_m)((y_0 = y_1 + 1 \wedge y_0 \neq x_m) \to$

$$x_n \cong \mathtt{seq}(rplaca(rplacd(z(y_1), \mathtt{NIL}), \mathtt{NIL}), z(y_0)).$$

The situation so described is illustrated in figure 13.

Lemma D2: z represents the product of the representations x and y iff $\exists z_0, x_0, y_0$ such that $z \cong z_0, x \cong x_0, y \cong y_0$ and $\otimes(x_0, y_0, z_0)$.

□**Theorem D**

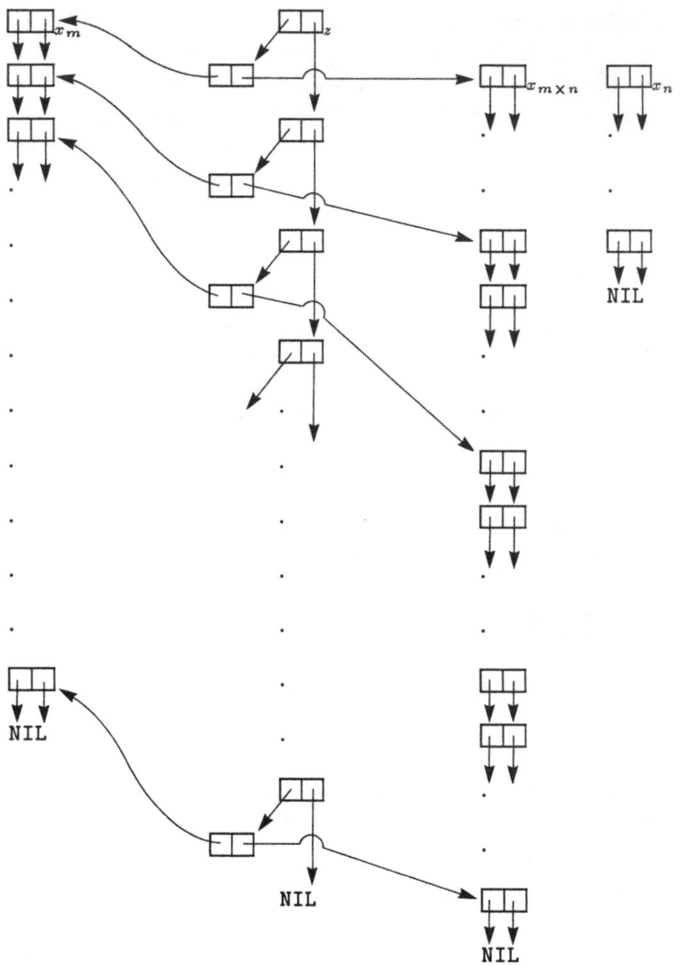

Figure 13. The Structure of z and $x_m, x_n, x_{m \times n}$

5.7. Previous Results

As we mentioned earlier the underlying data structure of pure Lisp can be thought of as a traditional first order structure:

$$< \mathbb{S}_{wf}, cons, car, cdr, atom, equal, \mathtt{T}, \mathtt{NIL} > .$$

It is thus a *static* object with quite nice properties. For example the theory of this structure has been shown to be decidable , (Tenney, 1972), (McKinsey and Tarski, 1946). Also in (Oppen, 1978) it is shown that the quantifier free part of this theory is decidable in linear time. Before we deal in any depth with the results of Oppen, and of Nelson and Oppen, (Nelson and Oppen, 1978a and 1978b), we shall generalize the decidability result above.

Definition: We define $\mathcal{L}^{\mathfrak{A}}_{pure}$ as follows. $\mathcal{L}^{\mathfrak{A}}_{pure}$ is a restricted version of $\mathcal{L}^{\mathfrak{A}}_{\equiv}$. We let

$$\mathbb{O}^{\mathfrak{A}}_{pure} = \{atom, atom{:}eq, cons, car, cdr, \phi_0, \ldots \phi_n, R^?_0, \ldots R^?_m\}.$$

The language of $\mathcal{L}^{\mathfrak{A}}_{pure}$ is then restricted to those expressions of $\mathcal{L}^{\mathfrak{A}}_{\equiv}$ that only contain operations from $\mathbb{O}^{\mathfrak{A}}_{pure}$. The quantifiers are similarly restricted to $\mathbb{M}_{wf}$. We then define $\mathbf{Th}_{pure}(\mathbb{M}_{\mathfrak{A}})$ to be the set of sentences true in this fragment of $\mathcal{L}^{\mathfrak{A}}_{\equiv}$. The generalization of the above decidability result is simply stated as:

Theorem: $\mathbf{Th}_{pure}(\mathbb{M}_{\mathfrak{A}})$ is recursive in $\mathbf{Th}(\mathfrak{A})$.

We begin by eliminating the need to consider the control primitives; `seq`, `let` and `if`. Firstly we define

$$e\downarrow \iff \exists x(e \equiv x).$$

Notice that the following schemata are valid in $\mathcal{L}^{\mathfrak{A}}_{pure}$:

1. $\mathtt{let}_{0\le i\le n}\{y_i \leftarrow e_i\}e \equiv e\{y_i \leftarrow e_i\}_{0\le i\le n}$ where the R.H.S. denotes the expression obtained by simultaneously replacing free occurences of y_i by e_i in e, provided that $e_i\downarrow$ for $0 \le i \le n$.
2. $\neg(\mathtt{let}_{0\le i\le n}\{y_i \leftarrow e_i\}e)\downarrow$ whenever there is an $0 \le i \le n$ such that $\neg(e_i\downarrow)$.
3. $\mathtt{seq}(e_0, \ldots, e_n) \equiv e_n$, as long as $e_0\downarrow, \ldots e_{n-1}\downarrow$
4. $\neg(\mathtt{seq}(e_0, \ldots, e_n)\downarrow)$, whenever there is an $0 \le i \le n$ such that $\neg(e_i\downarrow)$.
5. $\neg(\mathtt{if}(e_0, e_1, e_2)\downarrow)$, whenever $\neg(e_0\downarrow)$.
6. $\mathtt{if}(e_0, e_1, e_2) \equiv e_1$ whenever $e_0\downarrow$ and $e_0 \not\equiv \mathtt{NIL}$.
7. $\mathtt{if}(e_0, e_1, e_2) \equiv e_2$ whenever $e_0 \equiv \mathtt{NIL}$.

As we mentioned in Chapter 3 an equational theory for `if` can be given. For explicit results see (Bloom and Tindell, 1983) or (Guessarian and Meseguer, 1985). To state this equational theory we let

$$\bot = car(\mathtt{T}).$$

The rules of equational deduction are simply reflexivity, symmetry, transitivity, compatability with the operations, and full invariance; see (Bloom and Tindell, 1983). In their system, however, `if` is defined somewhat differently, namely

$$\mathtt{if}(x, y, z) = \begin{cases} z & \text{if } x = \mathtt{NIL} \\ y & \text{if } x = \mathtt{T} \\ \bot & \text{otherwise} \end{cases}$$

In other words to reduce our `if` to theirs we simply restrict ourselves to instances of the form

$$\mathtt{ifn}(eq(x, \mathtt{NIL}), y, z).$$

The axioms are then easily stated:

8. $\mathtt{if}(\mathtt{T}, x, y) \equiv x$
9. $\mathtt{if}(x, x, y) \equiv \mathtt{if}(x, \mathtt{T}, y)$
10. $\mathtt{if}(\mathtt{NIL}, x, y) \equiv y$
11. $\mathtt{if}(x, y, x) \equiv \mathtt{if}(x, y, \mathtt{NIL})$
12. $\mathtt{if}(\bot, x, y) \equiv \bot$
13. $\mathtt{if}(x, \bot, \bot) \equiv \bot$
14. **Premise Interchange Axiom:**

$$\mathtt{if}(x, \mathtt{if}(y, z, u), \mathtt{if}(y, v, w)) \equiv \mathtt{if}(y, \mathtt{if}(x, z, v), \mathtt{if}(x, u, w)).$$

15. **Redundancy Axiom:**

$$\mathtt{if}(x, \mathtt{if}(x, y, z), w) \equiv \mathtt{if}(x, y, w).$$

16. **Redundancy Axiom:**

$$\mathtt{if}(x, y, \mathtt{if}(x, y, w)) \equiv \mathtt{if}(x, y, w).$$

17. **Premise Simplification Axiom:**

$$\mathtt{if}(\mathtt{if}(x, y, z), u, v) \equiv \mathtt{if}(x, \mathtt{if}(y, u, v), \mathtt{if}(z, u, v)).$$

The facts 1. through 7. together with the observation that

$$\neg(e\downarrow) \iff (e \equiv car(\mathtt{T})),$$

provides us with a simple method of defining a translation, Γ, from $\mathcal{L}^{\mathfrak{A}}_{pure} \to \mathcal{L}^{\mathfrak{A}}_{pure}$ such that $\Gamma(\phi)$ contains none of the above control primitives and

$$(\Gamma(\phi) \leftrightarrow \phi) \in \mathbf{Th}_{pure}(\mathbb{M}_{\mathfrak{A}}).$$

It suffices as a consequence of the above that we need only show that the first-order theory of

$$< \mathbb{S}_{wf}, \phi_0, \ldots, \phi_n, R^?_0, \ldots, R^?_m, cons, car, cdr, atom, \mathtt{T}, \mathtt{NIL} >$$

is recursive in the first order theory of

$$\mathfrak{A} =< \mathbb{A}, \phi_0, \ldots, \phi_n, R^?_0, \ldots R^?_m, \mathtt{T}, \mathtt{NIL} > .$$

Rather than prove this directly it is much more convenient to prove:

Theorem: The first-order theory of

$$< \mathbb{S}_{wf}, \phi^*_0, \ldots, \phi^*_n, R^*_0, \ldots, R^*_m, cons, car, cdr, atom, \mathtt{T}, \mathtt{NIL} >$$

is recursive in the first order theory of

$$\mathfrak{A} =< \mathbb{A}, \phi^*_0, \ldots, \phi^*_n, R^*_0, \ldots R^*_m, \mathtt{T}, \mathtt{NIL} >,$$

both structures being regarded a relational.

This theorem follows from the following *decomposition* theorem. Suppose that $\mathfrak{F}$ is an operation on relational structures, such that if $\mathfrak{A}$ is a τ-structure then $\mathfrak{F}(\mathfrak{A})$ is a $(\tau_F \cup \tau)$-structure with the following properties:

1. A, the domain of $\mathfrak{A}$, is a unary relation in $\mathfrak{F}(\mathfrak{A})$. In what follows we will write $A\bar{x}$ to abbreviate the conjunction of Ax_i for $0 \leq i < |\bar{x}|$.
2. A is a set of *total indiscernables* in $\mathfrak{F}(\mathfrak{A})\downarrow_{\tau_F}$, see (Chang and Keisler, 1973) page 414.
3. $\mathfrak{A}$ is a submodel of $\mathfrak{F}(\mathfrak{A})\downarrow_{\tau}$.
4. If $\varrho \in \tau$ then

$$\mathfrak{F}(\mathfrak{A}) \models (\forall \bar{x}, y)(\underbrace{\varrho(\bar{x}) = y}_{\text{as a relation}} \rightarrow (A\bar{x} \wedge Ay)).$$

Theorem: $\mathbf{Th}(\mathfrak{F}(\mathfrak{A}))$ is recursive in the two theories $\mathbf{Th}(\mathfrak{A})$ and $\mathbf{Th}(\mathfrak{F}(\mathfrak{A})\downarrow_{\tau_F})$.

Proof of Theorem: Let T be the following theory

1. $\mathbf{Th}(\mathfrak{F}(\mathfrak{A})\downarrow_{\tau_F}$, a τ_F-theory.
2. $\mathbf{Th}(\mathfrak{A})\downarrow_A$, a $(\tau \cup \{A\})$-theory.
3. $\{(\forall \bar{x})(R\bar{x} \rightarrow A\bar{x}) \mid R \in \tau\}$, a $(\tau \cup \{A\})$-theory.

Here $\mathbf{Th}(\mathfrak{A})\downarrow_A$ is the set of sentences obtained from $\mathbf{Th}(\mathfrak{A})$ by relativizing all quantifiers to A. Let T_0 be the axioms given by 1, and let T_1 be those of 2, 3, and those of T_0 that are in the language $\{A\}$. Thus putting $\tau_0 = \tau_F$ and $\tau_1 = \tau \cup \{A\}$ we have that T_i is a complete τ_i-theory. We now show that $T = T_0 \cup T_1$ is a complete $(\tau_0 \cup \tau_1)$-theory. Clearly it is recursive in the two theories $\mathbf{Th}(\mathfrak{A})$ and $\mathbf{Th}(\mathfrak{F}(\mathfrak{A})\downarrow_{\tau_F})$.

Let $\Delta_A(\bar{x})$ denote the formula expressing that $A\bar{x}$ as well as the fact that the $\bar{x}$ are distinct. Also let $\Delta_A^c(\bar{x})$ denote the formula expressing that $\neg Ax_i$ for $0 \leq i < |\bar{x}|$, as well as the fact that the $\bar{x}$ are distinct.

Lemma: If $\phi_i(\bar{x}, \bar{y})$ is a quantifier free τ_i formula, for $i \in 2$ and

$$T \vdash (\exists \bar{x}\bar{y})(\Delta_A(\bar{x}) \wedge \Delta_A^c(\bar{y}) \wedge \phi_i(\bar{x}, \bar{y}))$$

for $i \in 2$, then

$$T \vdash (\exists \bar{x}\bar{y})(\Delta_A(\bar{x}) \wedge \Delta_A^c(\bar{y}) \wedge \phi_0(\bar{x}, \bar{y}) \wedge \phi_1(\bar{x}, \bar{y})).$$

Proof of Lemma: By completeness we have

$$T_i \vdash (\exists \bar{x}\bar{y})(\Delta_A(\bar{x}) \wedge \Delta_A^c(\bar{y}) \wedge \phi_i(\bar{x}, \bar{y}))$$

and by the indiscernability of A we have that

$$T_0 \vdash (\forall \bar{x})(\exists \bar{y})(\Delta_A(\bar{x}) \rightarrow (\Delta_A^c(\bar{y}) \wedge \phi_0(\bar{x}, \bar{y}))).$$

Furthermore if $\mathfrak{B} \models T_1$ and $\bar{b}_0, \bar{b}_1$ are such that

$$\mathfrak{B} \models \Delta_A^c(\bar{b}_i)$$

for $i \in 2$ then there is an automorphism of $\mathfrak{B}$ which is the identity on A and maps $\bar{b}_0$ to $\bar{b}_1$. Thus

$$T_1 \vdash (\exists \bar{x})(\forall \bar{y})(\Delta_A^c(\bar{y}) \rightarrow (\Delta_A(\bar{x}) \wedge \phi_1(\bar{x}, \bar{y}))).$$

Since

$$T \vdash (\exists \bar{x})\Delta_A(\bar{x})$$

and

$$T \vdash (\exists \bar{y})\Delta^c_A(\bar{y})$$

the result follows. $\square_{\mathbf{Lemma.}}$

The proof of the Theorem is now quite straightforward. Firstly observe that

Lemma: If $\mathfrak{B}_0$ and $\mathfrak{B}_1$ are both models of T then

$$\mathbf{Th}(\mathfrak{B}_0)_{B_0} \cup \mathbf{D}(\mathfrak{B}_1)_{B_1}$$

is consistent. Here $\mathbf{D}(\mathfrak{B})_B$ is the diagram of $\mathfrak{B}$.

Proof of Lemma: By compactness it suffices to prove that if $\mathfrak{B}_0 \models \psi$ and $\mathfrak{B}_1 \models (\exists \bar{z})\phi(\bar{z})$, where $\phi(\bar{x})$ is the conjunction of atomic and negated atomic formula, then $\psi \wedge (\exists \bar{z})\phi(\bar{z})$ is consistent. It now suffices to prove that

$$\mathfrak{B}_0 \models (\exists \bar{z})\phi(\bar{z}).$$

Split ϕ into $\phi_0(\bar{x}, \bar{y})$ and $\phi_1(\bar{x}, \bar{y})$ such that

$$\mathfrak{B}_1 \models (\exists \bar{x}\bar{y})(\Delta_A(\bar{x}) \wedge \Delta^c_A(\bar{y}) \wedge \phi_0(\bar{x}, \bar{y}) \wedge \phi_1(\bar{x}, \bar{y}))$$

and

$$\mathfrak{B}_1 \models (\exists \bar{x}\bar{y})(\Delta_A(\bar{x}) \wedge \Delta^c_A(\bar{y}) \wedge \phi_0(\bar{x}, \bar{y}) \wedge \phi_1(\bar{x}, \bar{y})) \rightarrow (\exists \bar{z})\phi(\bar{z}).$$

Thus

$$\mathfrak{B}_1 \models (\exists \bar{x}\bar{y})(\Delta_A(\bar{x}) \wedge \Delta^c_A(\bar{y}) \wedge \phi_i(\bar{x}, \bar{y}))$$

and

$$\mathfrak{B}_0 \models (\exists \bar{x}\bar{y})(\Delta_A(\bar{x}) \wedge \Delta^c_A(\bar{y}) \wedge \phi_i(\bar{x}, \bar{y}))$$

and the previous lemma gives the result. $\square_{\mathbf{Lemma.}}$

The theorem is then proven by simply constructing an alternating chain of models. $\square_{\mathbf{Theorem}}$

That the first order theory of

$$< \mathbb{S}_{wf}, cons, car, cdr, atom, equal, \mathtt{T}, \mathtt{NIL} >$$

is decidable does not immediately carry over to the non-well-founded case. The acyclicity plays an important role, since it is a well known result that the theory of a pairing function is undecidable. By a pairing function we simply mean a function, which we shall call *cons*, that satisfies the axioms

$$(\forall z)(\exists x, y)(cons(x, y) = z),$$

$$(\forall x, y, w, z)(cons(x, y) = cons(w, z) \rightarrow (x = w \wedge y = z)).$$

The work of Nelson and Oppen, (Oppen, 1978), (Nelson and Oppen, 1978a) and (Nelson and Oppen, 1978b), bridges this gap somewhat by studying quantifier free variations on this theory. Note that in the above theory the functions *car* and *cdr* are definable using quantifiers. For this and other reasons we include the functions explicitly in the quantifier free case. If we included them in the above system, the relevant axioms would be

$$(\forall x)(cons(car(x), cdr(x)) = x)$$

$$(\forall x, y)(car(cons(x, y)) = x)$$

$$(\forall x, y)(cdr(cons(x, y)) = y).$$

The relation *atom?* and the constant `NIL` also appear in the variations. We shall use equality to mean Lisp equality in the following sentences. In (Nelson and Oppen, 1978a) they give a decision procedure for the following set of axioms

$$car(cons(x, y)) = x$$

$$cdr(cons(x, y)) = y$$

$$\neg atom?(x) \rightarrow cons(car(x), cdr(x)) = x$$

$$\neg atom?(cons(x, y)).$$

Note that the axioms do not restrict the semantics to acyclic objects, so that a formula like

$$car(x) = x$$

is satisfiable. The decision procedure is based on determining the *congruence closure* of an equivalence relation $\sim$ on a directed graph with labeled vertices. It decides a conjunction of n atomic and negated atomic formula in $O(n^2)$ time. They also show that when the result of applying either *car* or *cdr* to an atom is specified the problem (of deciding a conjunction of n atomic and negated atomic formula) then becomes NP complete. For this last result the axioms they consider are

$$car(cons(x, y)) = x$$

$$cdr(cons(x, y)) = y$$

$$x \neq \texttt{NIL} \rightarrow cons(car(x), cdr(x)) = x$$

$$cons(x, y) \neq \texttt{NIL}.$$

On the other hand, when one adds axioms of acyclicity to the basic group a linear decision procedure is possible. The acyclicity axioms are all those formulas of the form

$$\theta(x) \neq x$$

where θ is any finite composition of the selector functions *car* and *cdr*.

5.7.1. Open Problems

Two related problems which we have not answered here are

1. Is $\mathbf{Th}^{\circ}_{\sim}(\mathsf{M}_{\mathfrak{A}})$ recursive in $\mathbf{Th}^{\circ}(\mathfrak{A})$, for $\sim$ either $\equiv$ or $\cong$?
2. Is $\mathbf{Th}^{+}_{\sim}(\mathsf{M}_{\mathfrak{A}})$ recursive in $\mathbf{Th}^{\circ}(\mathfrak{A})$, for $\sim$ either $\equiv$ or $\cong$, where $\mathbf{Th}^{+}_{\sim}(\mathsf{M}_{\mathfrak{A}})$ is the positive universal fragment of $\mathbf{Th}_{\sim}(\mathsf{M}_{\mathfrak{A}})$?

Chapter 6

Fragments of Lisp

In this chapter we use the equivalence relations to study the fragments of first-order Lisp introduced earlier. Recall that we defined three different sets of memory operations on $\mathbb{M}_{sexp}$, namely

$$\mathbb{O}_{sexp} = \{int, atom, add1, sub1, eq, cons, car, cdr, rplaca, rplacd\}$$

$$\mathbb{O}_{pure} = \{int, atom, add1, sub1, atom{:}eq, cons, car, cdr\}$$

$$\mathbb{O}_{pure+} = \{int, atom, add1, sub1, eq, cons, car, cdr\}$$

As usual we shall denote the memory structure with operations $\mathbb{O}_{sexp}$ simply by $\mathbb{M}_{sexp}$. To remind the reader we call the memory structure that has operations $\mathbb{O}_{pure}$ the *pure Lisp* memory structure and denote it by $\mathbb{M}_{pure}$. The memory structure with operations $\mathbb{O}_{pure+}$ is denoted by $\mathbb{M}_{pure+}$. Recall that the following program defines *eq* in terms of *atom:eq*, *atom* and *rplaca*, thus these are the only natural fragments.

```
defined:eq(x, y) ←
    if(or(atom(x), atom(y)),
      atom:eq(x, y),
      let{oldx ← car(x), oldy ← car(y)}
        seq(rplaca(x, T),
            rplaca(y, NIL),
            let{answer ← atom:eq(car(x), car(y))}
              seq(rplaca(x, oldx),
                  rplaca(y, oldy),
                  answer)))
```

Notice that these memory structures all have the same set of memories, consequently a simple comparison of functions definable in each structure is possible. In this section we examine some aspects of this comparison. We can summarize our results as follows. Firstly we show that any function definable in one of these fragments can actually be defined in any other fragment unless there is an obvious reason preventing this. There are only two such reasons. This result gives emphasis to the practical observation that the use of *eq* usually only increases speed, while the use of *rplaca* and *rplacd* improves space.

Secondly we relate the two equivalence relations, isomorphism and Lisp equality, on $\mathbb{M}_{sexp}$ to these fragments. We show that they are related in the sense that the behavior of a function in one of these fragments depends only on the equivalence class(es) of its arguments, for the appropriate equivalence relation. In the case of $\mathbb{M}_{pure}$ the appropriate relation is Lisp equality, while for $\mathbb{M}_{pure^+}$ and $\mathbb{M}_{sexp}$ it is isomorphism. In the $\mathbb{M}_{pure}$ case this indiscernability with respect to Lisp equality has many consequences. Because of the weakness of the equivalence relation one can define a natural non-trivial topology on the quotient space. Using this topology we can then prove two things. The first is that any purely definable function is continuous with respect to this topology; this has the immediate consequence of excluding many well-known functions from being purely definable. The second result in effect demonstrates that pure functions are essentially trivial on non well-founded objects, in that they are definable without recursion in an open neighborhood of any point. This again has the immediate consequence of excluding many functions from the already shrinking class of purely definable functions.

6.1. Equivalence Relations Revisited

We now give more model theoretic definitions of the two extensional equivalence relations . This is done by showing that they are maximal equivalence relations that are *indiscernable* with respect to the behavior of the functions defined in these fragments. In the following discussion L is either *pure*, *pure*$^+$ or *sexp*.

Definition: An equivalence relation on $\mathbb{M}_L$, $\sim$, is said to be an *L-congruence* if the following two conditions are met:

- $(\forall\, a_0, a_1 \in \mathbb{A})\ ((a_0\ ;\mu_0 \sim a_1\ ;\mu_1) \rightarrow (a_0 = a_1))$.
- If ϑ is a unary function defined in the L-definition D and $v_0\,;\mu_0 \sim v_1\,;\mu_1$ then whenever

$$\vartheta(v_0)\,;\mu_0 \gg^D w_0\ ;\mu_0^*$$

we must have that $\exists\ w_1\ ;\ \mu_1^*$ with

$$\vartheta(v_1)\ ;\ \mu_1 \gg^D w_1\ ;\ \mu_1^*$$

and

$$w_0\ ;\ \mu_0^* \sim w_1\ ;\ \mu_1^*.$$

An L-congruence is thus an equivalence relation that is simply equality on $\mathbb{A}$ and has the added property that unary L-functions preserve the relation. The model-theoretic definition of Lisp equality and isomorphism begins with the following observation.

Fact 2: There is a maximum L-congruence, which we denote by $\equiv_L$.

Theorem: $\equiv_{pure}$ is simply Lisp equality while $\equiv_{pure^+}$ and $\equiv_{sexp}$ are just isomorphism.

Proof of Theorem: The fact that $\equiv_{pure^+}$ and $\equiv_{sexp}$ are just $\cong$ follows easily from the proposition in 3.1. The proof for Lisp equality we delay until the next section. $\square_{\textbf{Theorem}}$

Recall that in Chapter 3 we proved two results. The first stated that isomorphism was roughly the smallest equivalence relation extending equality on atoms that was preserved by the destructive Lisp operations. The second stated that strong isomorphism was the weakest equivalence relation extending Lisp equality that had a substitution theorem. A similar result holds for Lisp equality, namely

Theorem: Restricting ourselves to $\mathbb{M}_{pure}$, suppose that $\sim$ is an equivalence relation on memory objects, memory object descriptions and expressions such that:

0. $e_0(\bar{v}_0)\ ;\ \mu_0 \sim e_1(\bar{v}_0)\ ;\ \mu_0$ implies that either both sides fail to denote, or else they denote memory objects which are $\sim$-related.
1. $(\forall \bar{v}\ ;\ \mu \in \mathbb{M}_{pure})(e_0(\bar{v})\ ;\ \mu \sim e_1(\bar{v})\ ;\ \mu) \iff e_0(\bar{x}) \sim e_1(\bar{x})$.
2. $(\forall\ a_0, a_1 \in \mathbb{A})\ ((a_0\ ;\ \mu_0 \sim a_1\ ;\ \mu_1) \rightarrow (a_0 = a_1))$.
3. The relation $\sim$ satisfies Leibniz's Law Suppose that $e_0(\bar{x}), e_1(\bar{x}), e(\bar{x}, y) \in \mathbb{M}_{pure}$. Then
$$e_0(\bar{x}) \sim e_1(\bar{x}) \rightarrow e(\bar{x}, e_0(\bar{x})) \sim e(\bar{x}, e_1(\bar{x})).$$

Then

$$e_0 \sim e_1 \rightarrow e_0 \equiv e_1.$$

6.2. The Structure of $\mathbb{M}_{pure}$ Definable Functions

We now concentrate on $\mathbb{M}_{wf}$ beginning with the following two remarks. $\mathbb{M}_{wf}$ factored out by $\equiv$, which we denote by $\mathbb{S}_{wf}$, is canonically isomorphic to the structure one obtains by closing $\mathbb{A}$ under a pairing operation; see for example (Moschovakis, 1969). Hence the celebrated isomorphism

$$\mathbb{S}_{wf} \cong \mathbb{A} \oplus (\mathbb{S}_{wf} \otimes \mathbb{S}_{wf}).$$

Secondly, for any memory object $v\,;\mu \in \mathbb{M}_{wf}$ there is a closed $\mathbb{M}_{pure}$ term e, i.e one with no free variables, which contains only the operation *cons*, and of course no function symbols, such that $e;\emptyset \gg v^*;\mu^*$ and $v;\mu \cong v^*;\mu^*$. Here $\emptyset$ denotes the empty memory. If we do not include the `let` construct in the set of terms, then we can only obtain $\equiv$ in this last result. Note that this result essentially means that the Skolem hull of $\mathbb{M}_{pure}$ or $\mathbb{M}_{pure+}$ over $\mathbb{A}$, being those objects constructible by terms with constants from $\mathbb{A}$, is $\mathbb{M}_{wf}$.

Fact 3: The following are equivalent.

1. $v_0\,;\mu_0 \in \mathbb{M}_{wf}$
2. There is a closed term e_0 in $\mathbb{M}_{pure}$ such that

$$e_0\,;\emptyset \gg v_1\,;\mu_1 \cong v_0\,;\mu_0$$

3. There is a closed term e_0 in $\mathbb{M}_{pure+}$ such that

$$e_0\,;\emptyset \gg v_1\,;\mu_1 \cong v_0\,;\mu_0$$

Proof of 1. → 2.:

Choose $v_0\,;\mu_0 \in \mathbb{M}_{wf}$. We prove this direction by induction on the number of shared cells in $\mathbf{Cells}_{\mu_0}(v_0)$, a shared cell being simply a cell $c \in \mathbb{C}$ for which there is more than one $\sigma \in \delta_{(v_0;\mu_0)}$ such that $(v_0\,;\mu_0)_\sigma = c$.

Base Case: This itself is proved by induction on $\mathbf{Cells}_{\mu_0}(v_0)$. The base case is then when $v_0 \in \mathbb{A}$ and the corresponding term is simply the constant symbol denoting v_0. The induction case is just as simple, letting $v_a = (v_0\,;\mu_0)_0$ and $v_d = (v_0\,;\mu_0)_1$ we can apply the induction hypothesis to obtain e_a and e_d. The required term is then $cons(e_a, e_d)$. It is because $v_0\,;\mu_0$ is well-founded and has no shared structure that enables us to conclude that this term evaluates to a memory object isomorphic to $v_0\,;\mu_0$. $\Box_{\textbf{Base Case}}$

Induction Step: Let the shared cells in $v_0\,;\mu_0$ be $c_0, \ldots c_n$ and assume that 1. implies 2. for objects with less structure sharing. By well-foundedness at least one of the c_i is such that $c_j \notin \mathbf{Cells}_{\mu_0}(c_i)$ whenever $j \neq i$. Let c_k be one such cell and let a_k be some atom that does not occur in $v_0 \,;\, \mu_0$. Now let $v_0^k \,;\, \mu_0^k$ be the memory object that is obtained by altering all the cells that contain c_k so that they now contain a_k. The shared structure in $v_0^k \,;\, \mu_0^k$ is simply $\{c_j \mid j \in n+1, j \neq k\}$. Thus we can use the induction hypothesis to obtain e_0^k. The required term is then

$$\mathtt{let}\{x_k \leftarrow e_k\}e_0^{k*}$$

where e_k is the term for $c_k \,;\, \mu_0$ and e_0^{k*} is the term obtained by replacing all occurences of a_k by x_k. That this term has the desired property is easily derived from the fact that e_0^k works for $v_0^k \,;\, \mu_0^k$.

$\square_{1.\rightarrow 2.}$

2. $\rightarrow$ 1.: This is a simple consequence of the fact that the pure memory operations preserve well-foundedness. That 2 is equivalent to 3 we take as self-evident. $\square_{\mathbf{Fact\ 3}}$.

Exercise: Remove the assumption that $\mathbb{A}$ is infinite from the above proof.

To prove the theorem following fact 2 and other results concerning the behavior of $\mathbb{M}_{pure}$ definable functions we need to develop some notation. In this section we write $e(v_0, \ldots, v_n)$ to mean that the elements of $\mathbb{V}$ that occur in e are amongst the v_i. Sometimes we tacitly assume the converse, namely that every v_i occurs in e. We now define a finite approximation to the relation $\equiv$, used in (Gordon, 1973) to show that certain well known Lisp functions are not definable using a certain *List iteration* functional; we shall use it in a slightly different manner to obtain similar results.

Definition: For $v_0, v_1 \in \mathbb{V}$ we say v_0 is *pointwise Lisp equal* to v_1 written, $v_0 \equiv_0 v_1$, iff either v_0 and $v_1 \in \mathbb{C}$ or else $v_0 = v_1$. Using this we define the notion of $v_0 \,;\, \mu_0$ being *pointwise Lisp equal to a depth n*, to mean that:

$$(\forall \sigma \in \cup_{i\in 2}\delta_{(v_i;\mu_i)})(|\sigma| \leq n \longrightarrow (v_0 \,;\, \mu_0)_\sigma \equiv_0 (v_1 \,;\, \mu_1)_\sigma).$$

We denote Lisp equality to a depth n by

$$v_0 \,;\, \mu_0 \equiv_n v_1 \,;\, \mu_1$$

and more generally if $\bar{v}_0 = [v_0^0, v_0^1, \ldots, v_0^m]$ and $\bar{v}_1 = [v_1^0, v_1^1, \ldots, v_1^m]$ then we write

$$\bar{v}_0 \,;\, \mu_0 \equiv_n \bar{v}_1 \,;\, \mu_1$$

to mean that $v_0^i \,;\, \mu_0 \equiv_n v_1^i \,;\, \mu_1$ for every $i \in m+1$.

Definition: We define the quotient spaces $\mathbb{S}_{pure}$ and $\mathbb{S}_{sexp}$ as follows:

itmx1. $\mathbb{S}_{pure} \underset{\text{df}}{=} \mathbb{M}_{sexp}/\equiv$.

2. $\mathbb{S}_{sexp} \underset{\text{df}}{=} \mathbb{M}_{sexp}/\cong$.

We now study $\mathbb{S}_{pure}$ in a little more detail. Our first step is to define a topology on it; this is done by providing the space with a metric.

Definition: Using $\equiv_n$ we can define a function $\mathbf{d}$ from $\mathbb{M}^{(2)}_{sexp}$ to the reals, $\mathbb{R}$, as follows:

$$\mathbf{d}(v\,;\mu, v^*\,;\mu^*) = \begin{cases} 0 & \text{if } v\,;\mu \equiv v^*\,;\mu^* \\ k^{-1} & \text{if } k \text{ is the least } n \text{ such that } v\,;\mu \not\equiv_n v^*\,;\mu^* \end{cases}$$

Notice that $\mathbf{d}$ is a metric on $\mathbb{S}_{pure}$, and a pseudo-metric on $\mathbb{M}_{sexp}$. With that in mind we define the notion of an open ball. For any $v^*\,;\mu^*$ and any $\epsilon > 0$ let

$$\mathbf{U}_\epsilon(v^*\,;\mu^*)$$

be the open ball of radius ϵ centered at $v^*\,;\mu^*$. Sometimes we regard $\mathbf{U}_\epsilon(v^*\,;\mu^*)$ as a subset of $\mathbb{M}_{sexp}$ rather than a subset of $\mathbb{S}_{pure}$, context should prevent confusion. By defining the distance between $[v_1, \ldots, v_n]\,;\mu$ and $[v_1^*, \ldots, v_n^*]\,;\mu^*$ to be

$$\mathbf{Max}_{1 \le i \le n} \ \mathbf{d}(v_i\,;\mu, v_i^*\,;\mu^*)$$

we obtain a metric for $\mathbb{S}^{(n)}_{pure}$ in the product topology.

As we have already remarked, $\mathbb{S}_{wf}$ is canonically isomorphic to the structure one obtains by closing $\mathbb{A}$ under a pairing object in the Moschovakis style, (Moschovakis, 1969). The functions that are induced on $\mathbb{S}_{wf}$ by $\mathbb{M}_{pure}$ definable functions are exactly the *prime computable* functions. $\mathbb{S}_{pure}$ is another story, however. The equivalence classes of $\equiv$ on non well-founded objects are somewhat richer than their well-founded counterparts. And the pure language is not strong enough to define many functions. The next fact states some elementary properties of the topology on $\mathbb{S}_{pure}$ induced by the metric $\mathbf{d}$.

Fact 4:

0. $\mathbb{S}_{pure}$ is not complete with this metric and hence not compact.

1. $\mathbb{S}_{wf}$ is the set of isolated points in $\mathbb{S}_{pure}$.

2. $\mathbb{S}_{wf}$ is dense in $\mathbb{S}_{pure}$.

3. $\mathbb{S}_{pure} - \mathbb{S}_{wf}$ is perfect, in other words it contains no isolated points.

4. $\mathbb{S}_{pure}$ is totally disconnected.

5. For any $s \in \mathbb{S}_{pure}$ and any $\epsilon > 0$ there is a $k \in \mathbb{N}$ such that $\mathbf{U}_\epsilon(s)$ is homeomorphic to

$$\mathbb{S}_{pure} \otimes \ldots \otimes \mathbb{S}_{pure} \qquad k \text{ times}$$

in the product topology, (here the empty product is taken to be the empty set). Conversely for any $k \in \mathbb{N}$ there is an $s \in \mathbb{S}_{pure}$ and an $\epsilon > 0$ such that $\mathbf{U}_\epsilon(s)$ is homeomorphic to

$$\mathbb{S}_{pure} \otimes \ldots \otimes \mathbb{S}_{pure} \qquad 2k \text{ times.}$$

Proof of Fact 4: The first follows from the simple observation that only a finite number of atoms can *occur in* an element of $\mathbb{S}_{pure}$. To prove 1. choose any $v\,;\mu$ that is well-founded and let k be the length of the longest element in $\delta_{(v;\mu)}$. Then the only element of $\mathbb{S}_{pure}$ in $\mathbf{U}_{(k+1)^{-1}}(v\,;\mu)$ is , the equivalence class of, $v\,;\mu$. In other words every other point in $\mathbb{S}_{pure}$ is further away than $(k+1)^{-1}$. The proof of 2 merely consists in defining successive well-founded approximations to a non well-founded object. Now 3 follows from the following observation:

Fact 5. If $c_0\,;\mu_0 \in \mathbb{M}_{sexp} - \mathbb{M}_{wf}$ then for any $k \in \mathbb{N}$ there is a $c_1\,;\mu_1 \in \mathbb{M}_{sexp}$ such that

$$c_0\,;\mu_0 \equiv c_1\,;\mu_1 \quad \text{and} \quad \mathbf{Cells}_{\mu_1}(c_1) > k.$$

This allows one to construct objects arbitrarily close to any particular non well-founded object. The proofs of 4 and 5 will be corollaries to Theorem A. $\square_{\mathbf{Fact\ 4}}$

The following is the main lemma of this section.

Main Lemma:

1. If D, e_0 and $\bar{v}_0\,;\mu_0$ are in $\mathbb{M}_{pure}$ and

$$e_0(\bar{v}_0)\,;\mu_0 \twoheadrightarrow^D \ldots \twoheadrightarrow^D e_n(\bar{v}_n)\,;\mu_n$$

is a single step reduction sequence of length n, and if $\bar{v}_0\,;\mu_0$ and $\bar{v}_0^*\,;\mu_0^*$ are pointwise $\equiv$ to a depth k , $k \geq n$, then

$$e_0(\bar{v}_0^*)\,;\mu_0^* \twoheadrightarrow^D \ldots \twoheadrightarrow^D e_n(\bar{v}_n^*)\,;\mu_n^*.$$

Furthermore $\bar{v}_n\,;\mu_n$ and $\bar{v}_n^*\,;\mu_n^*$ are pointwise Lisp equal to a depth $k-n$.

2. If D, e_0 and $\bar{v}_0\,;\mu_0$ are in $\mathbb{M}_{pure}$ and

$$e_0(\bar{v}_0)\,;\mu_0 \twoheadrightarrow^D \ldots \twoheadrightarrow^D \bar{v}_n{\downarrow_j}\,;\mu_n$$

is a single step reduction sequence of length n, and $c \in \delta_{\mu_0}$ is such that

$$(\forall \sigma)\ (|\sigma| \leq n \rightarrow c \neq (\bar{v}_0\!\downarrow_i ; \mu_0)_\sigma)$$

for all $i < |\bar{v}_0|$, then for any $w \in \mathbb{A} \oplus \delta_{\mu_0}$ we have that

$$e_0(\bar{v}_0) ; rplacx(c, w ; \mu_0) \twoheadrightarrow^D \ldots \twoheadrightarrow^D \bar{v}_n\!\downarrow_j ; setcxr(c, w ; \mu_n)$$

Proof of Main Lemma: We only prove the first part; the second is identical in form. The proof of part 1 is by induction on n.

Base Case ($n = 1$): In this case

$$e_0(\bar{v}_0) ; \mu_0 \twoheadrightarrow^D e_1(\bar{v}_1) ; \mu_1$$

and we must consider whether or not this is a primitive or congruence step. Suppose that $\bar{v}_0^*$ satisfies the hypothesis for $k \geq 1$.

Primitive Cases: Of the primitive cases the only non-trivial ones are the if and the memory operation cases.

Suppose $e_0(\bar{v}_0) = \mathtt{if}(\bar{v}_0\!\downarrow_j, e_{then}(\bar{v}_0), e_{else}(\bar{v}_0))$ then

$$\mathtt{if}(\bar{v}_0\!\downarrow_j, e_{then}(\bar{v}_0), e_{else}(\bar{v}_0)) ; \mu_0 \twoheadrightarrow^D \begin{cases} e_{then}(\bar{v}_0) ; \mu_0 & \text{if } \bar{v}_0\!\downarrow_j \neq \mathtt{NIL} \\ e_{else}(\bar{v}_0) ; \mu_0 & \text{if } \bar{v}_0\!\downarrow_j = \mathtt{NIL}. \end{cases}$$

because $\bar{v}_0 ; \mu_0 \equiv_k \bar{v}_0^* ; \mu_0^*$ with $k \geq 1$ we know that $\bar{v}_0\!\downarrow_j = \mathtt{NIL}$ iff $\bar{v}_0^*\!\downarrow_j = \mathtt{NIL}$, thus the result in this case follows. If $e_0(\bar{v}_0) = \vartheta(\bar{v}_0)$ then we must consider the following three cases.

1. $\vartheta = cons$
2. $\vartheta \in \{car, cdr\}$
3. $\vartheta \in \{int, atom, sub1, add1, atom{:}eq\}$

All are straightforward. Firstly notice that in all of these cases if $\vartheta(\bar{v}_0) ; \mu_0$ denotes then so will $\vartheta(\bar{v}_0^*) ; \mu_0^*$ simply because of the fact that $\bar{v}_0 ; \mu_0 \equiv_k \bar{v}_0^* ; \mu_0^*$ with $k \geq 1$. Thus we need only show that the resulting two memory objects, $\vartheta(\bar{v}_0 ; \mu_0)$ and $\vartheta(\bar{v}_0^* ; \mu_0^*)$, are Lisp equal to a depth $k - 1$. In case 1 we actually have Lisp equality to a depth $k + 1$ while in case three we have actual Lisp equality. It is only in case 2 that the bound $k - 1$ becomes relevant. $\Box_{\textbf{Primitive Cases}}$

Congruence Cases: To deal with the congruence cases it suffices to observe that a single step congruence reduction

$$e_0(\bar{v}_0) ; \mu_0 \twoheadrightarrow^D e_1(\bar{v}_1) ; \mu_1$$

must be *generated* in the following fashion: There is a subterm, $e_a(\bar{v}_0)$, of $e_0(\bar{v}_0)$ and a primitive single step reduction

$$e_a(\bar{v}_0)\ ;\ \mu_0 \twoheadrightarrow^{D} e_b(\bar{v}_1)\ ;\ \mu_1$$

such that the term $e_1(\bar{v}_1)$ is obtained from $e_0(\bar{v}_0)$ by simply replacing the appropriate occurrence of e_a by e_b. The result in this case then clearly follows from the primitive cases. $\Box_{\textbf{Base Case}}$

Induction Step: Is completely trivial. $\Box_{\textbf{Main Lemma}}$

The first corollary of the main lemma, theorem A, justifies the introduction of the topology on $\mathbb{S}_{pure}$.

Theorem A: If $f : \mathbb{M}_{sexp} \to \mathbb{M}_{sexp}$ is given by a pure definition, then the induced function from $\mathbb{S}_{pure} \to \mathbb{S}_{pure}$ is continuous.

Proof of Theorem A: Pick $v\ ;\ \mu \in \delta_f$ and let $v^*\ ;\ \mu^* = f(v)\ ;\ \mu$. Furthermore suppose that

$$f(v)\ ;\ \mu \gg v^*\ ;\ \mu^*$$

by a single step reduction sequence of length $n_{v;\mu}$. Given any $\epsilon = m^{-1} > 0$ we have, letting $\delta = (m + n_{v;\mu})^{-1}$, by the main lemma

$$f : \mathbf{U}_\delta(v\ ;\ \mu) \to \mathbf{U}_\epsilon(v^*\ ;\ \mu^*).$$

Thus the inverse image under f of an open set is open. $\Box_{\textbf{Theorem A}}$

Remark: Notice that we also have that n-ary functions are continuous in the product topology, by exactly the same proof.

Corollary 1: The *equal* function on $\mathbb{M}_{sexp}$ is not definable in $\mathbb{M}_{pure}$. By an *equal* function we simply mean a gentle program that only takes on the values T and NIL, and such that

$$equal(v_0, v_1)\ ;\ \mu \gg \mathtt{T}\ ;\ \mu \Longleftrightarrow v_0\ ;\ \mu \equiv v_1\ ;\ \mu.$$

Proof of Corollary 1: It suffices to observe that the function *equal* is not continuous. For pick $s \in \mathbb{S}_{pure} - \mathbb{S}_{wf}$ then there exists a sequence $\{s_i\}_{i \in \mathbb{N}}$ of elements of $\mathbb{S}_{wf}$ which converges to s. Therefore the sequence $\{[s, s_i]\}_{i \in \mathbb{N}}$ converges to $[s, s]$ in the product space. But for every $i \in \mathbb{N}$ we have that $equal(s, s_i) = \mathtt{NIL}$. $\Box_{\textbf{Corollary}}$

Corollary 2: The *elength* function on $\mathbb{M}_{elist}$ is not definable in $\mathbb{M}_{pure}$.

Proof of Corollary 2: Again it suffices to observe that *elength* is not continuous. $\Box_{\textbf{Corollary}}$

Corollary 3: (Proof of Fact 2 for the $\equiv_{pure}$ case) Two things must be shown. Firstly that $\equiv$ is a Pure-congruence, and secondly that two memory objects which are not Lisp equal cannot be identified by a Pure-congruence. The first fact follows from the main lemma and the fact that Lisp equal memory objects are pointwise $\equiv$ to a depth k for any $k \in \mathbb{N}$. The second is also as simple: if two memory objects $v_0 ; \mu_0$ and $v_1 ; \mu_1$ are not Lisp equal then for some *car-cdr* chain $\vartheta(x)$ we must have that

$$\vartheta(v_0) ; \mu_0 \gg w_0 ; \mu_0 \text{ and } \vartheta(v_1) ; \mu_1 \gg w_1 ; \mu_1,$$

where one of the w_i is in $\mathbb{A}$ and is distinct from the other. Consequently $v_0 ; \mu_0$ and $v_1 ; \mu_1$ cannot be identified by a Pure-congruence. $\square_{\textbf{Corollary}}$

Corollary 4: $\mathbb{S}_{pure}$ is totally disconnected.

Proof of Corollary 4: Suppose that s_0 and s_1 are distinct elements of $\mathbb{S}_{pure}$. Then it is a simple exercise to construct a purely defined total function

$$f_{s_0,s_1} : \mathbb{M}_{sexp} \to \{\mathtt{T}, \mathtt{NIL}\}$$

such that $f_{s_0,s_1}(s_0) = \mathtt{T}$ and $f_{s_0,s_1}(s_1) = \mathtt{NIL}$. The required open sets are thus simply $f^{-1}_{s_0,s_1}(\mathtt{T})$ and $f^{-1}_{s_0,s_1}(\mathtt{NIL})$. $\square_{\textbf{Corollary}}$

Corollary 5: If $v ; \mu \in \mathbb{M}_{sexp}$ is such that $\delta_{(v;\mu)}$ has exactly k elements, $\sigma_0, \ldots \sigma_{k-1}$, of length $n \in \mathbb{N}$, each having the property that $(v ; \mu)_{\sigma_i} \in \mathbb{C}$. Then $\mathbf{U}_{n-1}(v ; \mu)$ is homeomorphic to

$$\mathbb{S}_{pure} \otimes \ldots \otimes \mathbb{S}_{pure} \qquad 2k \text{ times}$$

in the product topology.

Proof of Corollary 5: For $v_0 ; \mu_0 \in \mathbf{U}_{n-1}(v ; \mu)$ define the mapping h by

$$h(v_0;\mu_0) = [(v_0;\mu_0)_{\sigma_0*0};\mu_0, (v_0;\mu_0)_{\sigma_0*1};\mu_0, \ldots, (v_0;\mu_0)_{\sigma_{k-1}*0};\mu_0, (v_0;\mu_0)_{\sigma_{k-1}*1};\mu_0].$$

Then it easy to verify that this is the desired homeomorphism. $\square_{\textbf{Corollary}}$

In fact functions specified by pure definitions satisfy an even stronger computational condition.

Definition: Let us say that a function f is *locally trivial* if for every $v ; \mu \in \mathbb{M}_{sexp} \cap \delta_f$ there is a $k \in \mathbb{N}$ and a pure term $e(x)$ such that

$$f(x) \simeq e(x) \qquad \text{on } \mathbf{U}_{k-1}(v ; \mu).$$

In other words a locally trivial function can, at an open neighborhood of any point, be defined without recursion. Thus the local behavior of such functions reduces to that of pure terms.

Theorem B: Every pure function is locally trivial.

Proof of Theorem B: Suppose that f is defined in the pure definition D. To prove this result we use two transformations on expressions. The first is the *unfolding* of an expression and the second is the *skeleton* of an expression; both have been defined previously. We can now describe the construction of the term. Pick $v ; \mu \in \delta_f$ and assume that $f(v) ; \mu \gg v^* ; \mu^*$ via a single step reduction sequence of length n. The desired term is then just

$$e = (f(x)^{\bowtie^{n+1}})^{\wr}.$$

That this term behaves in exactly the same way as f in the open ball of radius n^{-1} at $v ; \mu$ follows from the main lemma and simple properties of the unfolding and skeleton transformations. $\square_{\textbf{Theorem B}}$

Corollary 1: The *copy* function on $\mathbb{M}_{sexp}$ is not definable in $\mathbb{M}_{pure}$. Here by a *copy* function we mean a function that satisfies the following two conditions

1. $copy(x) \cong x$ on $\mathbb{M}_{sexp}$,
2. $\forall v ; \mu \in \mathbb{M}_{sexp}$, letting $copy(v) ; \mu \gg v^* ; \mu^*$, we have that $\emptyset = \mathbf{Cells}_{\mu}(v) \cap \mathbf{Cells}_{\mu^*}(v^*)$.

Proof of Corollary 1: This is a simple variation on the above fact and the second part of the main lemma. For suppose not; let $p{:}copy$ be a pure function that satisfies these two properties, and choose any $v ; \mu \in \mathbb{M}_{sexp} - \mathbb{M}_{wf}$. Assume that $p{:}copy(v) ; \mu \gg v^* ; \mu^*$ via a single step sequence of length k. Now by fact 5 there is a $v^+ ; \mu^+$ such that

- $v ; \mu \equiv v^+ ; \mu^+$
- $|\mathbf{Cells}_{\mu^+}(v^+)| > 2^{k+1}$.

Consequently

$$p{:}copy(v) ; \mu \equiv p{:}copy(v^+) ; \mu^+ \gg v^{+*} ; \mu^{+*}.$$

Now by assumption on $v^+ ; \mu^+$ there is a $c \in \mathbf{Cells}_{\mu^+}(v^+)$ such that $\forall \sigma\ |\sigma| < k+1 \rightarrow (v^+ ; \mu^+)_\sigma \neq c$. Now simply choose $a \in \mathbb{A}$ such that $\mu^+(v^+)\downarrow_0 \neq a$. Then by part two of the main lemma

$$p{:}copy(v^+) ; setcar(c, a ; \mu^+) \gg v^{+*} ; setcar(c, a ; \mu^{+*}).$$

But because $\mathbf{Cells}_{\mu^{+*}}(v^{+*})$ is disjoint from $\mathbf{Cells}_{\mu^+}(v^+)$, which contains c, we have that

$$v\,;\mu \equiv v^+\,;\mu^+ \cong v^{+*}\,;\mu^{+*} \cong v^{+*}\,;\mathit{setcar}(c, a\,;\mu^{+*}).$$

But this is ridiculous since by assumption

$$p{:}\mathit{copy}(v^+)\,;\mathit{setcar}(c, a\,;\mu^+) \cong v^+\,;\mathit{setcar}(c, a\,;\mu^+)$$

and

$$v^+\,;\mu^+ \not\cong v^+\,;\mathit{setcar}(c, a\,;\mu^+)$$

□**Corollary**

Remark: Note that almost exactly the same proof will work if we weaken the first property to

1. $\mathit{copy}(x) \equiv x$ on $\mathbb{M}_{sexp}$.

6.3. The Interrelationships

The three main results results concerning the relation between $\mathbb{M}_{sexp}$, $\mathbb{M}_{pure^+}$ and $\mathbb{M}_{pure}$ that we prove in this section are:

Theorem C: If $f : \mathbb{M}_{sexp}^{(n)} \to \mathbb{M}_{sexp}$ is definable in $\mathbb{M}_{sexp}$ then the following are equivalent:

- f preserves Lisp equality and maps $\mathbb{M}_{wf}^{(n)}$ to $\mathbb{M}_{wf}$.
- There is an $\mathbb{M}_{pure}$ definable function $f^* : \mathbb{M}_{sexp}^{(n)} \to \mathbb{M}_{sexp}$ such that

$$f(\bar{x}) \equiv f^*(\bar{x}) \qquad \text{on } \mathbb{M}_{wf}$$

Theorem D: If $f : \mathbb{M}_{sexp}^{(n)} \to \mathbb{M}_{sexp}$ is definable in $\mathbb{M}_{sexp}$ then the following are equivalent:

- f maps $\mathbb{M}_{wf}^{(n)}$ to $\mathbb{M}_{wf}$.
- There is an $\mathbb{M}_{pure^+}$ definable function $f^* : \mathbb{M}_{sexp}^{(n)} \to \mathbb{M}_{sexp}$ such that

$$f(\bar{x}) \cong f^*(\bar{x}) \qquad \text{on } \mathbb{M}_{wf}.$$

Furthermore if f maps $\mathbb{M}_{sexp}^{(n)}$ to $\mathbb{M}_{wf}$ then we can actually have that

$$f(\bar{x}) \cong f^*(\bar{x}) \qquad \text{on } \mathbb{M}_{sexp}.$$

Theorem E: If $f : \mathbb{M}^{(n)}_{sexp} \rightarrow \mathbb{M}_{sexp}$ is definable in $\mathbb{M}_{sexp}$ then the following are equivalent:

- f maps $\mathbb{M}^{(n)}_{wf}$ to $\mathbb{M}_{wf}$ and is gentle, i.e

$$\mathsf{seq}(f(\bar{x}), \bar{x}\downarrow_i) \simeq \bar{x}\downarrow_i$$

  for each $0 \leq i < |\bar{x}|$.

- There is an $\mathbb{M}_{pure^+}$ definable function $f^* : \mathbb{M}^{(n)}_{sexp} \rightarrow \mathbb{M}_{sexp}$ such that

$$f(\bar{x}) \simeq f^*(\bar{x}) \qquad \text{on } \mathbb{M}_{wf}.$$

These equivalences allow us to claim that there are only two possible reasons why a function definable in one fragment is not definable in an other. We outline the proof of theorem D; the proofs of theorems C and E are simple modifications of the same idea.

Proof of Theorem D: The proof divides itself into three separates steps; all in all they are essentially just tedious programming problems.

Step 1: In this step one constructs an $\mathbb{M}_{pure^+}$ definable function f_{code} which does the following: given a memory object $\bar{v}\ ;\ \mu \in \mathbb{M}_{sexp}$ it returns an object $f_{code}(\bar{v})\ ;\ \mu$ which codes up the memory value sequence $\bar{v}$ as well as the function μ on the finite set $\mathbf{Cells}_\mu(\bar{v})$. The details of this coding are not particularly important. One such possibility is that $f_{code}(\bar{v})\ ;\ \mu$ represents a pair, the first element of this pair is a list of length $|\bar{v}|$, the ith element of the list being the code for $\bar{v}\downarrow_i$. Then the second element of the pair could then be an alist consisting of argument-value pairs, the argument being a code for an element, c, of $\mathbf{Cells}_\mu(\bar{v})$ and the value being the codes for $\mu(c) = [v_a, v_d]$. The only requirement of this coding is that we can carry out the following:

Step 2: In this step we construct an $\mathbb{M}_{pure^+}$ definable function f_{eval} which, given *an internal form* $\bar{D}$, see (McCarthy and Talcott, 1980) or Chapter 9, of the $\mathbb{M}_{sexp}$ definition, D, of f evaluates the program on the code for the argument, $f_{code}(\bar{v})\ ;\ \mu$, rather than the argument itself. This enables the $\mathbb{M}_{pure^+}$ function to mimic the results of the operations *rplaca* and *rplacd* on the codes without actually needing to use them. The function f_{eval} should then return the code for the value, if there is one, thus leading us to step three.

Step 3: We now construct an $\mathbb{M}_{pure^+}$ function f_{decode} which given a code will construct an object isomorphic to the one described by the code. It is here that we must make use of the assumption that the range of our original function f is a subset of $\mathbb{M}_{wf}$. For otherwise, essentially by fact 3, such a decoding function would not exist.

Thus the required definition for f^* is loosely described by

$$f^*(\bar{x}) \leftarrow f_{decode}(f_{eval}(f, \bar{D}, f_{code}(\bar{x}))).$$

□**Theorem D**

The only modifications required for the proof of Theorem C is that now in the coding step we can only code up the Lisp equivalence class of the object. But since the function f (which by theorem D we may assume is $\mathbb{M}_{pure+}$ definable) preserves equality this need not worry us. It also allows us in the interpreter stage to assume that *eq* and *equal* are the same function. In other words we are assuming that the argument is the compact element of the equivalence class. The proof of theorem E is also a simple variation on this technique.

Chapter 7

Derivations and Transformations

This chapter is devoted to the subject of program transformation and derivation. As we have mentioned many times we view program derivation and program verification as duals of one another. Methods and insights in one area should give rise to corresponding methods and insights in the other. The contents of this chapter are rather tentative but nevertheless go some distance to realizing our thesis. Although we have tried to emphasize the relation between program derivation and program verification there is one important point where they are different, and this has the consequence of making the former rather more delicate and subtle than the latter. In program verification one deals with a fixed definition and proceeds by manipulating expressions. In program derivation one not only manipulates expressions but also definitions. Consequently one must deal with the behavior of an expression with respect to more than one definition. Comparing definitions is thus more central than simply comparing expressions with respect to some fixed definition.

In this chapter we define a set of program transformations based on those of Scherlis, (Scherlis, 1980), (Scherlis, 1981). Our rules will allow us to transform one program into another in a way that preserves the main function being defined, at least on the common domain of the program derived and the *specifying program.* The objects the rules apply to are not simply definitions, but include so called *expression procedures.* Expression procedures are central to the whole theory. The following quote is from (Scherlis, 1981).

> *The specialization technique we develop is based on a new approach to the transformation of applicative programs: We expand an ordinary language of recursive equations to include a generalized procedure construct - the expression procedure. This greatly enhances our ability to manipulate programs in the initial language. Indeed, the expression procedure provides a way of expressing information not just about the properties of the individual program elements, but also about the way they relate to each other. This ability to represent program-specific facts allows us to manipulate these facts in the same way as any other part of the program. Consequently, the set of transformation rules we require (not including simplification rules for the primitive symbols such as cons) is very small.*

An expression procedure represents a method for evaluating a specific class of expressions. An example of an expression procedure is

$$rev(\mathtt{u}) \circ \mathtt{v} \leftarrow \mathtt{ifn}(\mathtt{u}, \mathtt{v}, rev(cdr(\mathtt{u})) \circ cons(car(\mathtt{u}), \mathtt{v}).$$

This definition specifies a method for evaluating expressions which are of the form rev(u)ov where u and v are lists. Now, to evaluate an instance of the expression at run-time, an interpreter could, rather than evaluate the constituents of the expression in the usual way, use instead the expression procedure, and directly return a value. Note that since the else clause is an instance of the left hand side, this expression is recursive. That is, the expression procedure can be used to evaluate its own else clause.

Expression procedures are different from other procedures in several ways. First, their left hand sides are complex expressions which (as we will see below) already have meanings associated with them. This leads us to restrict our attention to expression procedures which are consistent - whose left and right hand sides are equivalent a priori. Thus given the usual definition of gcd, the expression procedure

$$gcd(\mathtt{x}, gcd(\mathtt{x}, \mathtt{y})) \leftarrow \mathtt{y}$$

is considered inconsistent, since the two sides of the definition are not always equivalent.

In addition, an expression procedure must represent a progressive method for computing the expression it defines. The expression procedure,

$$gcd(\mathtt{x}, \mathtt{y}) \leftarrow gcd(\mathtt{x}, \mathtt{y})$$

is not progressive since it introduces looping evaluation of terms whose values were previously effectively computable.

Consistency and progressiveness are properties of an expression procedure with respect to some given program. Consider, for example, the program,

```
a ← 3 ;  b ← 3
```

Either of the expression procedures,

```
a + b ← b + a   b + a ← a + b
```

is progressive with respect to the given program. After one has been added to the program, however, the other ceases to be progressive, since its addition would introduce looping evaluations where there were none previously.

In general, it may be quite difficult to establish consistency and progressiveness for arbitrary expression procedures. In our application, however we will introduce expression procedures in a systematic way, using transformation rules that guarantee new expression procedures to be both consistent and progressive.

Rather than simply manipulate definitions, the rules we shall consider act upon *definitions* that include expression procedures. We call these more general objects *derivation expressions*, the definition of which is as follows:

Definition: A *derivation expression* D is an expression of the form

$$D = \begin{cases} f_0(\bar{x}) \leftarrow & e_0 \\ \dots & \dots \\ f_m(\bar{x}) \leftarrow & e_m \\ e_0^* \leftarrow & e_1^* \\ \dots & \dots \\ e_{2n}^* \leftarrow & e_{2n+1}^* \end{cases}$$

where

$$D_{\text{standard}} = \begin{cases} f_0(\bar{x}) \leftarrow & e_0 \\ \dots & \dots \\ f_m(\bar{x}) \leftarrow & e_m \end{cases}$$

is a definition in the standard sense; we call this part of D the *standard part.* The function f_0 is called the main function in the definition.

$$D_{\text{expression}} = \begin{cases} e_0^* \leftarrow & e_1^* \\ \dots & \dots \\ e_{2n}^* \leftarrow & e_{2n+1}^* \end{cases}$$

is simply a collection of equations where the e_i^* are expressions. This part is called the *expression part.* Given such a definition D we say $t_0 \leftarrow t_1$ is an equation in D when it is in either the standard or the expression part. In other words

$$t_0 \leftarrow t_1 \in D = D_{\text{standard}} \cup D_{\text{expression}}.$$

In what follows we shall be evaluating expressions with respect to these more general objects; consequently we must modify our definition of $\gg^D$ accordingly. We shall also be comparing the behavior of one expression with respect to one derivation expression with that of another expression in the context of a second derivation expression. This again requires introducing some new terminology. This shall occupy us for the rest of this section.

Definition: Suppose that D is a derivation expression. Then we extend the reduction relation by adding the following clause to the primitive cases (cf 2.2.3).

$$e_0(\bar{v}) \,;\, \mu \twoheadrightarrow^D e_1(\bar{v}) \,;\, \mu \qquad \text{if } e_0(\bar{x}) \leftarrow e_1(\bar{x}) \in D \text{ is an expression procedure}$$

Note that, depending on D, the reduction relation $\gg^D$ may reduce an expression to many different values, depending on the *evaluation path.* Also one evaluation path may terminate in a value, while another may never terminate. We often view a memory object description $e \,;\, \mu$ as describing a tree, $\twoheadrightarrow^D$ being the *successor* function. Our terminology reflects this view; for example we shall speak of evaluation paths. These are of course just paths in the tree. If a derivation expression, D, has the property that for every memory object description $e \,;\, \mu$ every terminating evaluation path terminates at the same (or at least isomorphic) value, then we say it is *consistent.* If a derivation expression, D, has the property that for every memory object description $e \,;\, \mu$ either every evaluation path fails to terminate or else they all terminate at the same value, then we call it *progressive and consistent.* Derivation expressions which are not consistent are of very little interest to us. Consequently the following definition is restricted, for simplicity, to consistent derivation expressions. In comparing definitions and derivation expressions the following convention is useful.

Definition: Suppose that D_0, D_1 are derivation expressions, $e_0(\bar{x}), e_1(\bar{x})$ are expressions and $e_0(\bar{v}_0);\mu_0, e_1(\bar{v}_1);\mu_1$ are corresponding memory object descriptions. The function symbols occuring in e_i are assumed to be defined in the derivation expression D_i. Then we write

$$D_0, D_1 \vdash e_0 \,;\, \mu_0 \sim e_1 \,;\, \mu_1$$

to mean that whenever there is a terminating path in $e_0 \,;\, \mu_0$ with respect to $\gg^{D_0}$ there is a terminating path in $e_1 \,;\, \mu_1$ with respect to $\gg^{D_1}$ and these values are $\sim$-related (in the case of strong isomorphism we must also have that the original memories have been transformed appropriately) and vice versa. We shall also extend this notation to the expression case in the obvious fashion. Finally we shall write

$$D_0 \sim D_1$$

to mean that for every memory object description $e \,;\, \mu$ we have

$$D_0, D_1 \vdash e \,;\, \mu \sim e \,;\, \mu.$$

7.1. The Rules of Scherlis

We shall begin with a brief account of the rules we shall be generalizing. For more detail than included here the reader is advised to look at (Scherlis, 1980) or (Scherlis, 1981). The rules we state here are for pure Lisp, henceforth in this section all expressions and definitions, as well as derivation expressions will be assumed to be in $\mathbb{M}_{pure}$, unless explicitly stated to the contrary. In fact to be true to his system we shall also outlaw both `seq` and `let` since they are both redundant and, as far as the proofs in (Scherlis,1980), are troublesome. The plan of this section is as follows. We begin by making precise certain concepts necessary for the statement of the rules. Without further delay we then state the rules. Finally we give a simple example of their use. The first definition is that of a strict subexpression of an expression, a subexpression which must be evaluated in order to evaluate the whole.

Definition: The *strict subexpressions* of an expression e consist of the collection $\varrho(e)$ defined inductively as follows:

$$\varrho(e) = \begin{cases} \{e\} & \text{if } e \in \mathbb{X} \cup \mathbb{V}; \\ \{e\} \cup \varrho(e_0) & \text{if } e = \mathtt{if}(e_0, e_1, e_2) \\ \{e\} \cup \bigcup_i \varrho(e_i) & \text{if } e = \vartheta(e_0, \ldots e_m) \text{ with } \vartheta \in \mathbb{O} \cup \mathbb{F} \end{cases}$$

In (Scherlis, 1980) the following appears as lemma 1 in Chapter 2. It explains the notion of a strict subexpression.

Lemma: If an expression e (in memory μ) denotes then so must every strict subexpression.

Note that this lemma is on the face of it false if we include the control construct `let`. In that case the spirit of the lemma will remain the same; its statement however must, by force, be elaborated. This is simply because a strict subexpression of an expression, in the general situation, may have more free variables than the larger expression. In the general case the definition of the strict subexpressions of an expression, given in Chapter 2 and repeated here, are as follows.

Definition: The strict subexpressions of an expression e consist of the collection $\varrho(e)$ defined inductively as follows:

$$\varrho(e) = \begin{cases} \{e\} & \text{if } e \in \mathbb{X} \cup \mathbb{V}; \\ \{e\} \cup \varrho(e_0) & \text{if } e = \mathtt{if}(e_0, e_1, e_2) \\ \{e\} \cup \bigcup_i \varrho(e_i) & \text{if } e = \begin{cases} \vartheta(e_0, \ldots e_m) & \text{with } \vartheta \in \mathbb{O} \cup \mathbb{F} \text{ or} \\ \mathtt{seq}(e_0, \ldots e_m) \end{cases} \\ \{e\} \cup \bigcup_i \varrho(e_i) \cup \varrho(e_{body}) & \text{if } e = \mathtt{let}_{0 \le i \le m}\{y_i \leftarrow e_i\} e_{body} \end{cases}$$

Using this notion we can define the notion of an expression procedure being a proper definition instance of another expression procedure.

Definition: For a given program $e_{left}(\bar{\mathbf{x}}) \leftarrow e_{right}(\bar{\mathbf{x}})$ the pair

$$e_{left}(\bar{\mathbf{e}}) \leftarrow e_{right}(\bar{\mathbf{e}})$$

where $\bar{e} = [e_0, \ldots e_n]$ is a *proper definition instance* of $e_{left}(\bar{\mathbf{x}}) \leftarrow e_{right}(\bar{\mathbf{x}})$ if for each expression e_i, either x_i is a strict subexpression of e_{right}, or else evaluation of e_i always terminates.

The four rules can now be stated without difficulty.

Composition rule: Suppose that $e_0 \nleftarrow e_1$ is an equation in D. Composition produces a new program D^* that is the result of adding the new expression procedure

$$e(e_0^*) \nleftarrow e(e_1^*)$$

to D. For this rule to be applicable the variable z must occur only once in $e(z)$ and it must also be a strict subexpression. Also

$$e_0^* \nleftarrow e_1^*$$

must be a proper definition instance of

$$e_0 \nleftarrow e_1.$$

Application rule: Let $e_0 \nleftarrow e_1$ and $e \nleftarrow e^*(e_0^*)$ be equations in D, where z only occurs once in $e^*(z)$. Then the application rule allows us to obtain the program D^* which is D with the equation $e \nleftarrow e^*(e_0^*)$ replaced by the equation $e \nleftarrow e^*(e_1^*)$. Here again

$$e_0^* \nleftarrow e_1^*$$

must be a proper definition instance of

$$e_0 \nleftarrow e_1.$$

Abstraction rule: Let

$$e_0 \leftarrow e_0^*(e(\bar{e}))$$

$$\ldots\ldots$$

$$e_n \leftarrow e_n^*(e(\bar{e}))$$

be a collection of equations in a definition D such that $\bar{e} = [e^0, \ldots, e^n]$. $\bar{x} = [x_0, \ldots, x_n]$ is the set of free variables of e, and they all occur as strict subexpressions of e. Abstraction produces a new derivation expression D^* with these equations replaced by

$$e_0 \leftarrow e_0^*(f(\bar{e}))$$

$$\ldots\ldots$$

$$e_n \leftarrow e_n^*(f(\bar{e}))$$

$$f(\bar{x}) \not\leftarrow e(\bar{x})$$

where f is a new function symbol not in D. Note that this last equation is in the standard part of D^*.

Equation elimination rule: Any expression procedure can be dropped from a definition.

Simplification Rule: We refer the reader to (Scherlis, 1980) for a discussion of the simplification rule.

The following is the main result of (Scherlis, 1980) stated using our notation:

Theorem: Suppose that D_1 is derived from D_0 using the above rules as well as simplification. Then

$$D_0 \equiv D_1.$$

It is important to note that we cannot conclude that

$$D_0 \simeq D_1$$

or even

$$D_0 \cong D_1.$$

This is because of the way the abstraction rule has been formulated. The system we present will differ in this respect. Consider the following definition.

$$f(\mathrm{x}) \leftarrow cons(cons(\mathrm{x}, \mathrm{x}), cons(\mathrm{x}, \mathrm{x})).$$

Then abstraction allows us to form the following new definition

$$f(\mathrm{x}) \leftarrow cons(f_1(\mathrm{x}, \mathrm{x}), f_1(\mathrm{x}, \mathrm{x})),$$

$$f_1(\mathrm{y}) \leftarrow cons(\mathrm{y}, \mathrm{y}).$$

Another application produces:

$$f(\mathtt{x}) \leftarrow f_2(f_1(\mathtt{x},\mathtt{x}))$$

$$f_2(\mathtt{y}) \leftarrow cons(\mathtt{y},\mathtt{y})$$

$$f_1(\mathtt{y}) \leftarrow cons(\mathtt{y},\mathtt{y}).$$

Thus we have derived a program, D_1, from our original program, D_0, for which we only have

$$D_0, D_1 \vdash f(x) \equiv f(x).$$

We do however suspect that the following is true:

Conjecture: Suppose that D_1 is derived from D_0 using the above rules as well as simplification and that

$$D_0 \cong D_1.$$

Then in fact we have that

$$D_0 \simeq D_1.$$

7.1.1. An Example of a Derivation.

We finish this section by giving an example of a derivation. In this example we shall derive *reverse* from *slow:reverse*. Recall from Chapter 4 the respective definitions of these functions.

$$slow{:}reverse(\mathtt{y}) \leftarrow$$

$$\mathtt{ifn}(\mathtt{y},\mathtt{NIL}, append(slow{:}reverse(cdr(\mathtt{y})), cons(car(\mathtt{y}),\mathtt{NIL})))$$

$$reverse(\mathtt{y}) \leftarrow rev(\mathtt{y},\mathtt{NIL})$$

$$rev(\mathtt{y},\mathtt{x}) \leftarrow \mathtt{ifn}(\mathtt{y},\mathtt{x}, rev(cdr(\mathtt{y}), cons(car(\mathtt{y}),\mathtt{x}))))$$

Let us begin with the definition D_0, being

$$reverse(\mathtt{y}) \leftarrow \mathtt{ifn}(\mathtt{y},\mathtt{NIL}, append(reverse(cdr(\mathtt{y})), cons(car(\mathtt{y}),\mathtt{NIL}))).$$

Abstracting the recursive call

$$reverse(\mathtt{y}) \leftarrow \mathtt{ifn}(\mathtt{y},\mathtt{NIL}, append(rev_0(cdr(\mathtt{y})), cons(car(\mathtt{y}),\mathtt{NIL})))$$

$$rev_0(\mathtt{x}) \leftarrow reverse(\mathtt{x}).$$

Now using application with respect to the definition of *reverse* in the body of rev_0 gives

$$reverse(\mathtt{y}) \leftarrow \mathtt{ifn}(\mathtt{y},\mathtt{NIL}, append(rev_0(cdr(\mathtt{y})), cons(car(\mathtt{y}),\mathtt{NIL})))$$

$$rev_0(\mathtt{y}) \leftarrow \mathtt{ifn}(\mathtt{y},\mathtt{NIL}, append(rev_0(cdr(\mathtt{y})), cons(car(\mathtt{y}),\mathtt{NIL}))).$$

The derivation proceeds by specializing the auxiliary program rev_0 to the context $append(rev_0(x), y)$. This is done by using the composition rule.

$$\mathit{reverse}(\mathtt{y}) \leftarrow \mathtt{ifn}(\mathtt{y}, \mathtt{NIL}, \mathit{append}(\mathit{rev}_0(\mathit{cdr}(\mathtt{y})), \mathit{cons}(\mathit{car}(\mathtt{y}), \mathtt{NIL})))$$

$$\mathit{rev}_0(\mathtt{y}) \leftarrow \mathtt{ifn}(\mathtt{y}, \mathtt{NIL}, \mathit{append}(\mathit{rev}_0(\mathit{cdr}(\mathtt{y})), \mathit{cons}(\mathit{car}(\mathtt{y}), \mathtt{NIL})))$$

$$\mathit{append}(\mathit{rev}_0(\mathtt{x}), \mathtt{y}) \leftarrow$$

$$\mathit{append}(\mathtt{ifn}(\mathtt{x}, \mathtt{NIL}, \mathit{append}(\mathit{rev}_0(\mathit{cdr}(\mathtt{y})), \mathit{cons}(\mathit{car}(\mathtt{x}), \mathtt{NIL}))), \mathtt{y})$$

Simplifying using properties of `if` and *append* gives

$$\mathit{reverse}(\mathtt{y}) \leftarrow \mathtt{ifn}(\mathtt{y}, \mathtt{NIL}, \mathit{append}(\mathit{rev}_0(\mathit{cdr}(\mathtt{y})), \mathit{cons}(\mathit{car}(\mathtt{y}), \mathtt{NIL})))$$

$$\mathit{rev}_0(\mathtt{y}) \leftarrow \mathtt{ifn}(\mathtt{y}, \mathtt{NIL}, \mathit{append}(\mathit{rev}_0(\mathit{cdr}(\mathtt{y})), \mathit{cons}(\mathit{car}(\mathtt{y}), \mathtt{NIL})))$$

$$\mathit{append}(\mathit{rev}_0(\mathtt{x}), \mathtt{y}) \leftarrow$$

$$\mathtt{ifn}(\mathtt{x}, \mathtt{y}, \mathit{append}(\mathit{rev}_0(\mathit{cdr}(\mathtt{x})), \mathit{cons}(\mathit{car}(\mathtt{x}), \mathtt{y})))$$

Notice we have now obtained a tail recursive expression procedure, consequently the specialization procedure was successful. We proceed by renaming the complex expression $append(rev_0(x), y)$ to a new basic name $rev_1(x, y)$ by using abstraction and composition, and eliminating the redundant rev_0 function.

$$\mathit{reverse}(\mathtt{y}) \leftarrow \mathtt{ifn}(\mathtt{y}, \mathtt{NIL}, \mathit{rev}_1(\mathit{cdr}(\mathtt{y}), \mathit{cons}(\mathit{car}(\mathtt{y}), \mathtt{NIL})))$$

$$\mathit{rev}_1(\mathtt{x}, \mathtt{y}) \leftarrow \mathtt{ifn}(\mathtt{x}, \mathtt{y}, \mathit{rev}_1(\mathit{cdr}(\mathtt{x}), \mathit{cons}(\mathit{car}(\mathtt{x}), \mathtt{y})))$$

To obtain the definition of *reverse* above we simply abstract the bodies of both definitions into a new function rev_2

$$\mathit{reverse}(\mathtt{y}) \leftarrow \mathit{rev}_2(\mathtt{y}, \mathtt{NIL})$$

$$\mathit{rev}_1(\mathtt{x}, \mathtt{y}) \leftarrow \mathit{rev}_2(\mathtt{x}, \mathtt{y})$$

$$\mathit{rev}_2(\mathtt{x}, \mathtt{y}) \leftarrow \mathtt{ifn}(\mathtt{x}, \mathtt{y}, \mathit{rev}_1(\mathit{cdr}(\mathtt{x}), \mathit{cons}(\mathit{car}(\mathtt{x}), \mathtt{NIL})))$$

We then unfold the single rev_1 call in the body of rev_2 and eliminate the definition of rev_1 giving

$$\mathit{reverse}(\mathtt{y}) \leftarrow \mathit{rev}_2(\mathtt{y}, \mathtt{NIL})$$

$$\mathit{rev}_2(\mathtt{x}, \mathtt{y}) \leftarrow \mathtt{ifn}(\mathtt{x}, \mathtt{y}, \mathit{rev}_2(\mathit{cdr}(\mathtt{x}), \mathit{cons}(\mathit{car}(\mathtt{x}), \mathtt{y})))$$

as desired.

7.2. The Transformation Rules

Our rules are only a slight modification of those in (Scherlis, 1980). In fact we only modify two rules, the abstraction rule and the simplification rule. There are two reasons for altering the abstraction rule. The first is that since we are not restricting ourselves to pure Lisp the order of evaluation of terms is much more important in our case, consequently we cannot be so free-wheeling with substitutions. The second reason is that our rules are slightly weaker than those in (Scherlis, 1980), although when restricted to pure Lisp the difference disappears; this weakening prevents us from going from one definition to another definition that is only Lisp equal to the first. It is not such a tremendous weakening because we have the benefit of the `let` construct in our system. Our system also includes a generalization of the simplification rule which is used in (Scherlis, 1980) but never made completely explicit as a rule there. The reason we do this is because the simplification rule really only treated the underlying properties of the data operations as well as the control construct `if`. The three other main rules are principally concerned with function application. Consequently, since our control structure is much richer, we must include a rule, the equivalence rule, that allows us to make use of simple properties of these added control primitives. This rule allows us to be quite free-wheeling with properties of the control primitives and data operations. However it probably also allows us to introduce looping where there was none previously. To state this rule we need the following:

Definition: Two expressions $e_0(\bar{x})$ and $e_1(\bar{x})$, which may contain function symbols defined in D, are said to be ***strongly isomorphic independent of the definition*** D iff for every definition D^* (which provides definitions for the function symbols defined in D) we have

$$D^*, D^* \vdash e_0(\bar{x}) \simeq e_1(\bar{x}).$$

The idea behind this rule is quite simple; it is designed to eliminate those expressions which can only be shown to be strongly isomorphic by using *folding*. Every rule, other than folding, which we presented in the last section of chapter 3 preserves this stronger form of equivalence.

The first rule, being the generalization of the simplification rule, is then stated as:

Equivalence rule: Given a derivation expression, D, and an equation $t_0 \leftarrow t_1$ in D, if t_2 is an expression that is strongly equivalent to t_1 independent of the standard part of D then we can obtain a new derivation expression D^* from D by replacing the equation $t_0 \leftarrow t_1$ by $t_0 \leftarrow t_2$.

The next rule is our generalization of the abstraction rule:

Abstraction rule: Let

$$t_0 \leftarrow t_0^*(t(\bar{y}))$$

$$\cdots\cdots$$

$$t_n \leftarrow t_n^*(t(\bar{y}))$$

be a collection of equations in a definition D such that $\bar{y}$ is the set of free variables of t. Abstraction produces a new derivation expression D^* with these equations replaced by

$$t_0 \leftarrow t_0^*(f(\bar{y}))$$

$$\cdots\cdots$$

$$t_n \leftarrow t_n^*(f(\bar{y}))$$

$$f(\bar{y}) \leftarrow t(\bar{y})$$

where f is a new function symbol not in D. Note that this last equation is in the standard part of D^*.

The other three rules are the same as in the previous section, except of course they now apply to a wider class of expressions and definitions. We must also modify the definition of an expression procedure being a proper definition instance of a definition.

Definition: For a given program $e_{left}(\bar{\mathbf{x}}) \leftarrow e_{right}(\bar{\mathbf{x}})$ the pair

$$\mathtt{let}\{\bar{x} \leftarrow \bar{e}\}e_{left}(\bar{x}) \leftarrow \mathtt{let}\{\bar{x} \leftarrow \bar{e}\}e_{right}(\bar{x})$$

where $\bar{e} = [e_0, \ldots e_n]$ is a *proper definition instance* of $e_{left}(\bar{x}) \leftarrow e_{right}(\bar{x})$.

We make the following two conjectures concerning these rules.

Conjecture 1: Suppose D_1 is derived from D_0 using only the original simplification rule, the restricted abstraction rule and the three rules common to both systems. Then

$$D_0 \simeq D_1.$$

Conjecture 2: Suppose that D_1 is derived from D_0 using the rules above, and suppose that f is a function defined in both. Then letting $\delta_f^{D_i}$ be the domain of f with respect to the definition D_i we have that

$$D_0, D_1 \vdash f(\bar{x}) \simeq f(\bar{x}) \text{ on } \delta_f^{D_0} \cap \delta_f^{D_1}.$$

7.2.1. An Informal Derivation

We begin by giving an outline of a derivation that is more in the form of a verification. We then give the formal version of the derivation in our system. Consider the following derivation of a tail recursive append program from the traditional recursive one. We begin with the simple-minded definition of *append*:

$$append(x,y) \simeq$$
$$\simeq \mathtt{ifn}(x, y, cons(car(x), append(cdr(x), y)))$$

The first step is to break up the computation into single steps:

$$\begin{aligned}\simeq \mathtt{ifn}(&x,\\ &y,\\ &\mathtt{let}\{u \leftarrow append(cdr(x),y)\}\ cons(car(x),u))\end{aligned}$$

We can also break up the call to *cons* into two steps:

$$\begin{aligned}\simeq \mathtt{ifn}(&x,\\ &y,\\ &\mathtt{let}\{u \leftarrow append(cdr(x),y)\}\\ &\quad \mathtt{let}\{z \leftarrow cons(car(x),*)\}\ rplacd(z,u)),\end{aligned}$$

where $*$ is some term that does not depend on u.

We can now commute the *cons* since $*$ did not depend on u:

$$\begin{aligned}\simeq \mathtt{ifn}(&x,\\ &y,\\ &\mathtt{let}\{z \leftarrow cons(car(x),*)\}\\ &\quad \mathtt{let}\{u \leftarrow append(cdr(x),y)\}\ rplacd(z,u)),\end{aligned}$$

$$\begin{aligned}\simeq \mathtt{ifn}(&x,\\ &y,\\ &\mathtt{let}\{z \leftarrow cons(car(x),*)\}\\ &\quad \mathtt{let}\{val \leftarrow z\}\\ &\qquad \mathtt{let}\{u \leftarrow append(cdr(x),y)\}\\ &\qquad\quad \mathtt{seq}(rplacd(z,u), val))\end{aligned}$$

This last step separates the value returned from the operations, by creating another local variable. Such a step in general gives us more freedom to find tail recursive expressions. Now the smallest subexpression of this last term that we could possibly hope to obtain a tail recursive expression for is

$$\mathtt{let}\{u \leftarrow append(cdr(x), y)\}\mathtt{seq}(rplacd(z, u), val).$$

The task is thus to find a strongly isomorphic expression to this one which is tail recursive with respect to this expression. To begin with we have

$$
\begin{aligned}
&\mathtt{let}\{u \leftarrow append(x, y)\}\\
&\quad \mathtt{seq}(rplacd(z, u), val)) \simeq\\
&\quad \simeq \mathtt{let}\{u \leftarrow \mathtt{ifn}(x, y, cons(car(x), append(cdr(x), y)))\}\\
&\qquad\quad \mathtt{seq}(rplacd(z, u), val))\\
&\quad \simeq \mathtt{ifn}(x,\\
&\qquad\quad \mathtt{seq}(rplacd(z, y), val),\\
&\qquad\quad \mathtt{let}\{u \leftarrow cons(car(x), append(cdr(x), y))\}\\
&\qquad\qquad \mathtt{seq}(rplacd(z, u), val))\\
&\quad \simeq \mathtt{ifn}(x,\\
&\qquad\quad \mathtt{seq}(rplacd(z, y), val),\\
&\qquad\quad \mathtt{let}\{z_0 \leftarrow cons(car(x), *)\}\\
&\qquad\qquad \mathtt{let}\{u_0 \leftarrow append(cdr(x), y))\}\\
&\qquad\qquad\quad \mathtt{seq}(rplacd(z_0, u_0), rplacd(z, z_0), val))\\
&\quad \simeq \mathtt{ifn}(x,\\
&\qquad\quad \mathtt{seq}(rplacd(z, y), val),\\
&\qquad\quad \mathtt{let}\{z_0 \leftarrow cons(car(x), *)\}\\
&\qquad\qquad \mathtt{let}\{u_0 \leftarrow append(cdr(x), y))\}\\
&\qquad\qquad\quad \mathtt{seq}(rplacd(z, z_0), rplacd(z_0, u_0), val))\\
&\quad \simeq \mathtt{ifn}(x,\\
&\qquad\quad \mathtt{seq}(rplacd(z, y), val),\\
&\qquad\quad \mathtt{let}\{z_0 \leftarrow cons(car(x), *)\}\\
&\qquad\qquad \mathtt{seq}(rplacd(z, z_0)\\
&\qquad\qquad\quad \mathtt{let}\{u_0 \leftarrow append(cdr(x), y))\}\\
&\qquad\qquad\qquad \mathtt{seq}(rplacd(z_0, u_0), val))
\end{aligned}
$$

Thus we have succeeded in deriving a strongly isomorphic term that tail recursively calls the initial expression. Thus if we introduce a new function symbol,*app:it*, for the expression

$$\mathtt{let}\{u \leftarrow append(x, y)\}\mathtt{seq}(rplacd(z, u), val)),$$

which has x, y, z, val as its free variables, then the above shows that

```
app:it(x, y, z, val) ≃
    ≃ let{u ← append(cdr(x), y)}
          seq(rplacd(z, u), val)
    ≃ ifn(x,
          seq(rplacd(z, y), val),
          let{z0 ← cons(car(x), *)}
              seq(rplacd(z, z0)
                  app:it(cdr(x), y, z0, val)
```

Thus we arrive at the iterative version of the append program:

```
append(x, y) ←
    ifn(x,
        y,
        let{z ← cons(car(x), *)}
            let{val ← z}
                app:it(x, y, z, val))
```

```
app:it(x, y, z, val) ←
    ifn(x,
        seq(rplacd(z, y), val),
        let{z0 ← cons(car(x), *)}
            seq(rplacd(z, z0)
                app:it(cdr(x), y, z0, val)
```

7.2.2. The Formal Version of the Derivation

The previous derivation can be seen to be a valid one in our system by the following derivation: We begin with the initial definition

```
append(x, y) ← ifn(x, y, cons(car(x), append(cdr(x)), y)))
```

Using the composition rule we add to this the expression procedure

```
let{u ⤙ append(x, y)}seq(rplacd(z, u), val)) ←
    let{u ⤙ ifn(x, y, cons(car(x), append(cdr(x), y)))}
        seq(rplacd(z, u), val))
```

Then using the abstraction rule this expression procedure becomes:

```
let{u ⤙ append(x, y)}seq(rplacd(z, u), val)) ← app:it(x, y, z, val)
```

```
app:it(x, y, z, val) ←
    let{u ⤙ ifn(x, y, cons(car(x), append(cdr(x), y)))}
        seq(rplacd(z, u), val))
```

Using the equivalence rule this last equation becomes

```
app:it(x, y, z, val) ←
    ifn(x,
        seq(rplacd(z, y), val),
        let{z0 ⤙ cons(car(x), *)}
            seq(rplacd(z, z0)
                let{u0 ⤙ append(cdr(x), y))}
                    seq(rplacd(z0, u0), val))
```

The application rule allows us to transform this into

```
app:it(x, y, z, val) ←
    ifn(x,
        seq(rplacd(z, y), val),
        let{z0 ⤙ cons(car(x), *)}
            seq(rplacd(z, z0)
                app:it(cdr(x), y, z0, val)
```

The final result is obtained by using the equivalence rule, and then application.

Exercises:

1. Derive *copy:list* from *rec:copy:list*.
2. Derive *copy:queue* from *rec:copy:queue*.

Finally we ask a question we have not investigated. Can one derive *nconc* or *nreverse* from the following incomplete specifications?

1. $nconc(copy{:}list(x), y) \simeq append(x, y)$.
2. $nreverse(copy{:}list(x)) \simeq reverse(x)$.

Chapter 8

The Robson Marking Algorithm and Applications

In this chapter we verify the Robson marking algorithm, phase one of the so called Robson copying algorithm, by showing that it is strongly isomorphic to a very simple recursively defined algorithm. For an alternative proof of correctness see (Mason and Talcott, 1985). We shall also give two examples of the use of this program. In the first example we describe a transformation of a purely defined function, using this example to illustrate the process of pointer reversal and also to give a simple efficient way of implementing recursion with respect to the left first spanning tree of a graph, well-founded or not. The second example is the actual Robson copying algorithm, treated somewhat differently from that in (Mason and Talcott, 1985).

The marking algorithm is interesting in its own right since it is a more sophisticated algorithm than the Deutsch-Shorr-Waite marking algorithm, (Deutsch, 1968), (Schorr and Waite, 1967), and it can be used to implement recursion efficiently with respect to the left-first spanning tree of a graph. Although in our domain $\mathbb{M}_{sexp}$ there are no mark or field bits, this is of no particular importance since we shall use abstract syntax (McCarthy, 1962b) to hide this fact. The advantage of this is that we can isolate the necessary properties of the implementations of the abstract syntax that are required in the correctness proof. Thus, given a particular implementation of the algorithm we can simply check the correctness of the program by checking that the abstract syntax has the desired properties. We shall give two different interpretations to the abstract syntax, one for the transformation and one for the Robson copying algorithm.

The Robson marking algorithm, like the Deutsch-Schorr-Waite marking algorithm, uses pointer reversal to avoid using an explicit stack. Pointer reversal is a very powerful technique that is used in destructive memory programming. The idea is quite simple; the program destructively alters the structure it is operating on to store the information that a stack would normally be used for. In this case the algorithm scans the graph in a left-first fashion, marking cells as it proceeds. Since the cells are marked when they are first visited, looping or repeatedly scanning the same subgraph is avoided.

8.1. The Robson Marking Program

In the Robson marking algorithm the process of marking a cell consists of allocating a new cell and moving into this new cell the contents of the cell being marked. The cell being marked is then updated so that its car contains a mark and its cdr points to the new cell. Thus a cell prior to marking is depicted in figure 14, while the situation after marking is depicted in figure 15.

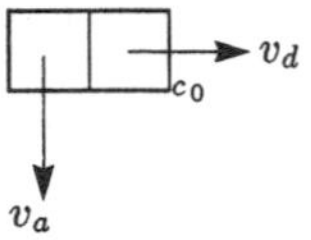

Figure 14. A Cons Cell Prior to Marking

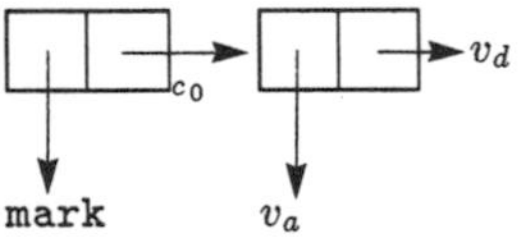

Figure 15. After Marking

Notice that since the old cell contains the mark, external pointers if they check can still access the old car and cdr. A mark is an object specially allocated before marking and so is recognizably not part of the structure to be marked. We use seven different marks to store more information than just simply whether or not the cell has been seen before. We shall denote these marks by `ER`, `EL`, `E10`, `M00`, `M01`, `M10`, `M11`, their meaning roughly being described by the following:

`EL` - Exploring the left hand side of the cell. If the car is not terminal, then while it is being marked the pointer to it will be utilized to store the previous stack. The cell itself then becomes the current stack.

ER - Exploring the right hand side after having explored the left hand side, which was neither atomic nor already marked. If the cdr is not terminal, then while it is being marked the pointer to it will be utilized to store the previous stack. The cell itself then becomes the current stack.

E10 - The left hand side is atomic or has been visited before, now exploring the right hand side.

M11 - Both the left and right hand side are either atoms or cells that were visited earlier in the left first scan; such cells are called *terminal*.

M01 - Only the right hand side was terminal and both sides have been completely visited.

M10 - Only the left hand side was terminal and both sides have been completely visited.

M00 - Neither the left nor the right were terminal, and both sides have been completely visited.

A cell that is marked either EL, ER or E10 resides on the stack, the inverted pointer chain. Marks may be either atoms or cells. The crucial point is that they must be distinct from one another and disjoint from the structure being marked. This will be assumed in the following. The actual definitions of the Robson algorithm are:

```
rmark(s) ← if(terminal(s), s, markcar(s, NIL))
markcar(s, stack) ←
    seq(mkmark(s, EL),
        let{t1 ← a(s)}
            if(terminal(t1),
                seq(setm(s, E10), markcdr(s, stack)),
                seq(seta(s, stack), markcar(t1, s))))
markcdr(s, stack) ←
    let{t2 ← d(s)}
        if(terminal(t2),
            ifs(eq(ER, m(s)), seq(setm(s, M01), pop:mark:stack(s, stack)),
                eq(E10, m(s)), seq(setm(s, M11), pop:mark:stack(s, stack)))
            seq(setd(s, stack), markcar(t2, s)))
```

```
pop:mark:stack(s, stack) ←
     ifn(stack,
          s,
          let{t1 ← a(stack), t2 ← d(stack)},
             ifs(eq(EL, m(stack)),
                  seq(setm(stack, ER),
                       seta(stack, s),
                       markcdr(stack, t1)),
                  eq(ER, m(stack)),
                  seq(setm(stack, M00),
                       setd(stack, s),
                       pop:mark:stack(stack, t2)),
                  eq(E10, m(stack)),
                  seq(setm(stack, M10),
                       setd(stack, s),
                       pop:mark:stack(stack, t2))))
```

The program as written above is a tail recursive definition, which uses the abstract syntax

$$m, a, d, seta, setd, mkmark, setm, marked, terminal\,.$$

The function *mkmark* does the job of allocating the new cell and placing the contents of the original cell in it, altering the original so that its car contains the appropriate mark and its cdr the new cell. *a* and *d* then access the old car and cdr, while *seta* and *setd* update them. *setm* just replaces the mark without allocating any new cells. *marked* determines whether the cell is marked and *m* returns the mark. *terminal* just checks whether a cell is terminal, namely whether it is an atom or an already marked cell. To be explicit we have the following definitions of these functions.

```
m(cell) ← car(cell)

a(cell) ← car(cdr(cell))

d(cell) ← cdr(cdr(cell))

mkmark(cell, m) ←

     let{t2 ← car(cell)}

          seq(rplaca(cell, m), rplacd(cell, cons(t2, cdr(cell))))
```

$setm(\texttt{cell}, \texttt{m}) \leftarrow rplaca(\texttt{cell}, \texttt{m})$

$seta(\texttt{cell}, \texttt{x}) \leftarrow rplaca(cdr(\texttt{cell}), \texttt{x})$

$setd(\texttt{cell}, \texttt{x}) \leftarrow rplacd(cdr(\texttt{cell}), \texttt{x})$

$marked(\texttt{cell}) \leftarrow memq(car(\texttt{cell}), (\texttt{ER}, \texttt{EL}, \texttt{E10}, \texttt{M11}, \texttt{M01}, \texttt{M10}, \texttt{M00}))$

$terminal(\texttt{cell}) \leftarrow \texttt{or}(atom(\texttt{cell}), marked(\texttt{cell}))$

In this example we shall prove that the above program does exactly the same job as a very simple recursive algorithm. Again we consider such a reduction as a form of verification. The simple recursive version is, using the same abstract syntax, the following program:

```
rec:rmark(s) ← if(terminal(s), s, seq(rec:rmark1(s), s))
rec:rmark1(s) ←
      seq(mkmark(s, EL),
          if(terminal(a(s)),
             if( terminal(d(s)),
                 setm(s, M11),
                 seq(setm(s, M10), rec:rmark1(d(s))))
             seq(rec:rmark1(a(s)),
              if(terminal(d(s)),
                 setm(s, M01),
                 seq(setm(s, M00), rec:rmark1(d(s)))))))
```

Theorem: $rmark(x) \simeq rec{:}mark(x)$

Before we prove this theorem we give two examples of the use of the marking program.

8.2. An Application of the Robson Marking Algorithm

In this example we shall describe a program transformation T which, given a pure Lisp function f with definition

$$
\begin{aligned}
&f(\mathtt{x},\mathtt{params}) \leftarrow \\
&\qquad \mathtt{if}(atom(\mathtt{x}), g(\mathtt{x},\mathtt{params}), h(f(car(\mathtt{x}),\mathtt{params}), \\
&\qquad\qquad f(cdr(\mathtt{x}),\mathtt{params}), \\
&\qquad\qquad \mathtt{x}, \\
&\qquad\qquad \mathtt{params})),
\end{aligned}
$$

here g and h are any previously defined pure Lisp functions, produces a function *Tf* that has the following properties:

- Whenever f is defined so is *Tf* and their values are Lisp equal.
- *Tf* is defined by a set of mutually tail recursive functions.
- *Tf* is gentle in the sense that its use of destructive memory operations is not visible from outside the function.
- *Tf* takes notice of any shared structure within x and does not duplicate calls to f. This gives *Tf* the ability to be exponentially faster than its pure counterpart. It also means that when f takes a value, *Tf* need not take an isomorphic value.
- As an added feature *Tf* can detect cyclicity in its x argument and terminate with some desired bell or whistle.
- *Tf* destructively alters x so that it can store the stack, the left-first spanning tree, and any precomputed value on the structure itself, thus using little space and allowing quick and easy access to the information so stored.

This destructive modification of x creates two complications the transformation must deal with, complications which of course slow down its performance.

- The first complication is that during the computation x, as we have already remarked, will be modified so that it can be used to store relevant information about it and the computation. This means that if the function h actually uses its x parameter during the computation then it must be made aware of these changes. We shall return to this point when we are able to discuss it in more detail.
- The second complication, again caused by the temporary modification of x, is more troublesome. If `params` share any structure with x then again this must be taken into account. However unlike the previous complication this is not at all easy to accomplish. For this reason we shall henceforth assume that there is no structure sharing between x and `params`.

The transformation that we describe here is an abstraction of the Robson copying algorithm (Robson, 1977). Being a generalization it fails to incorporate the *eureka* step , cf (Burstall and Darlington, 1977), which makes the Robson algorithm a bounded space algorithm.

8.3. A Description of the Transformation T

The transformed program *Tf* can naturally be divided up into three phases, the first and the last being independent of the nature of f, g and h. However we shall discuss them in order.

8.3.1. Phase 1: Marking x.

The marking algorithm used here is just phase one of the Robson copying algorithm, the only two modifications are to the abstract syntax.

- The *terminal* function is elaborated so as to detect cyclicity.
- The abstract syntax is modified so as to include a value cell.

Note that both these modifications only effect the abstract syntax; consequently as long as the new interpretation of the abstract syntax has the same properties as the old one, the marking theorem will hold in both cases.

The first modification is quite simple; during the marking process one can detect cyclicity with almost no effort. When a terminal cell is encountered that is marked either by `EL`, `ER` or `E10` we know that the structure in question is cyclic. The reason is simply that if the structure was well-founded then terminal cells would have to be completely marked, in other words be marked by either `M00`, `M01`, `M10` or `M11`. The second modification is as follows. When marking a cell here, two rather than one new cell is allocated. The first we shall call the value cell while the second we call the *a-d* cell. The old cell is modified so that its car points to a mark and its cdr points to the value cell. This new cell's car pointer is used to store values, originally set to a default value `no:value`, while it's cdr points to the second new cell, the *a-d* cell, which in turn is used to store the original cell's contents. v accesses the car of the value cell, and *setv* updates it. Thus if we begin

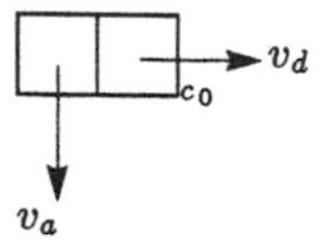

Figure 16. A Cons Cell Prior to Marking

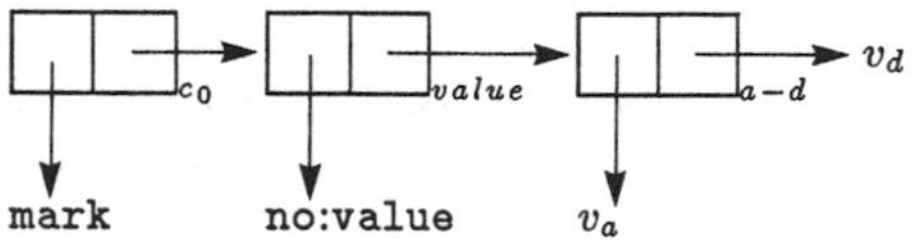

Figure 17. After Marking

with the situation depicted in figure 16, the situation after marking is portrayed in figure 17.

The actual definitions are as follows.

```
m(cell) ← car(cell)
v(cell) ← cadr(cell)
a(cell) ← caddr(cell)
d(cell) ← cdddr(cell)
mkmark(cell, m) ←
    let{t2 ← car(cell)}
        seq(rplaca(cell, m),
            rplacd(cell, cons(no:value, cons(t2, cdr(cell)))))
setm(cell, m) ← rplaca(cell, m)
setv(cell, v) ← rplaca(cdr(cell), v)
seta(cell, x) ← rplaca(cddr(cell), x)
```

$setd(\texttt{cell}, \texttt{x}) \leftarrow rplacd(cddr(\texttt{cell}), \texttt{x})$

$marked(\texttt{cell}) \leftarrow$

$\quad \texttt{if}(memq(car(\texttt{cell}), (\texttt{ER}, \texttt{EL}, \texttt{E10})),$

$\quad\quad \texttt{CYCLIC},$

$\quad\quad memq(car(\texttt{cell}), (\texttt{M11}, \texttt{M01}, \texttt{M10}, \texttt{M00})))$

$terminal(\texttt{cell}) \leftarrow \texttt{or}(atom(\texttt{cell}), marked(\texttt{cell}))$

In describing the next two phases we shall be content to describe the recursive versions of them. The we finish off this section with a brief description of the pointer reversing process, whereby one obtains the actual programs. For example the marking theorem of this section shows essentially that the Robson marking algorithm is simply a pointer reversing version of the recursively defined *rec:mark* program.

8.3.2. Phase 2 and 3: Computing $f(x)$ and Restoring x

Phase two of the transformation *Tf* is the program *comp:tf* that actually computes the value of the function *Tf*. It is then followed by *rstr*, the third phase, whose sole purpose is to restore x to its original state. The recursive versions of the algorithms are both instances of the following schema, perhaps the simplest example of recursion on the left first spanning tree.

$G(\texttt{s}, \texttt{params}) \leftarrow \texttt{if}(atom(\texttt{s}), g(\texttt{s}, \texttt{params}), G_1(\texttt{s}, \texttt{params}))$

$G_1(\texttt{s}, \texttt{params}) \leftarrow$

$\quad \texttt{let}\{\texttt{mark:bit} \leftarrow m(\texttt{s})\}$

$\quad\quad \texttt{seq}(\texttt{ifs}(eq(\texttt{mark:bit}, \texttt{M00}), \texttt{seq}(G_1(a(\texttt{s}), \texttt{params}),$

$\quad\quad\quad\quad\quad\quad G_1(d(\texttt{s}), \texttt{params}))$

$\quad\quad\quad eq(\texttt{mark:bit}, \texttt{M01}), G_1(a(\texttt{s}), \texttt{params}),$

$\quad\quad\quad eq(\texttt{mark:bit}, \texttt{M10}), G_1(d(\texttt{s}), \texttt{params}),$

$\quad\quad\quad eq(\texttt{mark:bit}, \texttt{M11}), \texttt{NIL}),$

$\quad\quad G_2(\texttt{s}, \texttt{params})))$

In the case of *rec:comp:tf* we have

- $G = rec{:}comp{:}tf$
- $G_1 = rec{:}comp{:}tf_1$

- G_2 has the following definition

```
G2(s, params) ←
      setv(s, t:h(val(a(s), params),
                  val(d(s), params),
                  s,
                  params))
val(s, params) ← if(atom(s), g(s, params), v(s))
```

While in the case of *rec:rstr* we have

- $G = rec{:}rstr$
- $G_1 = rec{:}rstr_1$
- $G_2(\mathtt{s}, \mathtt{params}) \nleftarrow rplacd(rplaca(\mathtt{s}, a(\mathtt{s}), d(\mathtt{s}))$

8.3.3. The Pointer Reversal Process.

It suffices to deal with the G, G_1, G_2 schema when both G_1 and G_2 are already tail recursive. So we shall treat only G_1 in this case. We shall also omit the parameters to simplify reading. The first and simplest way to transform such a program into a tail recursive program is to incorporate an explicit stack. In this case a frame need only consist of a single object, the father of the current value of s. The actual definitions are:

```
G1(s, stack) ←
    ifs(or(eq(m(s), M00),
           eq(m(s), M01)), G1(a(s), cons(s, stack)),
        eq(m(s), M10), G1(d(s), cons(s, stack)),
        eq(m(s), M11), pop:G1:stack(s, stack, G2(s))),
```

```
pop:G1:stack(s, stack, val) ←
    ifn(stack,
        val,
        let{father ← car(stack), mark ← m(car(stack))}
            ifs(and(eq(mark, M00), eq(s car(father))),
                    G1(d(father), stack),
                eq(mark, M00), pop:G1:stack(s, cdr(stack), G2(father)),
                eq(mark, M01), pop:G1:stack(s, cdr(stack), G2(father)),
                eq(mark, M10), pop:G1:stack(s, cdr(stack), G2(father))))
```

The next part of the process is aimed at eliminating the cons call when we push the stack. The first thing to notice is that, since we are treating recursion with respect to the left first spanning tree, the s cell will not be used in computing $G_1(a(\mathtt{s}), cons(\mathtt{s}, \mathtt{stack}))$ or $G_1(d(\mathtt{s}), cons(\mathtt{s}, \mathtt{stack}))$, except in one place. When s is marked M00 we use s to determine, in the *pop*:G_1:*stack* program, whether or not the *d* value has been computed. Rather than do this we can simply alter the mark, to say F00, when we are computing the *a* part of a M00 cell. Consequently while we are computing the *a* part of s we can use the *a* pointer of s to store the old stack. Similarly when we are computing the *d* part we can use the *d* pointer to store the stack. This eliminates the need to create a new cell when we push the stack. Of course when we pop the stack we must restore the contents. This leads to the following schema.

```
G1(s, stack) ←
    let{mark ← m(s), a:s ← a(s), d:s ← d(s)}
        ifs(eq(mark, M00), seq(seta(s, stack) setm(s, F00), G1(a:s, s)),
            eq(mark, M01), seq(seta(s, stack), G1(a:s, s)),
            eq(mark, M10), seq(setd(s, stack), G1(d:s, s)),
            eq(mark, M11), pop:G1:stack(s, stack, G2(s)))
```

```
pop:G1:stack(s, stack, val) ←
     ifn(stack,
          val,
          let{d:stack ← d(stack), a:stack ← a(stack), mark ← m(stack)}
              ifs(eq(mark, F00), seq(setm(stack, M00),
                                     setd(stack, a(stack)),
                                     seta(stack, s),
                                     G1(d:stack, stack)),
                  eq(mark, M00), seq(setd(stack, s),
                                     pop:G1:stack(stack, d:stack, G2(father)),
                  eq(mark, M01), seq(seta(stack, s),
                                     pop:G1:stack(stack, a:stack, G2(father)),
                  eq(mark, M10), seq(setd(stack, s),
                                     pop:G1:stack(stack, d:stack, G2(father))))
```

Thus we have obtained our tail recursive version, without using any more space, by incorporating the stack in the input.

8.3.4. Analysis of Tf and f

We simplify matters by only considering S-expressions which are Lisp equal up to different atomic values to *tree*(n) for some integer n.

```
tree(n) ← if(eq(n, 0), NIL, cons(tree(n − 1), tree(n − 1)))
```

There are many of these objects. For example we have the following simple exercise which shows that there are at least on the order of 2^n such objects.

Fact: $\forall m$ such that $n \leq m \leq 2^n - 1$ we have that there is a Lisp object containing only m cells which is Lisp equal to *tree*(n).

In fact this is a substantial underestimate since if we let $D(n)$ be the number of non-isomorphic lisp objects equal to *tree*($n+1$) and $D(n,k)$ be those of these that have exactly k cells which contain atoms then we have

- $D(n) = \sum_{i=1}^{2^n} D(n,i)$
- $D(n+1,k) = \sum_{i=1}^{2^n} \left\{ {2i \atop k} \right\}.D(n,i)$, where $\left\{ {n \atop k} \right\}$ is the Stirling number of the second kind, see (Knuth, 1968). In other words $\left\{ {n \atop k} \right\}$ is the number of partitions of a set with n elements into k non-empty subsets. So for example $D(0) = 1$, $D(1) = 2$, $D(2) = 17$, and $D(3) = 5482$.

If v is an object Lisp equal to *tree*($n+1$) we say that the *virtual size of* v is 2^n. The time to compute $f(v)$ is directly proportional to the virtual size of v

whereas that for Tf is proportion to the actual size. Thus in general when there is any substantial degree of structure sharing in x then the transformed program should out perform its pure parent. There are several questions raised by such an analysis. The most important, from a practical point of view, we shall not approach. We can describe for what sort of Lisp objects our transformed program out-performs its parent, but we cannot answer the question of how regularly such objects show up in actual practice.

In (Clark and Green ,1977) the following remarks are made:

A precise count of shared cells was not made at the same time as the other work reported here. A later measurement, however, using different versions of the programs and a different tracing technique, found that between 1.4 and 2.4 percent of each program's list cells were pointed to more than once. Most of these cells were pointed to just twice. The most frequently referenced cell in each program attracted between .1 and .5 percent of all list pointers (as many as several hundred pointers).

Although an interesting fact, it tells us little about the nature of this sharing, and consequently little about the above mentioned practical question. Another interesting observation made in (Clark and Green, 1977) is that pointers to atoms roughly obey Zipf's law. So although in our transformation we have not attempted to eliminate duplicate calls to g, such an optimization might be worthwhile if g is a lengthy or costly function.

8.4. The Robson Copying Algorithm

The next use of the Robson marking program is the one for which it was originally designed, namely as phase one of the Robson copying algorithm. In this example we use the first interpretation of the abstract syntax; namely, in marking only one new cell is allocated. We begin by a discussing how the program works. As Robson himself says of his own algorithm:

A new algorithm is presented which copies cyclic list structures using bounded workspace and linear time .... The distinctive feature of this algorithm is a technique for traversing the structure twice, using the same spanning tree in each case, first from left to right and then from right to left.

The first traversal of the structure corresponds precisely to the algorithm that we have called the Robson marking algorithm. Consequently we need now only describe the second traversal, best described as a *peeling* operation.

Recall that after the first traversal each cell is allocated a new cell, which we shall call its *image*. The original cell is modified so that its *car* part contains a mark denoting its place in the left-first spanning tree, while its *cdr* part contains its image. The image in turn contains the cell's original contents. Consequently each original cell now contains two more pieces of information, namely whether its *car* or its *cdr* is terminal in the Brouwer-Kleene ordering of the left-first spanning tree. This information allows the second traversal to use the same spanning tree, in the reverse order, without further marking. The crucial observation is that since the decision to follow a pointer depends on the mark in the cell containing it, rather than upon the cell pointed to, this traversal can remove the marks as it uses them. Furthermore since the *image* cell, which is used together with the original cell to store the mark and the original contents, is no longer required, this cell can be recycled and used as the corresponding cell in the copy. This storage optimization is similar in spirit to that done recently in the study of *tail recursion up to a cons*, see for example (Wadler, 1984), (Warren, 1980) or (Steele, 1977b).

```
copy(s) ← if(atom(s), s, peel(rmark(s), NIL)
peel(s, stack) ←
      let{nc ← cdr(s), t1 ← a(s), t2 ← d(s)}
         ifs(eq(M00, m(s)), seq(setm(s, F00),
                                 setd(s, stack),
                                 peel(t2, s)),
             eq(M01, m(s)), seq(setm(s, stack),
                                 seta(s, t2),
                                 setd(s, image(t2)),
                                 peel(t1, s)),
             eq(M10, m(s)), seq(setm(s, F10),
                                 setd(s, stack),
                                 peel(t2, s)),
             eq(M11, m(s)), seq(setm(s, t1),
                                 seta(s, image(t1)),
                                 setd(s, image(t2)),
                                 rplacd(s, t2),
                                 pop:peel:stack(s, stack, nc)))
```

```
pop:peel:stack(s, stack, newcel) ←
    ifn(stack,
        newcel,
        let{nc ← cdr(stack), oc ← car(stack), t1 ← a(stack), t2 ← d(stack)}
            ifs(eq(F00, m(stack)),seq(setm(stack, t2),
                                      setd(stack, newcel),
                                      seta(stack, s),
                                      peel(t1, stack)),
                eq(F10, m(stack)),seq(setm(stack, t1),
                                      seta(stack, image(t1)),
                                      setd(stack, newcel),
                                      rplacd(stack, s),
                                      pop:peel:stack(stack, t2, nc)),
                T,                seq(rplacd(stack, t1),
                                      setm(nc, newcel),
                                      setm(stack, s),
                                      pop:peel:stack(stack, oc, nc)))

image(l) ← if(atom(l), l, cdr(l))
```

In (Mason and Talcott, 1985) the following result is proved using explicit evaluation, induction and a sharp knife for dissecting the resulting memory.

Theorem: $copy(x) \cong x$ on $\mathbb{M}_{sexp}$. Furthermore if

$$copy(c)\,;\,\mu \gg c^*\,;\,\mu^*$$

then

1. $\mu = \mu^*$ on $\mathbf{Cells}_\mu(\mathrm{c})$
2. $\mathbf{Cells}_\mu(c) \cap \mathbf{Cells}_{\mu^*}(c^*) = \emptyset$
3. $|\delta_{\mu^*}| = |\delta_\mu| + |\mathbf{Cells}_\mu(c)|$

One could also show that it is strongly isomorphic to the following relatively simple recursively defined program. This we shall do later. It does however point out a weakness in our program, since the recursive version is not really very much simpler than the pointer reversing counterpart.

```
rec:copy(l) ←
     if(atom(l),
        l,
        seq(rec:mark(l), rec:peel(l)))
rec:peel(oldcel) ←
     let{newcel ← cdr(oldcel)}
     let{     newcar ← image(car(newcel)),
              newcdr ← image(cdr(newcel)),
              oldcar ← car(newcel),
              oldcdr ← cdr(newcel)}
     seq(ifs(eq(M00, m(oldcel)), seq(rec:peel(oldcdr), rec:peel(oldcar)),
              eq(M01, m(oldcel)), rec:peel(oldcar),
              eq(M10, m(oldcel)), rec:peel(oldcdr),
              eq(M11, m(oldcel)), NIL),
     rplaca(oldcel, oldcar),
     rplacd(oldcel, oldcdr),
     rplaca(newcel, newcar),
     rplacd(newcel, newcdr))
```

Peeling Theorem: If $x \cong rmark(y)$ for some y which does not contain any marks, then

$$peel(x, \mathtt{NIL}) \simeq rec{:}peel(x).$$

8.5. The Proof of the Marking Theorem

We now proceed with the proof of the following theorem,which is identical in spirit if not in detail to the proof given earlier of the Deutsch-Schorr-Waite marking algorithm.

Theorem: If x does not contain any marks, then

$$rmark(x) \simeq rec{:}mark(x)$$

Proof of Theorem: We prove the following lemma by induction on the size of

$$\mathbf{Unmarked}(s),$$

the set of unmarked cells reachable from s via paths through unmarked cells. For typographical reasons we shall refer to *pop:mark:stack* simply by *popstack*.

Lemma: $\mathit{markcar}(s, \mathit{stack}) \simeq \mathtt{seq}(\mathit{rec{:}mark1}(s), \mathit{popstack}(s, \mathit{stack}))$

To see that the result follows it suffices to observe that

$$\mathit{markcar}(s, \mathtt{NIL}) \simeq \mathtt{seq}(\mathit{rec{:}mark1}(s), \mathit{popstack}(s, \mathtt{NIL})) \simeq \mathtt{seq}(\mathit{rec{:}mark1}(s), s)$$

□Theorem

Proof of lemma: Although the proof seems long, it is in fact quite short. It consists of 20 simple transformations on a sizable program; hence its length.

$$
\begin{array}{l}
\mathit{markcar}(s, \mathit{stack}) \simeq \\
\quad \simeq \mathtt{seq}(\mathit{mkmark}(s, \mathtt{EL}), \\
\qquad\quad \mathtt{let}\{\mathtt{t1} \leftarrow a(s)\} \\
\qquad\qquad \mathtt{if}(\mathit{terminal}(\mathtt{t1}), \\
\qquad\qquad\quad \mathtt{seq}(\mathit{setm}(s, \mathtt{E10}), \mathit{markcdr}(s, \mathit{stack})), \\
\qquad\qquad\quad \mathtt{seq}(\mathit{seta}(s, \mathit{stack}), \mathit{markcar}(\mathtt{t1}, s))))
\end{array}
$$

evaluating the `let` gives

$$
\begin{array}{l}
\simeq \mathtt{seq}(\mathit{mkmark}(s, \mathtt{EL}), \\
\qquad \mathtt{if}(\mathit{terminal}(s_a), \\
\qquad\quad \mathtt{seq}(\mathit{setm}(s, \mathtt{E10}), \mathit{markcdr}(s, \mathit{stack})), \\
\qquad\quad \mathtt{seq}(\mathit{seta}(s, \mathit{stack}), \mathit{markcar}(s_a, s))))
\end{array}
$$

applying the induction hypothesis to the $\mathit{markcar}(s_a, s)$ call

$$
\begin{array}{l}
\simeq \mathtt{seq}(\mathit{mkmark}(s, \mathtt{EL}), \\
\qquad \mathtt{if}(\mathit{terminal}(s_a), \\
\qquad\quad \mathtt{seq}(\mathit{setm}(s, \mathtt{E10}), \mathit{markcdr}(s, \mathit{stack})), \\
\qquad\quad \mathtt{seq}(\mathit{seta}(s, \mathit{stack}), \mathtt{seq}(\mathit{rec{:}mark1}(s_a), \mathit{popstack}(s_a, s)))))
\end{array}
$$

removing nested `seq`s , unfolding the $\mathit{popstack}(s_a, s)$ call

```
≃ seq(mkmark(s, EL),
      if(terminal(s_a),
         seq(setm(s, E10), markcdr(s, stack)),
         seq(seta(s, stack),
             rec:mark1(s_a),
             ifn(s,
                 s_a,
                 let{t1 ← a(s), t2 ← d(s)},
                    ifs(eq(EL, m(s)),
                        seq(setm(s, ER), seta(s, s_a), markcdr(s, t1)),
                        eq(ER, m(s)),
                        seq(setm(s, M00), setd(s, s_a), popstack(s, t2)),
                        eq(E10, m(s)),
                        seq(setm(s, M10), setd(s, s_a), popstack(s, t2))
                        )))))
```

evaluating the `let` yields

```
≃ seq(mkmark(s, EL),
      if(terminal(s_a),
         seq(setm(s, E10), markcdr(s, stack)),
         seq(seta(s, stack),
             rec:mark1(s_a),
             ifs(eq(EL, m(s)),
                 seq(setm(s, ER), seta(s, s_a), markcdr(s, stack)),
                 eq(ER, m(s)),
                 seq(setm(s, M00), setd(s, s_a), popstack(s, s_d)),
                 eq(E10, m(s)),
                 seq(setm(s, M10), setd(s, s_a), popstack(s, s_d)))))))
```

simplifying the `if` using the fact that at this branch $m(\mathrm{s}) \simeq \mathtt{EL}$ gives:

$$
\begin{array}{l}
\simeq \mathtt{seq}(mkmark(s,\mathrm{EL}),\\
\qquad \mathtt{if}(terminal(s_a),\\
\qquad\quad \mathtt{seq}(setm(s,\mathtt{E10}), markcdr(s,stack)),\\
\qquad\quad \mathtt{seq}(seta(s,stack),\\
\qquad\qquad rec{:}mark1(s_a),\\
\qquad\qquad \mathtt{seq}(setm(s,\mathrm{ER}), seta(s,s_a), markcdr(s,stack)))))
\end{array}
$$

nested `seq` disposal, unfolding *markcdr*(s, stack) and commuting the *seta* s:

$$
\begin{array}{l}
\simeq \mathtt{seq}(mkmark(s,\mathrm{EL}),\\
\qquad \mathtt{if}(terminal(s_a),\\
\qquad\quad \mathtt{seq}(setm(s,\mathtt{E10}), markcdr(s,stack)),\\
\qquad\quad \mathtt{seq}(seta(s,stack),\\
\qquad\qquad seta(s,s_a),\\
\qquad\qquad rec{:}mark1(s_a),\\
\qquad\qquad setm(s,\mathrm{ER}),\\
\qquad\qquad \mathtt{let}\{\mathtt{t2} \leftarrow d(s)\}\\
\qquad\qquad\quad \mathtt{if}(terminal(\mathtt{t2}),\\
\qquad\qquad\qquad \mathtt{ifs}(eq(\mathrm{ER},m(s)),\\
\qquad\qquad\qquad\quad \mathtt{seq}(setm(s,\mathtt{M01}), popstack(s,stack)),\\
\qquad\qquad\qquad\quad eq(\mathtt{E10},m(s)),\\
\qquad\qquad\qquad\quad \mathtt{seq}(setm(s,\mathtt{M11}), popstack(s,stack)))\\
\qquad\qquad\qquad \mathtt{seq}(setd(s,stack), markcar(\mathtt{t2},s))))))
\end{array}
$$

evaluating the `let` and cancelling successive *seta* s yields:

$$
\begin{array}{l}
\simeq \mathtt{seq}(mkmark(s,\mathrm{EL}),\\
\qquad \mathtt{if}(terminal(s_a),\\
\qquad\quad \mathtt{seq}(setm(s,\mathtt{E10}), markcdr(s,stack)),\\
\qquad\quad \mathtt{seq}(rec{:}mark1(s_a),\\
\qquad\qquad setm(s,\mathrm{ER}),\\
\qquad\qquad \mathtt{if}(terminal(s_d),\\
\qquad\qquad\quad \mathtt{ifs}(eq(\mathrm{ER},m(s)), \mathtt{seq}(setm(s,\mathtt{M01}), popstack(s,stack)),\\
\qquad\qquad\qquad eq(\mathtt{E10},m(s)), \mathtt{seq}(setm(s,\mathtt{M11}), popstack(s,stack)))\\
\qquad\qquad\quad \mathtt{seq}(setd(s,stack), markcar(s_d,s))))))
\end{array}
$$

deleting vacuous `ifs` and using the induction hypothesis:

```
≃ seq(mkmark(s, EL),
      if(terminal(s_a),
         seq(setm(s, E10), markcdr(s, stack)),
         seq(rec:mark1(s_a),
             setm(s, ER),
             if(terminal(s_d),
                seq(setm(s, M01), popstack(s, stack)),
                seq(setd(s, stack),
                    seq(rec:mark1(s_d), popstack(s_d, s)))))))
```

nested seq disposal, unfolding and simplifying the *popstack*(s_d, s) call:

```
≃ seq(mkmark(s, EL),
      if(terminal(s_a),
         seq(setm(s, E10), markcdr(s, stack)),
         seq(rec:mark1(s_a),
             setm(s, ER),
             if(terminal(s_d),
                seq(setm(s, M01), popstack(s, stack)),
                seq(setd(s, stack),
                    rec:mark1(s_d),
                    seq(setm(s, M00), setd(s, s_d), popstack(s, stack)))))))
```

nested seq removal , commuting then cancelling *setd* s yields:

```
≃ seq(mkmark(s, EL),
      if(terminal(s_a),
         seq(setm(s, E10), markcdr(s, stack)),
         seq(rec:mark1(s_a),
             setm(s, ER),
             if(terminal(s_d),
                seq(setm(s, M01), popstack(s, stack)),
                seq(rec:mark1(s_d), setm(s, M00), popstack(s, stack))))))
```

We now concentrate on the terminal car branch:

markcar$(s, stack) \simeq$

unfolding the *markcdr*$(s, stack)$ call gives:

$$
\begin{aligned}
\simeq\ & \texttt{seq}(\mathit{mkmark}(s, \mathrm{EL}),\\
&\quad \texttt{if}(\mathit{terminal}(s_a),\\
&\qquad \texttt{seq}(\mathit{setm}(s, \texttt{E10}),\\
&\qquad\quad \texttt{if}(\mathit{terminal}(s_d),\\
&\qquad\qquad \texttt{ifs}(\mathit{eq}(\mathrm{ER}, m(s)), \texttt{seq}(\mathit{setm}(s, \texttt{M01}), \mathit{popstack}(s, \mathit{stack})),\\
&\qquad\qquad\qquad \mathit{eq}(\texttt{E10}, m(s)), \texttt{seq}(\mathit{setm}(s, \texttt{M11}), \mathit{popstack}(s, \mathit{stack})))\\
&\qquad\qquad \texttt{seq}(\mathit{setd}(s, \mathit{stack}), \mathit{markcar}(s_d, s)))\\
&\qquad \texttt{seq}(\mathit{rec{:}mark1}(s_a),\\
&\qquad\quad \mathit{setm}(s, \mathrm{ER}),\\
&\qquad\quad \texttt{if}(\mathit{terminal}(s_d),\\
&\qquad\qquad \texttt{seq}(\mathit{setm}(s, \texttt{M01}), \mathit{popstack}(s, \mathit{stack})),\\
&\qquad\qquad \texttt{seq}(\mathit{rec{:}mark1}(s_d), \mathit{setm}(s, \texttt{M00}), \mathit{popstack}(s, \mathit{stack})))))))
\end{aligned}
$$

simplifying the `ifs` by noting that $m(\mathrm{s}) \simeq \texttt{E10}$ at this point yields:

$$
\begin{aligned}
\simeq\ & \texttt{seq}(\mathit{mkmark}(s, \mathrm{EL}),\\
&\quad \texttt{if}(\mathit{terminal}(s_a),\\
&\qquad \texttt{seq}(\mathit{setm}(s, \texttt{E10}),\\
&\qquad\quad \texttt{if}(\mathit{terminal}(s_d),\\
&\qquad\qquad \texttt{seq}(\mathit{setm}(s, \texttt{M11}), \mathit{popstack}(s, \mathit{stack})))\\
&\qquad\qquad \texttt{seq}(\mathit{setd}(s, \mathit{stack}), \mathit{markcar}(s_d, s)))\\
&\qquad \texttt{seq}(\mathit{rec{:}mark1}(s_a),\\
&\qquad\quad \mathit{setm}(s, \mathrm{ER}),\\
&\qquad\quad \texttt{if}(\mathit{terminal}(s_d),\\
&\qquad\qquad \texttt{seq}(\mathit{setm}(s, \texttt{M01}), \mathit{popstack}(s, \mathit{stack})),\\
&\qquad\qquad \texttt{seq}(\mathit{rec{:}mark1}(s_d), \mathit{setm}(s, \texttt{M00}), \mathit{popstack}(s, \mathit{stack})))))))
\end{aligned}
$$

using the induction hypothesis on the $\mathit{markcar}(\mathrm{s_d}, \mathrm{s})$ call gives:

```
≃ seq(mkmark(s, EL),
      if(terminal(s_a),
         seq(setm(s, E10),
             if(terminal(s_d),
                seq(setm(s, M11), popstack(s, stack)))
                seq(setd(s, stack),
                    seq(rec:mark1(s_d), popstack(s_d, s))))
         seq(rec:mark1(s_a),
             setm(s, ER),
             if(terminal(s_d),
                seq(setm(s, M01), popstack(s, stack)),
                seq(rec:mark1(s_d), setm(s, M00), popstack(s, stack))))))
```

nested **seq** removal, unfolding and simplifying the *popstack*(s_d, s) call:

```
≃ seq(mkmark(s, EL),
      if(terminal(s_a),
         seq(setm(s, E10),
             if(terminal(s_d),
                seq(setm(s, M11), popstack(s, stack)))
                seq(setd(s, stack),
                    rec:mark1(s_d),
                    seq(setm(s, M10), setd(s, s_d), popstack(s, stack)))))
         seq(rec:mark1(s_a),
             setm(s, ER),
             if(terminal(s_d),
                seq(setm(s, M01), popstack(s, stack)),
                seq(rec:mark1(s_d), setm(s, M00), popstack(s, stack))))))
```

removing nested **seq**s, commuting then cancelling the successive *setd* s:

```
≃ seq(mkmark(s, EL),
        if(terminal(s_a),
           seq(setm(s, E10),
               if(terminal(s_d),
                  seq(setm(s, M11), popstack(s, stack)))
                  seq(rec:mark1(s_d),
                      setm(s, M10),
                      popstack(s, stack))))
           seq(rec:mark1(s_a),
               setm(s, ER),
               if(terminal(s_d),
                  seq(setm(s, M01), popstack(s, stack)),
                  seq(rec:mark1(s_d), setm(s, M00), popstack(s, stack)))))))
```

The final transformations are simple:

markcar(*s*, *stack*) ≃

removing redundant *setm* s produces:

```
≃ seq(mkmark(s, EL),
        if(terminal(s_a),
           if( terminal(s_d),
               seq(setm(s, M11), popstack(s, stack)))
               seq(rec:mark1(s_d),
                   setm(s, M10),
                   popstack(s, stack))))
           seq(rec:mark1(s_a),
               if( terminal(s_d),
                   seq(setm(s, M01), popstack(s, stack)),
                   seq(rec:mark1(s_d), setm(s, M00), popstack(s, stack))))))
```

commuting the *setm* s with the *rec:mark* calls gives:

$\simeq$ `seq`(*mkmark*(s, EL),
    `if`(*terminal*(s_a),
        `if`(*terminal*(s_d),
            `seq`(*setm*(s, M11), *popstack*(s, *stack*)))
            `seq`(*setm*(s, M10),
                rec:mark1(s_d),
                popstack(s, *stack*))))
        `seq`(*rec:mark1*(s_a),
            `if`(*terminal*(s_d),
                `seq`(*setm*(s, M01), *popstack*(s, *stack*)),
                `seq`(*setm*(s, M00), *rec:mark1*(s_d), *popstack*(s, *stack*)))))))

pulling the popstack out of the `if` and removing the s_a and s_d produces:

$\simeq$ `seq`(*mkmark*(s, EL),
    `if`(*terminal*($a(s)$),
        `if`(*terminal*($d(s)$),
            setm(s, M11),
            `seq`(*setm*(s, M10),
                rec:mark1($d(s)$))),
        `seq`(*rec:mark1*($a(s)$),
            `if`(*terminal*($d(s)$),
                setm(s, M01),
                `seq`(*setm*(s, M00), *rec:mark1*($d(s)$))))),
    popstack(s, *stack*))

folding gives the result:

$\simeq$ `seq`(*rec:mark1*(s), *popstack*(s, *stack*))

□Lemma

8.6. The Proof of the Peeling Theorem

In this section we sketch a proof of the following theorem.

Peeling Theorem: If $x \cong rmark(y)$ for some y which does not contain any marks, then

$$peel(x, \texttt{NIL}) \simeq rec{:}peel(x).$$

This theorem is a corollary of the following lemma:

Lemma: If s and $stack$ satisfy certain conditions (which we leave to the reader to express, see (Mason and Talcott, 1985) for hints) then

$$peel(s, stack) \simeq pop{:}peel{:}stack(s, stack, rec{:}peel(s)).$$

Proof of Lemma: The lemma is proved by induction. Again we leave it as an exercise for the reader to explicitly state the induction hypothesis (see (Mason and Talcott, 1985) for hints). The proof consists of thirteen steps, which we leave to the reader to annotate. Suppose that s satisfies the conditions and that s_a and s_d are its old car and old cdr respectively. Furthermore let s_n be its current cdr, and s_{na} and s_{nd} be the *image* of s_a and s_d, respectively. Then,

$$
\begin{aligned}
&peel(s, stack) \simeq \\
&\quad \simeq \mathtt{ifs}(eq(\mathtt{M00}, m(s)), \mathtt{seq}(setm(s, \mathtt{F00}), \\
&\qquad\qquad\qquad\qquad setd(s, stack), \\
&\qquad\qquad\qquad\qquad peel(s_d, s)), \\
&\qquad eq(\mathtt{M01}, m(s)), \mathtt{seq}(setm(s, stack), \\
&\qquad\qquad\qquad\qquad seta(s, s_d), \\
&\qquad\qquad\qquad\qquad setd(s, image(s_d)), \\
&\qquad\qquad\qquad\qquad peel(s_a, s)), \\
&\qquad eq(\mathtt{M10}, m(s)), \mathtt{seq}(setm(s, \mathtt{F10}), \\
&\qquad\qquad\qquad\qquad setd(s, stack), \\
&\qquad\qquad\qquad\qquad peel(s_d, s)), \\
&\qquad eq(\mathtt{M11}, m(s)), \mathtt{seq}(setm(s, s_a), \\
&\qquad\qquad\qquad\qquad seta(s, image(s_a)), \\
&\qquad\qquad\qquad\qquad setd(s, image(s_d)), \\
&\qquad\qquad\qquad\qquad rplacd(s, s_d), \\
&\qquad\qquad\qquad\qquad pop{:}peel{:}stack(s, stack, s_n)))
\end{aligned}
$$

$$
\begin{aligned}
\simeq \texttt{ifs}(&eq(\texttt{M00}, m(s)), \texttt{seq}(setm(s, \texttt{F00}),\\
&\qquad setd(s, stack),\\
&\qquad pop{:}peel{:}stack(s_d, s, rec{:}peel(s_d)))\\
&eq(\texttt{M01}, m(s)), \texttt{seq}(setm(s, stack),\\
&\qquad seta(s, s_d),\\
&\qquad setd(s, image(s_d)),\\
&\qquad pop{:}peel{:}stack(s_a, s, rec{:}peel(s_a)))\\
&eq(\texttt{M10}, m(s)), \texttt{seq}(setm(s, \texttt{F10}),\\
&\qquad setd(s, stack),\\
&\qquad pop{:}peel{:}stack(s_d, s, rec{:}peel(s_d)))\\
&eq(\texttt{M11}, m(s)), \texttt{seq}(setm(s, s_a),\\
&\qquad seta(s, image(s_a)),\\
&\qquad setd(s, image(s_d)),\\
&\qquad rplacd(s, s_d),\\
&\qquad pop{:}peel{:}stack(s, stack, s_n)))
\end{aligned}
$$

$$
\begin{aligned}
\simeq \mathtt{ifs}(&eq(\mathtt{M00}, m(s)), \mathtt{seq}(setm(s, \mathtt{F00}),\\
&\qquad setd(s, stack),\\
&\qquad rec{:}peel(s_d)\\
&\qquad setm(s, stack),\\
&\qquad setd(s, s_{nd}),\\
&\qquad seta(s, s_d),\\
&\qquad peel(s_a, s)),\\
&eq(\mathtt{M01}, m(s)), \mathtt{seq}(setm(s, stack),\\
&\qquad seta(s, s_d),\\
&\qquad setd(s, image(s_d)),\\
&\qquad rec{:}peel(s_a)\\
&\qquad rplacd(s, s_d),\\
&\qquad setm(s_n, s_{na}),\\
&\qquad setm(s, s_a),\\
&\qquad pop{:}peel{:}stack(s, stack, s_n)))\\
&eq(\mathtt{M10}, m(s)), \mathtt{seq}(setm(s, \mathtt{F10}),\\
&\qquad setd(s, stack),\\
&\qquad rec{:}peel(s_d)\\
&\qquad setm(s, s_a),\\
&\qquad seta(s, image(s_a)),\\
&\qquad setd(s, s_{nd}),\\
&\qquad rplacd(s, s_d),\\
&\qquad pop{:}peel{:}stack(s, stack, s_n)),\\
&eq(\mathtt{M11}, m(s)), \mathtt{seq}(setm(s, s_a),\\
&\qquad seta(s, image(s_a)),\\
&\qquad setd(s, image(s_d)),\\
&\qquad rplacd(s, s_d),\\
&\qquad pop{:}peel{:}stack(s, stack, s_n)))
\end{aligned}
$$

$$
\begin{aligned}
\simeq \mathtt{ifs}(&eq(\mathtt{M00}, m(s)), \mathtt{seq}(setm(s, \mathtt{F00}),\\
&\qquad setd(s, stack),\\
&\qquad rec{:}peel(s_d)\\
&\qquad setm(s, stack),\\
&\qquad setd(s, s_{nd}),\\
&\qquad seta(s, s_d),\\
&\qquad pop{:}peel{:}stack(s_a, s, rec{:}peel(s_a))),\\
&eq(\mathtt{M01}, m(s)), \mathtt{seq}(setm(s, stack),\\
&\qquad seta(s, s_d),\\
&\qquad setd(s, image(s_d)),\\
&\qquad rec{:}peel(s_a)\\
&\qquad rplacd(s, s_d),\\
&\qquad setm(s_n, s_{na}),\\
&\qquad setm(s, s_a),\\
&\qquad pop{:}peel{:}stack(s, stack, s_n)))\\
&eq(\mathtt{M10}, m(s)), \mathtt{seq}(setm(s, \mathtt{F10}),\\
&\qquad setd(s, stack),\\
&\qquad rec{:}peel(s_d)\\
&\qquad setm(s, s_a),\\
&\qquad seta(s, image(s_a)),\\
&\qquad setd(s, s_{nd}),\\
&\qquad rplacd(s, s_d),\\
&\qquad pop{:}peel{:}stack(s, stack, s_n)),\\
&eq(\mathtt{M11}, m(s)), \mathtt{seq}(setm(s, s_a),\\
&\qquad seta(s, image(s_a)),\\
&\qquad setd(s, image(s_d)),\\
&\qquad rplacd(s, s_d),\\
&\qquad pop{:}peel{:}stack(s, stack, s_n)))
\end{aligned}
$$

$$
\begin{aligned}
\simeq \mathtt{ifs}(&eq(\mathtt{M00}, m(s)), \mathtt{seq}(setm(s, \mathtt{F00}),\\
&\qquad setd(s, stack),\\
&\qquad rec{:}peel(s_d)\\
&\qquad setm(s, stack),\\
&\qquad setd(s, s_{nd}),\\
&\qquad seta(s, s_d),\\
&\qquad rec{:}peel(s_a),\\
&\qquad rplacd(s, s_d),\\
&\qquad setm(s_n, s_{na}),\\
&\qquad setm(s, s_a),\\
&\qquad pop{:}peel{:}stack(s, stack, s_n)))\\
&eq(\mathtt{M01}, m(s)), \mathtt{seq}(setm(s, stack),\\
&\qquad seta(s, s_d),\\
&\qquad setd(s, image(s_d)),\\
&\qquad rec{:}peel(s_a)\\
&\qquad rplacd(s, s_d),\\
&\qquad setm(s_n, s_{na}),\\
&\qquad setm(s, s_a),\\
&\qquad pop{:}peel{:}stack(s, stack, s_n)))\\
&eq(\mathtt{M10}, m(s)), \mathtt{seq}(setm(s, \mathtt{F10}),\\
&\qquad setd(s, stack),\\
&\qquad rec{:}peel(s_d)\\
&\qquad setm(s, s_a),\\
&\qquad seta(s, image(s_a)),\\
&\qquad setd(s, s_{nd}),\\
&\qquad rplacd(s, s_d),\\
&\qquad pop{:}peel{:}stack(s, stack, s_n)),\\
&eq(\mathtt{M11}, m(s)), \mathtt{seq}(setm(s, s_a),\\
&\qquad seta(s, image(s_a)),\\
&\qquad setd(s, image(s_d)),\\
&\qquad rplacd(s, s_d),\\
&\qquad pop{:}peel{:}stack(s, stack, s_n)))
\end{aligned}
$$

$$
\begin{aligned}
\simeq \texttt{ifs}(&eq(\texttt{M00}, m(s)), \texttt{seq}(rplaca(s, \texttt{F00}),\\
&\qquad rplacd(cdr(s), stack),\\
&\qquad rec{:}peel(s_d)\\
&\qquad rplaca(s, stack),\\
&\qquad rplacd(cdr(s), s_{nd}),\\
&\qquad rplaca(cdr(s), s_d),\\
&\qquad rec{:}peel(s_a),\\
&\qquad rplacd(s, s_d),\\
&\qquad rplaca(s_n, s_{na}),\\
&\qquad rplaca(s, s_a),\\
&\qquad pop{:}peel{:}stack(s, stack, s_n)))\\
&eq(\texttt{M01}, m(s)), \texttt{seq}(rplaca(s, stack),\\
&\qquad rplaca(cdr(s), s_d),\\
&\qquad rplacd(cdr(s), image(s_d)),\\
&\qquad rec{:}peel(s_a)\\
&\qquad rplacd(s, s_d),\\
&\qquad rplaca(s_n, s_{na}),\\
&\qquad rplaca(s, s_a),\\
&\qquad pop{:}peel{:}stack(s, stack, s_n)))\\
&eq(\texttt{M10}, m(s)), \texttt{seq}(rplaca(s, \texttt{F10}),\\
&\qquad rplacd(cdr(s), stack),\\
&\qquad rec{:}peel(s_d)\\
&\qquad rplaca(s, s_a),\\
&\qquad rplaca(cdr(s), image(s_a)),\\
&\qquad rplacd(cdr(s), s_{nd}),\\
&\qquad rplacd(s, s_d),\\
&\qquad pop{:}peel{:}stack(s, stack, s_n)),\\
&eq(\texttt{M11}, m(s)), \texttt{seq}(rplaca(s, s_a),\\
&\qquad rplaca(cdr(s), image(s_a)),\\
&\qquad rplacd(cdr(s), image(s_d)),\\
&\qquad rplacd(s, s_d),\\
&\qquad pop{:}peel{:}stack(s, stack, s_n)))
\end{aligned}
$$

$$
\begin{aligned}
\simeq \mathtt{ifs}(&eq(\mathtt{M00}, m(s)), \mathtt{seq}(rplaca(s, \mathtt{F00}),\\
&\qquad rplacd(s_n, stack),\\
&\qquad rec{:}peel(s_d)\\
&\qquad rplaca(s, stack),\\
&\qquad rplacd(s_n, s_{nd}),\\
&\qquad rplaca(s_n, s_d),\\
&\qquad rec{:}peel(s_a),\\
&\qquad rplacd(s, s_d),\\
&\qquad rplaca(s_n, s_{na}),\\
&\qquad rplaca(s, s_a),\\
&\qquad pop{:}peel{:}stack(s, stack, s_n)))\\
&eq(\mathtt{M01}, m(s)), \mathtt{seq}(rplaca(s, stack),\\
&\qquad rplaca(s_n, s_d),\\
&\qquad rplacd(s_n, s_{nd}),\\
&\qquad rec{:}peel(s_a)\\
&\qquad rplacd(s, s_d),\\
&\qquad rplaca(s_n, s_{na}),\\
&\qquad rplaca(s, s_a),\\
&\qquad pop{:}peel{:}stack(s, stack, s_n)))\\
&eq(\mathtt{M10}, m(s)), \mathtt{seq}(rplaca(s, \mathtt{F10}),\\
&\qquad rplacd(s_n, stack),\\
&\qquad rec{:}peel(s_d)\\
&\qquad rplaca(s, s_a),\\
&\qquad rplaca(s_n, s_{na}),\\
&\qquad rplacd(s_n, s_{nd}),\\
&\qquad rplacd(s, s_d),\\
&\qquad pop{:}peel{:}stack(s, stack, s_n)),\\
&eq(\mathtt{M11}, m(s)), \mathtt{seq}(rplaca(s, s_a),\\
&\qquad rplaca(s_n, s_{na})),\\
&\qquad rplacd(s_n, s_{nd}),\\
&\qquad rplacd(s, s_d),\\
&\qquad pop{:}peel{:}stack(s, stack, s_n)))
\end{aligned}
$$

$$
\begin{aligned}
\simeq \mathtt{ifs}(& eq(\mathtt{M00}, m(s)), \mathtt{seq}(\mathit{rec{:}peel}(s_d)\\
&\qquad \mathit{rec{:}peel}(s_a),\\
&\qquad \mathit{rplaca}(s, \mathtt{F00}),\\
&\qquad \mathit{rplaca}(s, \mathit{stack}),\\
&\qquad \mathit{rplaca}(s, s_a),\\
&\qquad \mathit{rplacd}(s, s_d),\\
&\qquad \mathit{rplaca}(s_n, s_d),\\
&\qquad \mathit{rplaca}(s_n, s_{na}),\\
&\qquad \mathit{rplacd}(s_n, \mathit{stack}),\\
&\qquad \mathit{rplacd}(s_n, s_{nd}),\\
&\qquad \mathit{pop{:}peel{:}stack}(s, \mathit{stack}, s_n)))\\
& eq(\mathtt{M01}, m(s)), \mathtt{seq}(\mathit{rec{:}peel}(s_a)\\
&\qquad \mathit{rplaca}(s, \mathit{stack}),\\
&\qquad \mathit{rplaca}(s, s_a),\\
&\qquad \mathit{rplacd}(s, s_d),\\
&\qquad \mathit{rplaca}(s_n, s_d),\\
&\qquad \mathit{rplaca}(s_n, s_{na}),\\
&\qquad \mathit{rplacd}(s_n, s_{nd}),\\
&\qquad \mathit{pop{:}peel{:}stack}(s, \mathit{stack}, s_n)))\\
& eq(\mathtt{M10}, m(s)), \mathtt{seq}(\mathit{rec{:}peel}(s_d)\\
&\qquad \mathit{rplaca}(s, \mathtt{F10}),\\
&\qquad \mathit{rplaca}(s, s_a),\\
&\qquad \mathit{rplacd}(s, s_d),\\
&\qquad \mathit{rplaca}(s_n, s_{na}),\\
&\qquad \mathit{rplacd}(s_n, \mathit{stack}),\\
&\qquad \mathit{rplacd}(s_n, s_{nd}),\\
&\qquad \mathit{pop{:}peel{:}stack}(s, \mathit{stack}, s_n)),\\
& eq(\mathtt{M11}, m(s)), \mathtt{seq}(\mathit{rplaca}(s, s_a),\\
&\qquad \mathit{rplacd}(s, s_d),\\
&\qquad \mathit{rplaca}(s_n, s_{na}),\\
&\qquad \mathit{rplacd}(s_n, s_{nd}),\\
&\qquad \mathit{pop{:}peel{:}stack}(s, \mathit{stack}, s_n)))
\end{aligned}
$$

$$
\begin{aligned}
\simeq \mathtt{ifs}(&eq(\mathtt{M00}, m(s)), \mathtt{seq}(rec{:}peel(s_d)\\
&\qquad rec{:}peel(s_a),\\
&\qquad rplaca(s, s_a),\\
&\qquad rplacd(s, s_d),\\
&\qquad rplaca(s_n, s_{na}),\\
&\qquad rplacd(s_n, s_{nd}),\\
&\qquad pop{:}peel{:}stack(s, stack, s_n)))\\
&eq(\mathtt{M01}, m(s)), \mathtt{seq}(rec{:}peel(s_a)\\
&\qquad rplaca(s, s_a),\\
&\qquad rplacd(s, s_d),\\
&\qquad rplaca(s_n, s_{na}),\\
&\qquad rplacd(s_n, s_{nd}),\\
&\qquad pop{:}peel{:}stack(s, stack, s_n)))\\
&eq(\mathtt{M10}, m(s)), \mathtt{seq}(rec{:}peel(s_d)\\
&\qquad rplaca(s, s_a),\\
&\qquad rplacd(s, s_d),\\
&\qquad rplaca(s_n, s_{na}),\\
&\qquad rplacd(s_n, s_{nd}),\\
&\qquad pop{:}peel{:}stack(s, stack, s_n)),\\
&eq(\mathtt{M11}, m(s)), \mathtt{seq}(rplaca(s, s_a),\\
&\qquad rplacd(s, s_d),\\
&\qquad rplaca(s_n, s_{na}),\\
&\qquad rplacd(s_n, s_{nd}),\\
&\qquad pop{:}peel{:}stack(s, stack, s_n)))
\end{aligned}
$$

$$
\begin{aligned}
\simeq \mathtt{seq}(&\mathtt{ifs}(eq(\mathtt{M00}, m(s)), \mathtt{seq}(rec{:}peel(s_d)\; rec{:}peel(s_a)),\\
&\quad eq(\mathtt{M01}, m(s)), \mathtt{seq}(rec{:}peel(s_a))\\
&\quad eq(\mathtt{M10}, m(s)), \mathtt{seq}(rec{:}peel(s_d))\\
&\quad eq(\mathtt{M11}, m(s)), \mathtt{seq}(\mathtt{NIL})),\\
&rplaca(s, s_a),\\
&rplacd(s, s_d),\\
&rplaca(s_n, s_{na}),\\
&rplacd(s_n, s_{nd}),\\
&pop{:}peel{:}stack(s, stack, s_n))
\end{aligned}
$$

$$
\begin{aligned}
&\simeq \mathtt{seq}(\mathtt{ifs}(eq(\mathtt{M00}, m(s)), \mathtt{seq}(rec{:}peel(s_d)\ rec{:}peel(s_a)),\\
&\qquad\qquad eq(\mathtt{M01}, m(s)), rec{:}peel(s_a)\\
&\qquad\qquad eq(\mathtt{M10}, m(s)), rec{:}peel(s_d)\\
&\qquad\qquad eq(\mathtt{M11}, m(s)), \mathtt{NIL}),\\
&\qquad rplaca(s, s_a),\\
&\qquad rplacd(s, s_d),\\
&\qquad rplaca(s_n, s_{na}),\\
&\qquad rplacd(s_n, s_{nd}),\\
&\qquad pop{:}peel{:}stack(s, stack, s_n))\\
&\simeq \mathtt{let}\{\mathtt{newcel} \leftarrow cdr(s)\}\\
&\qquad \mathtt{let}\{\mathtt{newcar} \leftarrow image(car(\mathtt{newcel})),\\
&\qquad\qquad \mathtt{newcdr} \leftarrow image(cdr(\mathtt{newcel})),\\
&\qquad\qquad \mathtt{oldcar} \leftarrow car(\mathtt{newcel}),\\
&\qquad\qquad \mathtt{oldcdr} \leftarrow cdr(\mathtt{newcel})\}\\
&\qquad \mathtt{seq}(\ \mathtt{ifs}(eq(\mathtt{M00}, m(s)), \mathtt{seq}(rec{:}peel(\mathtt{oldcdr}), rec{:}peel(\mathtt{oldcar})),\\
&\qquad\qquad\qquad eq(\mathtt{M01}, m(s)), rec{:}peel(\mathtt{oldcar}),\\
&\qquad\qquad\qquad eq(\mathtt{M10}, m(s)), rec{:}peel(\mathtt{oldcdr}),\\
&\qquad\qquad\qquad eq(\mathtt{M11}, m(s)), \mathtt{NIL}),\\
&\qquad\qquad rplaca(s, \mathtt{oldcar}),\\
&\qquad\qquad rplacd(s, \mathtt{oldcdr}),\\
&\qquad\qquad rplaca(\mathtt{newcel}, \mathtt{newcar}),\\
&\qquad\qquad rplacd(\mathtt{newcel}, \mathtt{newcdr}))\\
&\qquad\qquad pop{:}peel{:}stack(s, stack, s_n))\\
&\simeq \mathtt{seq}(rec{:}peel(s), pop{:}peel{:}stack(s, stack, s_n))\\
&\simeq pop{:}peel{:}stack(s, stack, rec{:}peel(s))
\end{aligned}
$$

□**Lemma.** □**Theorem.**

Chapter 9

Programs as Data and the Eval function

In this chapter we define the *internal* representation of Lisp programs as Lisp data and produce a version of the universal function *eval*. Because this *eval* program will be written in our external computation theory we shall have the luxury of truthfully asserting that *eval* defines our *internal* Lisp, as is often falsely claimed of other versions. *eval* plays both a theoretical and a practical role in Lisp. Historically, the list notation for Lisp functions and *eval* were first devised in order to show how easy it is to define a universal function in Lisp — the idea was to advocate Lisp as an alternative to Turing machines for doing the elementary theory of computability, see (McCarthy, 1963) or (McCarthy, 1960). S. R. Russell noted that *eval* could serve as an interpreter for Lisp and promptly programmed it in machine language with modifications to make it more practical. An interpreter based on *eval* has remained a feature of most Lisp systems. A detailed account of the evolution of the first interpreter can be found in (Stoyan, 1984).

The fact that Lisp programs are Lisp data is a very important feature of Lisp for other reasons than just the existence of a universal Lisp function. The following quote comes from (Barr and Feigenbaum, 1982).

> *One characteristic of LISP that is unique among high level programming languages and that seems particularly important in AI work is the representation of the programs themselves in the same data structure as all the other data, namely, list structure. This simple device has proved central to AI programs whose purpose is to manipulate other programs, sometimes themselves. For instance, a program that is to explain its line of reasoning must examine its operation in reaching a conclusion - it must determine what functions were called and with what values. Programs that learn to do some task, for another example, often involve procedures that create and modify new procedures to accomplish the task.*
>
> *The idea is simply that in most programming languages the executing program does not have access to the actual code, while any procedure in LISP can manipulate another procedure as easily as it can other data. For example, since the first element of a function call is the name of the function to be called, a general purpose procedure that returns the value of the first element of a list will, when applied to a function call like* `(TIMES X Y)`*, return the name of the function to be called,* `TIMES`*......*

Another ramification of the program-as-data idea is that the LISP programming environments tend to be extremely interactive: Since programs can be manipulated easily by other LISP programs, utilities such as program editors and debugging facilities can be written in LISP. Thus, they can be easily tailored by each programmer for a specific application or even used by a program to edit or monitor another program.

The representation of programs that we shall use is entirely standard, although some of the decisions regarding its semantics are be slightly non-standard. Programs will be represented by lists of lists in what has come to be called the *Cambridge Polish* notation. Actually our programs will be hereditary lists, lists of lists with no cellular structure sharing. Recall from Chapter 4 the following definition.

Definition: $c\,;\mu \in \mathbb{M}_{sexp}$ is in $\mathbb{M}_{hered}$ if the following two conditions hold

1. $(\forall c_0 \in \mathbf{Cells}_\mu(c))(c_0\,;\mu \in \mathbb{M}_{list})$.
2. $(\forall \sigma_0, \sigma_1)(((c\,;\mu)_{\sigma_0} = (c\,;\mu)_{\sigma_1} \ \wedge\ \sigma_0 \neq \sigma_1) \to (c\,;\mu)_{\sigma_0} \in \mathbb{A})$

Our Lisp programs will be a subset of $\mathbb{M}_{hered}$; there is no real reason why we forbid them to share structure. In fact if they did share structure whenever possible, execution time, due to the presence of self destructing macros, would be somewhat quicker. The only motivation we can give for this decision is that in the next chapter we shall examine a Lisp structure editor whose smooth operation requires that data, mostly programs, does not share structure. Thus editing one part of a program will not unexpectedlly alter another part. We begin by defining the representation of an expression $e(\bar{x}) \in \mathbb{E}$,

$$\mathtt{e(\bar{x})},$$

in $\mathbb{M}_{hered}$, by induction on the complexity of e. This definition is simply to give the reader some familiarity with our internal representation of programs. We shall formally define the language shortly; it will actually be explicitly richer than our external computation theory.

Definition: $\mathtt{e(\bar{x})}$, the internal representation of $e(\bar{x}) \in \mathbb{E}$, is defined to be

- `(QUOTE a)` if $e(\bar{x}) = \mathtt{a} \in \mathbb{A}$, `(QUOTE a)` is usually abbreviated to 'a,
- $\mathtt{X_i}$ if $e(\bar{x}) = x_i \in \mathbb{X}$,
- $\mathtt{(CONS\ e_0\ e_1)}$, $\mathtt{(EQ\ e_0\ e_1)}$, $\mathtt{(RPLACA\ e_0\ e_1)}$ or $\mathtt{(RPLACD\ e_0\ e_1)}$ if $e(\bar{e}) = \vartheta(e_0, e_1)$ and $\vartheta = cons, eq, rplaca$ or $rplacd$ respectively,
- $\mathtt{(CAR\ e_0)}$, $\mathtt{(CDR\ e_0)}$, $\mathtt{(INT\ e_0)}$, $\mathtt{(ADD1\ e_0)}$, $\mathtt{(SUB1\ e_0)}$ or $\mathtt{(ATOM\ e_0)}$ if $e(\bar{e}) = \vartheta(e_0)$ and $\vartheta = car, cdr, int, add1, sub1$ or $atom$ respectively,

- (SEQ e_0 $e_1 \ldots e_n$) if $e(\bar{x}) = \mathtt{seq}(e_0, e_1, \ldots, e_n)$,
- (f e_0 $e_1 \ldots$ e_n) if $e(\bar{x}) = f(e_0, e_1, \ldots, e_n)$ where $f \in \mathbb{F}$,
- (IF e_0 e_1 e_2) if $e(\bar{x}) = \mathtt{if}(e_0, e_1, e_2)$,
- (LET ((Y_0 e_0) ... (Y_n e_n))e_{body}) if $e(\bar{x}) = \mathtt{let}\{y_0 \leftarrow e_0, \ldots, e_n\}e_{body}$.

Here we are using standard notation introduced in Chapter 2. Namely, suppose $c_0 ; \mu_0 \in \mathbb{M}_{list}$ is a pure list such that

$$\mathbf{Spine}_{\mu_0}(c_0) = \{c_0 \ldots c_n\}$$

with $\mu_0(c_i) = [v_i \ , \ c_{i+1}]$ for $i \in n$ and $\mu_0(c_n) = [v_n \ , \ \mathtt{NIL}]$. Then we say $c_0 ; \mu_0$ represents the Lisp list

$$(\mathtt{v}_0 \quad \mathtt{v}_1 \quad \mathtt{v}_2 \ \ldots \mathtt{v}_n).$$

Thus when we say that the internal representation of

$$rplaca(x_0, x_1)$$

is

$$(\mathtt{RPLACA}\ \mathtt{X}_0\ \mathtt{X}_1)$$

we really mean that it is the value of

$$cons(\mathtt{RPLACA}, cons(\mathtt{X}_0, cons(\mathtt{X}_1, \mathtt{NIL})))$$

in the relevant or appropriate memory. Note that we are thus really only defining the isomorphism type of the internal representation. We shall return to this important point when the time is ripe. Also note that we are now making use of our assumptions, made way back in Chapter 2, concerning the set of atoms. We repeat them here for the convenience of the not so attentive reader. We often assume that the integers $\mathbb{Z}$ are contained in $\mathbb{A}$. $\mathbb{A}$ will always be assumed to contain two non-numeric atoms T and NIL. These atoms are used to represent *true* and *false*, NIL is also used to represent the empty list. We shall also assume that there are an unlimited collection of non-numeric atoms other than the two we just mentioned.

Examples:

- The following is the internal representation of the body of the *recursive:copy* program.

```
(IF (ATOM U)
    U
    (CONS (COPY (CAR U))
          (COPY (CDR U))))
```

- The following is the way we represent a single clause in a function definition. This example is of the *defined:eq* program of Chapter 3.

```
(DEFINED:EQ (X Y)
            (IF (OR (ATOM X) (ATOM Y))
                (ATOM:EQ X Y)
                (LET ((OLDX (CAR X))
                      (OLDY (CAR Y)))
                     (SEQ (RPLACA X T)
                          (RPLACA Y NIL)
                          (LET ((ANSWER (ATOM:EQ (CAR X)
                                                 (CAR Y))))
                               (SEQ (RPLACA X OLDX)
                                    (RPLACA Y OLDY)
                                    ANSWER))))))
```

The way we are representing programs illustrates another feature of Lisp that is in part an accidental consequence of the first implementation of Lisp. Parsing a Lisp program is essentially trivial. The following is from (McCarthy, 1978).

> *One can even conjecture that LISP owes its survival specifically to the fact that its programs are lists, which everyone, including me, has regarded as a disadvantage. Proposed replacements for LISP, e.g., POP-2 (Burstall, Collins, and Popplestone, 1968, 1971), abandoned this feature in favor of an ALGOL-like syntax leaving no target language for higher level systems.*

The fact that the syntax is trivial is exemplified by the manner in which we have printed the above programs. This method is known as *pretty printing*, items begining in the same column are at the same parenthetical level.

9.1. The Syntax of the Internal Programming Language

We shall now formally define the syntax and semantics of our internal Lisp. The semantics of the language is defined via our universal function or *interpreter*

eval.

We shall describe it informally in the next section and then, later, give a full external definition of it in our computation theory.

The following atoms will have special meaning in our language; they will be the internal names of the corresponding data operations,

`CAR CDR ATOM INT ADD1 SUB1 EQ CONS RPLACA RPLACD.`

The next group of atoms, also being special, will be the internal representation of certain control primitives. It is not the smallest set possible, but each primitive is important enough to warrant special attention,

`IF SEQ LET QUOTE EVAL DEFUN DEFMACRO.`

There are as the reader can easily see, more control constructs than in the external computation theory. We shall also include two mysterious functions in our language that will be used both in this chapter and the chapter following it. They are only mysterious in the sense that they connect our nice neat Lisp world with the horrors and torments of the real world. We shall make certain false assumptions about this external world when the time comes to describe their behavior. They are, without too much undue ceremony,

`READ` and `PRINT`.

The syntax of our internal programming language is now the subject of our attention. Our approach will be to define a class of S-expressions, $\mathbb{M}_{prog}$, that are well-formed programs.

Definition: We define $\mathbb{M}_{prog}$ to be the smallest set of memory objects closed under isomorphism satisfying the following closure conditions.

0. If $a \in \mathbb{A}$ and μ is any memory then $a \,;\, \mu \in \mathbb{M}_{prog}$.

1. If μ is any memory and $cons(\mathtt{READ}, \mathtt{NIL}) \,;\, \mu \gg v^* \,;\, \mu^*$ then $v^* \,;\, \mu^* \in \mathbb{M}_{prog}$. In other words anything isomorphic to

$$(\mathtt{READ}) \,;\, \mu^*$$

is in $\mathbb{M}_{prog}$.

2. If $v ; \mu \in \mathbb{M}_{prog}$ and $cons(\mathtt{PRINT}, cons(v, \mathtt{NIL})) ; \mu \gg v^* ; \mu^*$ then $v^* ; \mu^* \in \mathbb{M}_{prog}$. In other words anything isomorphic to

$$(\mathtt{PRINT}\ \ v) \,;\, \mu^*$$

is in $\mathbb{M}_{prog}$.

3. If a is an atom and $v_1 \,;\, \mu, \ldots v_n \,;\, \mu \in \mathbb{M}_{prog}$ and

$$cons(a, cons(v_1, \ldots cons(v_n, \mathtt{NIL}) \ldots)) \,;\, \mu \gg v^* \,;\, \mu^*$$

then $v^* \,;\, \mu^* \in \mathbb{M}_{prog}$. In other words anything isomorphic to

$$(a\ v_1\ \ldots\ v_n) \,;\, \mu^*$$

is in $\mathbb{M}_{prog}$. The next two clauses are simple elaborations on this rule.

4. If $v\,;\mu \in \mathbb{M}_{prog}, \theta$ is any one of the following atoms CAR, CDR, ATOM, INT, ADD1, SUB1, EVAL, and $cons(\theta, cons(v, \texttt{NIL}))\;;\mu \gg v^*\;;\mu^*$ then $v^*\;;\mu^* \in \mathbb{M}_{prog}$. In other words anything isomorphic to

$$(\theta\ v)\ ;\mu^*$$

is in $\mathbb{M}_{prog}$.

5. If $v_0;\mu, v_1;\mu \in \mathbb{M}_{prog}, \theta$ is any one of the following atoms EQ CONS RPLACA RPLACD and $cons(\theta, cons(v_0, cons(v_1, \texttt{NIL})));\mu \gg v^*;\mu^*$ then $v^*;\mu^* \in \mathbb{M}_{prog}$. In other words anything isomorphic to

$$(\theta\ v_0\ v_1)\ ;\mu^*$$

is in $\mathbb{M}_{prog}$.

6. If $v;\mu \in \mathbb{M}_{sexp}$ and $cons(\texttt{QUOTE}, cons(v, \texttt{NIL}));\mu \gg v^*;\mu^*$ then $v^*;\mu^* \in \mathbb{M}_{prog}$. In other words anything isomorphic to

$$(\texttt{QUOTE}\ \ v)\ ;\mu^*$$

is in $\mathbb{M}_{prog}$.

7. If $v_0;\mu, v_1;\mu, v_2;\mu \in \mathbb{M}_{prog}$ and $cons(\texttt{IF}, cons(v_0, cons(v_1, cons(v_2, \texttt{NIL}))));\mu \gg v^*\;;\mu^*$ then $v^*\;;\mu^* \in \mathbb{M}_{prog}$. In other words anything isomorphic to

$$(\texttt{IF}\ \ v_0\ v_1\ v_2)\ ;\mu^*$$

is in $\mathbb{M}_{prog}$.

8. If $n \in \mathbb{N}, v_1;\mu, \ldots, v_n;\mu \in \mathbb{M}_{prog}$ and $cons(\texttt{SEQ}, cons(v_1, \ldots, cons(v_n, \texttt{NIL})\ldots));$ $\mu \gg v^*\;;\mu^*$ then $v^*\;;\mu^* \in \mathbb{M}_{prog}$. In other words anything isomorphic to

$$(\texttt{SEQ}\ \ v_1\ \ldots\ v_n)\ ;\mu^*$$

is in $\mathbb{M}_{prog}$.

9. If $n \in \mathbb{N}, v\;;\mu, v_1\;;\mu, \ldots, v_n\;;\mu \in \mathbb{M}_{prog}$, $a_1, \ldots, a_n$ are distinct atoms, $cons(cons(a_1, cons(v_1, \texttt{NIL})), cons(\ldots cons(a_n, cons(v_n, \texttt{NIL})), \texttt{NIL})))\ldots) \gg v^*;$ μ^* and $cons(\texttt{LET}, cons(v^*, cons(v, \texttt{NIL})));\mu^* \gg v^{**};\mu^{**}$ then $v^{**};\mu^{**} \in \mathbb{M}_{prog}$. In other words anything isomorphic to

$$(\texttt{LET}\ \ ((a_1\ v_1)\ \ldots(a_n\ v_n))\ \ v)\ ;\mu^{**}$$

is in $\mathbb{M}_{prog}$.

10. If $n \in \mathbb{N}, v \,;\, \mu \in \mathbb{M}_{prog}$, $f, a_1, \ldots a_n$ are distinct atoms, and

$$cons(\mathtt{DEFUN}, cons(f, cons(cons(a_1, \ldots cons(a_n, \mathtt{NIL}) \ldots), cons(v, \mathtt{NIL})))) \,;\, \mu$$
$$\gg v^* \,;\, \mu^*$$

then $v^* \,;\, \mu^* \in \mathbb{M}_{prog}$. In other words anything isomorphic to

$$\mathtt{(DEFUN}\ f\ \mathtt{(}a_1\ \ldots\ a_n\mathtt{)}\quad v\mathtt{)} \,;\, \mu^*$$

is in $\mathbb{M}_{prog}$.

11. If $n \in \mathbb{N}, v \,;\, \mu \in \mathbb{M}_{prog}$, f, a are distinct atoms, and

$$cons(\mathtt{DEFMACRO}, cons(f, cons(cons(a, \mathtt{NIL}), cons(v, \mathtt{NIL})))) \,;\, \mu \gg v^* \,;\, \mu^*$$

then $v^* \,;\, \mu^* \in \mathbb{M}_{prog}$. In other words anything isomorphic to

$$\mathtt{(DEFMACRO}\ f\ \mathtt{(}a\mathtt{)}\ v\mathtt{)} \,;\, \mu^*$$

is in $\mathbb{M}_{prog}$.

9.2. The Semantics of the Internal Programming Language

We now describe the semantics of the constructs of this language in the order they are introduced above. We then finish this section by pointing out where our version of Lisp differs from more common versions such as Maclisp and Common Lisp.

9.2.1. Atoms, Variables and Environments

In our version of Lisp we are allowing symbols to have values associated with them. At any particular instant the set theoretical function that associates to each symbol its value is called the *current environment* or *current bindings*. There are three different ways to change the current environment, by using `LET`, `DEFUN`, or `DEFMACRO`. If the value of an atom has not been set by one of these devices then *it is its own value.* Thus initially all atoms evaluate to themselves. `DEFMACRO` and `DEFUN` are *dynamic* binding operations and `LET` is lexical. In what follows we shall let $\beta, \beta_0, \beta_1, \ldots$ range over environments or bindings. The reader is invited to think of them simply as either finite functions from

$$\mathbb{A} \to \mathbb{V},$$

or else memory objects that correspond to ***association lists*** or ***alists*** (these being pure lists of atom value pairs). The latter alternative is in fact how we shall implement them. Consequently we make the following definition of association lists.

Definition: The collection of association lists, $\mathbb{M}_{alist}$, is defined to be the smallest set of memory objects closed under isomorphism and satisfying the following conditions

1. For any memory μ we have $\mathtt{NIL}\,;\mu \in \mathbb{M}_{alist}$,
2. If $a \in \mathbb{A}, v\,;\mu \in \mathbb{M}_{sexp}, w\,;\mu \in \mathbb{M}_{alist}$ and $cons(cons(a,v),w)\,;\mu \gg v^*\,;\mu^*$ then $v^*\,;\mu^* \in \mathbb{M}_{alist}$.

Thus an alist can be thought of as a finite function, since it is simply a list of atom value pairs. To look up the value of an atom in an alist we use the following standard Lisp function,

```
assoc(atom, alist) ←
    ifn(alist,
        NIL,
        if(eq(atom, caar(alist)),
           car(alist),
           assoc(atom, cdr(alist)))).
```

Note that since *assoc* returns the pair rather than the value, when the alist does give the atom a value and `NIL` otherwise, we can distinguish between no value and a value of `NIL`. Also note that *assoc* returns the first pair (working from left to right) that it finds, so even though an atom may have several values associated with it, the first occurrence determines the value. Both of these facts are used heavily when manipulating association lists. In our applications we shall always assume that

```
((T . T) (NIL . NIL))
```

is, up to isomorphism a sublist of our alists. The reason we do this has nothing to do with the atoms `T` and `NIL` but rather with the dynamic function defining primitives (the fact that the alists are non-empty allows us the pleasure of destructively adding to them). We shall say more about this at the appropriate time.

Our program *eval* takes two arguments; the first is supposed to be an element of $\mathbb{M}_{prog}$ while the second is supposed to be an alist, in other words a member of

$\mathbb{M}_{alist}$. Thus our convention concerning atoms can be restated more formally by saying:

$$eval(a, \beta) \,;\, \mu \gg \begin{cases} cdr(v \,;\, \mu) & \text{if } assoc(a, \beta) \,;\, \mu \gg v \,;\, \mu \wedge v \neq \texttt{NIL}, \\ a \,;\, \mu & \text{otherwise.} \end{cases}$$

9.2.2. The READ and PRINT forms

We shall regard the READ form as the internal name for a new zero-ary memory operation, *read*. In real life it reads an S-expression from the terminal or file. In our Lisp we shall only assume that on each evaluation it produces a new S-expression in $\mathbb{M}_{prog}$. Explicitly, if μ is a memory then for some μ^* extending μ we have that

$$read() \,;\, \mu \gg v^* \,;\, \mu^*$$

$v^* \,;\, \mu^* \in \mathbb{M}_{prog}$ and that $\mathbf{Cells}_{\mu^*}(v^*) \cap \delta_\mu = \emptyset$. Similarly we regard PRINT as the internal name of a new unary memory operation *print*. In real life, evaluation of (PRINT v) will result in the evaluation of v and the printing of the resulting value to the terminal. The value of the (PRINT v) form in Maclisp is T. For our purpose it is sufficient to assume that *print* is the constant function,

$$print(v) \,;\, \mu \gg \texttt{T} \,;\, \mu.$$

We shall delve a little more into the nature of these operations in a subsequent section. The reader may have noticed in the description of the PRINT form, that evaluation of

$$(\texttt{PRINT}\ v) \,;\, \mu$$

in the appropriate current environment β does *not* correspond to the external evaluation of

$$print(v) \,;\, \mu,$$

but rather the external evaluation of

$$print(eval(v, \beta)) \,;\, \mu.$$

9.2.3. Function Application

This bring us appropriately to the discussion of the interpretation of function application and the internal form of definitions in our internal Lisp. Let us fix a system of function definitions

$$D = \begin{cases} f_0(\bar{x}_0) \leftarrow e_0 \\ \cdots\cdots \\ f_n(\bar{x}_n) \leftarrow e_n \end{cases}$$

for the purpose of discussion. Since our interpreter should be capable of knowing about such things, we define the *internal* form of this definition, denoted by D, to be any element of $\mathbb{M}_{alist}$ isomorphic to

$$((\mathtt{f}_0\ (\bar{\mathtt{x}}_0)\ \mathtt{e}_0) \ldots (\mathtt{f}_n\ (\bar{\mathtt{x}}_n)\ \mathtt{e}_n)).$$

We then allow the internal representation of this definition to be part of the current environment. Thus the value of the function symbol, $\mathtt{f}_0$, in an environment β is the list consisting of:

1. The list of its *internal* arguments, in traditional jargon its argument list,

   $$(\mathtt{X}_0\ \ \ldots\ \mathtt{X}_s)$$

   and
2. The internal form of its definition body.

   We can now explain the evaluation of

$$(\mathtt{f}_0\ \ v_0\ v_1\ \ldots\ v_s)\ ;\ \mu$$

in an environment, β, which includes the internal form of the above definition. This is done by explaining the behavior of

$$eval((\mathtt{f}_0\ \ v_0\ v_1\ \ldots\ v_s), \beta)\ ;\ \mu$$

which is defined to be

$$\begin{array}{l} \mathtt{let}\{f \leftarrow cdr(assoc(\mathtt{f}_0, \beta))\} \\ \quad \mathtt{let}\{z \leftarrow cons(cons(\mathtt{X}_0, eval(v_0, \beta)), \\ \qquad\qquad cons(cons(\mathtt{X}_1, eval(v_1, \beta)) \\ \qquad\qquad\qquad \ldots \\ \qquad\qquad\qquad\qquad cons(cons(\mathtt{X}_s, eval(v_s, \beta)), \beta)\} \\ \qquad eval(f, z). \end{array}$$

This can easily be explained in words: To evaluate

$$(\mathtt{f}_0\ \ v_0\ v_1\ \ldots\ v_s)$$

in a particular environment we first look up the internal form of the function body in that environment, then evaluate the arguments from left to right, again in that environment, and finally evaluate the *internal* form of the body of $\mathtt{f}_0$ in the new environment where the atoms in the, initial, argument list are now bound to these calculated values (the rest of the environment remains the same). The reason we mentioned that the argument list is the original one is due to our inclusion of making dynamic function definitions. We shall return to this point when we discuss **DEFUN**. We should also remark that if the body of a function definition has free variables other than those in its argument list, then those variables will have dynamic rather than lexical scope.

Memory operation application is treated in exactly the same way, except for the fact that we do not look up the value of the operation in the environment. Rather it has been fixed from the outset. Thus the evaluation of

$$(\texttt{CAR}\ v_0)\ ;\mu$$

in an environment β, $eval((\texttt{CAR}\ v_0),\beta)\,;\mu$, is simply $car(eval(v_0,\beta))\,;\mu$.

9.2.4. The QUOTE Form

In all cases, however, one thing should be clear. A function always evaluates its arguments, treating them as elements of $\mathbb{M}_{prog}$. For this reason it is convenient to have a simple form which will evaluate to an arbitrary memory object. For otherwise it would be impossible to have atomic constants. This is the job of the QUOTE form. (QUOTE v) evaluates to the piece of data v in the relevant memory. In symbols,

$$eval((\texttt{QUOTE}\ v),\beta)\,;\mu \gg v\,;\mu.$$

Note that QUOTE is not a function because it does not evaluate its arguments. It is thus really a control construct rather than an operation. It is traditional to abbreviate

(QUOTE v)

to 'v, for ease of reading.

9.2.5. The IF, SEQ and LET Forms

The interpretation of

if, seq, let,

should be no surprise, so we spend very little time on them.

$$eval((\texttt{IF}\ v_0\ v_1\ v_2),\beta)\,;\mu \simeq \texttt{if}(eval(v_0,\beta), eval(v_1,\beta), eval(v_2,\beta))\,;\mu$$

$$eval((\texttt{SEQ}\ v_1\ \ldots\ v_n),\beta)\,;\mu \simeq \texttt{seq}(eval(v_0,\beta),\ldots,eval(v_n,\beta))\,;\mu.$$

Finally

$$(\texttt{LET}\ ((\texttt{a}_0\ v_0)\ \ldots\ (\texttt{a}_n\ v_n))\ v)$$

will be strongly isomorphic to

$$\texttt{let}\{z \leftarrow cons(cons(\mathtt{a_0}, eval(v_0,\beta)),$$
$$cons(cons(\mathtt{a_1}, eval(v_1,\beta))$$
$$\ldots$$
$$cons(cons(\mathtt{a_n}, eval(v_n,\beta)),\beta)\}$$
$$eval(v, z).$$

Note that the binding variables in the binding expression of the `let` are not evaluated. Only the expressions they are to be bound to are evaluated. Also note that we are using the binding enviroments rather than substitution as a means of binding the variables. It has the same effect, is simpler to implement and extend, and it is more efficient to boot.

9.2.6. The EVAL, DEFUN and DEFMACRO Forms

We are now left with the task of explaining

EVAL DEFUN and DEFMACRO.

EVAL simply evaluates its single argument *twice* in the current environment. Thus for the form

$$\texttt{(EVAL}\ v\texttt{)}\ ;\mu$$

to denote in environment β we must have

$$eval(v,\beta)\ ;\mu \gg v^*\ ;\mu^*$$

and $v^*\ ;\mu^* \in \mathbb{M}_{prog}$. It is thus a way of treating *data as programs.* Note that (EVAL (QUOTE v) ; μ will evaluate to the same thing as $v\ ;\mu$. Explicitly

$$eval(\texttt{(EVAL}\ v\texttt{)},\beta)\ ;\mu \simeq eval(eval(v,\beta),\beta)\ ;\mu.$$

Both DEFUN and DEFMACRO are, as we have already said, dynamic function or macro definition forms. They allow us to add, dynamically, function and macro definitions to the current environment. Neither evaluates its arguments. Their behavior can be described in the following way. Suppose that `alist` is a current environment and `pair` is a pair, whose *car* is `f` and whose *cdr* is `val`. Then the function *destructively:add:bnds*(`pair`,`alist`) does the following. If `f` is given a value in `alist` then the result of the function call is the alist `alist` with the value of `f` destructively altered so that it is now `val`. If `f` is not given a value in `alist` then the result of the function call is

$$nconc(\texttt{alist}, cons(\texttt{pair}, \texttt{NIL})).$$

Note that because we are assuming our alists are non-empty, the value of this function call is the modified `alist`. The result of evaluating

$$\texttt{(DEFUN } f \texttt{ (}a_1 \ \ldots \ a_n\texttt{)} \quad v\texttt{)} \;;\; \mu$$

in the current environment, β, is the same as evaluating

$$\texttt{seq}(\textit{destructively:add:bnds}(\texttt{(}f \texttt{ (}a_1 \ \ldots \ a_n\texttt{)} \quad v\texttt{)}, \beta), f) \;;\; \mu.$$

Similarly the result of evaluating

$$\texttt{(DEFMACRO } f \texttt{ (}a\texttt{) } v\texttt{)} \;;\; \mu$$

in the current environment, β, is the same as evaluating

$$\texttt{seq}(\textit{destructively:add:bnds}(\texttt{(}f \texttt{ MACRO (}a\texttt{) } v\texttt{)}, \beta), f) \;;\; \mu.$$

Finally we must describe the difference between a *macro* definition and a normal function definition, since DEFUN makes a function definition and DEFMACRO makes a macro definition. We have already described the interpretation of function application so it suffices to describe the evaluation of a macro call. Suppose that β is the current environment and $assoc(f, \beta) \;;\; \mu$ is

$$\texttt{(}f \texttt{ MACRO (}a\texttt{) } v\texttt{)} \;;\; \mu.$$

Then evaluating

$$\texttt{(f } v_1 \ldots v_n\texttt{)} \;;\; \mu$$

is the same as evaluating (EVAL v) ; μ in the environment that binds a to (f $v_1 \ldots v_n$) ; μ. In other words we evaluate the body of the macro definition with its argument bound to the whole macro call. This evaluation should produce another program which is then evaluated. Thus a macro definition is a way dynamically extending the interpreter. The following example illustrates this by defining the internal form of the control primitive `ifn`. It is an example of a self destructing macro; it destructively alters the macro call to the defining form.

```
(DEFMACRO IFN (X)
   (LET ((THEN:CLAUSE (CADDR X))
     (SEQ (RPLACA X IF)
          (RPLACA (CDDR X) (CADDDR X))
          (RPLACA (CDDDR X) THEN:CLAUSE))))
```

Another, equally valid, example is the macro definition of the dynamic variable binding construct SETQ.

```
(DEFMACRO SETQ (X)
    (LET ((VAR (CADR X))
          (VAL (EVAL (CADDR X))))
       (CONS DEFUN (CONS VAR VAL))))
```

Thus the syntax of the SETQ form is

$$\texttt{(SETQ } \textit{var val}\texttt{)}.$$

It dynamically binds the unevaluated variable *var* to the result of evaluating *val*.

9.2.7. Where Our Lisp is Different

Our Lisp is different from standard versions of Lisp, such as Maclisp and Common Lisp, in many respects. We shall be satisfied with pointing out some of the most obvious differences.

Firstly, in most standard Lisps, atoms other than numbers and the booleans T and NIL, have no initial value. A variable binding operation must first be performed to give them one. Secondly the values of certain atoms are fixed. For example if we evaluated the following form in Maclisp

```
(LET ((T NIL)) T)
```

we would, rather than obtain the value NIL, receive the following error message, telling us that truth is eternal.

```
;(SETQ (T)) VERITAS AETERNA - DON'T SETQ T
```

As an aside we have noticed the following bug in Maclisp, when one evaluates

```
(LET ((NIL T)) NIL)
```

the answer NIL is returned, whereas if one evaluates

```
(SETQ NIL T)
```

one obtains the appropriate error message:

```
;(SETQ (NIL)) NIHIL EX NIHIL - DON'T SETQ NIL
```

Another difference is that we are storing the definition of a function in the value cell of the function. In Maclisp it is stored on the property list of the atom. It makes little difference, since we can still modify the definition of any function accessible to us. The following is a delightful example of this ability, taken from (McCarthy and Talcott, 1980). The following three forms, when evaluated in order, produce a *clever* version of the Fibonacci function.

```
(SETQ LST (CONS 1 (CONS 1 NIL)))
(DEFUN FIBON (N)
     (IF (OR (EQ N 0) (EQ N 1))
         1
         (FIBONLOOP N  LST)))
(DEFUN FIBONLOOP (N L)
     (IFN (CDDR L)
          (IF (EQ N 2)
              (CADR (RPLACD (CDR L)
                            (CONS (PLUS (CAR L)
                                        (CADR L))
                                  NIL)))
              (FIBONLOOP (SUB1 N)
                         (RPLACD (CDR L)
```

```
                                  (CONS (PLUS (CAR L)
                                              (CADR L))
                                        NIL))))
          (IF (EQ N 2)
              (CADDR L)
              (FIBONLOOP (SUB1 N) (CDR L)))))
```

If we now calculate (FIBON 5) we receive the answer 8. Not only that but now the definition of FIBON is

```
(FIBON (N)
     (IF (OR (EQ N 0) (EQ N 1))
         1
         (FIBONLOOP N '(1 1 2 3 5 8)))).
```

Thus FIBON, or at least its auxiliary program FIBONLOOP, destructively alters the second argument LST so that it stores any previously computed value. The nth element of LST corresponds to the value of (FIBON n). For example, after calculating (FIBON 10) the cell LST will then represent the pure list

(1 1 2 3 5 8 13 21 34 55 89).

Although this example is trivial it illustrates elegantly the reason why Lisp is *the* language for artificial intelligence. Note that FIBON has the free variable LST that is not in its argument list. This variable is scoped dynamically.

9.3. The Definition of *eval*

We now give a formal definition of our Lisp interpreter, *eval*. We also use it as an opportunity to illustrate some points in programming style. The first definition is of the main program *eval*. It is a very simply structured program that branches on the nature of the form it is evaluating. Note that it does almost no work itself, but rather decides what work needs to be done and then ships off the arguments to a function specialized for the job. It is thus a good example of obeying the ninth commandment of Lisp programming, (Friedman and Felleisen, 1986):

The Ninth Commandment Use help functions to abstract from representations.

Elsewhere in this work we have referred to these help functions as *abstract syntax*. There are at least two cosmetic uses for functions:

- To abstract away from representations.
- To emphasize the structure of control.

Note that once the appropriate specialist function has been chosen, it is usually unnecessary to remember the form *type*, and only the *body* of the form need be passed to the chosen function. It is only in the QUOTE and EVAL forms that the job of evaluating is so simple that no specialist function is needed.

```
eval(fm, bnds) ←
    if(atom(fm),
       let{val ← assoc(fm, bnds)}
           if(val, cdr(val), fm),
       let{f ← car(fm)}
           ifs(eq(f, SEQ),          seq:eval(body(fm), bnds),
               eq(f, LET),          let:eval(body(fm), bnds),
               eq(f, IF),           if:eval(body(fm), bnds),
               eq(f, DEFUN),        defun:eval(body(fm), bnds),
               eq(f, DEFMACRO),     defmacro:eval(body(fm), bnds),
               eq(f, QUOTE),        cadr(fm),
               eq(f, EVAL),         eval(eval(body(fm), bnds), bnds)
               memop(f),            memop:eval(f, body(fm), bnds),
               T,                   apply(fm, f, body(fm), bnds)))
```

9.3.1. The *seq:eval* Program

The first specialized function is *seq:eval*, which is passed a non-empty list of forms and the current environment. It must then evaluate each element of the list and return the value of the last element. This is easily done by recursion.

```
seq:eval(fm, bnds) ←
    if(cdr(fm),
       seq(eval(car(fm), bnds), seq:eval(cdr(fm), bnds)),
       eval(car(fm), bnds))
```

9.3.2. The *let:eval* Program

The function that evaluates a let form, *let:eval*, is just as simple, but requires the help of the auxiliary function *add:binds*. The function *let:eval* simply evaluates the let body in the environment that is obtained by calling *add:bnds* with the binding expression of the let and the current environment as arguments. Recall that the internal form of the binding expression is a list of lists, each sublist consisting of two elements, the first being the variable and the second being the expression whose value the variable should be bound to. The function *add:bnds* then produces a new environment in which the appropriate alist of variable value pairs has been appended on to the front. Thus these new values will over-ride any old values while the let body is being evaluated.

```
let:eval(fm, bnds) ←
    eval(cadr(fm), add:bnds(car(fm), bnds))

add:bnds(list, bnds) ←
    if(list,
       cons(cons(caar(list), eval(cadar(list), bnds))
            add:bnds(cdr(list), bnds)),
       bnds)
```

9.3.3. The *if:eval* Program

The function which evaluates the body of an IF, *if:eval*, is as simple as one could possibly want. It simply evaluates the test or predicate form and then evaluates the branch, returning it as the value.

```
if:eval(fm, bnds) ←
    if(eval(car(fm), bnds), eval(cadr(fm), bnds), eval(caddr(fm), bnds))
```

9.3.4. The *defun:eval* and *defmacro:eval* Programs

The dynamic function defining mechanisms are equally simple; they leave most of the work to an auxiliary function, *destructively:add:bnds*. In both cases they return the name of the function, or macro, being defined after they have destructively added its definition to the current environment.

The function *destructively:add:bnds* expects two arguments, the first being a pair while the second is a non-empty alist. What it does is quite simple; if the alist gives a value to the first element of the pair, then it simply destructively alters this value to be the second element of the pair, then returning the so modified alist. If, however, the alist does not give the first element of the pair a value, it then simply destructively adds this pair onto the end of the alist, in a way that makes sure that the result is also an alist. It is in this process that the initial alist must be non-empty for the function to make sense.

```
defun:eval(fm, bnds) ←
    seq(destructively:add:bnds(fm, bnds), car(fm))

defmacro:eval(fm, bnds) ←
    seq(destructively:add:bnds(rplacd(fm, cons(MACRO, cdr(fm))), bnds),
        car(fm))

destructively:add:bnds(pair, bnds) ←
    let{f ← car(pair), val ← cdr(pair)}
        let{old:bnd ← assoc(f, bnds)}
            if(old:bnd,
                rplacd(old:bnd, val),
                rplacd(last(bnds), cons(pair, NIL))
```

9.3.5. The *memop:eval* Program

The function *memop:eval* does the job of applying the memory operations, while the task of deciding whether a form was a memory operation call was that of the function *memop*. Both definitions are without subtlety.

```
memop:eval(f, args, bnds) ←
    ifs(eq(f, READ),   read(),
        eq(f, ATOM),   atom(eval(car(args), bnds)),
        eq(f, CAR),    car(eval(car(args), bnds)),
        eq(f, CDR),    cdr(eval(car(args), bnds)),
        eq(f, INT),    int(eval(car(args), bnds)),
        eq(f, SUB1),   sub1(eval(car(args), bnds)),
        eq(f, ADD1),   add1(eval(car(args), bnds)),
        eq(f, PRINT),  print(eval(car(args), bnds)),
        eq(f, EQ),     eq(eval(car(args), bnds), eval(cadr(args), bnds)),
        eq(f, CONS),   cons(eval(car(args), bnds), eval(cadr(args), bnds)),
        eq(f, RPLACA), rplaca(eval(car(args), bnds),
                              eval(cadr(args), bnds)),
        eq(f, RPLACD), rplacd(eval(car(args), bnds),
                              eval(cadr(args), bnds)))
```

```
memop(f) ←
    or(eq(f, ATOM), eq(f, EQ),      eq(f, CAR),
       eq(f, CDR),  eq(f, INT),     eq(f, ADD1),
       eq(f, SUB1), eq(f, PRINT),   eq(f, READ),
       eq(f, CONS), eq(f, RPLACA),  eq(f, RPLACD))
```

9.3.6. The *macro:eval* and *fun:eval* Programs

Finally we are left with the task of interpreting function and macro calls. This is done by a series of functions. *apply* determines whether or not the call is to a macro or a function. It then ships the call off to specialist functions, *macro:eval* in the case of a macro call, and *fun:eval* in the case of a function call. The actual task of determining whether the call is to a macro or not is the task of the *macro* function. We simply give the definition of these functions, and leave the the task of annotation to the reader.

```
apply(fm, f, args, bnds) ←
    if(macro(f, bnds), macro:eval(fm, bnds), fun:eval(f, args, bnds))


macro:eval(fm, bnds) ←
    let{d ← assoc(car(fm), bnds)}
        eval(eval(car(cdddr(d)), cons(cons(caddr(d), fm), bnds)), bnds)


fun:eval(f, args, bnds) ←
    let{d ← assoc(f, bnds)}
        eval(caddr(d), add:bnds(bnds:mk(cadr(d), args), bnds))


macro(f, bnds) ← eq(cadr(assoc(f, bnds)), MACRO)


body(fm) ← cdr(fm)
bnds:mk(vars, args) ←
    if(vars,
        cons(list(car(vars), car(args)),
             bnds:mk(cdr(vars), cdr(args))),
        NIL)
```

9.4. The Read-Eval-Print Loop

In this section we give a brief description of the *toplevel* of Lisp, the so called *read-eval-print* loop. Our simplified version of the *toplevel* consists of the three functions *read*,*eval* and *print* that read evaluate and print S-expressions. Thus when one are talking to Lisp the system is in a loop that consists of three programs

1. *read* reads what is typed and converts it into the corresponding internal list structure representation,

2. *eval* then evaluates the internal form in the current environment,

and

3. *print* then prints the result back to the terminal (or file, etc).

A real Lisp system does many other things too, such as storage management, error handling, provisions for editing function definitions, etc. However we shall be content with a very simple version:

$$lisp() \leftarrow$$
$$\quad \texttt{let}\{\texttt{bnds} \leftarrow cons(cons(\texttt{T},\texttt{T}), cons(cons(\texttt{NIL},\texttt{NIL}),\texttt{NIL}))\}$$
$$\quad\quad read{:}eval{:}print{:}loop(\texttt{bnds})$$

Here the auxiliary function *read:eval:print:loop* is exactly what it sounds like, namely

$$read{:}eval{:}print{:}loop(\texttt{bnds}) \leftarrow$$
$$\quad \texttt{seq}(print(eval(read(),\texttt{bnds}))$$
$$\quad\quad read{:}eval{:}print{:}loop(\texttt{bnds}))$$

The *read* program's job is to get from the input stream the next string of characters or tokens corresponding to the external representation of the S-expression. It then constructs the corresponding internal structure. Rather than deal with the issue of representing and manipulating character strings, our *read* and *print* programs are assumed to satisfy reasonable approximations, at least in respect to their observable behavior. A more detailed approach can be found in (McCarthy and Talcott, 1980, 1985).

9.5. Correctness of the *eval* Program

We finish off this chapter by pointing out the partial correctness of our interpreter. The actual proof is left to the reader as it is not difficult.

Theorem: Suppose that $e(\bar{x})$ is an expression with respect to a definition D, $\bar{v}\ ;\ \mu \in \mathbb{M}_{sexp}$ with $|\bar{x}| = n = |\bar{v}|$. Suppose further that $\mathtt{D}\ ;\ \mu$ is an internal representation of D and suppose finally that $v^*\ ;\ \mu$ is isomorphic to

$$\mathtt{e}(\bar{v})\ ;\ \mu.$$

Then

$$D_{eval}, D \vdash eval(v^*, \mathtt{D})\ ;\ \mu \simeq e(\bar{v})\ ;\ \mu.$$

Note that we are not proving anything concerning the control constructs that are in the internal language, but not in the external one. This is not to say that we could not, just that we do not.

Chapter 10

Editing Data Efficiently

In this chapter we shall describe and prove properties of an interactive Lisp editor. The editor and the treatment are based on the editor in (McCarthy and Talcott, 1980), which in turn is based on the Maclisp editor. The following is from (McCarthy and Talcott, 1980).

> *An important part of any LISP system is an interactive editor. With the help of the editor you can write and modify programs. Some editors allow you to evaluate expressions without leaving the editing environment. They may also provide facilities for editing S-expressions other than programs. The fact that LISP programs are S-expressions with a very simple syntax means that is easy to write a simple but powerful LISP program editor in LISP.*

This is the subject of this chapter. Before we begin describing the actual code for the editor, it is perhaps appropriate if we discuss what is desirable in such an entity. Suppose that we wished to edit an S-expression `s`. The most obvious question that should first be answered is : *What does it mean to edit* `s`? This is easily answered when one thinks of the case when `s` is a program. Editing a program is to a large extent synonomous with *debugging* it. Thus we would like to be able to change items, add items, delete items and make structural changes. This immediately entails that we should be able to move around within `s`. This is done by maintaining a pointer to some location in the structure. The thing pointed to is called the *current S-expression* and the variable pointing to it is called `cs`. The editor should then have commands that allow us to change this pointer, in other words to move around the S-expression. Moving around essentially boils down to two different operations; the first is when we wish to delve deeper within the current expression and the second is when we wish to *step back* and perhaps edit some other portion of `s` that is not a substructure of the present current expression. For this purpose it is desirable to keep track of our path *down* to `cs` so that we can at any stage backtrack and then follow another path. This is done by what we call the `chain`. The editor would not be much help if it did not allow one to *look* at the current expression and so we should be able to print it (to the terminal). Nor would it be useful if it did not allow us to exit it once we have finished editing; for this reason we include a quit command.

As we have already said we should be able to insert and delete elements of the current expression. Indeed this is all we need to be able to convert any non-atomic program into any other non-atomic program. But of course an editor that only had the above commands would hardly deserve the title of *user friendly.* Consequently we include other features which are useful in the course of editing a program. As we have already said, a principal application of the editor is to *debug* programs. Debugging is often a trial and error exercise, and so for this reason we allow calling the Lisp interpreter from within. An important feature of the editor is that many of the commands are destructive. In fact one might consider it to be an essential feature. For if we did not edit destructively, each alteration to `s` would require us to copy, with the necessary modifications, the entire structure. This of course would produce an editor that tried the patience of its most patient users. Furthermore since the point of editing a structure is to change it, avoiding destructive operations seems counter intuitive. Nevertheless the destructive operations are all *safe* in the sense that for any command there is an inverse command, one that will undo the previous one. We shall not actually implement an *undo* command, but its existence or possibility will be the subject of our attention.

Since our programs are elements of $\mathbb{M}_{hered}$, we have designed our editor to operate on such objects. It will actually work for all S-expressions but sometimes with unexpected and surprising results. One other important difference between our version of the editor and the one found in (McCarthy and Talcott, 1980) other than style, is that we do absolutely no *error checking.* Commands given to our editor are assumed to make sense. This is mainly because we are concerned with the behavior of the operations and not that of the operator (who is assumed to be infallible). We list the commands here, giving an extremely brief description of them. We shall give much more detailed descriptions when we actually come to define them and their consequences.

10.1. Commands

The commands that we shall implement and study in our interactive Lisp editor are:

- `ok`, exit the editor.
- `print`, print the current expression.
- `n`, where `n` is any integer. This alters the pointer `cs` so that it points to the `n`th element of the current `cs`.
- `up`, move the `cs` pointer to its previous value in the path down, the sublist of `s` which contains `cs` as an element. We call this objects the parent of `cs`.

- `left`, assuming that `cs` points to an element of a list, this command moves the `cs` pointer so that it points to the element to the left, in this *parent* list, of its current value.
- `right`, same as for `left` except that it move `cs` to the right.
- `lpi`, move the left parenthesis of `cs` in. This splices the first element of `cs` into its parent in the position `cs` occupies.
- `rpi`, move the right parenthesis of `cs` in. This splices the last element of `cs` into the next position in the parent.
- `lpo`, move the left parenthesis of `cs` out. This splices the element before `cs` in the parent onto the front of `cs`.
- `rpo`, move the right parenthesis of `cs` out. This splices the element to the right in the parent onto the end of `cs`.
- `(d n)`, delete the `n`th element from `cs`, numbering them from 1 to the length of the `cs`.
- `(i x n)` insert `x` into the `n`th position in `cs`, again numbering them from 1 to the length of `cs`.
- Any other S-expression will be evaluated by Lisp interpreter in the current environment.

We shall describe the commands in more detail when it comes time to give their definitions.

10.2. The Code for the Editor

In this section we shall give the actual definition of the editor. It will be within the internal programming language that we introduced in the previous chapter. However for ease of reading we no longer insist on everything being in `CAPITALS`. The principal program in the definition of the editor is called

`editloop`.

It is similar to the read-eval-print loop, in that within the loop it reads a command, executes it and then calls itself again. In the case of *read:eval:print:loop* the only argument passed between calls to itself was the current environment. In the case of the editor it is the state, `state`. The state consists of a pure list that stores three objects. The first is the S-expression being edited, the second is the current

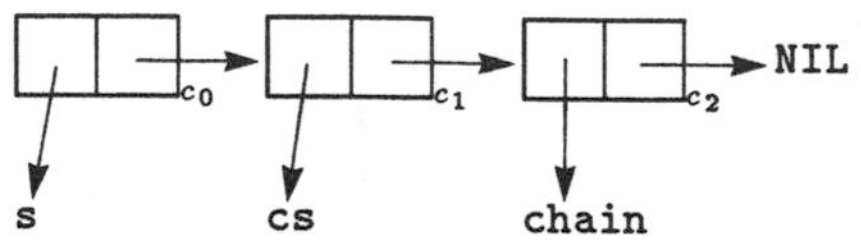

Figure 18. The Nature of **state**

expression and the third is the chain. Thus the variable `state` will point to an object of the form depicted in figure 18.

As usual we shall use abstract syntax to hide the actual details of this representation. Thus we have the following, self-explanatory, definitions.

```
(defun set:s (state val) (seq (rplaca state val) state))
(defun set:cs (state val) (seq (rplaca (cdr state) val) state))
(defun set:chain (state val)
   (seq (rplaca (cddr state) val) state))
(defun get:s (state) (car state))
(defun get:cs (state) (cadr state))
(defun get:chain (state) (caddr state)).
```

The variable `chain`, as we have already said, stores the path down to the current expression. Explicitly `chain` is a pure list (actually it is an alist), which is non-empty when the values of `s` and `cs` are different and `NIL` otherwise. Note that `s` and `cs` being different correspond to the situation when we have already descended *into* `s`. When `chain` is non-empty its first element is a pair `(n . e)`. Here `e` is the expression, or piece of data, which immediately contains the current expression `cs`, and n is the position of `cs` in the list `e`. The second element, if there is one, is again a pair. The second element of the pair is the *father* or *parent* of `e` and the first element of the pair corresponds to the position of `e` within its parent. This continues in the obvious fashion until we reach the top, `s`. The abstract syntax for chains simply consists of the following three programs.

```
(defun position (chain) (caar chain))
(defun parent   (chain) (cdar chain))
(defun set:position (chain n) (rplaca (car chain) n)).
```

We make the convention that the *car* of a list is the first element, and in general the nth element of the list `x` is computed by the following program.

```
(defun element (x n)
  (if (and (> n 1) (cdr x))
      (element (cdr x) (sub1 n))
      (car x))).
```

To invoke the editor on an object within the read-eval-print-loop of Lisp one simply calls the function `editor` on something which evaluates to that object. Thus to edit the definition of a function `f` it suffices to evaluate `(editor f)`, since the value of `f` in our Lisp *is* its definition. The state is initialized so that both `s` and `cs` correspond to the value of `f`, and the `chain` is of course `NIL`. This is reflected in the following definition.

```
(defun editor (s)
  (if (atom s) 'no-edit (editloop (list s s NIL)))).
```

The `editloop` is then given by the following definition. It first prints a prompt, in this case `>`, to the terminal to inform the operator that it is waiting for a command. It then reads in the command, obtains the relevant information from the `state` and then acts upon the command. Note that if the command is `ok` the editloop does not call itself but simply returns, the possibly modified, `s`. If the command is not the quit command then the editloop calls a specialized function to execute the command. Each of these specialized functions returns the resulting state. This explains why the `ifs` part of the program is within the recursive `editloop` call. Thus we are utilizing the fact that internal Lisp programs evaluate their arguments. Note that just in the case of the *eval* program there are some commands which are so simple to execute that no specialized program is required. In this case executing either a print statement, and exit statement, or a call to the Lisp interpreter requires no specialized function.

```
(defun editloop (state)
  (seq (print '>)
       (let ((cmd   (read))
             (s     (get:s state))
             (cs    (get:cs state))
             (chain (get:chain state)))
         (if (eq cmd 'ok)
             s
             (editloop
              (ifs (eq cmd 'print)   (seq (print cs) state)
                   (int cmd)
                   (edit:down cmd s cs chain state)
                   (eq cmd 'up)      (up s cs chain state)
                   (eq cmd 'left)    (left s cs chain state)
                   (eq cmd 'right)   (right s cs chain state)
                   (eq cmd 'lpi)     (lpi s cs chain state)
                   (eq cmd 'lpo)     (lpo s cs chain state)
                   (eq cmd 'rpi)     (rpi s cs chain state)
                   (eq cmd 'rpo)     (rpo s cs chain state)
                   (and (not (atom cmd)) (eq (car cmd) 'i))
                   (i (cadr cmd)
                      (caddr cmd)
                      s
                      cs
                      chain
                      state)
                   (and (not (atom cmd)) (eq (car cmd) 'd))
                   (d (cadr cmd) s cs chain state)
                   T                 (seq (print (eval cmd))
                                          state)))))).
```

10.2.1. Coherent States

We now begin describing the specialized editing programs, the commands that they execute as well as the definition of a legal command. We begin by defining the notion of a coherent state, since the notion of a legal command requires it.

Definition: Suppose that state $\in \mathbb{M}_{sexp}$ is a pure list of length 3, it is said to be a *coherent state* if the following hold. Letting s $\simeq$ *get:s*(state), cs $\simeq$ *get:cs*(state) and chain $\simeq$ *get:chain*(state),

1. chain $\in \mathbb{M}_{alist}$,

2. $\mathtt{s} = \mathtt{cs}$ iff $\mathtt{chain} = \mathtt{NIL}$,

and now supposing that $\mathtt{chain} \neq \mathtt{NIL}$ we also have

3. $element(parent(\mathtt{chain}), position(\mathtt{chain})) \simeq \mathtt{cs}$,
4. $parent(last(\mathtt{chain})) \simeq \mathtt{s}$,
5. $(\forall c_1, c_2 \in \mathbf{Spine}(\mathtt{chain}))$

$$(cdr(c_1) \simeq c_2) \rightarrow element(parent(c_2), position(c_2)) \simeq c_1,$$

6. $(\forall c \in \mathbf{Spine}(\mathtt{chain})) parent(c) \in \mathbb{M}_{hered}$.

The idea of a coherent state is quite simple. It is a state reached from the initial one, `(s s NIL)`, via a sequence of legal commands. In fact this is the principal loop invariant that we shall prove later. Namely

Theorem: Executing a legal command takes coherent states to coherent states.

In the following descriptions we shall assume that `state` is a coherent state and that `s`, `cs` and `chain` are its respective components.

10.2.2. The Integer Commands

The first type of command that we shall consider is the integer command. If `n` is a positive integer and `cs` is a list of length greater than or equal to `n`, then `n` is a legal command. The specialized program that executes it is `editdown`. What `editdown` does is to produce a new state of the form

```
(s (element cs n) (cons (n . cs) chain).
```

In other words the state is changed so that the new current expression is the `n`th element of `cs` and the chain is modified by adding the pair `(n . cs)` to the front of the original one. The actual definition of `editdown` is

```
(defun edit:down (n s cs chain state)
  (seq (set:cs state (element cs n))
       (set:chain state (cons (cons n cs) chain)))).
```

The process can be pictured as follows, supposing that prior to execution of the `n` command the situation is as depicted in figure 19, then after execution the situation is depicted in figure 20.

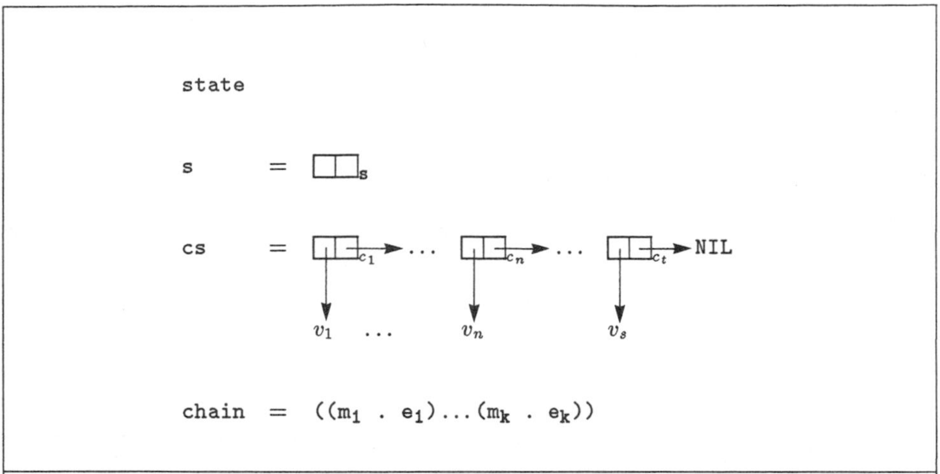

Figure 19. Prior to Execution on **n**

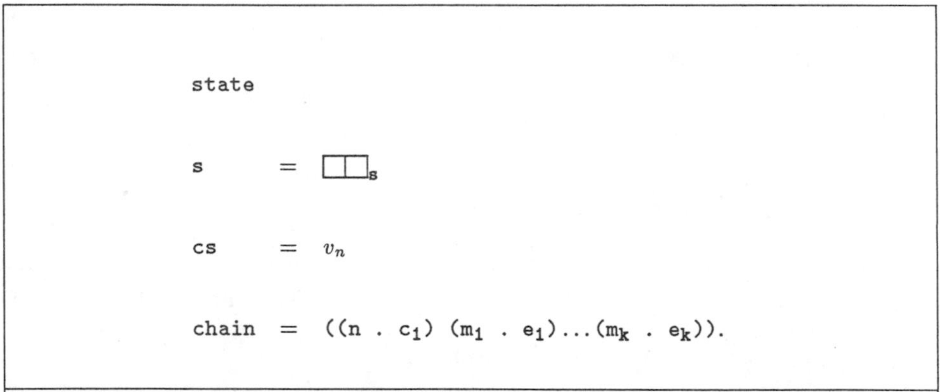

Figure 20. After Execution

10.2.3. The Up Command

The next command is the up command, which is legal as long as the `chain` is not `NIL`. The up command is the inverse of a legal integer command. After executing the up command the new current expression is the parent of the old current expression, and the new chain is the old chain with the first element removed. The actual definition is the following.

```
(defun up (s cs chain state)
  (seq (set:cs state (parent chain))
       (set:chain state (cdr chain)))).
```

10.2.4. The Move Right Command

The move right command, `right`, is legal as long as `cs` is not the rightmost, or last element, of *parent*(`chain`). Explicitly, we require that

$$length(parent(\texttt{chain})) > position(\texttt{chain}).$$

The result of executing the `right` command is that the state is altered so that the new current expression is the next element of *parent*(`chain`) after the appropriate occurrence of the old `cs`. The chain must also be modified so that the first element of the first pair is one larger than previously. The command is executed by the following definition.

```
(defun right (s cs chain state)
  (let ((n (add1 (position chain))))
    (seq (set:cs state (element (parent chain) n))
         (set:position chain n)
         state))).
```

10.2.5. The Move Left Command

The move left command, `left`, is the inverse of the move right command. It is legal as long as `cs` is not the first element of *parent*(`chain`). Explicitly, we require that

$$position(\texttt{chain}) \neq 1.$$

The result of executing the `left` command is that the state is altered so that the new current expression is the element of *parent*(`chain`) prior to the appropriate occurrence of the old `cs`. The chain must also be modified so that the first element of the first pair is one smaller than previously. The command is executed by the following definition.

```
(defun left (s cs chain state)
  (let ((n (sub1 (position chain))))
    (seq (set:cs state (element (parent chain) n))
         (set:position chain n)
         state))).
```

10.2.6. The Move the Left Parenthesis In Command

The *move the left parenthesis in command*, `lpi`, is legal as long as neither `cs` is atomic nor `chain` in `NIL`. What it does is to splice the first element of `cs` into the parent of `cs`, at the position previously occupied by `cs`. The cdr of `cs` is then moved to the next position to the right of the new element in the parent. Thus the parent will become a list, one element longer than it was originally. The new `cs` is the *cdr* of the old. To help with visualizing this operation suppose that the situation is as pictured in figure 21, then the situation after executing the `lpi` command is depicted in figure 22.

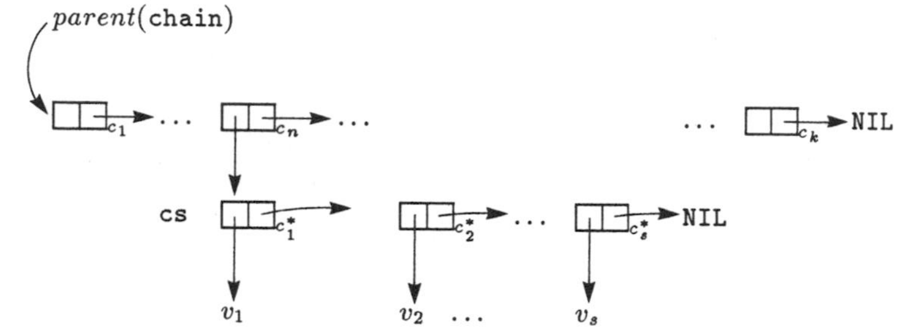

Figure 21. Prior to `lpi`

Notice that no new cells are created in performing this modification. The actual definition of the operation is as follows; it utilizes an auxiliary program called `spine` which simply returns the nth element of the spine (numbering them from 1 to the length of the argument, which is supposed to be a list).

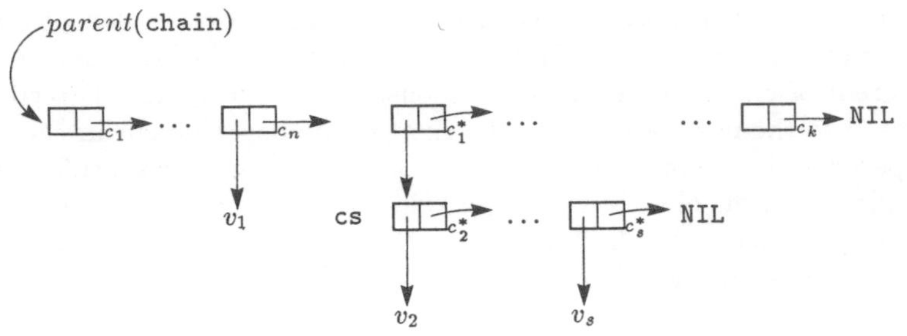

Figure 22. After lpi

```
(defun lpi (s cs chain state)
  (let ((pos (spine (parent chain) (position chain))))
    (seq (rplaca pos (car cs))
         (rplaca cs (cdr cs))
         (rplacd cs (cdr pos))
         (rplacd pos cs)
         (set:position chain (add1 (position chain)))
         (set:cs state (car cs)))))
```

```
(defun spine (x n)
  (if (and (> n 1) (cdr x))
      (spine (cdr x) (sub1 n))
      x)).
```

10.2.7. The Move the Left Parenthesis Out Command

The *move the left parenthesis out command*, lpo, is the inverse of the lpi command. It is legal as long as the chain is not NIL, the cs is a (possibly empty) list and cs is not the first element of its parent. Execution of a legal lpo command does the following; it physically removes the element prior to cs in the parent, from

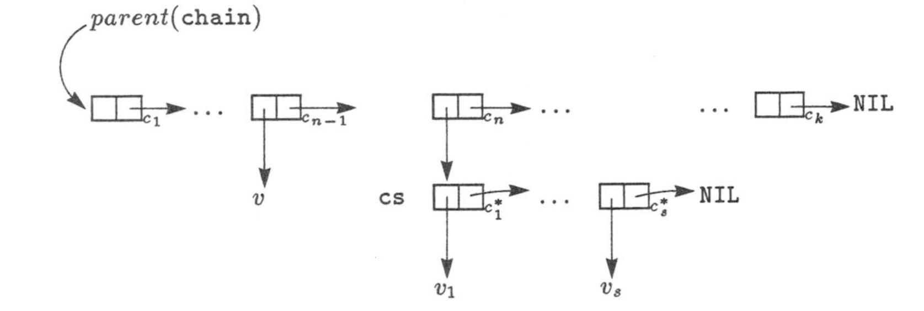

Figure 23. Prior to `lpo`

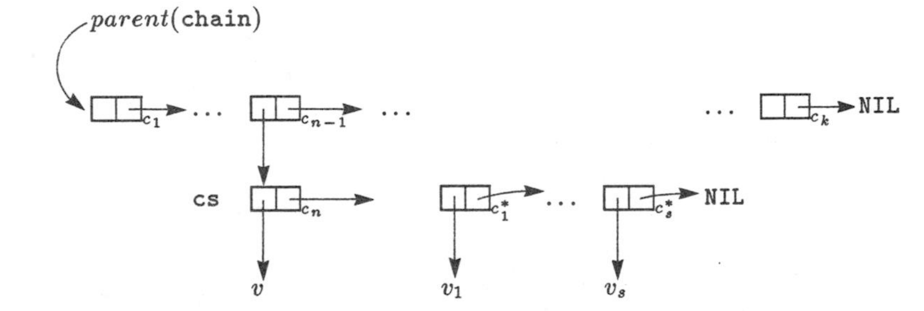

Figure 24. After `lpo`

the parent, and adds it to the front of `cs`. Again we can illustrate this operation for clarity. Suppose that the situation is as pictured in figure 23, then after executing `lpo` the situation is as depicted in figure 24.

Note that the parent of `cs` is shortened by one and that no new cells are created. The actual definition is the following.

```
(defun lpo (s cs chain state)
  (let ((n (sub1 (position chain))))
    (let ((pos (spine (parent chain) n)))
      (let ((pos1 (cdr pos)))
        (seq (rplacd pos (cdr pos1))
             (rplacd pos1 cs)
             (rplaca pos1 (car pos))
             (rplaca pos pos1)
             (set:position chain  n)
             (set:cs state pos1))))))).
```

10.2.8. The Move the Right Parenthesis In Command

The *move the right parenthesis in*, rpi, is legal as long as chain is not NIL and cs is not atomic. It is similar to the lpi command except that it splices the last element of cs into the position *after* cs in the parent. The definition is then, using the auxiliary program chop:

```
(defun rpi (s cs chain state)
  (let ((pos  (spine (parent chain) (position chain))))
    (ifn (cdr cs)
         (seq (rplaca pos NIL)
              (rplacd cs (cdr pos))
              (rplacd pos cs)
              (set:cs state NIL))
         (let ((last (chop cs)))
           (seq (rplacd last (cdr pos))
                (rplacd pos last)
                state))))).
```

The auxiliary program chop destructively removes the last element of the spine of the list, returning the deleted cell:

```
(defun chop (x) (chp x (cdr x)))
(defun chp (x y)
  (ifn (cdr y) (seq (rplacd x NIL) y) (chp y (cdr y)))).
```

10.2.9. The Move the Right Parenthesis Out Command

The *move the right parenthesis out command*, rpi, is the inverse of the rpi command. It is legal as long as chain is not NIL, cs is a list and is not the last element of its parent. The definition is thus:

```
(defun rpo (s cs chain state)
  (let ((pos (spine (parent chain) (position chain))))
    (let ((pos1 (cdr pos)))
      (seq (rplacd pos (cdr pos1))
           (rplacd pos1 NIL)
           (ifn cs
                (seq (rplaca pos pos1)
                     (set:cs state pos1))
                (set:cs state (nconc cs pos1))))))).
```

10.2.10. The Delete Command

The delete command, (d n), deletes the nth element from cs. It is thus only legal when there is an nth element. Thus cs should not be atomic and n should be less than or equal to the length of cs. The definition is stated simply as:

```
(defun d (n s cs chain state)
  (if (eq n 1)
      (let ((pos (cdr cs)))
        (ifn chain
             (set:s (set:cs state pos) pos)
             (seq (rplaca (spine (parent chain) (position chain))
                          pos)
                  (set:cs state pos))))
      (seq (rplacd (spine cs (sub1 n)) (cdr (spine cs n)))
           state))).
```

Actually there is a subtle point here: it is impossible to remove the very first cell in s and still have s point to the modified result. For this reason we shall also make (d 1) illegal when cs = s.

10.2.11. The Insert Command

The insert command, `(i n x)`, inserts `x` into the `n`th position in `cs`. If there is already an element occupying the `n`th position it is, of course, moved to the right. The command is legal as long as `cs` is not atomic, `x` does not share any cells with `s`, and `n` is less than or equal to one plus the length of `cs`. In other words one can insert `x` *into* `cs` or add it to the end.

```
(defun i (n x s cs chain state)
  (let ((tmp (cons x (spine cs n))))
    (if (eq n 1)
        (ifn chain
             (set:s (set:cs state tmp) tmp)
             (seq (rplaca (spine (parent chain) (position chain))
                          tmp)
                  (set:cs state tmp)))
        (seq (rplacd (spine cs (sub1 n)) tmp)
             state)))).
```

Just as in the case of the delete command we also make `(i 1 x)` illegal when `cs` = `s`.

10.2.12. Legal Commands

We finish off this section by summarizing the definition of a legal command. Suppose that `state` is a coherent state and that `s`,`cs` and `chain` are its respective components. Then we can define when a command `cmd` is legal with respect to this state as follows.

Definition: The command `cmd` is legal iff

1. `cmd` = `n`, `cs` is not atomic and $length($`cs`$) \geq n$.
2. `cmd` = `up` and `chain` is not `NIL`.
3. `cmd` = `left`, `chain` is not `NIL` and $position($`chain`$) \neq 1$.
4. `cmd` = `right`, `chain` is not `NIL` and $length(parent($`chain`$)) > position($`chain`$)$.
5. `cmd` = `lpi`, `cs` is not atomic and `chain` is not `NIL`.
6. `cmd` = `lpo`, `cs` is a list, `chain` is not `NIL` and $position($`chain`$) \neq 1$.
7. `cmd` = `rpi`, `cs` is not atomic and `chain` is not `NIL`.

8. cmd $=$ rpo, cs is a list, chain is not NIL and

$$position(\texttt{chain}) < length(parent(\texttt{chain}).$$

9. cmd $=$ (d n), $length(\texttt{cs}) \geq$ n and if s $=$ cs then n $\neq 1$.
10. cmd $=$ (i n x), cs is not atomic, x does not share any cells with s, n $\leq$ $1 + length(\texttt{cs})$ and if s $=$ cs then n $\neq 1$.

10.3. A Sample Editing Session

In this section we give a simple example of the use of the editor, based on a lecture given by Carolyn Talcott. Suppose that while within the read-eval-print loop we make the following definition, of a program similar to spine. In fact we want the program to perform exactly the same task as spine, although it is written in a more Maclisp-ish dialect.

```
(DEFUN NTHT (U N)
  (COND ((GREATERP N 1) (NTHTAIL (CDR U) (SUB1 N)))
        (T U) ))
```

However it soon becomes apparent that our definition of ntht is defective in two ways. The most obvious is that we have misspelt ntht in the recursive call. The second mistake is that we do not check to make sure that U is not the empty list before we take its *cdr*. The correct definition should then be:

```
(DEFUN NTHT (U N)
  (COND ((AND (GREATERP N 1) (NOT (NULL (CDR U))))
         (NTHT (CDR U) (SUB1 N)))
        (T U) )).
```

Realizing our mistake we wish to correct the program, using the interactive Lisp editor. This is done by calling the program editor on the atom ntht. The first thing we shall correct is the misspelt recursive call. Consequently we descend into the code.

```
(editor ntht)
> 2
```

Rather than do anything hasty we print the current expression and decide what to do next.

```
> print
(COND ((GREATERP N 1)
       (NTHTAIL (CDR U) (SUB1 N)))
      (T U))
```

The next step is to descend further into the structure, namely to the second element of the current expression.

```
> 2
```

Again we print the current expression.

```
> print
((GREATERP N 1) (NTHTAIL (CDR U) (SUB1 N)))
```

The misspelt call is in the second element of the current expression and so again we descend and print.

```
> 2
> print
(NTHTAIL (CDR U) (SUB1 N))
```

We can now make the correction. This is done in two steps. The first is to delete the misspelt word.

```
> (d 1)
```

The second is to insert the correct version, and print the result to make sure we have done what we intended.

```
> (i 1 ntht)
> print
(NTHT (CDR U) (SUB1 N))
```

We now wish to correct the logical error. That is, we want to change the `(GREATERP N 1)` test to the correct version, namely `(AND (GREATERP N 1) (NOT (NULL (CDR U))))`. The first thing to do is to ascend.

```
> up
> print
((GREATERP N 1) (NTHT (CDR U) (SUB1 N)))
```

We can now insert the second conjunction. This is done in two steps. We first insert a list containing this clause into the second position, and then move the left parenthesis of this inserted clause out.

```
> (i 2 ((not (null (cdr u)))))
> print
((GREATERP N 1) ((NOT (NULL (CDR U)))) (NTHT (CDR U) (SUB1 N)))
> 2
> print
((NOT (NULL (CDR U))))
> lpo
> print
((GREATERP N 1) (NOT (NULL (CDR U))))
```

All we need do now is to insert the `and` and we have repaired the program.

```
> (i 1 and)
```

```
> print
(AND (GREATERP N 1) (NOT (NULL (CDR U))))
> up
> print
((AND (GREATERP N 1) (NOT (NULL (CDR U))))
 (NTHT (CDR U) (SUB1 N)))
```

However while we are still in the editor it seems wise to examine the program to make sure we have not overlooked anything.

```
> up
> print
(COND ((AND (GREATERP N 1) (NOT (NULL (CDR U))))
       (NTHT (CDR U) (SUB1 N)))
      (T U))
> up
> print
((U N)
 (COND ((AND (GREATERP N 1) (NOT (NULL (CDR U))))
        (NTHT (CDR U) (SUB1 N)))
       (T U)))
```

Everything appears in order so we exit the editor.

```
> ok
((U N)
 (COND ((AND (GREATERP N 1) (NOT (NULL (CDR U))))
        (NTHT (CDR U) (SUB1 N)))
       (T U)))
```

We can give an idea of what goes on while we are editing. The structure of the state initially is represented in the following picture:

```
s =
  ((U N)
   (COND ((GREATERP N 1)
          (NTHTAIL (CDR U) (SUB1 N)))
         (T U)))
cs = s
chain = NIL.
```

After descending into the structure using the following three integer commands

2 2 1

the state becomes

```
cs = (GREATERP N 1)
chain =
```

```
((1 (GREATERP N 1) (NTHTAIL (CDR U) (SUB1 N)))
 (2 COND ((GREATERP ..) (NTHTAIL ..)) (T U))
 (2 (U N) ...) ).
```

If we then execute the move right command,

```
rt,
```

the state is transformed into

```
cs = (NTHTAIL (CDR U) (SUB1 N))
chain =
  ((2 (GREATERP N 1) (NTHTAIL (CDR U) (SUB1 N)))
   (2 COND ((GREATERP ..) (NTHTAIL ..)) (T U))
   (2 (U N) ...)
  ).
```

10.4. Proving Properties of the Editor

In this section we prove several properties of the editor. We begin by dividing the commands into two separate groups, the atomic commands, and the list commands. The atomic commands are those which are actually atoms. Namely

```
up n left right lpi lpo rpi rpo.
```

The list commands are those which are actually lists,

```
(d n)  (i n x).
```

Notice we are ignoring the `print` and `ok` commands. The reason for this is quite simple. There is nothing interesting, other than the obvious, to prove about them. The first result that we shall prove other than the coherent state theorem (that executing a legal command takes coherent states to coherent states) demonstrates that each command has an inverse. We first formulate the result for the case of the atomic commands.

Definition: Suppose that `state` is a coherent state, `s`, `cs` and `chain` are its respective components, and `cmd` is an atomic command other than `n` or `up`, then we define $\texttt{cmd}^{-1}$ as follows,

$$\texttt{cmd}^{-1} = \begin{cases} \texttt{left} & \text{if } \texttt{cmd} = \texttt{right}, \\ \texttt{right} & \text{if } \texttt{cmd} = \texttt{left}, \\ \texttt{lpi} & \text{if } \texttt{cmd} = \texttt{lpo}, \\ \texttt{lpo} & \text{if } \texttt{cmd} = \texttt{lpi}, \\ \texttt{rpi} & \text{if } \texttt{cmd} = \texttt{rpo}, \\ \texttt{rpo} & \text{if } \texttt{cmd} = \texttt{rpi}. \end{cases}$$

Using this definition we can state the theorem as:

The Atomic Command Inverse Theorem: Suppose that state is a coherent state, s, cs and chain are its respective components, and cmd is a legal atomic command other than n or up, and *cmd* is the external form of its definition. Then

$$\texttt{state} \simeq$$

$$\texttt{seq}(\mathit{cmd}(\texttt{s}, \texttt{cs}, \texttt{chain}, \texttt{state}),$$
$$\quad \mathit{cmd}^{-1}(\mathit{get{:}s}(\texttt{state}), \mathit{get{:}cs}(\texttt{state}), \mathit{get{:}chain}(\texttt{state}), \texttt{state})).$$

Remark: In the case of the n and up commands the situation is not quite as simple. We only get strong isomorphism in one direction. Explicitly

The Integer Command Inverse Theorem: Suppose that state is a coherent state, s, cs and chain are its respective components, and n is a legal atomic command. Then

$$\texttt{state} \simeq$$

$$\texttt{seq}(\mathit{edit{:}down}(\texttt{n}, \texttt{s}, \texttt{cs}, \texttt{chain}, \texttt{state}),$$
$$\quad \mathit{up}(\mathit{get{:}s}(\texttt{state}), \mathit{get{:}cs}(\texttt{state}), \mathit{get{:}chain}(\texttt{state}), \texttt{state})).$$

Whereas when $\mathit{position}(\texttt{chain}) = \texttt{n}$, we only have that

$$\texttt{state} \cong$$

$$\texttt{seq}(\mathit{up}(\texttt{s}, \texttt{cs}, \texttt{chain}, \texttt{state}),$$
$$\quad \mathit{edit{:}down}(\texttt{n}, \mathit{get{:}s}(\texttt{state}), \mathit{get{:}cs}(\texttt{state}), \mathit{get{:}chain}(\texttt{state}), \texttt{state})).$$

Exercise: Explain why, supposing that state is a coherent state, s, cs and chain are its respective components, and up is a legal atomic command and that $\mathit{position}(\texttt{chain}) = \texttt{n}$, we do not have that

$$\texttt{state} \simeq$$

$$\texttt{seq}(\mathit{up}(\texttt{s}, \texttt{cs}, \texttt{chain}, \texttt{state}),$$
$$\quad \mathit{edit{:}down}(\texttt{n}, \mathit{get{:}s}(\texttt{state}), \mathit{get{:}cs}(\texttt{state}), \mathit{get{:}chain}(\texttt{state}), \texttt{state})).$$

A similar situation holds in the case of the list commands. Namely

The List Command Inverse Theorem: Suppose that `state` is a coherent state, `s`, `cs` and `chain` are its respective components, and `(i n x)` is a legal list command. Then

$$\texttt{state} \simeq$$

$$\texttt{seq}(i(\texttt{n}, \texttt{x}, \texttt{s}, \texttt{cs}, \texttt{chain}, \texttt{state}),$$
$$d(\texttt{n}, get{:}s(\texttt{state}), get{:}cs(\texttt{state}), get{:}chain(\texttt{state}), \texttt{state})).$$

Whereas when $element(\texttt{chain}, \texttt{n}) = \texttt{x}$, we only have that

$$\texttt{state} \cong$$

$$\texttt{seq}(d(\texttt{n}, \texttt{s}, \texttt{cs}, \texttt{chain}, \texttt{state}),$$
$$i(\texttt{n}, \texttt{x}, get{:}s(\texttt{state}), get{:}cs(\texttt{state}), get{:}chain(\texttt{state}), \texttt{state})).$$

The coherent state theorem is then stated in the following fashion. We split it into several cases for ease of reading.

The Atomic Command Coherent State Theorem: Suppose that `state` is a coherent state, `s`, `cs` and `chain` are its respective components, and `cmd` is a legal atomic command other than `n`,and *cmd* is the external form of its definition. Then

$$cmd(\texttt{s}, \texttt{cs}, \texttt{chain}, \texttt{state})$$

is also a coherent state.

The Integer Command Coherent State Theorem: Suppose that `state` is a coherent state, `s`, `cs` and `chain` are its respective components, and `n` is a legal command. Then

$$edit{:}down(\texttt{n}, \texttt{s}, \texttt{cs}, \texttt{chain}, \texttt{state})$$

is also a coherent state.

The List Command Coherent State Theorem: Suppose that `state` is a coherent state, `s`, `cs` and `chain` are its respective components.

1. If `(d n)` is a legal command then

   $$d(\texttt{n}, \texttt{s}, \texttt{cs}, \texttt{chain}, \texttt{state})$$

   is also a coherent state.

2. If `(i n x)` is a legal command then

   $$i(\texttt{n}, \texttt{x}, \texttt{s}, \texttt{cs}, \texttt{chain}, \texttt{state})$$

   is also a coherent state.

We leave the proofs of the coherent state theorems to the reader and concentrate on the inverse theorems.

10.4.1. Proof of the Inverse Theorems

Rather than prove every equation we content ourselves with proving a small but representative sample, namely the following three lemmas.

Lemma 1: Suppose that `state` is a coherent state, `s`, `cs` and `chain` are its respective components, and `n` is a legal atomic command. Then

$$\texttt{state} \simeq$$

$$\texttt{seq}(\textit{edit:down}(\texttt{n}, \texttt{s}, \texttt{cs}, \texttt{chain}, \texttt{state}),$$
$$\quad \textit{up}(\textit{get:s}(\texttt{state}), \textit{get:cs}(\texttt{state}), \textit{get:chain}(\texttt{state}), \texttt{state}))$$

Proof of lemma 1: Assume the hypotheses of the lemma. Then

$$\texttt{seq}(\textit{edit:down}(\texttt{n}, \texttt{s}, \texttt{cs}, \texttt{chain}, \texttt{state}),$$
$$\quad \textit{up}(\textit{get:s}(\texttt{state}), \textit{get:cs}(\texttt{state}), \textit{get:chain}(\texttt{state}), \texttt{state}))$$
$$\simeq \texttt{seq}(\textit{set:cs}(\texttt{state}, \textit{element}(\texttt{cs}, \texttt{n})),$$
$$\quad \textit{set:chain}(\texttt{state}, \textit{cons}(\textit{cons}(\texttt{n}, \texttt{cs}), \texttt{chain})),$$
$$\quad \textit{up}(\textit{get:s}(\texttt{state}), \textit{get:cs}(\texttt{state}), \textit{get:chain}(\texttt{state}), \texttt{state})),$$

by unfolding and simplifying the `edit:down` call.

$$\simeq \texttt{let}\{\texttt{cell} \leftarrow \textit{cons}(\textit{cons}(\texttt{n}, \texttt{cs}), \texttt{chain})\},$$
$$\quad \texttt{seq}(\textit{set:cs}(\texttt{state}, \textit{element}(\texttt{cs}, \texttt{n})),$$
$$\qquad \textit{set:chain}(\texttt{state}, \texttt{cell}),$$
$$\qquad \textit{up}(\textit{s}, \textit{element}(\texttt{cs}, \texttt{n}), \texttt{cell}, \texttt{state})),$$

by introducing a `let` and evaluating the arguments to the up call.

$$\simeq \texttt{let}\{\texttt{cell} \leftarrow \textit{cons}(\textit{cons}(\texttt{n}, \texttt{cs}), \texttt{chain})\},$$
$$\quad \texttt{seq}(\textit{set:cs}(\texttt{state}, \textit{element}(\texttt{cs}, \texttt{n})),$$
$$\qquad \textit{set:chain}(\texttt{state}, \texttt{cell}),$$
$$\qquad \textit{set:cs}(\texttt{state}, \textit{parent}(\texttt{cell})),$$
$$\qquad \textit{set:chain}(\texttt{state}, \textit{cdr}(\texttt{cell}))),$$

by unfolding and simplifying the up call.

$$\simeq \texttt{let}\{\texttt{cell} \leftarrow \textit{cons}(\textit{cons}(\texttt{n}, \texttt{cs}), \texttt{chain})\},$$
$$\quad \texttt{seq}(\textit{set:cs}(\texttt{state}, \textit{element}(\texttt{cs}, \texttt{n})),$$
$$\qquad \textit{set:chain}(\texttt{state}, \texttt{cell}),$$
$$\qquad \textit{set:cs}(\texttt{state}, \texttt{cs}),$$
$$\qquad \textit{set:chain}(\texttt{state}, \texttt{chain}))),$$

by evaluating the components of cell.

$$\simeq \texttt{let}\{\texttt{cell} \leftarrow cons(cons(\texttt{n}, \texttt{cs}), \texttt{chain})\},$$
$$\texttt{seq}(set{:}cs(\texttt{state}, element(\texttt{cs}, \texttt{n})),$$
$$set{:}cs(\texttt{state}, \texttt{cs}),$$
$$set{:}chain(\texttt{state}, \texttt{cell}),$$
$$set{:}chain(\texttt{state}, \texttt{chain}))),$$

by commuting the set operations.

$$\simeq \texttt{let}\{\texttt{cell} \leftarrow cons(cons(\texttt{n}, \texttt{cs}), \texttt{chain})\},$$
$$\texttt{seq}(set{:}cs(\texttt{state}, \texttt{cs}),$$
$$set{:}chain(\texttt{state}, \texttt{chain}))),$$

by cancelling redundant sets.

$$\simeq \texttt{seq}(set{:}cs(\texttt{state}, \texttt{cs}),$$
$$set{:}chain(\texttt{state}, \texttt{chain}))),$$

by eliminating a redundant let.

$$\simeq \texttt{state}.$$

□Lemma 1

Lemma 2: Suppose that state is a coherent state, s, cs and chain are its respective components, and left is a legal atomic command. Then

$$\texttt{state} \simeq$$
$$\texttt{seq}(left(\texttt{s}, \texttt{cs}, \texttt{chain}, \texttt{state}),$$
$$right(get{:}s(\texttt{state}), get{:}cs(\texttt{state}), get{:}chain(\texttt{state}), \texttt{state}))$$

Proof of lemma 2: Assume the hypotheses of the lemma. Then

$$\texttt{seq}(left(\texttt{s}, \texttt{cs}, \texttt{chain}, \texttt{state}),$$
$$right(get{:}s(\texttt{state}), get{:}cs(\texttt{state}), get{:}chain(\texttt{state}), \texttt{state}))$$
$$\simeq \texttt{seq}(\texttt{let}\{\texttt{n} \leftarrow position(\texttt{chain})\}$$
$$\texttt{seq}(set{:}cs(\texttt{state}, element(parent(\texttt{chain}), sub1(\texttt{n}))),$$
$$set{:}position(\texttt{chain}, sub1(\texttt{n})),$$
$$\texttt{state}),$$
$$right(get{:}s(\texttt{state}), get{:}cs(\texttt{state}), get{:}chain(\texttt{state}), \texttt{state})),$$

by unfolding the call to left.

```
≃ let{n ← position(chain)}
      seq(set:cs(state, element(parent(chain), sub1(n))),
          set:position(chain, sub1(n)),
          state,
          right(s, element(parent(chain), sub1(n)), chain, state)),
```

by simplifying the arguments to the `right` call.

```
≃ let{n ← position(chain)}
      seq(set:cs(state, element(parent(chain), sub1(n))),
          set:position(chain, sub1(n)),
          state,
          let{m ← add1(position(chain))}
              seq(set:cs(state, element(parent(chain), m)),
                  set:position(chain, m),
                  state)),
```

by unfolding and simplifying the call to `right`,

renaming the lexical variable to avoid clashes.

```
≃ let{n ← position(chain)}
      seq(set:cs(state, element(parent(chain), sub1(n))),
          set:position(chain, sub1(n)),
          let{m ← n}
              seq(set:cs(state, element(parent(chain), m)),
                  set:position(chain, m),
                  state)),
```

by simplifying the binding expression of the inner `let`.

```
≃ let{n ← position(chain)}
      seq(set:cs(state, element(parent(chain), sub1(n))),
          set:position(chain, sub1(n)),
          set:cs(state, cs),
          set:position(chain, n)
          state)),
```

by eliminating the `let` and collapsing nested `seq`s.

$$\simeq \texttt{let}\{\texttt{n} \leftarrow position(\texttt{chain})\}$$
$$\texttt{seq}(set{:}cs(\texttt{state}, element(parent(\texttt{chain}), sub1(\texttt{n}))),$$
$$set{:}cs(\texttt{state}, \texttt{cs}),$$
$$set{:}position(\texttt{chain}, sub1(\texttt{n})),$$
$$set{:}position(\texttt{chain}, \texttt{n}),$$
$$\texttt{state})),$$

by commuting various **sets**.

$$\simeq \texttt{let}\{\texttt{n} \leftarrow position(\texttt{chain})\}$$
$$\texttt{seq}(set{:}cs(\texttt{state}, \texttt{cs}),$$
$$set{:}position(\texttt{chain}, \texttt{n}),$$
$$\texttt{state})),$$

by eliminating redundant **sets**.

$$\simeq \texttt{seq}(set{:}cs(\texttt{state}, \texttt{cs}),$$
$$set{:}position(\texttt{chain}, position(\texttt{chain})),$$
$$\texttt{state})),$$

by eliminating the **let**.

$$\simeq \texttt{state},$$

finally eliminating the redundant **sets**.

□**Lemma 2**

Lemma 3: Suppose that state is a coherent state, s, cs and chain are its respective components, and n is a legal atomic command. Then

$$\texttt{state} \simeq$$
$$\texttt{seq}(lpo(\texttt{s}, \texttt{cs}, \texttt{chain}, \texttt{state}),$$
$$lpi(get{:}s(\texttt{state}), get{:}cs(\texttt{state}), get{:}chain(\texttt{state}), \texttt{state})).$$

Proof of lemma 3: Assume the hypothesis of the lemma. Then

$$\texttt{seq}(lpo(\texttt{s}, \texttt{cs}, \texttt{chain}, \texttt{state}),$$
$$lpi(get{:}s(\texttt{state}), get{:}cs(\texttt{state}), get{:}chain(\texttt{state}), \texttt{state}))$$

```
≃ seq(let{n ← sub1(position(chain))}
          let{pos ← spine(parent(chain), n)}
              let{pos1 ← cdr(pos)}
                  seq(rplacd(pos, cdr(pos1)),
                      rplacd(pos1, cs),
                      rplaca(pos1, car(pos)),
                      rplaca(pos, pos1),
                      set:position(chain, n),
                      set:cs(state, pos1)),
      lpi(get:s(state), get:cs(state), get:chain(state), state)),
```

by unfolding the `lpo` call.

```
≃ seq(let{n ← sub1(position(chain))}
          let{pos ← spine(parent(chain), n)}
              let{pos1 ← cdr(pos)}
                  seq(rplacd(pos, cdr(pos1)),
                      rplacd(pos1, cs),
                      rplaca(pos1, car(pos)),
                      rplaca(pos, pos1),
                      set:position(chain, n),
                      set:cs(state, pos1)),
      lpi(s, get:cs(state), chain, state)),
```

by simplifying the arguments to the `lpi` call.

```
≃ let{n ← sub1(position(chain))}
      let{pos ← spine(parent(chain), n)}
          let{pos1 ← cdr(pos)}
              seq(rplacd(pos, cdr(pos1)),
                  rplacd(pos1, cs),
                  rplaca(pos1, car(pos)),
                  rplaca(pos, pos1),
                  set:position(chain, n),
                  set:cs(state, pos1),
                  lpi(s, pos1, chain, state)),
```

by pulling the `let` out and further simplifying the arguments to the `lpi` call.

```
≃ let{n ← sub1(position(chain))}
      let{pos ← spine(parent(chain), n)}
          let{pos1 ← cdr(pos)}
              seq(rplacd(pos, cdr(pos1)),
                  rplacd(pos1, cs),
                  rplaca(pos1, car(pos)),
                  rplaca(pos, pos1),
                  set:position(chain, n),
                  set:cs(state, pos1),
                  let{npos ← spine(parent(chain), position(chain))}
                      seq(rplaca(npos, car(pos1)),
                          rplaca(pos1, cdr(pos1)),
                          rplacd(pos1, cdr(pos)),
                          rplacd(npos, pos1),
                          set:position(chain, add1(position(chain))),
                          set:cs(state, car(pos1)))),
```

by unfolding the `lpi` call and renaming variables to avoid clashes.

```
≃ let{n ← sub1(position(chain))}
      let{pos ← spine(parent(chain), n)}
          let{pos1 ← cdr(pos)}
              seq(rplacd(pos, cdr(pos1)),
                  rplacd(pos1, cs),
                  rplaca(pos1, car(pos)),
                  rplaca(pos, pos1),
                  set:position(chain, n),
                  set:cs(state, pos1),
                  let{npos ← spine(parent(chain), n)}
                      seq(rplaca(npos, car(pos1)),
                          rplaca(pos1, cs),
                          rplacd(pos1, cdr(pos)),
                          rplacd(npos, pos1),
                          set:position(chain, add1(n)),
                          set:cs(state, cs)))),
```

by simplifying the binding expression of the inner `let`.

```
≃ let{n ← sub1(position(chain))}
      let{pos ← spine(parent(chain), n)}
          let{pos1 ← cdr(pos)}
              seq(rplacd(pos, cdr(pos1)),
                  rplacd(pos1, cs),
                  rplaca(pos1, car(pos)),
                  rplaca(pos, pos1),
                  set:position(chain, n),
                  set:cs(state, pos1),
                  let{npos ← pos}
                      seq(rplaca(npos, car(pos1)),
                          rplaca(pos1, cs),
                          rplacd(pos1, cdr(pos)),
                          rplacd(npos, pos1),
                          set:position(chain, add1(n)),
                          set:cs(state, cs)))),
```

again by simplifying the binding expression of the innermost `let`.

```
≃ let{n ← sub1(position(chain))}
      let{pos ← spine(parent(chain), n)}
          let{pos1 ← cdr(pos)}
              seq(rplacd(pos, cdr(pos1)),
                  rplacd(pos1, cs),
                  rplaca(pos1, car(pos)),
                  rplaca(pos, pos1),
                  set:position(chain, n),
                  set:cs(state, pos1),
                  rplaca(pos, car(pos1)),
                  rplaca(pos1, cs),
                  rplacd(pos1, cdr(pos)),
                  rplacd(pos, pos1),
                  set:position(chain, add1(n)),
                  set:cs(state, cs)))),
```

finally eliminating the innermost let.

```
≃ let{n ← sub1(position(chain))}
    let{pos ← spine(parent(chain), n)}
      let{pos1 ← cdr(pos)}
        seq(rplacd(pos, cdr(pos1)),
            rplacd(pos1, cs),
            rplaca(pos1, car(pos)),
            rplaca(pos, pos1),
            rplaca(pos, car(pos1)),
            rplaca(pos1, cs),
            rplacd(pos1, cdr(pos)),
            rplacd(pos, pos1),
            set:position(chain, n),
            set:cs(state, pos1),
            set:position(chain, add1(n)),
            set:cs(state, cs)))),
```

by commuting various sets.

```
≃ let{n ← sub1(position(chain))}
    let{pos ← spine(parent(chain), n)}
      let{pos1 ← cdr(pos)}
        seq(rplacd(pos, cdr(pos1)),
            rplacd(pos1, cs),
            rplaca(pos1, car(pos)),
            rplaca(pos, car(pos1)),
            rplaca(pos1, cs),
            rplacd(pos1, cdr(pos)),
            rplacd(pos, pos1),
            set:position(chain, n),
            set:position(chain, add1(n)),
            set:cs(state, pos1),
            set:cs(state, cs)))),
```

again by commuting sets.

```
≃ let{n ← sub1(position(chain))}
      let{pos ← spine(parent(chain), n)}
          let{pos1 ← cdr(pos)}
              seq(rplacd(pos, cdr(pos1)),
                  rplacd(pos1, cs),
                  rplaca(pos1, car(pos)),
                  rplaca(pos, car(pos)),
                  rplaca(pos1, cs),
                  rplacd(pos1, cdr(pos)),
                  rplacd(pos, pos1),
                  set:position(chain, add1(n)),
                  set:cs(state, cs)))),
```

cancelling the redundant **sets** and making use of the fact that at the second *rplaca* *car*(pos1)=*car*(pos).

```
≃ let{n ← sub1(position(chain))}
      let{pos ← spine(parent(chain), n)}
          let{pos1 ← cdr(pos)}
              seq(rplacd(pos, cdr(pos1)),
                  rplacd(pos1, cs),
                  rplaca(pos1, car(pos)),
                  rplaca(pos1, cs),
                  rplaca(pos, car(pos)),
                  rplacd(pos1, cdr(pos)),
                  rplacd(pos, pos1),
                  set:position(chain, add1(n)),
                  set:cs(state, cs)))),
```

by eliminating redundant operations and commuting others.

$$
\begin{aligned}
\simeq\ & \texttt{let}\{\texttt{n} \leftarrow \mathit{sub}1(\mathit{position}(\texttt{chain}))\}\\
&\quad \texttt{let}\{\texttt{pos} \leftarrow \mathit{spine}(\mathit{parent}(\texttt{chain}), \texttt{n})\}\\
&\qquad \texttt{let}\{\texttt{pos1} \leftarrow \mathit{cdr}(\texttt{pos})\}\\
&\qquad\quad \texttt{seq}(\mathit{rplacd}(\texttt{pos}, \mathit{cdr}(\texttt{pos1})),\\
&\qquad\qquad \mathit{rplacd}(\texttt{pos1}, \texttt{cs}),\\
&\qquad\qquad \mathit{rplacd}(\texttt{pos1}, \mathit{cdr}(\texttt{pos})),\\
&\qquad\qquad \mathit{rplaca}(\texttt{pos1}, \texttt{cs}),\\
&\qquad\qquad \mathit{rplacd}(\texttt{pos}, \texttt{pos1}),\\
&\qquad\qquad \mathit{set{:}position}(\texttt{chain}, \mathit{add}1(\texttt{n})),\\
&\qquad\qquad \mathit{set{:}cs}(\texttt{state}, \texttt{cs})))),
\end{aligned}
$$

again by cancellation.

$$
\begin{aligned}
\simeq\ & \texttt{let}\{\texttt{n} \leftarrow \mathit{sub}1(\mathit{position}(\texttt{chain}))\}\\
&\quad \texttt{let}\{\texttt{pos} \leftarrow \mathit{spine}(\mathit{parent}(\texttt{chain}), \texttt{n})\}\\
&\qquad \texttt{let}\{\texttt{pos1} \leftarrow \mathit{cdr}(\texttt{pos})\}\\
&\qquad\quad \texttt{seq}(\mathit{rplacd}(\texttt{pos}, \mathit{cdr}(\texttt{pos1})),\\
&\qquad\qquad \mathit{rplacd}(\texttt{pos1}, \mathit{cdr}(\texttt{pos})),\\
&\qquad\qquad \mathit{rplaca}(\texttt{pos1}, \texttt{cs}),\\
&\qquad\qquad \mathit{rplacd}(\texttt{pos}, \texttt{pos1}),\\
&\qquad\qquad \mathit{set{:}position}(\texttt{chain}, \mathit{add}1(\texttt{n})),\\
&\qquad\qquad \mathit{set{:}cs}(\texttt{state}, \texttt{cs})))),
\end{aligned}
$$

the same again, once more.

$$
\begin{aligned}
\simeq\ & \texttt{let}\{\texttt{n} \leftarrow \mathit{sub}1(\mathit{position}(\texttt{chain}))\}\\
&\quad \texttt{let}\{\texttt{pos} \leftarrow \mathit{spine}(\mathit{parent}(\texttt{chain}), \texttt{n})\}\\
&\qquad \texttt{let}\{\texttt{pos1} \leftarrow \mathit{cdr}(\texttt{pos})\}\\
&\qquad\quad \texttt{seq}(\mathit{rplacd}(\texttt{pos}, \mathit{cdr}(\texttt{pos1})),\\
&\qquad\qquad \mathit{rplacd}(\texttt{pos1}, \mathit{cdr}(\texttt{pos1})),\\
&\qquad\qquad \mathit{rplaca}(\texttt{pos1}, \texttt{cs}),\\
&\qquad\qquad \mathit{rplacd}(\texttt{pos}, \texttt{pos1}),\\
&\qquad\qquad \mathit{set{:}position}(\texttt{chain}, \mathit{add}1(\texttt{n})),\\
&\qquad\qquad \mathit{set{:}cs}(\texttt{state}, \texttt{cs})))),
\end{aligned}
$$

by using the fact that at the second *rplacd* the *cdr* of pos is also the *cdr* of pos1.

```
≃ let{n ← sub1(position(chain))}
      let{pos ← spine(parent(chain), n)}
          let{pos1 ← cdr(pos)}
              seq(rplacd(pos, cdr(pos1)),
                  rplaca(pos1, cs),
                  rplacd(pos, pos1),
                  set:position(chain, add1(n)),
                  set:cs(state, cs)))),
```

by eliminating the redundant alteration to the *cdr* of pos1.

```
≃ let{n ← sub1(position(chain))}
      let{pos ← spine(parent(chain), n)}
          let{pos1 ← cdr(pos)}
              seq(rplacd(pos, cdr(pos1)),
                  rplacd(pos, pos1),
                  rplaca(pos1, cs),
                  set:position(chain, add1(n)),
                  set:cs(state, cs)))),
```

by commuting operations.

```
≃ let{n ← sub1(position(chain))}
      let{pos ← spine(parent(chain), n)}
          let{pos1 ← cdr(pos)}
              seq(rplacd(pos, pos1),
                  rplaca(pos1, cs),
                  set:position(chain, add1(n)),
                  set:cs(state, cs)))),
```

by eliminating redundant operations.

```
≃ let{n ← sub1(position(chain))}
      let{pos ← spine(parent(chain), n)}
          let{pos1 ← cdr(pos)}
              seq(rplaca(pos1, cs),
                  set:position(chain, add1(n)),
                  set:cs(state, cs)))),
```

eliminating the first *rplacd*, since *cdr*(pos)=pos1.

$$\simeq \texttt{let}\{\texttt{n} \leftarrow sub1(position(\texttt{chain}))\}$$
$$\quad \texttt{let}\{\texttt{pos} \leftarrow spine(parent(\texttt{chain}), \texttt{n})\}$$
$$\quad\quad \texttt{let}\{\texttt{pos1} \leftarrow cdr(\texttt{pos})\}$$
$$\quad\quad\quad \texttt{seq}(set{:}position(\texttt{chain}, add1(\texttt{n})),$$
$$\quad\quad\quad\quad set{:}cs(\texttt{state}, \texttt{cs})))),$$

eliminating useless `lets`.

$$\simeq \texttt{let}\{\texttt{n} \leftarrow sub1(position(\texttt{chain}))\}$$
$$\quad \texttt{seq}(set{:}position(\texttt{chain}, add1(\texttt{n})),$$
$$\quad\quad set{:}cs(\texttt{state}, \texttt{cs})))),$$

again by eliminating a `let`.

$$\simeq \texttt{seq}(set{:}position(\texttt{chain}, add1(sub1(position(\texttt{chain})))),$$
$$\quad set{:}cs(\texttt{state}, \texttt{cs})),$$

using a simple arithmetic fact.

$$\simeq \texttt{seq}(set{:}position(\texttt{chain}, position(\texttt{chain})),$$
$$\quad set{:}cs(\texttt{state}, \texttt{cs}))))$$
$$\simeq \texttt{state}.$$

□**Lemma 3.**

Chapter 11

Conclusions

This work has provided a precise but elegant framework for reasoning about programs which destructively manipulate their data. In the foundational respect it is entirely new. It is an implicit aim of this work to show that the verification, specification and transformation of programs are not, and should not be, distinct enterprises. Thus we view our work as a contribution, however small, to *inferential programming* as described in (Scherlis and Scott, 1983).

The work itself is relatively complete insofar as it achieves its initial aims. It only raises a small number of important or interesting unanswered questions, other than those in the tentative chapter on program transformations. It is, however, a mere stepping stone in the whole scheme of things, and we finish by summarizing our results and then pointing out two areas of research that would follow on naturally from this body of work.

11.1. Summary

This work presents a framework for reasoning about, and proving properties of, programs which destructively alter their underlying data. Unlike its rivals the theory neatly separates control from data and provides a foundation for verification, derivation and transformation. In this book we have tried to emphasize the interplay between these areas. Indeed we believe that the old paradigm, see (Burstall, 1974),

$$\text{Verification} = \text{Hand Simulation} + \text{Induction},$$

should be replaced by one which is closer to the aims and spirit of *inferential* programming. Namely

$$\text{Verification} = \text{Transformation} + \text{Induction}.$$

One of the implicit aims of this work was to justify this paradigm. A virtue of this paradigm is that it emphasizes the role of transformation rather than the low-level hand simulation approach. Transformations developed and studied in the process of verification are equally applicable in the more productive process of derivation. The style is also more amenable to automation than the hand simulation variety. The dominance of the hand simulation school is largely a consequence of their preoccupation with extensional relations. To retain a transformational approach in the transition from purely applicative languages to those with side effects one must also make the transition from extensional to intensional equivalence relations. Thus we claim that the limitations of the hand simulation school rests upon their mistaken emphasis on extensionality.

The explicit aim of this work was to develop a theory just as elegant as that which exists for pure Lisp. The most important principle in pure Lisp is Leibniz's Law; *equal* expressions can be replaced by *equal* expressions to obtain an *equal* expression:

Leibniz's Law

$$e_0(\bar{x}) \equiv e_1(\bar{x}) \;\rightarrow\; e(\bar{x}, e_0(\bar{x})) \equiv e(\bar{x}, e_1(\bar{x})).$$

This principle has the consequence that correctness proofs in pure Lisp are very much of the *transformation* plus *induction* variety. The content of Leibniz's Law is that it lays the foundation for a calculus of program transformations; any program that is obtained from another by replacing a portion by another Lisp equal one is guaranteed to have all the extensional properties the original had. It also allows equational verification and derivation. The underlying semantics can be pushed somewhat into the background, serving merely as a *justification* for the transformations and induction principles involved.

One of the problems in developing a theory for destructive Lisp is the failure of Leibniz's Law. This is because evaluating the same expression twice will more often than not give different results. Thus simple syntactic manipulations, on the face of it, seem prohibited in the destructive case. This does much to explain why the vast majority of verification proofs of destructive programs in the literature are of the hand simulation variety. Thus a first step in justifying our paradigm is to recover Leibniz's Law in some form. This was done by making the transition from extensional relations to intensional ones.

To define the semantics we introduced the notion of a memory structure. The equivalence relations were then defined within this model theoretic framework. A distinction was made between intensional relations and extensional relations. The former class turned out to have a much more manageable theory than the latter. The principal intensional relation studied was *strong isomorphism*, $\simeq$. Its properties allow for elegant verification proofs in a style similar to that of pure Lisp, and very much of the transformation plus induction variety.

Substitution Theorem: If $e^0_{body}(\bar{x}, \bar{y}) \simeq e^1_{body}(\bar{x}, \bar{y})$, $|\bar{x}| = k+1$ and $e^0_i(\bar{y}) \simeq e^1_i(\bar{y})$, for $0 \leq i \leq k$ then

$$\mathtt{let}_{0 \leq i \leq k}\{x_i \leftarrow e^0_i(\bar{y})\} e^0_{body}(\bar{x}, \bar{y}) \simeq \mathtt{let}_{0 \leq i \leq k}\{x_i \leftarrow e^1_i(\bar{y})\} e^1_{body}(\bar{x}, \bar{y}).$$

This provided a wealth of syntactic manipulations that preserve strong isomorphism, and we spent some time enumerating them in Chapter 3. Some of the more important control properties are:

Sequencing : $\mathtt{seq}_{0\leq i<k}(e_i^0(\bar{y})) \simeq \mathtt{seq}_{0\leq i<k}(e_i^1(\bar{y}))$.

Composition : $\vartheta(e_0^0(\bar{y}),\ldots,e_{k-1}^0(\bar{y})) \simeq \vartheta(e_0^1(\bar{y}),\ldots,e_{k-1}^1(\bar{y}))$.

Branching : $\mathtt{if}(e_0^0(\bar{y}),e_1^0(\bar{y}),e_2^0(\bar{y})) \simeq \mathtt{if}(e_0^1(\bar{y}),e_1^1(\bar{y}),e_2^1(\bar{y}))$.

Unfolding : $e(\bar{x}) \simeq e^{\bowtie}(\bar{x})$.

These properties give a foundation for a calculus of program transformations; any program that is obtained from another by replacing a portion by another strongly isomorphic one is guaranteed to be strongly isomorphic to the original one:

Leibniz's Law: Supposing $e_i(\bar{x}), e(\bar{x},y)$ are expressions, $i \in 2$, then,

$$e_0(\bar{x}) \simeq e_1(\bar{x}) \ \rightarrow\ e(\bar{x},e_0(\bar{x})) \simeq e(\bar{x},e_1(\bar{x})).$$

A plethora of verification proofs of both simple and complex programs was given using the intensional equivalence relation. All of these proofs were of the transformation plus induction variety. In contrast, we gave some verification proofs of programs, using the extensional relations. Because the Substitution Theorem fails for these extensional relations, the proofs were necessarily of the hand simulation variety.

In a more theoretical light, we also proved that the equivalence relations introduced here are decidable, and used them to study the expressive powers of certain fragments of Lisp.

11.2. Richer Languages

The area of research that we are most immediately interested in to follow up on this work is that of incorporating high level constructs into our language, and enlarging the framework accordingly. Three examples are:

1. Closures, allowing functions or functionals to be passed as arguments and returned as values. We have recently done some work in this area that suggests this is not such a difficult extension.

2. Continuations, allowing for non-functional control constructs such as `Note` (Talcott, 1985a) that make continuations, i.e. the remaining part of the computation, first class objects. There is good reason to believe that this will be somewhat more difficult than the previous problem.

3. Concurrency, allowing for concurrent evaluation by introducing primitives like `QLAMBDA`, `QLET` (Gabriel and McCarthy, 1984) and, in the spirit of actors, (Hewitt, 1977) `SEND` (Mason, Talcott and Weyhrauch, 1984).

It is our belief that the most fruitful approach that can be taken in these examples is the study of the *equivalence* of programs, to prove that programs with these high level constructs are equivalent to programs without them. The simple programs play the role of specifications and the proofs of equivalence the role either as verifications or derivations of the more complex programs. Operations or transformations on programs from one language to another are central to the whole approach. *Operations on programs need meanings to transform and meanings to preserve,* (Talcott, 1985b, 1986), and the study of various notions of equivalence is simply a study of the various *meanings*. This variety of languages and interpretations should exist within a single framework. They should be *compatible* in the sense that the value returned by a program should be the same in each interpretation. They should also be *coherent* in that one can move gracefully between interpretations and have systematic methods for *deriving* one interpretation from another. The fact the target languages and specification languages are supersets or subsets of one another permits special interpretation of fragments (Talcott, 1986). This approach emphasizes the role of transformation, the new paradigm; in the long term it is a contribution to inferential programming, seen as the unification of programming, program verification, program derivation and program transformation.

11.3. Foundations for the Analogy

In this work we have tried to show that verification and derivation should be thought of as *duals*. We have concentrated on verification only because it is much simpler than derivation. In Chapter 7 we scratched the surface of the problem of program derivation. There is much more to be done here. In (Scherlis and Scott, 1983) the authors suggest the following analogy between programming and mathematics:

Mathematics		*Programming*
problem	...	specification
theorem	...	program
proof	...	program derivation

Thus it remains to develop a firm foundation for these analogies. This is a large scale project and we are not too embarrassed by our modest initial contributions. As they say in (Scherlis and Scott, 1983):

We shall not arrive at inferential programming overnight, however, because the very act of producing a complete derivation requires a programmer to express some of his previously unexpressed intuitions.

Bibliography

Aho, A. V., Hopcroft, J. E., and Ullman, J. D. 1974. *The Design and Analysis of Computer Algorithms.* London: Addison-Wesley.

Barr, A., and Feigenbaum, E. A. 1982. *The Handbook of Artificial Intelligence.* Vol. 2. Los Altos, Calif.: William Kaufmann.

Bloom, S., and Tindell, R. 1983. Varieties of if-then-else. *SIAM Journal of Computing,* 12:677–707.

Brooks, R. A., and Gabriel, R. P. 1984. A Critique of Common LISP. *1984 ACM Symposium on LISP and Functional Programming,* 1–8.

Burstall, R. M. 1972. Some Techniques for Proving Correctness of Programs which Alter Data Structures. In B. Meltzer and D. Mitchie (Eds.), *Machine Intelligence 7.* Edinburgh: Edinburgh University Press, 23–50.

Burstall, R. M. 1974. Program Proving as Hand Simulation with a Little Induction. *Proceedings IFIP Congress,* 308–312.

Burstall, R. M. and Darlington, J. 1977. A Transformation System for Developing Recursive Programs. *Journal of the ACM,* 24:1.

Cartwright, R. 1976. *A Practical Formal Semantic Definition and Verification System for Typed LISP.* Doctoral dissertation, Stanford University.

Cartwright, R. 1978. First Order Semantics: A Natural Programming Logic for Recursively Defined Functions. Tech. Rep. No. TR78–339, Cornell University.

Cartwright, R., Hood, R., and Matthews, P, 1981. Paths: An Abstract Alternative to Pointers. *Conference Record of the Eighth Annual ACM Symposium on Principles of Programming Languages,* 14–28.

de Champeaux, D. 1978. SUBSTAD: For Fast Substitution in LISP, with an Application on Unification. *Information Processing Letters,* 7:58–62.

de Champeaux, D., and de Bruin, J. 1981. Symbolic Evaluation of LISP Functions with Side Effects for Verification. In de Bakker and van Vliet, (Eds.), *Algorithmic Languages.* New York: North Holland, 271–291.

Chang, C. C., and Keisler, H. J. 1973. *Model Theory.* New York: North Holland.

Clark, D. W., and Green, C. C. 1977. An Empirical Study of List Structure in LISP. *Communications of the ACM,* 20:78–86.

Deutsch, L. P. 1969. **K**, 1:417.

Floyd, R. W. 1967. Assigning Meanings to Programs. In J. T. Schwartz (Ed.), *Proceedings of the Symposium in Applied Mathematics 19.* Providence, R.I.: A.M.S, 19–32.

Friedman, D. P, and Felleisen, M. 1986. *The Little LISPer.* Chicago: Science Research Associates.

Friedman, H. 1971. Algorithmic Procedures, Generalized Turing Algorithms, and Elementary Recursion Theory. *Logic Colloquium '69.* New York: North Holland, 316–389.

Gabriel, R. P. and McCarthy, J. 1984. Queue-based Multi-processing LISP. *1984 ACM Symposium on LISP and Functional Programming.*

Goad, C. A. 1980. *Computational Uses of the Manipulation of Formal Proofs.* Doctoral dissertation, Stanford University.

Gordon, M. J. C. 1973. An Investigation of lit: where $\text{lit}((a_1, \ldots, a_n), a_{n+1}, f) = f(a_1, f(a_2, \ldots, f(a_n, a_{n+1})) \ldots))$. A.I. Memo No. MIP-R-101, Edinburgh University.

Gries, D. 1979. The Schorr-Waite Graph Marking Algorithm. *Acta Informatica,* 11:223–232.

Guessarian, I. and Meseguer, J. 1985. On the Axiomatization of if-then-else. Rep. No. CSLI–85–20, Center for the Study of Language and Information, Stanford University.

Hewett, C. 1977. Viewing Control Structures as Patterns of Passing Messages. *Artificial Intelligence,* 8:323–363.

Hillis, D. W. 1985. *The Connection Machine.* Cambridge, Mass: The MIT Press.

Hoare, C. A. R. 1972. Proof of Correctness of Data Representations. *Acta Informatica,* 1:271–281.

Hood, R. and Matthews, P. 1980. Real Time Queue Operations in Pure LISP. C.S. Rep. No. TR80–433, Cornell University.

Knuth, D. E., 1973. *The Art of Computer Programming.* (Vol. 1, 2nd ed.). Reading, Mass.: Addison-Wesley.

Kowaltowski, T. 1973. *Correctness of Programs Manipulating Data Structures.* Doctoral dissertation, University of California, Berkeley.

McCarthy, J. 1960. Recursive Functions of Symbolic Expressions and their Computation by Machine, Part 1. *Communications of the ACM,* Vol. 3.

McCarthy, J., et al. 1962a. *LISP 1.5 Programmers' Manual.* Cambridge, Mass: The MIT Press.

McCarthy, J. 1962b. Towards a Mathematical Science of Computation. *Proceedings of IFIP Congress 62,* 21–28.

McCarthy, J. 1963. A Basis for a Mathematical Theory of Computation. In Braffort and Hershberg (Eds.), *Computer Programming and Formal Systems.* Amsterdam: North Holland.

McCarthy, J. 1978. History of LISP. *ACM SIGPLAN Notices,* 13:217–223.

McCarthy, J. 1980. LISP-Notes on Its Past and Future. *Conference Record of the 1980 LISP Conference,* v–viii.

McCarthy, J., and Cartwright, R. 1979. Recursive Programs as Functions in a First Order Theory. AI Memo AIM–324, Stanford University.

McCarthy, J., and Talcott, C. L. 1980. *LISP Programming and Proving.* Course Notes, Stanford University.

McCarthy, J., and Talcott, C. L. 1985. LISP Programming and Proving. Course Notes, Stanford University.

McKinsey, J. C. C., and Tarski, A. 1946. On Closed Elements in Closure Algebras. *Ann. of Math.,* 47:1.

Manna, Z., and Waldinger, R. 1977. Is Sometimes Better Than Always? Intermittent Assertions in Proving Program Correctness. *Communications of the ACM,* 21:159–172.

Mason, I. A. 1985. Memories of LISP. Abstracts of Contributed Papers, Annual meeting of the Association of Symbolic Logic, *Journal of Symbolic Logic,* (to appear).

Mason, I. A. 1986. Equivalence of First Order LISP Programs, Proving Properties of Destructive Programs via Transformation. *Proceedings of the First Symposium on Logic in Computer Science,* Massachusetts Institute of Technology.

Mason, I. A., and Talcott, C. L. 1985. Memories of S-expressions. Rep. No. STAN-CS-85-1057, Computer Science Dept., Stanford University.

Mason, I. A., Talcott, C. L., and Weyhrauch, R. 1984. SEUS a New Programming Language for Multiprocessing. Unpublished manuscript.

Milner, R. 1971. An Algebraic Definition of Simulation Between Programs. Rep. No. STAN-CS-71-205, Computer Science Dept., Stanford University.

Morris, Jr., J. H. 1972. Verification-Orientated Language Design. Tech. Rep. 7, Computer Science Dept., University of California, Berkeley.

Morris, J. M. 1979. Traversing Binary Trees Simply and Cheaply. *Information Processing Letters,* 9:197–200.

Moschovakis, Y. N. 1969. Abstract First Order Computability I. *Trans. Amer. Math. Soc.,* 138:427–464.

Nelson, G., and Oppen, D. C. 1978a. Fast Decision Algorithms Based on Congruence Relations. AI Memo AIM–309, Stanford University.

Nelson, G., and Oppen, D. C. 1978b. Simplification by Cooperating Procedures. AI Memo AIM–311, Stanford University.

Oppen, D. C. 1978. Reasoning about Recursively Defined Data Structures. AI Memo AIM–314, Stanford University.

Pitman, K. M. 1980, Special Forms in LISP. Conference Record of the 1980 LISP Conference, 179–187.

Pitman, K. M. 1983. The revised Maclisp Manual. LCS Tech. Rep. No. TR-295, Massachusetts Institute of Technology.

Poupon, J., and Wegbreit, B. 1972. Covering Functions. Center for Research in Computing Technology, Harvard University. Unpublished manuscript.

Robson, J. M. 1977. A Bounded Storage Algorithm for Copying Cyclic Structures. *Communications of the ACM,* 20:431–433.

Scherlis, W. L. 1980. *Expression Procedures and Program Derivation.* Doctoral dissertation, Stanford University.

Scherlis, W. L. 1981. Program Improvement by Internal Specialization. *Conference Record of the Eighth Annual ACM Symposium on Principles of Programming Languages,* 41–49.

Scherlis, W. L., and Scott, D. S. 1983. First Steps Towards Inferential Programming. In R. E. A. Mason (Ed.), *Information Processing 83.* New York: North Holland.

Schorr, H., and Waite, W. M. 1967. An Efficient Machine-Independent Procedure for Garbage Collection in Various List Structures. *Communications of the ACM,* 10:501–506.

Steele, G. L., et al, 1984. *Common LISP.* Bedford, Mass.: Digital Press.

Steele, G. L. 1976a. LAMBDA: The Ultimate Declarative. Tech. Rep., Massachusetts Institute of Technology.

Steele, G. L. 1976b. RABBIT: A Compiler for SCHEME. Tech. Rep., Massachusetts Institute of Technology.

Steele, G. L. 1977. LAMBDA: The Ultimate Goto. *Proceedings of the Annual ACM Conference,* 153–162

Steele, G. L., and Sussman, G. J. 1976. LAMBDA: The Ultimate Imperative. Tech. Rep., Massachusetts Institute of Technology.

Stoyan, H. 1984. Early LISP History (1956–59). *1984 ACM Symposium on LISP and Functional Programming,* 299–310.

Suzuki, N. 1976. *Automatic Verification of Programs with Complex Data Structures.* Doctoral dissertation, Stanford University.

Suzuki, N. 1982. Analysis of Pointer Rotation. *Communications of the ACM,* 25:330–335.

Talcott, C. L. 1983. *SEUS Reference Manual.* Unpublished manuscript.

Talcott, C. L. 1985a. *The Essence of RUM.* Doctoral dissertation, Stanford University.

Talcott, C. L. 1985b. Derived Properties and Derived Programs. Unpublished manuscript.

Talcott, C. L. 1986. Notes on Transformations. Unpublished manuscript.

Tenney. 1972. *Decidable Pairing Functions.* Doctoral dissertation, Cornell University.

Topor, R. W. 1979. The Correctness of the Shorr-Waite List Marking Algorithm. *Acta Informatica,* 11:211–221.

Touretzky, D. S. 1983. A Summary of Maclisp Functions and Flags. (5th ed.) Tech. Rep., Computer Science Dept., Carnegie-Mellon University.

Touretzky, D. S. 1984, *LISP: A Gentle Introduction to Symbolic Computation.* New York: Harper and Row.

Tucker, J. V., et al. 1980. Finite Algorithmic Procedures and Inductive Definability. *Math Scand,* 46:62–76.

Wadler, P. 1984. Listlessness Is Better than Lazyness. *1984 ACM Symposium on LISP and Functional Programming,* 45–53.

Warren 1980, An Improved Prolog Implementation which Optimizes Tail-Recursion. AI Rep. No. 141, University of Edinburgh.

CSLI Reports

The following titles have been published in the CSLI Reports series. These reports may be obtained from CSLI Publications, Ventura Hall, Stanford University, Stanford, CA 94305.

Research Program on Situated Language. Rep. No. CSLI–84–1. (*NC*)

The Situation in Logic–I. Jon Barwise. Rep. No. CSLI–84–2. (*$2.00*)

Coordination and How to Distinguish Categories. Ivan Sag, Gerald Gazdar, Thomas Wasow, and Steven Weisler. Rep. No. CSLI–84–3. (*$3.50*)

Belief and Incompleteness. Kurt Konolige. Rep. No. CSLI–84–4. (*$4.50*)

Equality, Types, Modules and Generics for Logic Programming. Joseph Goguen and José Meseguer. Rep. No. CSLI–84–5. (*$2.50*)

Lessons from Bolzano. Johan van Benthem. Rep. No. CSLI–84–6. (*$1.50*)

Self-propagating Search: A Unified Theory of Memory. Pentti Kanerva. Rep. No. CSLI–84–7. (*$9.00*)

Reflection and Semantics in LISP. Brian Cantwell Smith. Rep. No. CSLI–84–8. (*$2.50*)

The Implementation of Procedurally Reflective Languages. Jim des Rivières and Brian Cantwell Smith. Rep. No. CSLI–84–9. (*$3.00*)

Parameterized Programming. Joseph Goguen. Rep. No. CSLI–84–10. (*$3.50*)

Morphological Constraints on Scandinavian Tone Accent. Meg Withgott and Per-Kristian Halvorsen. Rep. No. CSLI–84–11. (*$2.50*)

Partiality and Nonmonotonicity in Classical Logic. Johan van Benthem. Rep. No. CSLI–84–12. (*$2.00*)

Shifting Situations and Shaken Attitudes. Jon Barwise and John Perry. Rep. No. CSLI–84–13. (*$4.50*)

Aspectual Classes in Situation Semantics. Robin Cooper. Rep. No. CSLI–85–14-C. (*$4.00*)

Completeness of Many-Sorted Equational Logic. Joseph Goguen and José Meseguer. Rep. No. CSLI–84–15. (*$2.50*)

Moving the Semantic Fulcrum. Terry Winograd. Rep. No. CSLI–84–17. (*$1.50*)

On the Mathematical Properties of Linguistic Theories. C. Raymond Perrault. Rep. No. CSLI–84–18. (*$3.00*)

A Simple and Efficient Implementation of Higher-order Functions in LISP. Michael P. Georgeff and Stephen F.Bodnar. Rep. No. CSLI–84–19. (*$4.50*)

On the Axiomatization of "if-then-else". Irène Guessarian and José Meseguer. Rep. No. CSLI–85–20. (*$3.00*)

The Situation in Logic–II: Conditionals and Conditional Information. Jon Barwise. Rep. No. CSLI–84–21. (*$3.00*)

Principles of OBJ2. Kokichi Futatsugi, Joseph A. Goguen, Jean-Pierre Jouannaud, and José Meseguer. Rep. No. CSLI–85–22. (*$2.00*)

Querying Logical Databases. Moshe Vardi. Rep. No. CSLI–85–23. (*$1.50*)

Computationally Relevant Properties of Natural Languages and Their Grammar. Gerald Gazdar and Geoff Pullum. Rep. No. CSLI–85–24. (*$3.50*)

An Internal Semantics for Modal Logic: Preliminary Report. Ronald Fagin and Moshe Vardi. Rep. No. CSLI–85–25. (*$2.00*)

The Situation in Logic–III: Situations, Sets and the Axiom of Foundation. Jon Barwise. Rep. No. CSLI–85–26. (*$2.50*)

Semantic Automata. Johan van Benthem. Rep. No. CSLI–85–27. (*$2.50*)

Restrictive and Non-Restrictive Modification. Peter Sells. Rep. No. CSLI–85–28. (*$3.00*)

Equations, Schemata and Situations: A Framework for Linguistic Semantics. Jens Erik Fenstad, Per-Kristian Halvorsen, Tore Langholm, and Johan van Benthem. Rep. No. CSLI–85–29. (*$7.00*)

Institutions: Abstract Model Theory for Computer Science. J. A. Goguen and R. M. Burstall. Rep. No. CSLI–85–30. (*$4.50*)

A Formal Theory of Knowledge and Action. Robert C. Moore. Rep. No. CSLI–85–31. (*$5.50*)

Finite State Morphology: A Review of Koskenniemi (1983). Gerald Gazdar. Rep. No. CSLI–85–32. (*$1.50*)

The Role of Logic in Artificial Intelligence. Robert C. Moore. Rep. No. CSLI–85–33. (*$2.00*)

Applicability of Indexed Grammars to Natural Languages. Gerald Gazdar. Rep. No. CSLI–85–34. (*$2.00*)

Commonsense Summer: Final Report. Jerry R. Hobbs, et al.. Rep. No. CSLI–85–35. (*$12.00*)

Limits of Correctness in Computers. Brian Cantwell Smith. Rep. No. CSLI–85–36. (*$2.50*)

On the Coherence and Structure of Discourse. Jerry R. Hobbs. Rep. No. CSLI–85–37. (*$3.00*)

The Coherence of Incoherent Discourse. Jerry R. Hobbs and Michael H. Agar. Rep. No. CSLI–85–38. (*$2.50*)

The Structures of Discourse Structure. Barbara Grosz and Candace L. Sidner. Rep. No. CSLI–85–39. *($4.50)*

A Complete Type-free, Second-order Logic and its Philosophical Foundations. Christopher Menzel. Rep. No. CSLI–86–40. *($4.50)*

Possible-world Semantics for Autoepistemic Logic. Robert C. Moore. Rep. No. CSLI–85–41. *($2.00)*

Deduction with Many-Sorted Rewrite. José Meseguer and Joseph A. Goguen. Rep. No. CSLI–85–42. *($1.50)*

On Some Formal Properties of Metarules. Hans Uszkoreit and Stanley Peters. Rep. No. CSLI–85–43. *($1.50)*

Language, Mind, and Information. John Perry. Rep. No. CSLI–85–44. *($2.00)*

Is Computation Formal? Brian Cantwell Smith. Rep. No. CSLI–86–45. *(Forthcoming)*

Constraints on Order. Hans Uszkoreit. Rep. No. CSLI–86–46. *($3.00)*

Linear Precedence in Discontinuous Constituents: Complex Fronting in German. Hans Uszkoreit. Rep. No. CSLI–86–47. *($2.50)*

A Compilation of Papers on Unification-Based Grammar Formalisms, Parts I and II. Stuart M. Shieber, Fernando C.N. Pereira, Lauri Karttunen, and Martin Kay. Rep. No. CSLI–86–48. *($4.00)*

An Algorithm for Generating Quantifier Scopings. Jerry R. Hobbs and Stuart M. Shieber. Rep. No. CSLI–86–49. *($2.50)*

Verbs of Change, Causation, and Time. Dorit Abusch. Rep. No. CSLI–86–50. *($2.00)*

Noun-Phrase Interpretation. Mats Rooth. Rep. No. CSLI–86–51. *($2.50)*

Noun Phrases, Generalized Quantifiers and Anaphora. Jon Barwise. Rep. No. CSLI–86–52. *($2.50)*

Circumstantial Attitudes and Benevolent Cognition. John Perry. Rep. No. CSLI–86–53. *($1.50)*

A Study in the Foundations of Programming Methodology: Specifications, Institutions, Charters and Parchments. Joseph A. Goguen and R. M. Burstall. Rep. No. CSLI–86–54. *($2.50)*

Quantifiers in Formal and Natural Languages. Dag Westerståhl. Rep. No. CSLI–86–55. *($7.50)*

Intentionality, Information, and Matter. Ivan Blair. Rep. No. CSLI–86–56. *($3.00)*

Graphs and Grammars. William Marsh. Rep. No. CSLI–86–57. *($2.00)*

Computer Aids for Comparative Dictionaries. Mark Johnson. Rep. No. CSLI–86–58. *($2.00)*

The Relevance of Computational Linguistics. Lauri Karttunen. Rep. No. CSLI–86–59. *($2.50)*

Grammatical Hierarchy and Linear Precedence. Ivan A. Sag. Rep. No. CSLI–86–60. *($3.50)*

D-PATR: A Development Environment for Unification-Based Grammars. Lauri Karttunen. Rep. No. CSLI–86–61. *($4.00)*

A Sheaf-Theoretic Model of Concurrency. Luís F. Monteiro and Fernando C. N. Pereira. Rep. No. CSLI–86–62. *($3.00)*

CSLI Lecture Notes

The titles in this series are distributed by the University of Chicago Press and may be purchased in academic or university bookstores or ordered directly from the distributor at 5801 Ellis Avenue, Chicago, Illinois 60637.

A Manual of Intensional Logic. Johan van Benthem. Lecture Notes No. 1. (*Paper $8.95*)

Emotions and Focus. Helen Fay Nissenbaum. Lecture Notes No. 2. (*Paper $8.95*)

Lectures on Contemporary Syntactic Theories. Peter Sells. Lecture Notes No. 3. (*Paper $11.95* *Cloth $23.95*)

An Introduction to Unification-Based Approaches to Grammar. Stuart M. Shieber. Lecture Notes No. 4. (*Paper $8.95* *Cloth $17.95*)

Facts. Ken Olson. Lecture Notes No. 6. (*Forthcoming*)

Lecture Notes on Non-Well-Founded Sets. Peter Aczel. Lecture Notes No. 7. (*Forthcoming*)